Annual Recipes
2010

INCLUDING PILLSBURY BAKE-OFF® CONTEST WINNERS

Pillsbury Annual Recipes 2010

Our recipes have been tested in the Pillsbury Kitchens and meet our standards of easy preparation, reliability and great taste.

For more great recipes, visit pillsbury.com

Copyright © 2010 General Mills, Inc.
Minneapolis, Minnesota

All rights reserved. No part of this book may be reproduced or transmitted in any form or by any means, electronic or mechanical, including photocopying, recording, or by any information storage and retrieval system, without permission in writing from the publisher.

PUBLISHED BY
Taste of Home Books
Reiman Media Group, Inc.
5400 S. 60th St., Greendale, WI 53129
www.tasteofhome.com

Printed in U.S.A.

Taste of Home® is a registered trademark of Reiman Media Group, Inc.

Bake-Off® is a registered trademark of General Mills.

The trademarks referred to herein are trademarks of General Mills, Inc., or its affiliates, except as noted.

Yoplait® is a registered trademark of YOPLAIT Marques Internationales SAS (France) used under license.

All recipes were originally published in different form by Pillsbury Easy Meals™ Magazine and Pillsbury® Magazines, both trademarks of General Mills, Inc.

International Standard Book Number (10):
0-89821-761-X
International Standard Book Number (13):
978-0-89821-761-2
International Standard Serial Number:
1930-7349

CREDITS
General Mills, Inc.
EDITORIAL DIRECTOR: JEFF NOWAK
PUBLISHING MANAGER: CHRISTINE GRAY
COOKBOOK EDITOR: GRACE WELLS
DIGITAL ASSETS MANAGER: CARRIE JACOBSON
PRODUCTION MANAGER: MICHELLE TUFTS
RECIPE DEVELOPMENT AND TESTING: PILLSBURY TEST KITCHENS
PHOTOGRAPHY: GENERAL MILLS PHOTO STUDIO

Reiman Media Group, Inc.
EDITOR IN CHIEF: CATHERINE CASSIDY
VICE PRESIDENT, EXECUTIVE EDITOR/BOOKS: HEIDI REUTER LLOYD
CREATIVE DIRECTOR: ARDYTH COPE
SENIOR EDITOR/BOOKS: MARK HAGEN
EDITOR: MICHELLE BRETL
ART DIRECTOR: GRETCHEN TRAUTMAN
CONTENT PRODUCTION SUPERVISOR: JULIE WAGNER
LAYOUT DESIGNERS: KATHY CRAWFORD, NANCY NOVAK, EMMA ACEVEDO
GRAPHIC DESIGN ASSOCIATE: HEATHER MEINEN
PROOFREADERS: LINNE BRUSKEWITZ, AMY GLANDER

CREATIVE DIRECTOR/CREATIVE MARKETING: JAMES PALMEN
VICE PRESIDENT/BOOK MARKETING: DAN FINK
CHIEF MARKETING OFFICER: LISA KARPINSKI

Reader's Digest Association, Inc.
PRESIDENT AND CHIEF EXECUTIVE OFFICER: MARY G. BERNER
PRESIDENT, U.S. AFFINITIES: SUZANNE M. GRIMES
SVP, CHIEF MARKETING OFFICER: AMY J. RADIN
PRESIDENT, GLOBAL CONSUMER MARKETING: DAWN M. ZIER

COVER PHOTOGRAPHY: REIMAN PUBLICATIONS PHOTO STUDIO
  PHOTOGRAPHER: ROB HAGEN
  FOOD STYLIST: KAITLYN BESASIE
  SET STYLIST: JENNIFER BRADLEY VENT

FRONT COVER PHOTOGRAPHS:
Savory Brisket Stew, Pg. 196; Chicken Saltimbocca, Pg. 135; Feta and Tomato Crostini, Pg. 43; Pear-Walnut Crumble Pie, Pg. 335; and Rotisserie Chicken Salad with Cherries and Gorgonzola, Pg. 138.

PAGE 5 PHOTOGRAPHS:
Berry-Peach Cobbler, Pg. 328; Spicy Chunky Beef Chili, Pg. 193; Pumpkin Truffle Pound Cake with Browned Butter Icing, Pg. 321; and Roast Turkey, Pg. 276.

BACK COVER PHOTOGRAPHS:
Caramelized Onion and Mushroom Tartlets, Pg. 47; Garden-Style Red Rice, Pg. 124; Pear-Rum Crisp, Pg. 183; and Pot Roast and Vegetables, Pg. 185.

contents

"Plan Your Meals Every Day With This Annual Pillsbury Cookbook!"

introduction

Whether you want a fast yet family-pleasing dinner for a busy weeknight or a festive feast for a holiday, you'll find the perfect choices here inside *Pillsbury Annual Recipes 2010*. In fact, you can use this indispensable cookbook to plan and create every menu you need every day of the week.

The fifth edition of our popular series, this can't-miss collection takes the best from the 2009 Pillsbury Classic® Cookbooks to give you hundreds of mouth-watering recipes and expert kitchen tips—more than 400 in all! And because each delicious dish carries the trusted name of Pillsbury, you can rest assured each is a proven winner.

To locate the exact types of recipes you need, simply choose from 12 big chapters jam-packed with scrumptious selections. For example, on weekend mornings, turn to the Breakfast & Brunch chapter for a.m. sensations such as Ham and Chile Brunch Pizza (p. 16).

Looking for something wholesome to tide over the kids? Rely on Mini Bacon-Cheese Cups (p. 63) and more in the Snacks & Munchies chapter. Or see Appetizers & Beverages for Smoked Salmon Spread (p. 49) and other impressive hors d'oeuvres for parties.

Putting a home-cooked dinner on the table has never been easier thanks to entrees such as Chicken Bruschetta (p. 158) in Main Dishes. For a tasty pairing, add Perfect

Mashed Potatoes (p. 114) from Side Dishes & More...or Brie, Lettuce and Tomato Salad (p. 92) from Salads & Sandwiches.

Any day can be a south-of-the-border party when you fix the Family Fiesta chapter's Mexican fare, including Ground Beef Fajitas (p. 235). Want to keep things super-simple? Give supper a jump-start with ready-when-you-get-home Harvest Pork Stew (p. 175) in Slow Cooker Sensations.

Special occasions call for extra-special foods—and Cozy Holiday Favorites is brimming with memorable ideas. Thrill family and friends with Christmas Tree Vegetable Platter (p. 291). Or, count on Potluck Pleasers to wow the crowd with Ham and Cheese Pull-Apart Sandwich Loaf (p. 258).

Don't forget the sweet treats! Everyone will save room when you whip up delights from the Cookies, Bars & Candies and Delectable Desserts chapters. Indulge in Triple-Nut Toffee (p. 311) and Key Lime Cheesecake Pie (p. 342).

Because every recipe includes a gorgeous color photo and step-by-step directions, even novice cooks can serve up success. Plus, many dishes use brand-name convenience products you've enjoyed for years, and each dish has been approved by the pros in the Pillsbury Test Kitchens.

It's all here for you in *Pillsbury Annual Recipes 2010*. And there's more! Read on...

AT-A-GLANCE ICONS

If you're like most family cooks, you have less time than ever to spend in the kitchen. You need to find the recipes right for you, and fast!

Maybe you're most interested in dishes that are especially fuss-free to prepare...or are on the healthier side...or were winners from the famous Pillsbury Bake-Off® Contest. To quickly locate these types of dishes, look for the following icons located next to the recipe title:

EASY RECIPE

These dishes use 6 ingredients or less OR are ready to cook in 20 minutes or less OR are ready to eat in 30 minutes or less.

LOW-FAT RECIPE

These dishes contain 10 grams of fat or less (main dishes) or 3 grams of fat or less (all other recipes).

PILLSBURY BAKE-OFF® RECIPE

These dishes were judged award-winners in a Pillsbury Bake-Off® Contest.

We've also included "Prep" and "Ready in..." times, so you'll know exactly how long it takes to prepare each dish from start to finish. And to provide even more at-a-glance information, we've featured Nutrition Facts with the majority of this book's recipes.

HELPFUL INDEXES

This easy-to-use cookbook is indexed in two convenient ways. Look up any major ingredient in the general index, which starts on page 346, and you'll see a comprehensive list of the recipes in which it is included. For instance, if you'd like a main dish with chicken, turn to "chicken" in the general index to find dozens of flavorful options.

The alphabetical index starts on page 344. Once you've found a few favorite recipes for your family, you can easily find them by title the next time you want to make them.

Or, perhaps you just want to page through and look at all of the taste-tempting photos until you discover a new recipe that's perfect for you. No matter which Pillsbury favorite you choose to serve, it's certain to become a permanent, much-loved part of your kitchen collection!

Breakfast & Brunch

From coffee cakes to egg bakes, these
a.m. sensations will wake up taste buds.

MINI PEAR BRIE BITES
PG. 12

RASPBERRY-PEACH
ICED TEA SMOOTHIES
PG. 10

HAM AND CHILE BRUNCH PIZZA
PG. 16

ARTICHOKE-SPINACH STRATA
PG. 13

Almond-Apricot Crescent Ring

PREP TIME: 20 MINUTES (READY IN 40 MINUTES)
SERVINGS: 6

e EASY

CRESCENT RING

- 1 can (8 oz) Pillsbury® refrigerated crescent dinner rolls or 1 can (8 oz) Pillsbury® Crescent Recipe Creations™ refrigerated flaky dough sheet
- 2 tablespoons butter or margarine, softened
- 2 tablespoons packed brown sugar
- 1/4 cup chopped dried apricots
- 1/3 cup chopped almonds

GLAZE

- 1/2 cup powdered sugar
- 2 to 3 teaspoons milk

1) Heat oven to 375°F. Spray large cookie sheet with cooking spray. Unroll dough on work surface (if using crescent rolls, pinch the seams to seal); press into 12x8-inch rectangle.

2) In small bowl, mix butter, brown sugar and apricots. Spread to within 1/2 inch of dough edges. Sprinkle with almonds.

3) Starting with long side of rectangle, roll up; pinch edge to seal. With serrated knife, cut into 12 slices. Arrange slices on cookie sheet in a circle, overlapping slightly.

4) Bake 15 to 20 minutes or until golden brown. Cool 5 minutes. Remove from cookie sheet to cooling rack.

5) In small bowl, mix glaze ingredients until thin enough to drizzle. Drizzle over warm crescent ring.

HIGH ALTITUDE (3500-6500 FT.): No change.

Nutrition Information Per Serving:	
Calories: 280	From Fat: 120
Total Fat	14g
Saturated Fat	5g
Trans Fat	0g
Cholesterol	10mg
Sodium	330mg
Total Carbohydrate	35g
Dietary Fiber	1g
Sugars	20g
Protein	3g

Asparagus-Potato Brunch Bake

PREP TIME: 15 MINUTES (READY IN 50 MINUTES)   EASY
SERVINGS: 8

1 tablespoon butter or margarine

1 cup sliced green onions

8 eggs

$1/2$ cup fat-free (skim) milk

3 cups frozen southern-style diced hash brown potatoes (from 32-oz bag), thawed

2 cups chopped lean cooked ham ($1/2$ lb)

1 box (9 oz) Green Giant® frozen asparagus cuts, thawed, drained

1 cup shredded Cheddar cheese (4 oz)

Salt and pepper to taste

Nutrition Information Per Serving:		
Calories: 270	From Fat: 120	
Total Fat		13g
Saturated Fat		6g
Trans Fat		0g
Cholesterol		245mg
Sodium		530mg
Total Carbohydrate		19g
Dietary Fiber		2g
Sugars		3g
Protein		18g

1) Heat oven to 350°F. Generously spray 13x9-inch (3-quart) baking dish with cooking spray. In 8-inch skillet, melt butter over medium heat. Cook onions in butter 2 to 3 minutes, stirring occasionally, until tender.

2) In large bowl, mix eggs and milk until blended. Stir in cooked onions, potatoes, ham and asparagus. Pour into baking dish. Top with cheese.

3) Bake 30 to 35 minutes or until set. Season to taste with salt and pepper.

HIGH ALTITUDE (3500-6500 FT.): No change.

Raspberry-Peach Iced Tea Smoothies

PREP TIME: 5 MINUTES (READY IN 5 MINUTES)
SERVINGS: 4 (ABOUT 1 CUP EACH)

e EASY   **lf** LOW FAT

1 cup frozen whole raspberries without syrup (about 4½ oz)

¾ cup milk

2 tablespoons sugar-free low-calorie peach instant iced tea mix

1 container (6 oz) Yoplait® Original 99% Fat Free white chocolate raspberry yogurt

1 bag (16 oz) frozen sliced peaches without syrup, 2 slices reserved and thawed

1) In blender or food processor, place the raspberries, milk, iced tea mix and yogurt. Cover; blend on high speed 10 to 20 seconds or until smooth.

2) Add half of the peach slices; cover and blend on high speed until smooth. Add remaining peaches; cover and blend until smooth. Pour into 4 glasses.

3) Garnish glasses with peach pieces. Serve immediately.

HIGH ALTITUDE (3500-6500 FT.): No change.

Nutrition Information Per Serving:		
Calories: 140	From Fat: 15	
Total Fat		2g
Saturated Fat		1g
Trans Fat		0g
Cholesterol		5mg
Sodium		45mg
Total Carbohydrate		26g
Dietary Fiber		5g
Sugars		18g
Protein		4g

tip

This smoothie can also be served in a small bowl as a refreshing dessert. Or, sprinkle it with granola for a hearty breakfast treat.

Caramel-Glazed Apple Bread

PREP TIME: 20 MINUTES (READY IN 2 HOURS 55 MINUTES)
SERVINGS: 2 LOAVES (12 SLICES EACH)

EASY

BREAD

- 1½ cups shredded peeled baking apples (2 large)
- 1 cup packed brown sugar
- ½ cup buttermilk
- ½ cup vegetable oil
- 4 eggs, lightly beaten
- 3 cups all-purpose flour
- ½ cup chopped pecans
- 2 teaspoons baking soda
- 2 teaspoons ground cinnamon
- 1 teaspoon salt
- 1 teaspoon ground nutmeg

GLAZE

- 2 tablespoons butter or margarine
- ¼ cup packed brown sugar
- 1 tablespoon milk
- ½ cup powdered sugar, sifted

1) Heat oven to 350°F. Grease bottoms only of 2 (8x4-inch) loaf pans with cooking spray or shortening.

2) In large bowl, stir together apples, 1 cup brown sugar, the buttermilk, oil and eggs. Stir in remaining bread ingredients just until dry ingredients are moistened. Pour into pans.

3) Bake 45 to 55 minutes or until toothpick inserted in the center comes out clean. Cool 10 minutes on cooling rack. Loosen sides of loaves from pans; remove from pans and place top sides up on cooling rack. Cool completely, about 1 hour.

4) In 1-quart saucepan, melt butter over medium heat. Stir in ¼ cup brown sugar. Heat to boiling, stirring constantly; reduce heat to low. Boil and stir 2 minutes. Stir in milk. Heat to boiling; remove from heat. Cool to lukewarm, about 30 minutes.

5) Gradually stir powdered sugar into glaze mixture. Place saucepan of glaze in bowl of cold water. Beat with spoon until smooth and thin enough to drizzle. If glaze becomes too stiff, stir in additional milk, ½ teaspoon at a time, or heat over low heat, stirring constantly. Drizzle glaze over loaves. Wrap tightly and store at room temperature up to 4 days, or refrigerate up to 10 days.

HIGH ALTITUDE (3500-6500 FT.): Heat oven to 375°F. Bake 45 to 50 minutes.

Nutrition Information Per Serving:	
Calories: 200	From Fat: 70
Total Fat	8g
Saturated Fat	2g
Trans Fat	0g
Cholesterol	40mg
Sodium	230mg
Total Carbohydrate	27g
Dietary Fiber	1g
Sugars	15g
Protein	3g

Mini Pear Brie Bites

PREP TIME: 25 MINUTES (READY IN 45 MINUTES)
SERVINGS: 24 APPETIZERS

1 can (8 oz) Pillsbury® refrigerated crescent dinner rolls or 1 can (8 oz) Pillsbury® Crescent Recipe Creations™ refrigerated flaky dough sheet

1 pear, peeled, finely chopped (about 1¹/₂ cups)

1 tablespoon packed brown sugar

¹/₈ teaspoon ground red pepper (cayenne), if desired

1 tablespoon honey

1 round (8 oz) Brie cheese, rind removed, cut into 24 (¹/₂-inch) chunks

¹/₃ cup finely chopped pecans

1) Heat oven to 375°F. Grease or spray 24 mini muffin cups. Unroll dough on work surface (if using crescent rolls, pinch the seams to seal); press into 12x8-inch rectangle. Cut into 6 rows by 4 rows to make 24 squares. Gently press squares into mini muffin cups (dough will not completely cover inside of cup; do not press too much).

2) In small bowl, mix the chopped pear, brown sugar, red pepper and honey. Place 1 Brie cheese chunk in each cup. Top with 1 heaping teaspoon pear mixture. Sprinkle with pecans.

3) Bake 15 to 20 minutes or until the edges are deep golden brown. Cool 5 minutes; remove from muffin pans. Serve warm.

HIGH ALTITUDE (3500-6500 FT.): No change.

Nutrition Information Per Serving:	
Calories: 80	From Fat: 45
Total Fat	5g
Saturated Fat	2.5g
Trans Fat	0g
Cholesterol	10mg
Sodium	135mg
Total Carbohydrate	7g
Dietary Fiber	0g
Sugars	3g
Protein	2g

Blueberry-Pomegranate Smoothies

PREP TIME: 5 MINUTES (READY IN 5 MINUTES)
SERVINGS: 2 (3/4 CUP EACH)

❸ EASY   **❶ LOW FAT**

1 cup frozen blueberries

¹/₂ cup pomegranate juice

¹/₂ cup soy milk

1) In blender or food processor, place all ingredients. Cover; blend on high speed about 1 minute or until smooth. Pour into 2 glasses. Serve immediately.

HIGH ALTITUDE (3500-6500 FT.): No change.

Nutrition Information Per Serving:	
Calories: 140	From Fat: 15
Total Fat	2g
Saturated Fat	0g
Trans Fat	0g
Cholesterol	0mg
Sodium	40mg
Total Carbohydrate	28g
Dietary Fiber	4g
Sugars	21g
Protein	3g

Artichoke-Spinach Strata

PREP TIME:	20 MINUTES (READY IN 5 HOURS 30 MINUTES)
SERVINGS:	8

🄴 EASY

2 teaspoons olive or vegetable oil

1 cup finely chopped red bell pepper (1 medium)

$1/2$ cup finely chopped onion (1 medium)

2 garlic cloves, finely chopped

1 can (14 oz) quartered artichoke hearts, drained, coarsely chopped ($1^1/2$ cups)

1 box (9 oz) Green Giant® frozen spinach, thawed, squeezed to drain

8 cups cubed (1 inch) rustic round bread (about 1 lb)

$1^1/2$ cups shredded Monterey Jack cheese (6 oz)

6 eggs

$2^1/2$ cups milk

$1/2$ teaspoon ground mustard

1 teaspoon salt

$1/4$ teaspoon pepper

$1/2$ cup shredded Parmesan cheese (2 oz)

1) In 10-inch nonstick skillet, heat oil over medium heat. Add bell pepper, onion and garlic; cook about 6 minutes, stirring occasionally, until tender. Remove from heat. Stir in artichokes and spinach; set aside.

2) Spray 13x9-inch (3-quart) glass baking dish with cooking spray. Arrange bread cubes in dish. Spoon vegetable mixture evenly over bread cubes; sprinkle with Monterey Jack cheese.

3) In medium bowl, beat eggs, milk, mustard, salt and pepper with wire whisk until blended; pour evenly over the bread, vegetables and Monterey Jack cheese. Sprinkle with Parmesan cheese. Cover tightly with foil; refrigerate at least 4 hours but no longer than 24 hours.

4) Heat oven to 350°F. Bake covered 30 minutes. Uncover and bake 20 to 30 minutes longer or until top is golden brown and knife inserted in center comes out clean. Let stand 10 minutes before cutting.

HIGH ALTITUDE (3500-6500 FT.): Bake covered 40 minutes. Uncover; bake 25 to 35 minutes longer.

Nutrition Information Per Serving:		
Calories: 390	From Fat:	150
Total Fat		17g
Saturated Fat		8g
Trans Fat		0.5g
Cholesterol		190mg
Sodium		980mg
Total Carbohydrate		35g
Dietary Fiber		7g
Sugars		12g
Protein		24g

Summer's Bounty Smoothies

PREP TIME: 10 MINUTES (READY IN 10 MINUTES)
SERVINGS: 2 (1 CUP EACH)

e EASY   **f** LOW FAT

1 ripe banana, peeled, cut into chunks

1 ripe nectarine, peeled, pitted and quartered

4 to 5 large fresh strawberries, cut in half

1 cup strawberry frozen yogurt

1) In blender or food processor, place all ingredients. Cover; blend on high speed 20 to 30 seconds or until smooth. Pour into 2 glasses. Serve immediately.

HIGH ALTITUDE (3500-6500 FT.): No change.

Nutrition Information Per Serving:

Calories:	240	From Fat:	25
Total Fat			2.5g
Saturated Fat			1.5g
Trans Fat			0g
Cholesterol			5mg
Sodium			75mg
Total Carbohydrate			47g
Dietary Fiber			3g
Sugars			36g
Protein			7g

tip

For a nutritional boost, try adding one tablespoon of wheat germ or Fiber One® cereal to this easy recipe.

Mixed-Berry Coffee Cake

PREP TIME: 15 MINUTES (READY IN 1 HOUR)
SERVINGS: 8

€ EASY

COFFEE CAKE

- ¾ cup granulated sugar
- ¼ cup butter or margarine, softened
- 1 egg
- ½ cup milk
- 1½ cups all-purpose flour
- 2 teaspoons baking powder
- ½ teaspoon salt
- 2 tablespoons granulated sugar
- 1 teaspoon ground cinnamon
- 1½ cups mixed fresh berries (such as blueberries, raspberries and blackberries)
- ⅓ cup sliced almonds

GLAZE

- ½ cup powdered sugar
- ¼ teaspoon vanilla
- 2 to 3 teaspoons milk

1) Heat oven to 350°F. Grease and flour the bottom and side of 9-inch round cake pan, or spray with baking spray with flour.

2) In large bowl, beat ¾ cup granulated sugar, the butter and egg with electric mixer on medium speed until fluffy. Beat in milk just until blended. Stir in flour, baking powder and salt. Spread batter in pan.

3) In medium bowl, stir together 2 tablespoons granulated sugar and the cinnamon. Add berries; toss with the cinnamon-sugar mixture until well coated. Spoon berry mixture over batter. Sprinkle with almonds.

4) Bake 35 to 45 minutes or until toothpick inserted in center of cake comes out clean.

5) In small bowl, mix glaze ingredients until smooth and thin enough to drizzle. Drizzle glaze over warm coffee cake. Serve warm.

HIGH ALTITUDE (3500-6500 FT.): Bake 45 to 50 minutes.

Nutrition Information Per Serving:	
Calories: 310	From Fat: 80
Total Fat	9g
Saturated Fat	4.5g
Trans Fat	0g
Cholesterol	45mg
Sodium	330mg
Total Carbohydrate	53g
Dietary Fiber	2g
Sugars	32g
Protein	5g

Ham and Chile Brunch Pizza

JENNIFER KAVANAGH | EASTON, PENNSYLVANIA

Pillsbury Bake-Off®   BAKE-OFF® CONTEST 40, 2002

PREP TIME:	15 MINUTES (READY IN 30 MINUTES)
SERVINGS:	4

e EASY

1 can (13.8 oz) Pillsbury® refrigerated classic pizza crust

6 eggs

¼ teaspoon salt

⅛ teaspoon pepper

1 tablespoon butter or margarine

1 cup julienne-cut strips or chopped cooked ham

1 can (4.5 oz) Old El Paso® chopped green chiles

1½ cups shredded Monterey Jack cheese (6 oz)

2 tablespoons chopped fresh cilantro, if desired

1) Heat oven to 425°F. Grease 14-inch pizza pan with shortening. Unroll dough; place in pan. Starting at the center, press out dough to edge of pan to form crust. Bake 6 to 8 minutes or until the crust begins to brown.

2) Meanwhile, in medium bowl, beat eggs, salt and pepper with wire whisk. In 10-inch skillet, melt butter over medium heat. Add eggs; cook 1 to 2 minutes, stirring frequently, until eggs are firm but still moist.

3) Remove partially baked crust from oven. Spoon and spread eggs over crust. Top with ham, chiles and cheese.

4) Return to oven; bake 8 to 12 minutes longer or until crust is deep golden brown. Sprinkle with cilantro before serving.

HIGH ALTITUDE (3500-6500 FT.): In Step 1, bake 8 to 10 minutes. In Step 4, bake 10 to 14 minutes longer.

Nutrition Information Per Serving:		
Calories: 610	From Fat:	270
Total Fat		30g
Saturated Fat		14g
Trans Fat		0g
Cholesterol		385mg
Sodium		1820mg
Total Carbohydrate		49g
Dietary Fiber		2g
Sugars		8g
Protein		35g

Zucchini-Carrot Bread with Creamy Honey Spread

PREP TIME: 25 MINUTES (READY IN 3 HOURS 5 MINUTES)
SERVINGS: 2 LOAVES (12 SLICES EACH)

BREAD

1½ cups shredded zucchini (2 medium)

1½ cups shredded carrots (3 medium)

1½ cups sugar

⅔ cup vegetable oil

4 eggs

1½ cups all-purpose flour

1½ cups whole wheat flour

2 teaspoons baking soda

1½ teaspoons ground cinnamon

1 teaspoon salt

¾ teaspoon ground cloves

SPREAD

1 package (8 oz) cream cheese, softened

¼ cup honey

2 teaspoons grated orange or lemon peel

1) Heat oven to 350°F. Grease bottoms only of 2 (8x4-inch) loaf pans or 1 (9x5-inch) loaf pan with shortening or cooking spray.

2) In large bowl, mix the zucchini, carrots, sugar, oil and eggs with wire whisk. Stir in remaining bread ingredients. Divide batter evenly between pans.

3) Bake 8-inch loaves 1 hour to 1 hour 15 minutes, 9-inch loaf 1 hour 15 minutes to 1 hour 30 minutes, or until toothpick inserted in center comes out clean. Cool 10 minutes in pans on cooling rack.

4) Loosen sides of loaves from pans; remove from pans and place top sides up on cooling rack. Cool completely, about 1 hour.

5) In small bowl, beat the spread ingredients with electric mixer on medium speed until smooth and fluffy. Serve with sliced bread. Cover; refrigerate any remaining spread. Wrap loaves tightly and store at room temperature up to 4 days, or refrigerate up to 10 days.

HIGH ALTITUDE (3500-6500 FT.): Heat oven to 375°F.

Nutrition Information Per Serving:	
Calories: 220 From Fat: 90	
Total Fat	11g
Saturated Fat	3.5g
Trans Fat	0g
Cholesterol	45mg
Sodium	250mg
Total Carbohydrate	28g
Dietary Fiber	1g
Sugars	16g
Protein	3g

Double-Orange Scones with Orange Butter

PREP TIME: 15 MINUTES (READY IN 35 MINUTES)
SERVINGS: 8 SCONES

SCONES

     2 cups all-purpose flour

     3 tablespoons sugar

 2½ teaspoons baking powder

     2 teaspoons grated orange peel

 ⅓ cup butter or margarine

 ½ cup mandarin orange segments
       (from 11-oz can), chopped, drained

 ¼ cup milk

     1 egg, slightly beaten

     1 tablespoon sugar

ORANGE BUTTER

 ½ cup butter or margarine, softened

     2 tablespoons orange marmalade

1) Heat oven to 400°F. Lightly spray cookie sheet with cooking spray.

2) In large bowl, mix flour, 3 tablespoons sugar, the baking powder and orange peel. Cut in ⅓ cup butter, using pastry blender or fork, until mixture looks like coarse crumbs. Add orange segments, milk and egg; stir with fork just until mixture leaves side of bowl and soft dough forms.

3) Place dough on floured surface. Knead lightly 10 times. On cookie sheet, roll or pat dough into 7-inch round. Sprinkle with 1 tablespoon sugar. Cut into 8 wedges; separate slightly.

4) Bake 15 to 20 minutes or until golden brown. Meanwhile, in small bowl, beat ½ cup butter until light and fluffy; stir in the marmalade. Serve butter with warm scones.

HIGH ALTITUDE (3500-6500 FT.): Decrease baking powder to 2 teaspoons. Bake 17 to 22 minutes.

Nutrition Information Per Serving:	
Calories: 340	From Fat: 180

Total Fat	20g
Saturated Fat	12g
Trans Fat	1g
Cholesterol	50mg
Sodium	300mg
Total Carbohydrate	36g
Dietary Fiber	1g
Sugars	10g
Protein	4g

Cappuccino Smoothies

PREP TIME: 10 MINUTES (READY IN 10 MINUTES)
SERVINGS: 4 (1 CUP EACH)

EASY

- 2 tablespoons instant coffee granules or crystals
- 2 tablespoons hot water
- 1 pint (2 cups) vanilla ice cream
- 1/4 cup instant chocolate milk mix
- 1 1/2 cups milk

1) In small bowl, mix instant coffee and hot water; stir until dissolved.

2) In blender or food processor, place the coffee mixture and remaining ingredients. Cover; blend on medium speed about 20 seconds or until smooth.

3) Pour into 4 glasses or mugs. Serve the smoothies immediately.

HIGH ALTITUDE (3500-6500 FT.): No change.

Nutrition Information Per Serving:

Calories:	240	From Fat:	90
Total Fat			10g
Saturated Fat			6g
Trans Fat			0g
Cholesterol			40mg
Sodium			120mg
Total Carbohydrate			32g
Dietary Fiber			1g
Sugars			26g
Protein			6g

tip

To give this smoothie even more mocha flavor, use coffee ice cream instead. Or, sprinkle each serving with unsweetened baking cocoa.

Egg and Sausage Breakfast Ring

PREP TIME: 20 MINUTES (READY IN 50 MINUTES)
SERVINGS: 8

e EASY

½ lb bulk pork sausage

⅓ cup sliced green onions

⅓ cup chopped red bell pepper

5 eggs

¼ teaspoon salt

⅛ teaspoon pepper

1 package (3 oz) cream cheese, softened

2 cans (8 oz each) Pillsbury®
refrigerated crescent dinner rolls or
2 cans (8 oz each) Pillsbury®
Crescent Recipe Creations™
refrigerated flaky dough sheet

½ cup shredded Cheddar-Monterey
Jack cheese blend (2 oz)

1 egg, beaten

1 teaspoon sesame seed

1) Heat oven to 375°F. Spray large cookie sheet with cooking spray. In 10-inch nonstick skillet, cook sausage and onions over medium-high heat 5 to 8 minutes or until thoroughly cooked; drain. Stir in red bell pepper; cook until tender. Remove from pan.

2) In small bowl, beat 5 eggs, the salt and pepper. Add egg mixture to skillet; cook over medium heat, stirring occasionally from outside edge to center. Cook until eggs are set but still moist. Stir in sausage mixture and cream cheese.

3) Unroll both cans of dough. Place the dough on cookie sheet, long sides overlapping, to form 14x13-inch rectangle; firmly press the edges to seal. Spoon egg mixture down center to within ½ inch of edges. Sprinkle with cheese. Starting at longest side, roll up; press edges to seal. Shape into a circle; pinch ends to seal. Cut six 2-inch slits around top of dough. Brush dough with egg; sprinkle with sesame seed. Bake 25 to 30 minutes or until deep golden brown.

HIGH ALTITUDE (3500-6500 FT.): Bake 20 to 25 minutes.

Nutrition Information Per Serving:		
Calories: 480	From Fat: 280	
Total Fat		31g
Saturated Fat		13g
Trans Fat		0g
Cholesterol		250mg
Sodium		1000mg
Total Carbohydrate		34g
Dietary Fiber		0g
Sugars		8g
Protein		17g

Chai Latte Tea Mix

PREP TIME:	15 MINUTES (READY IN 15 MINUTES)
SERVINGS:	18 (1 CUP PREPARED TEA EACH)

e EASY

2	cups dry nondairy creamer
1½	cups unsweetened instant tea mix
1½	cups packed dark brown sugar
½	cup powdered sugar
2	teaspoons ground ginger
2	teaspoons ground cinnamon
1	teaspoon ground cardamom
1	teaspoon ground cloves

Nutrition Information Per Serving:

Calories:	150	From Fat:	35
Total Fat			4g
Saturated Fat			3.5g
Trans Fat			0g
Cholesterol			0mg
Sodium			30mg
Total Carbohydrate			29g
Dietary Fiber			0g
Sugars			27g
Protein			1g

1) In large bowl, stir all ingredients until blended. In food processor, blend about 2 cups mixture at a time 30 to 45 seconds or until mixture looks like fine powder.

2) To serve, place ¼ cup tea mixture in mug. Add 1 cup hot water; stir until dissolved. (Recipe makes 4½ cups mix.)

HIGH ALTITUDE (3500-6500 FT.): No change.

Melon-Raspberry Smoothies

PREP TIME:	5 MINUTES (READY IN 5 MINUTES)
SERVINGS:	2 (3/4 CUP EACH)

e EASY   **f LOW FAT**

1	cup cubed cantaloupe or honeydew melon
1	cup fresh raspberries
1	container (6 oz) Yoplait® Original 99% Fat Free strawberry mango yogurt
2	tablespoons milk
1	tablespoon sugar

Nutrition Information Per Serving:

Calories:	180	From Fat:	15
Total Fat			1.5g
Saturated Fat			0.5g
Trans Fat			0g
Cholesterol			5mg
Sodium			60mg
Total Carbohydrate			37g
Dietary Fiber			4g
Sugars			30g
Protein			4g

1) In blender or food processor, place all ingredients. Cover; blend on high speed 20 to 30 seconds or until smooth. Pour into 2 glasses. Serve the smoothies immediately.

HIGH ALTITUDE (3500-6500 FT.): No change.

Maple Cream Coffee Treat

RETA EBBINK | TORRANCE, CALIFORNIA

BAKE-OFF® CONTEST 28, 1978

PREP TIME: 15 MINUTES (READY IN 50 MINUTES)
SERVINGS: 20 SWEET ROLLS

e EASY

1 cup packed brown sugar

½ cup chopped nuts

⅓ cup maple-flavored syrup or dark corn syrup

¼ cup butter or margarine, melted

1 package (8 oz) cream cheese, softened

¼ cup powdered sugar

2 tablespoons butter or margarine, softened

½ cup coconut

2 cans (12 oz each) Pillsbury® Grands!® Jr. Golden Layers® refrigerated buttermilk biscuits

1) Heat oven to 350°F. In an ungreased 13x9-inch pan, mix brown sugar, nuts, syrup and ¼ cup butter; spread evenly in the bottom of pan. In small bowl, beat cream cheese, powdered sugar and 2 tablespoons butter with spoon until smooth. Stir in coconut.

2) Separate biscuit dough into 20 biscuits; press or roll each into 4-inch round. Spoon 1 tablespoon cream cheese mixture down center of each biscuit round to within ¼ inch of the edge. Overlap sides of dough over filling, forming finger-shaped rolls; arrange seam side down in 2 rows of 10 rolls each over the brown sugar mixture in the pan.

3) Bake 25 to 30 minutes or until deep golden brown. Cool 5 minutes. Turn pan upside down onto sheet of foil or waxed paper, or onto serving platter; remove pan. Serve warm. Cover and refrigerate any remaining sweet rolls.

HIGH ALTITUDE (3500-6500 FT.): Bake 30 to 35 minutes.

Nutrition Information Per Serving:

Calories:	270	From Fat:	130
Total Fat			15g
Saturated Fat			7g
Trans Fat			2g
Cholesterol			20mg
Sodium			430mg
Total Carbohydrate			32g
Dietary Fiber			0g
Sugars			17g
Protein			3g

Shrimp and Egg Brunch Bake

PREP TIME: 25 MINUTES (READY IN 1 HOUR 5 MINUTES)
SERVINGS: 10

EGG MIXTURE

- 3 tablespoons butter or margarine
- 1/2 cup chopped onion
- 1/2 cup chopped green bell pepper
- 12 eggs, beaten
- 6 oz (1 1/2 cups) cooked shrimp
- 1 cup sliced fresh mushrooms

SAUCE

- 2 tablespoons butter or margarine
- 2 tablespoons all-purpose flour
- 1 1/4 cups half-and-half
- 1 cup shredded Swiss cheese (4 oz)
- 1/4 cup grated Parmesan cheese
- 3 tablespoons dry white wine or chicken broth

TOPPING

- 1 can (8 oz) Pillsbury® refrigerated crescent dinner rolls
- 1 tablespoon butter or margarine, melted
- 1 tablespoon chopped fresh parsley

1) Heat oven to 350°F. Lightly grease 12x8-inch (2-quart) glass baking dish. In 10-inch skillet, melt 3 tablespoons butter over medium heat. Add onion and bell pepper; cook and stir until crisp-tender. Add eggs; cook, stirring occasionally, just until eggs are set but still moist. Fold in shrimp and mushrooms.

2) In 2-quart saucepan, melt 2 tablespoons butter. Add the flour; cook and stir until smooth and bubbly. Gradually add half-and-half, cooking and stirring until mixture boils and thickens. Add Swiss cheese, Parmesan cheese and wine; stir until smooth. Fold sauce into egg mixture. Pour into baking dish.

3) Remove dough from can in 2 rolled sections. Do not unroll dough. Cut each roll into 6 slices; cut each slice in half. Arrange 20 slices flat edge down around edges of pan; arrange remaining 4 slices in center. In small bowl, mix 1 tablespoon melted butter and the parsley; brush over dough.

4) Bake 25 to 35 minutes or until eggs are set and crust is golden brown. Let stand 5 minutes before serving. Garnish as desired.

HIGH ALTITUDE (3500-6500 FT.): Bake 28 to 33 minutes.

Nutrition Information Per Serving:	
Calories: 360	From Fat: 230
Total Fat	26g
Saturated Fat	13g
Trans Fat	1.5g
Cholesterol	330mg
Sodium	420mg
Total Carbohydrate	14g
Dietary Fiber	0g
Sugars	5g
Protein	18g

Dried Fruit and Cinnamon Batter Bread

PREP TIME: 15 MINUTES (READY IN 3 HOURS)
SERVINGS: 1 LOAF (16 SLICES)

e EASY

BREAD

- 3 cups all-purpose flour
- 1/4 cup granulated sugar
- 1 teaspoon salt
- 2 teaspoons ground cinnamon or cardamom
- 1 package fast-acting dry yeast (2 1/4 teaspoons)
- 1 1/4 cups very warm water (120°F to 130°F)
- 1/4 cup butter or margarine, melted
- 1 egg
- 1 cup diced dried fruit and raisin mixture (from 7-oz bag)

GLAZE

- 1/2 cup powdered sugar
- 1/4 teaspoon vanilla
- 2 to 3 teaspoons milk

1) Spray bottom and sides of 9x5-inch loaf pan with cooking spray.

2) In large bowl, mix 2 cups of the flour, the granulated sugar, salt, cinnamon and yeast. Add water, butter and egg. Beat with electric mixer on medium speed 3 minutes, scraping bowl frequently. Stir in dried fruit and remaining 1 cup flour to make a stiff batter.

3) Spread batter in pan; pat into shape with floured hands. Cover loosely with plastic wrap lightly sprayed with cooking spray; let rise in warm place 45 to 60 minutes or until doubled in size.

4) Heat oven to 375°F. Remove plastic wrap. Bake 40 to 45 minutes or until loaf sounds hollow when tapped. Immediately remove from pan and place top side up on cooling rack. Cool completely, about 1 hour.

5) In small bowl, mix glaze ingredients until smooth and thin enough to drizzle. Drizzle glaze over top of loaf.

HIGH ALTITUDE (3500-6500 FT.): No change.

Nutrition Information Per Serving:		
Calories: 170	From Fat:	30
Total Fat		3.5g
Saturated Fat		2g
Trans Fat		0g
Cholesterol		20mg
Sodium		170mg
Total Carbohydrate		31g
Dietary Fiber		1g
Sugars		11g
Protein		3g

Sweet Potato Streusel Muffins

PREP TIME: 25 MINUTES (READY IN 45 MINUTES)
SERVINGS: 15 MUFFINS

MUFFINS

1½   cups all-purpose flour
¾   cup cornmeal
½   cup granulated sugar
¼   cup chopped peanuts
¼   cup golden raisins
3   teaspoons baking powder
1   teaspoon ground nutmeg
2   eggs
1   cup mashed cooked sweet potato (1 small to medium; about 10 to 12 oz)
⅔   cup milk
2   tablespoons vegetable oil

TOPPING

3   tablespoons packed brown sugar
2   tablespoons chopped peanuts
1   tablespoon butter or margarine, softened

1) Heat oven to 400°F. Spray 15 regular-size muffin cups with cooking spray. In medium bowl, mix flour, cornmeal, granulated sugar, ¼ cup peanuts, the raisins, baking powder and nutmeg.

2) In medium bowl, beat eggs slightly. Stir in sweet potato, milk and oil until well blended. Add to dry ingredients all at once; stir just until dry ingredients are moistened. (Batter will be lumpy.) Fill muffin cups ¾ full.

3) In small bowl, mix the topping ingredients. Sprinkle topping evenly over the muffins.

4) Bake 15 to 20 minutes or until toothpick inserted in the center comes out clean. Remove from pan. Serve warm.

HIGH ALTITUDE (3500-6500 FT.): No change.

Nutrition Information Per Serving:	
Calories: 200	From Fat: 50
Total Fat	6g
Saturated Fat	1.5g
Trans Fat	0g
Cholesterol	30mg
Sodium	135mg
Total Carbohydrate	32g
Dietary Fiber	1g
Sugars	13g
Protein	4g

BAYOU SHRIMP WITH
LEMON-ROSEMARY AIOLI
PG. 42

Appetizers & Beverages

Dazzle guests with scrumptious yet easy hors d'oeuvres, the kinds that get everyone talking—and munching!

CARAMELIZED ONION AND
MUSHROOM TARTLETS
PG. 47

THREE-CHEESE PARTY WHEEL
PG. 33

THAI TURKEY ROLLS WITH
PEANUT SAUCE
PG. 40

Festive Fillo Crab Cups

PREP TIME: 15 MINUTES (READY IN 15 MINUTES)
SERVINGS: 30 APPETIZERS

e EASY   **f** LOW FAT

2 cans (6 oz each) lump crabmeat, drained, flaked

¼ cup mayonnaise or salad dressing

¼ cup sour cream

3 tablespoons finely chopped celery

2 tablespoons finely chopped fresh chives

1 tablespoon finely chopped fresh dill weed

1 teaspoon lemon juice

½ teaspoon grated lemon peel

¼ teaspoon salt

½ teaspoon Worcestershire sauce

¼ teaspoon red pepper sauce

2 packages (2.1 oz each) frozen mini fillo shells (15 shells each)

Additional fresh dill weed sprigs, if desired

Fresh lemon slices, cut into quarters, if desired

1) In medium bowl, stir together all ingredients except fillo shells, additional dill weed and lemon slices until well mixed. Cover; refrigerate until ready to serve.

2) Spoon about 1 rounded tablespoon crab mixture into each fillo shell. Garnish each with dill weed sprig and lemon slices. Serve immediately.

HIGH ALTITUDE (3500-6500 FT.): No change.

Nutrition Information Per Serving:

Calories:	45	From Fat:	25
Total Fat			3g
Saturated Fat			0g
Trans Fat			0g
Cholesterol			10mg
Sodium			75mg
Total Carbohydrate			2g
Dietary Fiber			0g
Sugars			0g
Protein			2g

Cheese and Fruit Plate

PREP TIME: 15 MINUTES (READY IN 15 MINUTES)
SERVINGS: 18 (1-1/2 OZ CHEESE, 1-2 STRAWBERRIES, 1-2 APRICOTS, 4 CRACKERS & SCANT 2 TBSP SPREAD EACH)

 EASY

FIG SPREAD

- 1 bag (9 oz) dried Mission figs (about 24 medium figs), chopped
- 1 bag (2½ oz) hazelnuts (filberts), chopped (about ⅓ cup)
- 1 jar (12 oz) apricot preserves

CHEESE AND FRUIT

- 1 piece (8 oz) Gouda cheese
- 1 piece (8 oz) blue cheese
- 1 round (8 oz) Brie cheese
- 1 container (1 lb) fresh strawberries (about 24)
- 1 bag (7 oz) dried apricots
- 64 whole wheat crackers
- Fresh parsley sprigs

1) In small serving bowl, mix spread ingredients until blended.

2) To serve, place cheeses on decorative platter; surround with strawberries, apricots and crackers. Garnish with parsley sprigs. Serve with fig spread.

HIGH ALTITUDE (3500-6500 FT.): No change.

Nutrition Information Per Serving:	
Calories: 330	From Fat: 130

Total Fat	14g
Saturated Fat	7g
Trans Fat	0g
Cholesterol	35mg
Sodium	460mg
Total Carbohydrate	40g
Dietary Fiber	4g
Sugars	24g
Protein	11g

Crab and Pepper Jack Tostaditos

PREP TIME:	40 MINUTES (READY IN 50 MINUTES)	(lf) LOW FAT
SERVINGS:	54 APPETIZERS	

1 teaspoon vegetable oil

¼ cup finely chopped yellow bell pepper

¼ cup sliced green onions (4 medium)

¼ cup finely chopped poblano chile

1 package (8 oz) salad-style imitation crabmeat, finely chopped

½ cup shredded pepper Jack cheese (2 oz)

¼ cup Old El Paso® Thick 'n Chunky salsa

½ bag (10-oz size) bowl-shaped white corn tortilla chips (54 chips)

⅓ cup crumbled cotija or feta cheese (about 1½ oz)

½ ripe medium avocado, pitted, peeled and cut into 54 small slices

1) Heat oven to 375°F. In 10-inch skillet, heat oil over medium-high heat. Add the bell pepper, onions and chile; cook 3 to 4 minutes, stirring frequently, until soft. Remove from skillet; place in medium bowl. Stir in imitation crabmeat, pepper Jack cheese and salsa until well mixed.

2) Place tortilla chips, hollow side up, on ungreased large cookie sheet. Spoon 1 heaping teaspoon crabmeat mixture into each tortilla chip. Top each evenly with cotija cheese.

3) Bake 6 to 8 minutes or until pepper Jack cheese in crabmeat mixture is melted. Place on serving plate; garnish each with avocado slice.

HIGH ALTITUDE (3500-6500 FT.): No change.

Nutrition Information Per Serving:	
Calories: 30	From Fat: 15
Total Fat	1.5g
Saturated Fat	0g
Trans Fat	0g
Cholesterol	0mg
Sodium	85mg
Total Carbohydrate	3g
Dietary Fiber	0g
Sugars	0g
Protein	1g

Mojito Slush

PREP TIME: 20 MINUTES (READY IN 4 HOURS 45 MINUTES)
SERVINGS: 14 (3/4 CUP EACH)

🅔 EASY   🅕 LOW FAT

3 cups water

1 cup sugar

¾ cup fresh lime juice (from about 5 limes)

¾ cup light rum

½ cup lightly packed fresh mint leaves

1½ cups ginger ale

Mint sprigs, if desired

Nutrition Information Per Serving:		
Calories: 100	From Fat:	0
Total Fat		0g
Saturated Fat		0g
Trans Fat		0g
Cholesterol		0mg
Sodium		5mg
Total Carbohydrate		18g
Dietary Fiber		0g
Sugars		17g
Protein		0g

1) In 1½-quart saucepan, heat water and sugar over medium heat about 2 minutes or until sugar is dissolved. Cool completely, about 30 minutes.

2) In 8-cup blender, place sugar water, lime juice, rum and mint leaves (if smaller blender, do in batches). Cover; blend on high speed about 20 seconds or until mint is finely chopped.

3) Pour mixture into 13x9-inch (3-quart) glass baking dish. Freeze 4 to 6 hours, using fork to break apart ice crystals every 2 hours.

4) To serve, spoon ½ cup mixture into each glass; pour ¼ cup ginger ale over each. Stir. If desired, garnish with mint sprigs.

HIGH ALTITUDE (3500-6500 FT.): No change.

Caramelized Chili Shrimp

PREP TIME: 5 MINUTES (READY IN 15 MINUTES)
SERVINGS: 12 (ABOUT 2 SHRIMP EACH)

🅔 EASY   🅕 LOW FAT

½ cup sugar

1 tablespoon all-purpose flour

1 teaspoon kosher (coarse) salt

1 teaspoon chili powder

⅛ teaspoon chipotle chili powder or ground red pepper (cayenne)

1 garlic clove, finely chopped

1 lb uncooked large shrimp (21 to 30 shrimp), peeled with tails left on, deveined

¼ medium fresh lime

1) Heat oven to 500°F. Line 15x10x1-inch pan with foil; spray foil with cooking spray.

2) In a resealable 1-gallon food-storage plastic bag, mix all ingredients except shrimp and lime. Add shrimp; seal bag and shake to coat with sugar mixture. Arrange shrimp with sugar mixture in single layer in pan.

3) Bake 7 to 9 minutes or until sugar is caramelized. Remove from oven. Using pancake turner, turn shrimp; squeeze juice from lime over shrimp. Place on serving platter; serve immediately.

HIGH ALTITUDE (3500-6500 FT.): No change.

Nutrition Information Per Serving:		
Calories: 60	From Fat:	0
Total Fat		0g
Saturated Fat		0g
Trans Fat		0g
Cholesterol		55mg
Sodium		260mg
Total Carbohydrate		9g
Dietary Fiber		0g
Sugars		8g
Protein		6g

Ceviche-Style Shrimp Cocktail

PREP TIME: 15 MINUTES (READY IN 1 HOUR 15 MINUTES)
SERVINGS: 10 (3/4 CUP EACH)

e EASY

1½ lb cooked deveined peeled medium shrimp, thawed if frozen, tail shells removed

1 large avocado, pitted, peeled and diced

1 medium cucumber, peeled, diced

¾ cup finely chopped red onion

¾ cup sliced green onions (12 medium)

2 plum (Roma) tomatoes, chopped

1 serrano chile, seeded, chopped

½ cup finely chopped fresh cilantro

¾ cup ketchup

½ cup Bloody Mary mix

⅓ cup seasoned tomato-clam cocktail

⅓ cup fresh lime juice

1 teaspoon salt

½ teaspoon garlic salt

Few drops red pepper sauce, if desired

Saltine crackers, if desired

1) In large bowl, place shrimp, avocado, cucumber, onions, tomatoes, chile and cilantro; toss gently to mix.

2) In medium bowl, mix remaining ingredients except crackers until blended. Pour over shrimp mixture, stirring to mix.

3) Cover and refrigerate 1 to 2 hours to marinate. Spoon ¾ cup shrimp mixture into each of 10 glasses. Serve with saltine crackers.

HIGH ALTITUDE (3500-6500 FT.): No change.

Nutrition Information Per Serving:

Calories:	170	From Fat:	70
Total Fat			8g
Saturated Fat			1g
Trans Fat			0g
Cholesterol			95mg
Sodium			650mg
Total Carbohydrate			13g
Dietary Fiber			4g
Sugars			7g
Protein			12g

tip

This Latin-American inspired appetizer is typically paired with saltine crackers, but oyster crackers could be used as well.

Three-Cheese Party Wheel

PREP TIME: 15 MINUTES (READY IN 15 MINUTES)
SERVINGS: 20 (2 TABLESPOONS SPREAD AND 4 CRACKERS EACH)

ⓔ EASY

1 container (8 oz) Swiss almond cold-pack cheese food

1 container (8 oz) sharp Cheddar cold-pack cheese food

1 container (8 oz) chives-and-onion cream cheese spread

1/4 cup sliced almonds, toasted if desired

1/4 cup finely chopped fresh parsley

80 assorted crackers

Fresh currants, if desired

1) On sheet of waxed paper, spread Swiss almond cheese into 5-inch round, about 1/2 inch thick. With small metal spatula, smooth side and top.

2) Evenly spread Cheddar cheese over Swiss cheese; smooth side and top.

3) Evenly spread cream cheese spread over top; smooth side and top to even layers. Sprinkle almonds over the top; press in lightly. Press parsley into side of cheese wheel. Serve immediately, or wrap in waxed paper and refrigerate until serving time.

4) To serve, place cheese wheel on serving plate; arrange crackers around cheese. Garnish with currants.

HIGH ALTITUDE (3500-6500 FT.): No change.

Nutrition Information Per Serving:	
Calories: 180	From Fat: 120
Total Fat	14g
Saturated Fat	7g
Trans Fat	0g
Cholesterol	30mg
Sodium	440mg
Total Carbohydrate	8g
Dietary Fiber	0g
Sugars	0g
Protein	7g

Coffee-Crusted Beef Tenderloin with Dijon Cream

PREP TIME: 30 MINUTES (READY IN 5 HOURS)
SERVINGS: 24 APPETIZERS

2 teaspoons instant coffee granules

½ teaspoon coarsely ground pepper

¼ teaspoon salt

1 lb beef tenderloin (center cut)

1 tablespoon vegetable oil

1 tablespoon Dijon mustard

½ cup mayonnaise or salad dressing

½ teaspoon salt

4 large leaf lettuce leaves, torn into 24 small pieces

2 whole-grain French dinner rolls, cut into 24 (¼-inch) slices

24 small thyme sprigs

1) Heat oven to 450°F. In small bowl, mix coffee granules, pepper and ¼ teaspoon salt. Sprinkle evenly over all sides of beef.

2) In 10-inch nonstick skillet, heat oil over medium-high heat. Add beef; cook 3 minutes. Turn beef; cook 2 to 3 minutes longer or until very dark brown. Place beef in 9-inch square pan (or deep-dish pie pan). Insert ovenproof meat thermometer so tip is in center of beef.

3) Bake 25 to 30 minutes or until the thermometer reads 140°F. Remove from oven. Let stand 5 minutes. Wrap in foil; refrigerate until cold, at least 4 hours or overnight.

4) Meanwhile, in small bowl, mix mustard, mayonnaise and ½ teaspoon salt. Cover; refrigerate Dijon cream until serving time.

5) To serve, cut beef into 12 thin slices; cut each slice in half. Place 1 lettuce piece on each bread slice; top each with beef slice and heaping teaspoon Dijon cream. Garnish with thyme sprigs.

HIGH ALTITUDE (3500-6500 FT.): No change.

Nutrition Information Per Serving:		
Calories: 80	From Fat: 50	
Total Fat		6g
Saturated Fat		1g
Trans Fat		0g
Cholesterol		10mg
Sodium		150mg
Total Carbohydrate		2g
Dietary Fiber		0g
Sugars		0g
Protein		5g

Roasted Vegetables with Roasted Pepper Hummus

PREP TIME: 35 MINUTES (READY IN 45 MINUTES)
SERVINGS: 20 (1 TABLESPOON HUMMUS AND 5 PIECES VEGETABLES EACH)   (f) LOW FAT

ROASTED PEPPER HUMMUS

1 can (15 oz) Progresso® chickpeas (garbanzo beans), drained, liquid reserved

1/4 cup roasted red bell peppers (from 7-oz jar)

1 tablespoon white wine vinegar or lemon juice

1 tablespoon olive oil

1 medium garlic clove, peeled

Salt, if desired

VEGETABLES

7 to 8 green onions, tops trimmed

2 medium red bell peppers, cut into 1½-inch pieces

½ lb fresh asparagus spears, trimmed

½ lb fresh sugar snap pea pods

1 package (8 oz) fresh whole mushrooms

1 tablespoon olive or vegetable oil

½ teaspoon seasoned salt

1) Heat oven to 450°F. In food processor, place chickpeas. Cover; process with quick on-and-off motions until smooth, adding enough reserved liquid (about ¼ cup) to make a creamy mixture. Add roasted peppers, vinegar, 1 tablespoon oil and the garlic; process until smooth. If desired, season with salt to taste. Spoon into serving bowl. Let stand 30 minutes to blend flavors, or cover and refrigerate until serving time.

2) In large bowl, toss vegetables with 1 tablespoon oil to coat evenly. Arrange in ungreased 15x10x1-inch pan; sprinkle with seasoned salt.

3) Bake 7 to 10 minutes or until crisp-tender. Serve warm vegetables with hummus as a dip, or refrigerate vegetables at least 8 hours or overnight and serve with hummus.

HIGH ALTITUDE (3500-6500 FT.): In Step 3, bake 10 to 13 minutes.

Nutrition Information Per Serving:		
Calories: 60	From Fat: 20	
Total Fat		2g
Saturated Fat		0g
Trans Fat		0g
Cholesterol		0mg
Sodium		65mg
Total Carbohydrate		8g
Dietary Fiber		2g
Sugars		2g
Protein		2g

Camembert and Cherry Pastry Puffs

PREP TIME: 20 MINUTES (READY IN 40 MINUTES)
SERVINGS: 36 APPETIZERS

e EASY

1 sheet frozen puff pastry
(from 17.3-oz package), thawed

1/4 cup dried cherries, finely chopped

3 tablespoons cherry preserves

4 oz Camembert cheese (do not
remove rind), cut into 1/4x1/4-inch
pieces

2 tablespoons finely chopped pecans
or hazelnuts

Nutrition Information Per Serving:

Calories:	60	From Fat:	35
Total Fat			3.5g
Saturated Fat			1.5g
Trans Fat			0g
Cholesterol			10mg
Sodium			45mg
Total Carbohydrate			5g
Dietary Fiber			0g
Sugars			1g
Protein			1g

1) Heat oven to 400°F. Spray 36 mini muffin cups with cooking spray. On lightly floured surface, unfold pastry sheet. Cut sheet into 6 rows by 6 rows to get 36 (1½-inch) squares. Lightly press 1 square into center of each muffin cup, pressing center to bottom of cup with finger. Bake 10 minutes.

2) Meanwhile, in small bowl, mix cherries and cherry preserves until well blended; set aside.

3) Press centers of pastry cups with handle of wooden spoon; bake 6 to 8 minutes longer or until golden brown.

4) Immediately press pastry cups in center again. Fill each cup with about 1 heaping teaspoon cheese; top with 1/4 teaspoon cherry mixture. Sprinkle evenly with pecans.

5) Bake 2 to 4 minutes or just until cheese is melted. Carefully remove from muffin cups; place on serving platter. Serve warm.

HIGH ALTITUDE (3500-6500 FT.): No change.

Strawberry Margarita Slush

PREP TIME: 10 MINUTES (READY IN 8 HOURS 10 MINUTES)
SERVINGS: 10 (1 CUP EACH)

e EASY   f LOW FAT

1 bag (16 oz) frozen unsweetened whole strawberries, slightly thawed

1/3 cup sugar

1 can (12 oz) frozen limeade concentrate

1½ cups water

1½ cups tequila

4 cups lemon-lime carbonated beverage, chilled

Nutrition Information Per Serving:

Calories:	250	From Fat:	0
Total Fat			0g
Saturated Fat			0g
Trans Fat			0g
Cholesterol			0mg
Sodium			10mg
Total Carbohydrate			42g
Dietary Fiber			1g
Sugars			32g
Protein			0g

1) In blender, place the strawberries, sugar and limeade concentrate. Cover; blend on high speed until strawberries are chopped and mixture is blended. Slowly add 1/2 to 1 cup of the water, blending well.

2) Pour into nonmetal freezer container. Add remaining 1/2 to 1 cup water, tequila and 1½ cups of the carbonated beverage; mix well. Cover container; freeze 8 hours or overnight until icy, stirring 2 or 3 times after 2 hours.

3) To serve, stir mixture; spoon into 10 glasses. Top each serving with 1/4 cup carbonated beverage.

HIGH ALTITUDE (3500-6500 FT.): No change.

Caramelized-Onion Squares with Olives

PREP TIME: 15 MINUTES (READY IN 35 MINUTES)
SERVINGS: 24 APPETIZERS

 EASY

1 tablespoon olive or vegetable oil

1 tablespoon butter or margarine

1 large onion, cut in half, thinly sliced

2 tablespoons fresh thyme leaves

1 can (8 oz) Pillsbury® Crescent Recipe Creations™ refrigerated flaky dough sheet or 1 can (8 oz) Pillsbury® refrigerated crescent dinner rolls

1½ cups shredded Gruyère cheese (6 oz)

2 tablespoons coarsely chopped pitted kalamata olives

2 tablespoons coarsely chopped roasted red bell peppers

1) In 12-inch skillet, heat oil and butter over medium heat until butter is melted. Add onion and thyme; cook about 10 minutes, stirring frequently, until onion is golden brown. Remove from the heat.

2) Heat oven to 375°F. Roll dough into 12x10-inch rectangle. Cut dough in half lengthwise. On ungreased cookie sheet, place dough pieces about 2 inches apart.

3) Bake about 10 minutes or until light golden brown. Cool slightly, about 2 minutes.

4) Top each baked crust with cheese, caramelized onions, olives and roasted peppers. Bake 4 to 6 minutes longer or until cheese is melted. Using pizza cutter or serrated knife, cut each into 12 squares. Serve warm.

HIGH ALTITUDE (3500-6500 FT.): No change.

Nutrition Information Per Serving:

Calories: 70	From Fat: 45
Total Fat	5g
Saturated Fat	2.5g
Trans Fat	0g
Cholesterol	10mg
Sodium	110mg
Total Carbohydrate	5g
Dietary Fiber	0g
Sugars	1g
Protein	2g

tip

Patience is truly a virtue when you are caramelizing these onions. If you rush them, they won't taste as sweet.

Shrimp Cakes with Wasabi Mayo

PREP TIME: 50 MINUTES (READY IN 1 HOUR 5 MINUTES)
SERVINGS: 12 (1 SHRIMP CAKE AND 2 TEASPOONS WASABI MAYO EACH)

SHRIMP CAKES

- 1 lb uncooked shrimp, peeled (tail shells removed), deveined
- 1 tablespoon reduced-sodium soy sauce
- 1 tablespoon fresh lime juice
- 1/2 teaspoon grated gingerroot
- 1 garlic clove, finely chopped
- 1 egg white
- 2 cups Progresso® panko crispy bread crumbs
- 2 tablespoons finely chopped red bell pepper
- 1 small jalapeño chile, seeded, finely chopped
- 5 tablespoons vegetable oil

WASABI MAYO

- 1/2 cup mayonnaise or salad dressing
- 1 teaspoon wasabi paste
- 1/2 teaspoon reduced-sodium soy sauce

1) Line cookie sheet with cooking parchment paper; line serving platter with paper towels. In food processor, coarsely chop shrimp. Add 1 tablespoon soy sauce, the lime juice, gingerroot, garlic and egg white; process with on-and-off pulses until well mixed. Gradually add 1 cup of the bread crumbs, processing with pulses until mixture is well blended. Remove shrimp mixture from processor; place in medium bowl. Stir in bell pepper and chile.

2) Divide shrimp mixture into 12 equal portions. Shape each portion into patty, 2½ inches in diameter. Place remaining 1 cup bread crumbs on plate. Lightly press both sides of each patty into crumbs to coat evenly; place on cookie sheet. Refrigerate 20 minutes. Discard any remaining bread crumbs.

3) Meanwhile, in small bowl, mix wasabi mayo ingredients until well blended. Cover; refrigerate until serving time.

4) In 10-inch skillet, heat 2 to 3 tablespoons oil over medium-high heat about 2 minutes or until hot. Working in batches, cook the patties in oil 8 to 12 minutes, turning once, until thoroughly cooked and golden brown. Remove patties from skillet to paper towel-lined platter; cover to keep warm. Repeat with remaining 2 tablespoons oil and remaining patties. Serve with wasabi mayo.

HIGH ALTITUDE (3500-6500 FT.): In Step 4, heat oil over medium heat. Cook patties 8 to 10 minutes.

Nutrition Information Per Serving:	
Calories: 210	From Fat: 130
Total Fat	14g
Saturated Fat	2g
Trans Fat	0g
Cholesterol	55mg
Sodium	210mg
Total Carbohydrate	14g
Dietary Fiber	0g
Sugars	1g
Protein	7g

Mexican Plum-Tomato Cups

PREP TIME: 15 MINUTES (READY IN 15 MINUTES)
SERVINGS: 20 APPETIZERS

ⓔ EASY   ⓕ LOW FAT

TOMATO CUPS

- 10 medium plum (Roma) tomatoes
- 1 ripe large avocado, pitted, peeled and finely chopped (about 1 cup)
- ½ cup finely chopped cucumber
- 1 medium jalapeño chile, seeded, finely chopped
- 3 to 4 tablespoons chopped fresh cilantro or parsley
- 2 tablespoons lime juice
- ½ teaspoon salt

TOPPING

- ½ cup sour cream
- 2 teaspoons whipping cream or milk
- ½ teaspoon grated lime peel
- ½ teaspoon salt

1) Cut each tomato in half crosswise. Using teaspoon, scoop out seeds and pulp from each tomato half, leaving enough tomato for a firm shell. If necessary, cut small slice from the bottom so the tomato half stands upright.

2) In medium bowl, mix remaining tomato cup ingredients. In small bowl, mix topping ingredients. Spoon about 1 tablespoon avocado mixture into each tomato shell. Top each with about 1 teaspoon topping.

HIGH ALTITUDE (3500-6500 FT.): No change.

Nutrition Information Per Serving:	
Calories: 35	From Fat: 25
Total Fat	2.5g
Saturated Fat	1g
Trans Fat	0g
Cholesterol	0mg
Sodium	125mg
Total Carbohydrate	2g
Dietary Fiber	1g
Sugars	1g
Protein	0g

Thai Turkey Rolls with Peanut Sauce

PREP TIME: 25 MINUTES (READY IN 40 MINUTES)
SERVINGS: 12 APPETIZERS

TURKEY ROLLS

1 can (8 oz) Pillsbury® refrigerated crescent dinner rolls or 1 can (8 oz) Pillsbury® Crescent Recipe Creations™ refrigerated flaky dough sheet

1 tablespoon vegetable oil

¼ lb ground turkey

¼ cup chopped drained water chestnuts (from 8-oz can)

¼ cup shredded carrot

2 tablespoons chopped fresh cilantro

1 garlic clove, finely chopped

2 tablespoons apricot preserves

2 teaspoons soy sauce

½ teaspoon ground ginger

¼ teaspoon crushed red pepper flakes

1 egg, beaten

SAUCE

¼ cup creamy peanut butter

2 tablespoons orange marmalade

2 tablespoons water

2 tablespoons soy sauce

¼ teaspoon ground ginger

¼ teaspoon crushed red pepper flakes

1) Heat oven to 375°F. Spray large cookie sheet with cooking spray. Unroll dough on work surface (if using crescent rolls, pinch the seams to seal); press into 12x9-inch rectangle. Cut dough into 12 rectangles.

2) In 10-inch nonstick skillet, heat oil over medium-high heat until hot. Add turkey; cook 4 to 5 minutes, stirring occasionally, until no longer pink. Stir in the water chestnuts, carrot, cilantro, garlic, apricot preserves, soy sauce, ginger and red pepper flakes. Spoon about 1 tablespoon turkey mixture onto long side of each dough rectangle to within ¼ inch of short ends. Starting with long side, roll up. Pinch edges to seal. Place seam side down on cookie sheet. Brush with egg.

3) Bake 10 to 15 minutes or until deep golden brown. Remove from cookie sheet.

4) Meanwhile, in 1-quart saucepan, heat sauce ingredients over low heat, stirring until hot. Remove from heat. Serve with turkey rolls.

HIGH ALTITUDE (3500-6500 FT.): No change.

Nutrition Information Per Serving:		
Calories: 150	From Fat:	70
Total Fat		8g
Saturated Fat		2.5g
Trans Fat		0g
Cholesterol		25mg
Sodium		390mg
Total Carbohydrate		15g
Dietary Fiber		0g
Sugars		6g
Protein		5g

Sangria

PREP TIME: 10 MINUTES (READY IN 3 HOURS)
SERVINGS: 12 (3/4 CUP EACH)

e EASY   **(f)** LOW FAT

1 cup sugar

1 cup fresh lemon juice

1 cup orange juice

1/2 cup orange-flavored liqueur

2 bottles (750 ml each) Burgundy wine

1 lemon, sliced

1 orange, sliced

Nutrition Information Per Serving:		
Calories: 220	From Fat:	0
Total Fat		0g
Saturated Fat		0g
Trans Fat		0g
Cholesterol		0mg
Sodium		10mg
Total Carbohydrate		28g
Dietary Fiber		0g
Sugars		23g
Protein		0g

1) In 4-quart nonmetal container, mix sugar, lemon juice, orange juice, liqueur and wine. Refrigerate several hours.

2) Just before serving, pour into pitcher; add lemon and orange slices. Serve in glasses over ice.

HIGH ALTITUDE (3500-6500 FT.): No change.

Prosciutto Spinach Pinwheels

PREP TIME: 20 MINUTES (READY IN 35 MINUTES)
SERVINGS: 24 PINWHEELS

e EASY   **(f)** LOW FAT

1 can (8 oz) Pillsbury® refrigerated crescent dinner rolls or 1 can (8 oz) Pillsbury® Crescent Recipe Creations™ refrigerated flaky dough sheet

1 package (4 oz) thinly sliced prosciutto

1 box (9 oz) Green Giant® frozen spinach, thawed, squeezed to drain

1/4 cup shredded Asiago cheese

1 garlic clove, finely chopped

1 tablespoon onion, finely chopped

1 egg, beaten

Nutrition Information Per Serving:		
Calories: 50	From Fat:	25
Total Fat		2.5g
Saturated Fat		1g
Trans Fat		0g
Cholesterol		15mg
Sodium		170mg
Total Carbohydrate		5g
Dietary Fiber		0g
Sugars		0g
Protein		2g

1) Heat oven to 375°F. Spray large cookie sheet with cooking spray. Unroll dough on work surface (if using crescent rolls, pinch seams to seal); press into 12x8-inch rectangle. Arrange prosciutto evenly over rectangle.

2) In small bowl, mix remaining ingredients except the egg. Spoon spinach mixture evenly over prosciutto. Starting with longest side, roll up; pinch long side to seal. With serrated knife, cut into 24 slices. Place cut side down on cookie sheet. Brush with egg.

3) Bake 10 to 15 minutes or until golden brown. Remove from cookie sheets. Serve warm.

HIGH ALTITUDE (3500-6500 FT.): No change.

Bayou Shrimp with Lemon-Rosemary Aioli

PREP TIME: 15 MINUTES (READY IN 15 MINUTES)
SERVINGS: 32 (1 SHRIMP AND 3/4 TEASPOON AIOLI EACH)

🅔 EASY

AIOLI

- 1/2 cup mayonnaise or salad dressing
- 2 tablespoons extra-virgin olive oil
- 1 medium garlic clove, finely chopped
- 2 to 3 teaspoons lemon juice
- 1 teaspoon grated lemon peel
- 1/2 teaspoon chopped fresh rosemary leaves

SHRIMP

- 2 teaspoons extra-virgin olive oil
- 1 lb uncooked deveined peeled medium shrimp with tails left on (about 32 shrimp)
- 3/4 teaspoon seafood seasoning
- Garnish, if desired
- Fresh rosemary sprigs
- Lemon wedges

1) In small bowl, mix aioli ingredients until well blended.

2) Heat 12-inch nonstick skillet over medium-high heat. Add 2 teaspoons oil; tilt skillet to lightly coat bottom. Add shrimp; sprinkle evenly with seafood seasoning. Cook 3 to 5 minutes, stirring frequently, until shrimp are pink.

3) To serve, place shrimp and any cooking juices on serving platter. Arrange sprigs of rosemary and lemon wedges on platter. Serve with aioli and if desired, toothpicks.

HIGH ALTITUDE (3500-6500 FT.): No change.

Nutrition Information Per Serving:		
Calories: 45	From Fat:	35
Total Fat		4g
Saturated Fat		0.5g
Trans Fat		0g
Cholesterol		20mg
Sodium		60mg
Total Carbohydrate		0g
Dietary Fiber		0g
Sugars		0g
Protein		2g

Feta and Tomato Crostini

PREP TIME: 20 MINUTES (READY IN 30 MINUTES)   ● EASY
SERVINGS: 16 CROSTINI

1 can (8 oz) Pillsbury® refrigerated crescent dinner rolls or 1 can (8 oz) Pillsbury® Crescent Recipe Creations™ refrigerated flaky dough sheet

1 tablespoon olive oil

1 garlic clove, finely chopped

1 medium plum (Roma) tomato, seeded and chopped

¼ cup chopped pitted kalamata olives

¼ cup crumbled feta cheese

1 tablespoon chopped fresh basil leaves

1 teaspoon olive oil

¼ teaspoon salt

¼ teaspoon pepper

1) Heat oven to 375°F. Spray large cookie sheets with cooking spray. Open can of dough; do not unroll. With serrated knife, cut dough into 16 slices. Flatten slices to 2-inch circles.

2) In small bowl, mix 1 tablespoon olive oil and the garlic; brush on tops of dough circles. Place on cookie sheet.

3) Bake 10 to 15 minutes or until deep golden brown.

4) Meanwhile, in small bowl, mix remaining ingredients. Spoon slightly less than 1 tablespoon tomato mixture on each crostini. Serve immediately.

HIGH ALTITUDE (3500-6500 FT.): No change.

Nutrition Information Per Serving:	
Calories: 70	From Fat: 35
Total Fat	4g
Saturated Fat	1.5g
Trans Fat	0g
Cholesterol	0mg
Sodium	190mg
Total Carbohydrate	6g
Dietary Fiber	0g
Sugars	1g
Protein	1g

Kalamata Olives and Sun-Dried Tomatoes on Cream Cheese

PREP TIME: 10 MINUTES (READY IN 10 MINUTES)
SERVINGS: 10 (2 TABLESPOONS SPREAD AND 4 CRACKERS EACH)

 EASY

20 pitted kalamata olives, finely chopped ($^1/_3$ cup)

2 tablespoons finely chopped, drained sun-dried tomatoes in oil

1 tablespoon oil from sun-dried tomatoes

2 tablespoons chopped fresh basil leaves

1 teaspoon cider vinegar

$^1/_8$ teaspoon crushed red pepper flakes

1 medium garlic clove, finely chopped

1 package (8 oz) cream cheese, softened

Additional fresh basil leaves, if desired

40 assorted crackers

1) In small bowl, stir together all ingredients except cream cheese, additional basil leaves and crackers.

2) To serve, place softened cream cheese on serving platter. Using small metal spatula, spread cream cheese into 8-inch round. Spoon olive mixture over cheese. Serve with crackers.

HIGH ALTITUDE (3500-6500 FT.): No change.

Nutrition Information Per Serving:	
Calories: 160	From Fat: 120
Total Fat	13g
Saturated Fat	6g
Trans Fat	0g
Cholesterol	25mg
Sodium	210mg
Total Carbohydrate	9g
Dietary Fiber	0g
Sugars	0g
Protein	3g

Feta-Herb Puff Pastry Wedges

PREP TIME: 5 MINUTES (READY IN 1 HOUR 5 MINUTES)
SERVINGS: 32 APPETIZERS

 EASY

1 sheet frozen puff pastry (from 17.3-oz package)

$^1/_4$ cup basil pesto

$^1/_3$ cup crumbled feta cheese

2 tablespoons pine nuts

2 tablespoons coarsely chopped fresh basil leaves

1) Let the puff pastry stand at room temperature 40 minutes to thaw.

2) Heat oven to 400°F. Unfold pastry on work surface. Using pastry brush, brush pesto evenly over all of pastry, including edges. Cut pastry into 16 squares; cut each square in half diagonally, making 32 triangles.

3) Lightly spray 2 large cookie sheets with cooking spray. Gently arrange pastry wedges on cookie sheets. Sprinkle with feta cheese and pine nuts.

4) Bake 5 minutes. Reduce oven temperature to 350°F. Bake 8 to 10 minutes, until edges are golden brown. Top wedges with basil. Serve warm.

HIGH ALTITUDE (3500-6500 FT.): No change.

Nutrition Information Per Serving:	
Calories: 60	From Fat: 40
Total Fat	4.5g
Saturated Fat	1.5g
Trans Fat	0g
Cholesterol	10mg
Sodium	55mg
Total Carbohydrate	4g
Dietary Fiber	0g
Sugars	0g
Protein	1g

French Country Pâté

PREP TIME: 25 MINUTES (READY IN 10 HOURS 50 MINUTES)
SERVINGS: 34 (1/2 SLICE EACH)

LOW FAT

2 teaspoons olive or vegetable oil

1/2 cup finely chopped onion (1 medium)

1 teaspoon herbes de Provence

2 garlic cloves, finely chopped

1/4 teaspoon salt

1/8 teaspoon freshly ground pepper

1/4 cup dry white wine

1/2 lb extra-lean (at least 90%) ground beef

1/2 lb lean ground pork

1/4 cup Progresso® plain bread crumbs

2 tablespoons pine nuts, toasted

2 tablespoons chopped fresh parsley

1 tablespoon finely chopped fresh chives

5 slices bacon (about 1/3 lb)

1) In 10-inch skillet, heat oil over medium-high heat 1 to 2 minutes or until hot. Add onion; cook 2 to 3 minutes, stirring occasionally, until onion begins to soften. Stir in herbes de Provence, garlic, salt and pepper; cook 2 minutes. Stir in wine. Increase heat to high; cook 2 to 3 minutes or until no liquid remains in skillet. Cool completely, about 10 minutes.

2) Heat oven to 350°F. In large bowl, mix beef, pork, bread crumbs, pine nuts, parsley, chives and cooled onion mixture until thoroughly combined. Shape into 5-inch-long loaf, packing mixture tightly to hold together. Wrap bacon around loaf to cover, with ends of bacon slices all on bottom of loaf.

3) Place loaf, bacon seam side down, on rack in roasting pan. Bake 1 hour 15 minutes to 1 hour 25 minutes or until thermometer inserted in center of loaf reads 160°F.

4) Remove the loaf from oven. Cover loosely with tent of foil; cool completely, about 1 hour. Refrigerate at least 8 hours or overnight. Using serrated knife, cut into 17 (1/4-inch) slices; cut each slice in half to serve.

HIGH ALTITUDE (3500-6500 FT.): No change.

Nutrition Information Per Serving:

Calories:	40	From Fat:	25
Total Fat			2.5g
Saturated Fat			1g
Trans Fat			0g
Cholesterol			10mg
Sodium			55mg
Total Carbohydrate			1g
Dietary Fiber			0g
Sugars			0g
Protein			3g

Smoked Salmon Spread

PREP TIME: 10 MINUTES (READY IN 1 HOUR 10 MINUTES)
SERVINGS: 24 (2 TABLESPOONS SPREAD AND 4 CRACKERS EACH)

ⓔ EASY

2 packages (8 oz each) cream cheese, softened

1 cup sour cream

1 teaspoon lemon-pepper seasoning

2 tablespoons chopped fresh dill weed

4 oz smoked salmon, flaked

$1/2$ cup finely chopped red bell pepper

Fresh dill weed sprigs

96 crackers

1) Line 3-cup bowl or pan with plastic wrap, letting plastic wrap hang over edge. In large bowl, stir together cream cheese, $1/2$ cup of the sour cream, the lemon-pepper seasoning and chopped dill weed until well blended.

2) Spoon $1/2$ of cream cheese mixture by heaping tablespoonfuls into bowl; spread and press into bottom of bowl. Top with salmon. Spoon remaining cheese mixture by tablespoonfuls over salmon; spread over salmon layer. Fold plastic wrap over the top of cheese to cover completely; press top layer of cheese onto salmon. Refrigerate 1 hour.

3) Remove plastic wrap from the top of cheese mixture. Place serving plate upside down on bowl; turn plate and bowl over. Remove bowl and plastic wrap. Using rubber spatula, spread the remaining $1/2$ cup sour cream over cheese mixture. Spoon bell pepper over sour cream. Garnish with dill weed sprigs. Serve with crackers.

HIGH ALTITUDE (3500-6500 FT.): No change.

Nutrition Information Per Serving:		
Calories: 150	From Fat:	110
Total Fat		12g
Saturated Fat		6g
Trans Fat		0g
Cholesterol		30mg
Sodium		210mg
Total Carbohydrate		8g
Dietary Fiber		0g
Sugars		0g
Protein		3g

Caramelized Onion and Mushroom Tartlets

PREP TIME: 40 MINUTES (READY IN 40 MINUTES)
SERVINGS: 24 APPETIZERS

1 can (8 oz) Pillsbury® refrigerated crescent dinner rolls or 1 can (8 oz) Pillsbury® Crescent Recipe Creations™ refrigerated flaky dough sheet

1 tablespoon olive oil

1 large sweet onion (about 8 oz), thinly sliced (about 3 cups)

2 teaspoons chopped fresh thyme leaves or 1 teaspoon dried thyme

1 tablespoon packed brown sugar

2 tablespoons white wine or chicken broth

1 cup chopped fresh mushrooms

1/3 cup chopped walnuts

1/3 cup shredded Asiago cheese

1) Heat oven to 375°F. Unroll the dough on work surface (if using crescent rolls, pinch the seams to seal); cut into 24 (2-inch) squares. Press 1 square in the bottom and up the side of each of 24 ungreased mini muffin cups.

2) In 10-inch skillet, heat oil over medium heat. Add sweet onion and thyme; cook 8 to 10 minutes, stirring frequently. Reduce heat to medium-low; cook 6 to 9 minutes, stirring constantly, until onions are caramelized. Stir in brown sugar and wine; cook 2 to 3 minutes, stirring constantly, until liquid is gone. Stir in mushrooms. Spoon about 1 tablespoon onion-mushroom mixture into each cup. Top with walnuts and cheese.

3) Bake 12 to 15 minutes or until golden brown. Remove tartlets from pan immediately. Serve warm.

HIGH ALTITUDE (3500-6500 FT.): No change.

Nutrition Information Per Serving:

Calories:	70	From Fat:	40
Total Fat			4.5g
Saturated Fat			1g
Trans Fat			0.5g
Cholesterol			0mg
Sodium			90mg
Total Carbohydrate			6g
Dietary Fiber			0g
Sugars			2g
Protein			1g

tip

Be sure to store goat cheese in the refrigerator, tightly wrapped in plastic wrap. Keep it away from eggs, butter and other foods that might easily pick up strong flavors.

Roasted Red Bell Pepper and Goat Cheese Bites

PREP TIME: 30 MINUTES (READY IN 40 MINUTES)
SERVINGS: 32 APPETIZERS   LOW FAT

1 Pillsbury® refrigerated pie crust (from 15-oz box), softened as directed on box

1 container (5 oz) goat cheese

2/3 cup roasted red bell peppers (from 15-oz jar), drained, patted dry with paper towel and cut into 1/2-inch pieces

2 1/2 teaspoons finely chopped fresh oregano leaves

2 teaspoons extra-virgin olive oil

1/4 to 1/2 teaspoon garlic powder

Small fresh oregano leaves

1) Heat oven to 400°F. Line 2 large cookie sheets with cooking parchment paper. On floured work surface, unroll pie crust. Using 1 3/4-inch round cookie or canapé cutter, cut out 32 rounds; place about 1/2 inch apart on cookie sheets.

2) Spread about 1 teaspoon goat cheese on each dough round. Bake 10 to 12 minutes or until edges are light golden brown.

3) Meanwhile, in medium bowl, stir together chopped roasted peppers, finely chopped oregano, oil and garlic powder until well blended.

4) Immediately top each baked cheese-topped round with 1 teaspoon red pepper mixture; place on serving platter. Garnish each with oregano leaf. Serve warm or at room temperature.

HIGH ALTITUDE (3500-6500 FT.): No change.

Nutrition Information Per Serving:		
Calories: 40	From Fat:	25
Total Fat		3g
Saturated Fat		1.5g
Trans Fat		0g
Cholesterol		0mg
Sodium		45mg
Total Carbohydrate		3g
Dietary Fiber		0g
Sugars		0g
Protein		1g

Prosciutto and Creamy Blue Cheese Pear Slices

PREP TIME: 10 MINUTES (READY IN 10 MINUTES)
SERVINGS: 12 APPETIZERS

EASY **LOW FAT**

1 oz cream cheese, softened

1 oz crumbled blue cheese (about 8 teaspoons)

1 ripe (not firm) medium pear, cut in half lengthwise, cut into 12 slices

6 thin slices prosciutto, cut in half lengthwise

Nutrition Information Per Serving:	
Calories: 40	From Fat: 20
Total Fat	2g
Saturated Fat	1g
Trans Fat	0g
Cholesterol	10mg
Sodium	150mg
Total Carbohydrate	2g
Dietary Fiber	0g
Sugars	2g
Protein	2g

1) In small bowl, stir the cream cheese and blue cheese, using rubber spatula, until well blended.

2) Spread rounded 1/2 teaspoon cheese mixture on each pear slice. Starting at one end of each pear slice, wrap 1 prosciutto strip in spiral fashion around pear slice.

HIGH ALTITUDE (3500-6500 FT.): No change.

Crab-Filled Crescent Wontons

PREP TIME: 20 MINUTES (READY IN 35 MINUTES)
SERVINGS: 24 WONTONS

EASY **LOW FAT**

1 can (8 oz) Pillsbury® refrigerated crescent dinner rolls or 1 can (8 oz) Pillsbury® Crescent Recipe Creations™ refrigerated flaky dough sheet

1 package (3 oz) cream cheese, softened

3/4 cup chopped cooked crabmeat

1 tablespoon chopped green onion (1 medium)

1/8 to 1/4 teaspoon ground red pepper (cayenne)

1 egg white, beaten

1) Heat oven to 375°F. Spray cookie sheet with cooking spray. Unroll dough on work surface (if using crescent rolls, pinch the seams to seal); cut into 6 rows by 4 rows to make 24 squares.

2) In small bowl, mix the cream cheese, crabmeat, onion and red pepper. Spoon about 1 teaspoon crab mixture 1/2 inch from 1 corner of 1 square. Starting with same corner, fold the dough over filling, and tuck end tightly underneath filling; continue rolling to within 1/2 inch of opposite corner. Lightly brush exposed corner with egg white. Roll the moistened corner of dough over roll; press to seal. Place on cookie sheet. Brush with egg white. Repeat with remaining squares and filling.

3) Bake 10 to 15 minutes or until golden brown. Remove from cookie sheet. Serve warm.

HIGH ALTITUDE (3500-6500 FT.): Bake 12 to 17 minutes.

Nutrition Information Per Serving:	
Calories: 50	From Fat: 25
Total Fat	3g
Saturated Fat	1.5g
Trans Fat	0g
Cholesterol	10mg
Sodium	100mg
Total Carbohydrate	4g
Dietary Fiber	0g
Sugars	0g
Protein	1g

Snacks & Munchies

When it comes to casual parties or just tiding over the family until dinner, these small bites go over big.

SHRIMP COCKTAIL DEVILED EGGS
PG. 62

BEER CHEESE DIP
PG. 63

MINI GREEK BURGERS
PG. 53

POT STICKERS WITH
SWEET SOY DIPPING SAUCE
PG. 61

Chile and Olive Pizza Snacks

PREP TIME: 10 MINUTES (READY IN 30 MINUTES)
SERVINGS: 32 APPETIZERS

EASY   **LOW FAT**

1 can (13.8 oz) Pillsbury® refrigerated classic pizza crust

1 tablespoon chopped fresh or 1 teaspoon dried oregano leaves

1 cup shredded provolone cheese (4 oz)

2 oz red onion, cut into 4 ($\frac{1}{4}$-inch-thick) slices (about $\frac{1}{4}$ of large onion)

$\frac{1}{2}$ cup coarsely chopped jalapeño-stuffed green olives (about 10 olives)

2 teaspoons olive or vegetable oil

1 poblano chile (5 oz), seeded, cut into thin rounds (about 2 cups)

1) Heat oven to 400°F. Spray cookie sheet with cooking spray. On cookie sheet, unroll pizza dough into about 16x9-inch rectangle. Top evenly with the oregano, cheese, onion and olives.

2) Heat 10-inch nonstick skillet over medium-high heat. Add oil and chile rounds; cook 3 to 4 minutes, stirring frequently, until edges of chile rounds begin to lightly brown.

3) Arrange chile rounds evenly over pizza toppings; press down gently. Bake 13 to 17 minutes or until edges of crust are golden brown.

4) Remove the pizza from cookie sheet to cutting board. Cut into 8 rows by 4 rows to make 32 pieces. Serve warm.

HIGH ALTITUDE (3500-6500 FT.): No change.

Nutrition Information Per Serving:

Calories:	50	From Fat:	20
Total Fat			2g
Saturated Fat			1g
Trans Fat			0g
Cholesterol			0mg
Sodium			160mg
Total Carbohydrate			7g
Dietary Fiber			0g
Sugars			0g
Protein			2g

Mini Greek Burgers

PREP TIME: 30 MINUTES (READY IN 30 MINUTES)
SERVINGS: 16 SANDWICHES

🅮 EASY

SAUCE

¾ cup Yoplait® Fat Free plain yogurt (from 2-lb container)

1 teaspoon grated lemon peel

1 garlic clove, finely chopped

¼ teaspoon salt

¼ teaspoon dried dill weed

BURGERS

1 lb lean (at least 80%) ground beef

¼ cup Progresso® plain bread crumbs

1 tablespoon balsamic vinegar

2 teaspoons finely grated lemon peel

2 teaspoons fresh lemon juice

1 teaspoon dried oregano leaves

1 teaspoon dried thyme leaves

½ teaspoon salt

3 garlic cloves, finely chopped

BREADS AND TOPPINGS

16 mini (2½-inch) pita breads (from one 7-oz bag)

½ medium cucumber, cut into very thin slices

¼ small red onion, cut into bite-size strips

1) In small bowl, mix sauce ingredients. Cover; refrigerate until ready to use.

2) In large bowl, mix burger ingredients until well mixed. Shape beef mixture into 16 patties, about ¼ inch thick.

3) Place 8 patties in 12-inch nonstick skillet; cook over medium-low heat about 3 minutes. Turn patties; cook 2 to 4 minutes longer or until meat thermometer inserted in center of patties reads 160°F. Remove patties from skillet; cover to keep warm. Repeat with remaining patties.

4) With serrated knife, cut pita breads in half horizontally. Place the patties on the bottom halves of breads. Top each patty with about 2 teaspoons sauce, several slices of cucumber and strips of onion. Cover with top halves of breads. Serve immediately.

HIGH ALTITUDE (3500-6500 FT.): No change.

Nutrition Information Per Serving:		
Calories: 90	From Fat:	30
Total Fat		3.5g
Saturated Fat		1.5g
Trans Fat		0g
Cholesterol		20mg
Sodium		190mg
Total Carbohydrate		8g
Dietary Fiber		0g
Sugars		1g
Protein		6g

Magic Dragon Puffs

PREP TIME: 20 MINUTES (READY IN 50 MINUTES)
SERVINGS: 30 APPETIZERS

EASY   **LOW FAT**

¾ cup water

¼ cup butter or margarine, cut up

½ teaspoon salt

¾ cup all-purpose flour

3 eggs

¼ cup grated Parmesan cheese

2 tablespoons finely chopped fresh chives

2 tablespoons finely chopped fresh basil leaves

Nutrition Information Per Serving:

Calories:	35	From Fat:	20
Total Fat			2.5g
Saturated Fat			1.5g
Trans Fat			0g
Cholesterol			25mg
Sodium			70mg
Total Carbohydrate			2g
Dietary Fiber			0g
Sugars			0g
Protein			1g

1) Heat oven to 425°F. Line 2 cookie sheets with cooking parchment paper. In 2-quart saucepan, heat water, butter and salt to rolling boil over medium heat. When butter is melted, remove from heat; stir in flour all at once until blended.

2) Return to medium heat; cook 1 to 1½ minutes, stirring constantly, until dough forms a ball and leaves a slight film on side of pan.

3) Remove from heat; stir in eggs, one at a time, stirring until thoroughly mixed. Stir in the Parmesan cheese, chives and basil. On cookie sheets, drop by heaping teaspoonfuls 2 inches apart into 1¼-inch mounds, making 30 mounds.

4) Bake about 20 minutes or until golden brown and set. Remove from oven; with tip of sharp knife, make small slit in side of each puff to allow steam to escape. Bake 5 to 8 minutes longer or until dry and firm.

HIGH ALTITUDE (3500-6500 FT.): In Step 4, for second bake time, bake 4 to 7 minutes.

Garlicky Cheese Bites

PREP TIME: 15 MINUTES (READY IN 35 MINUTES)
SERVINGS: 24 (1 APPETIZER AND 1 TABLESPOON SAUCE EACH)

EASY   **LOW FAT**

1 can (8 oz) Pillsbury® refrigerated garlic-flavored breadsticks

4 sticks (0.75 oz each) mozzarella string cheese

2 tablespoons grated Parmesan cheese

1½ cups marinara sauce, heated

Nutrition Information Per Serving:

Calories:	60	From Fat:	25
Total Fat			3g
Saturated Fat			1g
Trans Fat			0g
Cholesterol			0mg
Sodium			200mg
Total Carbohydrate			7g
Dietary Fiber			0g
Sugars			2g
Protein			2g

1) Heat oven to 350°F. Spray 24 mini muffin cups with cooking spray. Unroll breadstick dough. Cut dough crosswise into thirds; separate into 24 strips. Cut each cheese stick into 6 equal pieces (24 pieces total).

2) Place 1 cheese piece on short end of each dough strip; roll up cheese piece in dough. Pinch and seal dough to completely cover cheese. Place rolls, seam sides down, in muffin cups. Turn rolls in cups to coat all sides with cooking spray. Lightly sprinkle with Parmesan cheese.

3) Bake 15 to 18 minutes or until puffed and golden brown. Remove from pans to serving platter. Serve warm with marinara sauce for dipping.

HIGH ALTITUDE (3500-6500 FT.): No change.

Sneaky Snake Pinwheels

PREP TIME: 20 MINUTES (READY IN 1 HOUR 20 MINUTES)
SERVINGS: ABOUT 16

EASY

tip

Look for flatbread in the deli department of your grocery store. Or, instead of using flatbread, try 8-inch round tortillas.

2 squares ($7\frac{1}{4}$x$8\frac{3}{4}$ inch) flatbread (from 8-oz package)

1 package (3 oz) cream cheese, softened

Half a medium red bell pepper, chopped (about $\frac{1}{4}$ cup)

4 leaves romaine lettuce

24 thin slices hard salami (about $4\frac{1}{2}$ oz)

Half a large pickle, cut lengthwise into 4 spears (from 32-oz jar kosher dill pickle halves)

2 small red bell pepper pieces, cut into snakelike tongues

1) Spread each flatbread with half of the cream cheese to within 1 inch from edge of bread. Sprinkle each with 2 tablespoons chopped bell pepper.

2) Top each with 2 leaves romaine lettuce and 12 thin salami slices, leaving 1-inch border on both long sides of each. Place 2 pickle slices end to end lengthwise on each flatbread. Tightly roll up flatbread.

3) Wrap flatbread rolls individually in plastic wrap. Refrigerate at least 1 hour but no longer than 24 hours. With serrated knife, cut into 1-inch slices; secure each slice with a toothpick. Arrange on large platter in a twisty snakelike shape. Arrange front piece at angle slightly away from the body to look like head, place 1 red pepper piece on underside of pinwheel to look like tongue. Arrange rear piece at angle for end of snake.

HIGH ALTITUDE (3500-6500 FT.): No change.

Nutrition Information Per Serving:

Calories:	100	From Fat:	40
Total Fat			4.5g
Saturated Fat			2g
Trans Fat			0g
Cholesterol			15mg
Sodium			260mg
Total Carbohydrate			11g
Dietary Fiber			2g
Sugars			1g
Protein			4g

Rosemary Turkey Squares

PREP TIME:	20 MINUTES (READY IN 45 MINUTES)	e EASY
SERVINGS:	6 SANDWICHES	

1 package (3 oz) cream cheese, softened

2 tablespoons milk

1 tablespoon butter or margarine, softened

2 cups cubed cooked turkey breast

1 teaspoon chopped fresh rosemary leaves or 1/2 teaspoon dried rosemary leaves, crushed

2 tablespoons chopped green onions (2 medium)

2 tablespoons finely chopped red bell pepper

1 can (8 oz) Pillsbury® refrigerated crescent dinner rolls or 1 can (8 oz) Pillsbury® Crescent Recipe Creations™ refrigerated flaky dough sheet

1 egg, beaten

1 tablespoon grated Parmesan cheese

1) Heat oven to 375°F. Grease cookie sheet. In medium bowl, beat cream cheese, milk and butter with electric mixer on medium speed until smooth. Stir in turkey, rosemary, green onions and red bell pepper.

2) Unroll dough on work surface (if using crescent rolls, pinch the seams to seal); cut into 4 rows by 3 rows to make 12 squares. Spoon about 1/3 cup turkey mixture onto center of each of 6 squares. Top with remaining squares; firmly press edges with fork. Place on cookie sheet.

3) Brush the tops with egg; sprinkle with Parmesan cheese. Bake 20 to 25 minutes or until golden brown.

HIGH ALTITUDE (3500-6500 FT.):
Bake 15 to 20 minutes.

Nutrition Information Per Serving:

Calories:	270	From Fat:	130
Total Fat			15g
Saturated Fat			8g
Trans Fat			0g
Cholesterol			95mg
Sodium			410mg
Total Carbohydrate			17g
Dietary Fiber			0g
Sugars			4g
Protein			18g

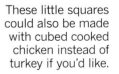

These little squares could also be made with cubed cooked chicken instead of turkey if you'd like.

Cheesy Chicken 'n Spinach Pinwheels

PREP TIME: 25 MINUTES (READY IN 40 MINUTES)
SERVINGS: 20 PINWHEELS

1 box (9 oz) Green Giant® frozen spinach

1 tablespoon olive oil

1/4 cup finely chopped onion

1 garlic clove, finely chopped

2 slices bacon, crisply cooked, crumbled

1/2 cup finely chopped cooked chicken

3/4 cup shredded Asiago cheese

1/4 cup mayonnaise or salad dressing

1 can (8 oz) Pillsbury® refrigerated crescent dinner rolls or 1 can (8 oz) Pillsbury® Crescent Recipe Creations™ refrigerated flaky dough sheet

1 egg, beaten

1) Heat oven to 375°F. Spray cookie sheet with cooking spray. Cook spinach in microwave as directed on box. Drain spinach in strainer; cool 5 minutes. Carefully squeeze with paper towel to drain well.

2) In 10-inch skillet, heat oil over medium heat. Add onion and garlic; cook 2 to 3 minutes, stirring occasionally, until crisp-tender. Remove from heat. Stir in the spinach, bacon, chicken, cheese and mayonnaise.

3) Unroll dough on work surface (if using crescent rolls, pinch seams to seal). Spread spinach mixture on rectangle to within 1/2 inch of edges. Starting at long side of rectangle, roll up; seal long edge. With serrated knife, cut into 20 slices. Place cut side down on cookie sheet. Brush with egg.

4) Bake 10 to 15 minutes or until golden brown. Remove from cookie sheet. Serve warm.

HIGH ALTITUDE (3500-6500 FT.): No change.

Nutrition Information Per Serving:	
Calories: 100	From Fat: 60
Total Fat	7g
Saturated Fat	2.5g
Trans Fat	0g
Cholesterol	20mg
Sodium	180mg
Total Carbohydrate	6g
Dietary Fiber	0g
Sugars	1g
Protein	3g

Spicy Thai Pizza

PREP TIME: 25 MINUTES (READY IN 25 MINUTES)
SERVINGS: 4

e EASY

1 package (10 oz) prebaked Italian pizza crusts (8 inch)

¼ cup peanut sauce

1½ cups chopped cooked chicken breast

½ cup shredded carrot

2 medium green onions, chopped (2 tablespoons)

2 tablespoons coarsely chopped peanuts, if desired

⅔ cup finely shredded mozzarella cheese

2 tablespoons chopped fresh cilantro

1) Heat gas or charcoal grill. Spread each pizza crust with 2 tablespoons of the peanut sauce. Top each pizza with chicken, carrot, onions and peanuts. Sprinkle with cheese.

2) Place sheet of heavy-duty foil on grill; place pizzas on foil over medium heat. Cover grill; cook 8 to 10 minutes, moving pizzas around grill every 2 minutes to prevent bottoms from burning, until cheese is melted. Sprinkle with cilantro.

HIGH ALTITUDE (3500-6500 FT.): Cook over medium-low heat.

Nutrition Information Per Serving:

Calories:	390	From Fat:	130
Total Fat			14g
Saturated Fat			6g
Trans Fat			0g
Cholesterol			60mg
Sodium			550mg
Total Carbohydrate			35g
Dietary Fiber			2g
Sugars			2g
Protein			30g

Chicken Alfredo Pizza

PREP TIME: 25 MINUTES (READY IN 25 MINUTES)
SERVINGS: 4

e EASY

1 package (10 oz) prebaked Italian pizza crusts (8 inch)

¼ cup Alfredo sauce

1½ cups chopped cooked chicken breast

½ cup shredded carrot

2 medium green onions, chopped (2 tablespoons)

⅔ cup finely shredded Gruyére cheese

2 tablespoons chopped fresh cilantro

1) Heat gas or charcoal grill. Spread each pizza crust with 2 tablespoons of the Alfredo sauce. Top each pizza with chicken, carrot and onions. Sprinkle with cheese.

2) Place sheet of heavy-duty foil on grill; place pizzas on foil over medium heat. Cover grill; cook 8 to 10 minutes, moving pizzas around grill every 2 minutes to prevent bottoms from burning, until cheese is melted. Sprinkle with cilantro.

HIGH ALTITUDE (3500-6500 FT.): Cook over medium-low heat.

BBQ Chicken Pizza

PREP TIME: 25 MINUTES (READY IN 25 MINUTES)
SERVINGS: 4

e EASY

1 package (10 oz) prebaked Italian pizza crusts (8 inch)

¼ cup barbecue sauce

1½ cups chopped cooked chicken breast

2 medium green onions, chopped (2 tablespoons)

⅔ cup finely shredded Cheddar cheese

2 tablespoons chopped fresh cilantro

1) Heat gas or charcoal grill. Spread each pizza crust with 2 tablespoons of the barbecue sauce. Top each pizza with chicken and onions. Sprinkle with cheese.

2) Place sheet of heavy-duty foil on grill; place pizzas on foil over medium heat. Cover grill; cook 8 to 10 minutes, moving pizzas around grill every 2 minutes to prevent bottoms from burning, until cheese is melted. Sprinkle with cilantro.

HIGH ALTITUDE (3500-6500 FT.): Cook over medium-low heat.

tip

On a rainy day, these pizzas can easily be made in the oven. Heat oven to 450°F. Bake on an ungreased cookie sheet 8 to 10 minutes.

Curry Chicken Triangles

PREP TIME: 25 MINUTES (READY IN 40 MINUTES)
SERVINGS: 24 APPETIZERS

2 cans (8 oz each) Pillsbury®
  refrigerated crescent dinner rolls
  or 2 cans (8 oz each) Pillsbury®
  Crescent Recipe Creations™
  refrigerated flaky dough sheet

1 package (3 oz) cream cheese,
  softened

1 tablespoon milk

2 tablespoons apricot preserves

1 cup finely chopped cooked chicken

½ cup shredded Cheddar cheese (2 oz)

¼ cup chopped drained water
  chestnuts (from 8-oz can)

3 tablespoons chopped green onions
  (3 medium)

2 teaspoons curry powder

1 egg, beaten

2 tablespoons chopped almonds

1) Heat oven to 375°F. Spray large cookie
   sheet with cooking spray. Unroll both
   cans of dough on work surface (if using
   crescent rolls, pinch seams to seal);
   press each to form 12x9-inch rectangle.
   Cut each into 12 squares.

2) In medium bowl, beat cream cheese,
   milk and apricot preserves with electric
   mixer on medium speed until smooth.
   Stir in chicken, cheese, water chestnuts,
   onions and curry powder.

3) Spoon about 1 tablespoon chicken mixture in center of each square. Fold
   dough over filling; press edges with a fork. Place on cookie sheet. Brush
   with beaten egg; sprinkle with almonds. Bake 10 to 15 minutes or until
   deep golden brown.

HIGH ALTITUDE (3500-6500 FT.): Bake 12 to 17 minutes.

Nutrition Information Per Serving:	
Calories: 110	From Fat: 50
Total Fat	6g
Saturated Fat	3g
Trans Fat	0g
Cholesterol	20mg
Sodium	180mg
Total Carbohydrate	10g
Dietary Fiber	0g
Sugars	3g
Protein	4g

Pot Stickers with Sweet Soy Dipping Sauce

PREP TIME: 40 MINUTES (READY IN 40 MINUTES)
SERVINGS: 24 (1 POT STICKER AND 1 TEASPOON SAUCE EACH)

 LOW FAT

POT STICKERS

- 1/2 lb lean ground pork
- 1/2 cup chopped green onions (8 medium)
- 1 tablespoon grated gingerroot
- 24 wonton skins (about 3 1/4-inch square)
- 3 tablespoons vegetable oil

SAUCE

- 2 tablespoons sugar
- 2 tablespoons reduced-sodium soy sauce
- 2 tablespoons rice vinegar
- 2 tablespoons water
- 1/2 teaspoon sesame oil
- 1/8 to 1/4 teaspoon crushed red pepper flakes

Nutrition Information Per Serving:		
Calories: 60	From Fat:	30
Total Fat		3g
Saturated Fat		1g
Trans Fat		0g
Cholesterol		5mg
Sodium		95mg
Total Carbohydrate		6g
Dietary Fiber		0g
Sugars		1g
Protein		2g

1) Line cookie sheet with cooking parchment paper. In small bowl, mix pork, onions and gingerroot.

2) Working with 1 wonton skin at a time, place 1 heaping teaspoon pork mixture on center of each wonton skin. Moisten edges of wonton skin with water; fold in half over filling to form triangle and seal sides. Bring 2 ends together to form a "hat" shape (see photo). Place pot stickers on cookie sheet; cover with damp towel to keep from drying out.

3) In Dutch oven, heat 3 quarts water to boiling. Add half of the pot stickers; boil about 5 minutes or until edges of wonton skins are clear. Using slotted spoon, remove pot stickers from water; drain thoroughly on paper towels. Repeat with remaining pot stickers.

4) Meanwhile, in small bowl, mix sauce ingredients until sugar is dissolved; set aside.

5) In a 12-inch nonstick skillet, heat 2 tablespoons of the oil over medium heat. Add half of pot stickers; cook 2 to 3 minutes or until crisp and golden brown on the bottom. Turn; cook 2 to 3 minutes longer or until browned and crisp. Using pancake turner, remove pot stickers from oil; place on serving platter. Repeat with remaining tablespoon oil and remaining pot stickers. Serve warm with sauce.

HIGH ALTITUDE (3500-6500 FT.): In Step 5, cook pot stickers 5 to 7 minutes on each side.

tip

Be sure to drain the pot stickers on paper towels to remove most of the moisture before adding them to the oil in the skillet.

Shrimp Cocktail Deviled Eggs

PREP TIME: 25 MINUTES (READY IN 1 HOUR 25 MINUTES)
SERVINGS: 24

12 eggs

1/3 cup mayonnaise or salad dressing

3 tablespoons finely chopped fresh chives

1 tablespoon cocktail sauce

1/2 teaspoon salt

1/8 teaspoon pepper

24 cooked tiny to small shrimp (61 to 70 shrimp), peeled, deveined (tail shells removed, if desired)

1) In Dutch oven, place eggs in single layer; carefully add enough cold water to cover eggs by about 1 inch. Cover; heat to boiling. Remove from heat; let stand 15 minutes. Drain. Immediately place eggs in cold water with ice cubes or run cold water over eggs until completely cooled. To remove shell, crackle it by tapping gently all over; roll between hands to loosen. Peel, starting at the large end.

2) Cut eggs in half lengthwise. Carefully remove egg yolks to medium bowl; place egg white halves on a serving platter. Mash yolks with fork; stir in mayonnaise, 1 tablespoon of the chives, the cocktail sauce, salt and pepper until well blended.

3) Using decorating bag fitted with open star tip, carefully pipe yolk mixture into each egg white half. Cover; refrigerate at least 30 minutes to blend flavors.

4) Before serving, garnish eggs with shrimp; sprinkle with remaining 2 tablespoons chives.

HIGH ALTITUDE (3500-6500 FT.): No change.

Nutrition Information Per Serving:

Calories:	60	From Fat:	45
Total Fat			5g
Saturated Fat			1g
Trans Fat			0g
Cholesterol			115mg
Sodium			115mg
Total Carbohydrate			0g
Dietary Fiber			0g
Sugars			0g
Protein			4g

Mini Bacon-Cheese Cups

PREP TIME: 15 MINUTES (READY IN 35 MINUTES)
SERVINGS: 16 APPETIZERS

e EASY

1 Pillsbury® refrigerated pie crust (from 15-oz box), softened as directed on box

1 package (3 oz) cream cheese, softened

1 whole egg

1 egg yolk

1/4 cup chopped green onions (4 medium)

3 oz shredded Swiss cheese (about 2/3 cup)

8 slices precooked bacon (from 2.2-oz package), chopped (about 1/2 cup)

Additional finely chopped green onions, if desired

1) Heat oven to 425°F. Spray 16 mini muffin cups with cooking spray. Unroll pie crust on work surface. Using 2 1/2-inch round cutter, cut 16 rounds from crust; discard any remaining crust. Place 1 crust round in each muffin cup, pressing down gently to form cup.

2) In blender or food processor, blend or process cream cheese, whole egg, egg yolk and 1/4 cup green onions until almost smooth. Divide mixture evenly among crust-lined muffin cups (about 2 teaspoons each). Top each evenly with Swiss cheese and bacon.

3) Bake 9 to 11 minutes or until edges are light golden brown. Cool 5 minutes; remove cups from pan. Garnish each with additional onions.

HIGH ALTITUDE (3500-6500 FT.): No change.

Nutrition Information Per Serving:

Calories:	100	From Fat:	70
Saturated Fat			3.5g
Trans Fat			0g
Cholesterol			40mg
Sodium			110mg
Total Carbohydrate			5g
Dietary Fiber			0g
Sugars			0g
Protein			3g

Beer Cheese Dip

PREP TIME: 20 MINUTES (READY IN 20 MINUTES)
SERVINGS: 16 (ABOUT 1/4 CUP DIP WITHOUT DIPPERS)

e EASY

1 garlic clove, peeled, cut in half

1/4 cup butter or margarine

1/4 cup all-purpose flour

1 can or bottle (12 oz) regular or nonalcoholic beer

6 cups shredded mild Cheddar cheese (1 1/2 lb)

Assorted dippers such as cubes of bread, cubes of ham, green onions, apple wedges and pretzel twists, if desired

Green onion, chopped, if desired

Nutrition Information Per Serving:

Calories:	210	From Fat:	150
Total Fat			17g
Saturated Fat			11g
Trans Fat			0g
Cholesterol			50mg
Sodium			280mg
Total Carbohydrate			2g
Dietary Fiber			0g
Sugars			0g
Protein			11g

1) Rub inside of 3-quart saucepan with the cut sides of garlic; discard garlic. Add butter to pan; melt over low heat. Stir in flour; cook 2 minutes, stirring constantly. Stir in beer. Increase heat to medium-high; heat to boiling. Boil 2 to 3 minutes, stirring constantly, until mixture is thick and smooth.

2) Reduce heat to low. Add the cheese, about 1/2 cup at a time, stirring until cheese is melted and mixture is smooth.

3) Transfer cheese mixture to fondue pot. Immediately place fondue pot over flame. Serve with dippers. Garnish dip with onions.

HIGH ALTITUDE (3500-6500 FT.): No change.

Baked Artichoke and Jalapeño Cheese Spread

PREP TIME: 10 MINUTES (READY IN 30 MINUTES)
SERVINGS: 18 (2 TABLESPOONS SPREAD AND 4 CRACKERS EACH)

e EASY

1 package (8 oz) cream cheese, softened

1/2 cup mayonnaise or salad dressing

1 jar (6 oz) marinated artichoke hearts, drained, coarsely chopped

1/4 cup finely chopped red bell pepper

8 to 10 Old El Paso® pickled jalapeño slices (from 12-oz jar), drained, chopped

1/2 cup grated Parmesan cheese

1/3 cup Progresso® panko crispy bread crumbs

72 wafer crackers

1) Heat oven to 400°F. Spray 9-inch glass pie plate with cooking spray.

2) In medium bowl, stir together cream cheese and mayonnaise. Stir in the artichokes, bell pepper and jalapeños. Reserve 1 tablespoon of the cheese; stir remaining cheese into artichoke mixture.

3) Spread cheese mixture evenly in bottom of pie plate. Sprinkle evenly with bread crumbs and reserved tablespoon cheese.

4) Bake about 20 minutes or just until top is lightly golden. Serve warm with crackers.

HIGH ALTITUDE (3500-6500 FT.): In Step 4, bake about 25 minutes.

Nutrition Information Per Serving:

Calories:	190	From Fat:	120
Total Fat			13g
Saturated Fat			4.5g
Trans Fat			1g
Cholesterol			20mg
Sodium			290mg
Total Carbohydrate			13g
Dietary Fiber			0g
Sugars			1g
Protein			3g

Artichoke 'n Bacon Crescent Squares

PREP TIME: 20 MINUTES (READY IN 1 HOUR 5 MINUTES)
SERVINGS: 32 APPETIZERS

e EASY

2 cans (8 oz each) Pillsbury® refrigerated crescent dinner rolls or 2 cans (8 oz each) Pillsbury® Crescent Recipe Creations™ refrigerated flaky dough sheet

1 package (8 oz) cream cheese, softened

¼ cup shredded Parmesan cheese

1 tablespoon chopped fresh parsley

1 tablespoon mayonnaise or salad dressing

1 cup chopped fresh spinach

2 jars (6 to 7 oz each) marinated artichoke hearts, drained, coarsely chopped

6 slices bacon, crisply cooked, crumbled

1 cup seeded diced plum (Roma) tomatoes

½ cup diced red bell pepper

1) Heat oven to 375°F. Unroll both cans of dough. Place in ungreased 15x10x1-inch pan, long sides overlapping to fit pan. Press in bottom and up sides of pan to form crust.

2) Bake 10 to 15 minutes or until golden brown. Cool completely, about 30 minutes.

3) In small bowl, beat cream cheese, Parmesan cheese, parsley and mayonnaise with electric mixer on medium speed until smooth. Spread over cooled crust. Top with the remaining ingredients. Serve immediately, or cover and refrigerate up to 2 hours. Cut into 8 rows by 4 rows.

HIGH ALTITUDE (3500-6500 FT.): Bake 15 to 20 minutes.

Nutrition Information Per Serving:

Calories:	100	From Fat:	60
Total Fat			6g
Saturated Fat			3g
Trans Fat			0g
Cholesterol			10mg
Sodium			210mg
Total Carbohydrate			8g
Dietary Fiber			0g
Sugars			2g
Protein			2g

Cheesy Olive Bread

PREP TIME:	5 MINUTES (READY IN 15 MINUTES)
SERVINGS:	16 APPETIZERS

🌀 EASY

1 cracker bread, about 12 inches in diameter (from 15¾-oz package)

1½ cups shredded Italian cheese blend (6 oz)

⅓ cup pitted kalamata olives, cut in half

1 tablespoon chopped fresh basil leaves

1) Heat oven to 375°F. Place cracker bread on large cookie sheet. Sprinkle Italian cheese and olives over entire top of cracker bread.

2) Bake 4 to 6 minutes or until the Italian cheese is melted. Top with the chopped fresh basil.

3) Break cracker bread into small pieces, or cut into 3-inch squares (4 rows by 4 rows) with pizza cutter or chef's knife. Serve warm.

HIGH ALTITUDE (3500-6500 FT.): No change.

Nutrition Information Per Serving:

Calories:	100	From Fat:	30
Total Fat			3.5g
Saturated Fat			2g
Trans Fat			0g
Cholesterol			10mg
Sodium			240mg
Total Carbohydrate			12g
Dietary Fiber			3g
Sugars			0g
Protein			4g

All-American Cracker Bread

PREP TIME: 5 MINUTES (READY IN 15 MINUTES)
SERVINGS: 16 APPETIZERS

EASY

1 cracker bread, about 12 inches in diameter (from 15¾-oz package)

1½ cups shredded Cheddar cheese (6 oz)

6 slices bacon, cooked and crumbled

1 tablespoon chopped fresh parsley

1) Heat oven to 375°F. Place cracker bread on large cookie sheet. Sprinkle Cheddar cheese and bacon over entire top of cracker bread.

2) Bake 4 to 6 minutes or until the Cheddar cheese is melted. Top with the chopped fresh parsley.

3) Break cracker bread into small pieces, or cut into 3-inch squares (4 rows by 4 rows) with pizza cutter or chef's knife. Serve warm.

HIGH ALTITUDE (3500-6500 FT.): No change.

Mexican Cracker Bread

PREP TIME: 5 MINUTES (READY IN 15 MINUTES)
SERVINGS: 16 APPETIZERS

EASY

1 cracker bread, about 12 inches in diameter (from 15¾-oz package)

1½ cups shredded taco cheese blend (6 oz)

1 plum (Roma) tomato, seeded and finely chopped

1 tablespoon chopped fresh cilantro

1) Heat oven to 375°F. Place cracker bread on large cookie sheet. Sprinkle taco cheese and tomatoes over entire top of cracker bread.

2) Bake 4 to 6 minutes or until the taco cheese is melted. Top with the chopped fresh cilantro.

3) Break cracker bread into small pieces, or cut into 3-inch squares (4 rows by 4 rows) with pizza cutter or chef's knife. Serve warm.

HIGH ALTITUDE (3500-6500 FT.): No change.

tip

Look near the deli section of your grocery store for cracker bread. It's often near the gourmet crackers.

SOUTHWEST PULLED-PORK
SANDWICHES
PG. 75

Salads & Sandwiches

From refreshing fruit bowls to unbeatable burgers, the rave-winning recipes here are sure to please.

NAPA CABBAGE SLAW
PG. 87

TURKEY AND RICE SALAD
PG. 88

CHICKEN NIÇOISE
SALAD SANDWICHES
PG. 98

Open-Face Chicken Pitas

PREP TIME: 30 MINUTES (READY IN 30 MINUTES)
SERVINGS: 4

2 cups shredded deli rotisserie chicken, without skin (from 2- to 2½-lb chicken)

1 teaspoon Greek seasoning

4 Greek-style pita fold breads (7 inch)

⅓ cup refrigerated hummus

½ cup chopped cucumber

2 plum (Roma) tomatoes, chopped (1 cup)

½ cup crumbled feta cheese (2 oz)

Plain yogurt or sour cream, if desired

1 green onion, sliced (1 tablespoon)

1) In medium microwavable bowl, mix the chicken and Greek seasoning. Microwave uncovered on High 1 to 2 minutes, stirring once or twice, until hot. Cover to keep warm.

2) Heat pita folds as directed on package. Spread each pita fold with about 1 tablespoon hummus. Top with ½ cup warm chicken, the cucumber, tomatoes and cheese. Serve topped with yogurt and onion.

HIGH ALTITUDE (3500-6500 FT.): No change.

Nutrition Information Per Serving:		
Calories: 400	From Fat: 100	
Total Fat		11g
Saturated Fat		4g
Trans Fat		0g
Cholesterol		75mg
Sodium		950mg
Total Carbohydrate		46g
Dietary Fiber		3g
Sugars		2g
Protein		30g

Tilapia Salad with Strawberry-Pineapple Salsa

PREP TIME: 30 MINUTES (READY IN 30 MINUTES)
SERVINGS: 4

(If) LOW FAT

SALSA

- 1 can (8 oz) crushed pineapple in juice, drained, juice reserved
- 2 cups fresh strawberries, stems removed, halved
- 1/2 cup diced cucumber
- 1/4 cup chopped fresh mint leaves
- 2 tablespoons tarragon or wine vinegar
- 2 medium green onions, thinly sliced (2 tablespoons)

TILAPIA AND SALAD

- 4 tilapia or other mild-flavored fish fillets (5 oz each)

  Cooking spray
- 1/2 teaspoon seasoned salt
- 1/4 teaspoon smoked paprika, if desired
- 4 cups loosely packed fresh spinach

1) Set aside 2 tablespoons pineapple juice. In small bowl, mix the pineapple and remaining juice with the other salsa ingredients.

2) Set oven control to broil. On rack in broiler pan, place fish; spray tops of fish with cooking spray. Sprinkle tops of fish with 2 tablespoons reserved pineapple juice, seasoned salt and smoked paprika. Broil with tops 4 to 6 inches from heat 6 to 8 minutes or until fish flakes easily with fork.

3) Meanwhile, on each of 4 plates, arrange 1 cup spinach. Place fish on spinach. Spoon salsa over fish and spinach.

HIGH ALTITUDE (3500-6500 FT.): No change.

Nutrition Information Per Serving:

Calories:	210	From Fat:	25
Total Fat			3g
Saturated Fat			0.5g
Trans Fat			0g
Cholesterol			75mg
Sodium			310mg
Total Carbohydrate			17g
Dietary Fiber			3g
Sugars			13g
Protein			28g

Wheat Berry, Grilled Corn and Spinach Salad

PREP TIME: 20 MINUTES (READY IN 2 HOURS)
SERVINGS: 6 (1 CUP EACH)

ⓔ EASY

$3^1/_2$ cups water

1 cup uncooked wheat berries

$^1/_2$ teaspoon salt

2 medium ears fresh sweet corn, husks and silk removed

1 cup cherry tomatoes, cut in half

2 cups baby spinach leaves

$^1/_4$ cup chopped onion

2 tablespoons white vinegar

1 teaspoon grated orange peel

2 tablespoons orange juice

2 tablespoons vegetable oil

1 tablespoon honey

1 teaspoon salt

$^1/_8$ teaspoon ground red pepper (cayenne)

1) In 2-quart saucepan, heat water, wheat berries and salt to a rolling boil over high heat. Reduce the heat to low; cover and simmer $1^1/_4$ to $1^1/_2$ hours or until wheat berries are tender. Drain; rinse with cold water to cool. Drain well.

2) Heat gas or charcoal grill. Place corn on grill over medium-high heat. Cover grill; cook 12 to 15 minutes, turning frequently, until tender. Cool slightly; cut corn from ears to measure about 2 cups.

3) In large bowl, stir together the wheat berries, corn, halved cherry tomatoes, spinach and onion.

4) In 1-cup measuring cup, mix vinegar, orange peel, orange juice, oil, honey, salt and red pepper with wire whisk. Stir into wheat berry mixture. Let stand 15 minutes before serving.

HIGH ALTITUDE (3500-6500 FT.): No change.

Nutrition Information Per Serving:		
Calories: 180	From Fat:	50
Total Fat		6g
Saturated Fat		1g
Trans Fat		0g
Cholesterol		0mg
Sodium		610mg
Total Carbohydrate		27g
Dietary Fiber		4g
Sugars		6g
Protein		4g

Peach-Berry Bellini Salad

PREP TIME: 15 MINUTES (READY IN 1 HOUR 45 MINUTES)
SERVINGS: 4

e EASY   **f** LOW FAT

¼ cup orange juice

3 tablespoons sugar

4 medium peaches (1 lb), peeled, pitted and cut into chunks

1 cup fresh raspberries or blackberries

2 cups sparkling wine or lemon-lime carbonated beverage

1) In large bowl, stir together the orange juice and sugar. Stir in the peaches and raspberries.

2) Divide fruit mixture evenly among four 6-oz custard cups. Cover; freeze at least 1 hour.

3) About 30 minutes before serving, remove custard cups from freezer. Let stand until slightly thawed. Transfer the fruit mixture to four 8-oz champagne saucers or margarita glasses. Pour sparking wine over fruit. Serve immediately.

HIGH ALTITUDE (3500-6500 FT.): No change.

Nutrition Information Per Serving:

Calories:	230	From Fat:	5
Total Fat			0.5g
Saturated Fat			0g
Trans Fat			0g
Cholesterol			0mg
Sodium			5mg
Total Carbohydrate			32g
Dietary Fiber			4g
Sugars			28g
Protein			2g

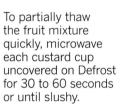

tip

To partially thaw the fruit mixture quickly, microwave each custard cup uncovered on Defrost for 30 to 60 seconds or until slushy.

Jicama, Zucchini and Red Pepper Salad

PREP TIME:	20 MINUTES (READY IN 20 MINUTES)	⊖ EASY
SERVINGS:	4 (1 CUP EACH)	

DRESSING

3 tablespoons red wine vinegar

3 tablespoons olive or vegetable oil

1 teaspoon sugar

$^1/_2$ teaspoon ground cumin

$1^1/_2$ teaspoons chopped fresh oregano or $^1/_4$ teaspoon dried oregano leaves

$^1/_4$ teaspoon salt

1 garlic clove, crushed

SALAD

1 medium zucchini, cut into $1^1/_2$x$^1/_4$x$^1/_4$-inch strips

1 medium red bell pepper, cut into $1^1/_2$x$^1/_4$-inch strips

$^1/_2$ small jicama, peeled, cut into $1^1/_2$x$^1/_4$x$^1/_4$-inch strips

4 lettuce leaves

1) In small jar with tight-fitting lid, shake dressing ingredients.

2) In large bowl, mix zucchini, bell pepper and jicama. Pour dressing over mixture; stir gently.

3) Arrange lettuce on 4 individual salad plates or large serving platter. Spoon salad mixture over lettuce.

HIGH ALTITUDE (3500-6500 FT.): No change.

Nutrition Information Per Serving:		
Calories: 140	From Fat:	90
Total Fat		10g
Saturated Fat		1.5g
Trans Fat		0g
Cholesterol		0mg
Sodium		160mg
Total Carbohydrate		9g
Dietary Fiber		3g
Sugars		3g
Protein		1g

Southwest Pulled-Pork Sandwiches

PREP TIME: 15 MINUTES (READY IN 8 HOURS 15 MINUTES)
SERVINGS: 12 SANDWICHES

e EASY

1 boneless pork shoulder or butt roast (3 lb), trimmed of fat

¼ cup packed brown sugar

1 teaspoon salt

2 teaspoons dried thyme leaves

2 teaspoons red pepper sauce

2 garlic cloves, finely chopped

1 can (6 oz) tomato paste

1 can (4.5 oz) Old El Paso® chopped green chiles

12 hamburger buns, split

1) Spray 3- to 4-quart slow cooker with cooking spray. Place pork in slow cooker. In small bowl, mix brown sugar, salt, thyme, pepper sauce, garlic, tomato paste and chiles. Spread the mixture over pork.

2) Cover; cook on Low heat setting 8 to 9 hours.

3) Remove the pork from slow cooker; place on large plate. Shred pork with 2 forks; return to slow cooker and mix well. Spoon ½ cup pork mixture on the bottom half of each bun. Cover with top halves of buns.

Nutrition Information Per Serving:	
Calories: 370	From Fat: 140
Total Fat	16g
Saturated Fat	5g
Trans Fat	0g
Cholesterol	75mg
Sodium	610mg
Total Carbohydrate	29g
Dietary Fiber	1g
Sugars	9g
Protein	29g

Buffalo Pepper-Chicken Sandwiches

PREP TIME: 35 MINUTES (READY IN 55 MINUTES)
SERVINGS: 4

1/3 cup Buffalo wing sauce or red
pepper sauce

1/2 teaspoon black and red pepper blend

4 boneless skinless chicken breasts
(4 to 5 oz each)

1 tablespoon vegetable oil

1/4 cup blue cheese dressing

4 kaiser rolls, split

4 slices (1 oz each) Swiss cheese

4 slices tomato

4 lettuce leaves

1) In a 13x9-inch (3-quart) glass baking dish, mix the Buffalo wing sauce and pepper blend.

2) Between pieces of plastic wrap or waxed paper, place each chicken breast smooth side down; gently pound with flat side of meat mallet or rolling pin until about 1/4 inch thick. Add chicken to sauce in baking dish; turn to coat both sides with sauce. Cover; refrigerate 20 minutes to marinate.

3) In 12-inch skillet, heat oil over medium heat. Add the chicken; cook 10 to 13 minutes, turning once, until no longer pink in center.

4) Spread 1 tablespoon dressing on bottom half of each roll. Top with chicken, cheese, tomato, lettuce and tops of rolls.

HIGH ALTITUDE (3500-6500 FT.): No change.

Nutrition Information Per Serving:

Calories:	550	From Fat:	250
Total Fat			28g
Saturated Fat			8g
Trans Fat			1g
Cholesterol			115mg
Sodium			1270mg
Total Carbohydrate			30g
Dietary Fiber			1g
Sugars			2g
Protein			44g

Chicken Waldorf Salad

PREP TIME: 20 MINUTES (READY IN 20 MINUTES)
SERVINGS: 4 (1-1/4 CUPS EACH)

🌀 EASY

2 cups cubed deli rotisserie chicken
breast (from 2- to 2 1/2-lb chicken)

2 medium unpeeled apples, cubed
(2 cups)

2 medium stalks celery, sliced (1 cup)

1 cup red seedless grapes, cut in half

1/3 cup slivered almonds, toasted

1/4 cup refrigerated coleslaw dressing

4 leaf lettuce leaves

1 tablespoon thinly sliced chives

1) In large bowl, mix all ingredients except the lettuce leaves and chives. Place 1 lettuce leaf on each of 4 serving plates; spoon salad onto lettuce. Sprinkle with chives.

HIGH ALTITUDE (3500-6500 FT.): No change.

Nutrition Information Per Serving:

Calories:	300	From Fat:	120
Total Fat			14g
Saturated Fat			2.5g
Trans Fat			0g
Cholesterol			65mg
Sodium			560mg
Total Carbohydrate			23g
Dietary Fiber			3g
Sugars			18g
Protein			22g

Pico de Gallo Salad

PREP TIME: 25 MINUTES (READY IN 25 MINUTES)
SERVINGS: 6

e EASY

DRESSING

- 2 tablespoons chopped fresh cilantro
- 3 tablespoons vegetable oil
- 2 tablespoons lime juice
- 1 teaspoon sugar
- 1/4 teaspoon salt
- 1/8 teaspoon ground red pepper (cayenne)

SALAD

- 2 oranges, peeled, sliced crosswise
- 1/2 cucumber, thinly sliced
- 1 small red and/or yellow bell pepper, cut into thin strips
- 1/2 medium jicama, peeled, julienned (matchstick-cut) 3x1/4x1/4 inch (about 2 cups)
- 1/8 teaspoon chili powder, if desired

  Fresh cilantro sprigs, if desired

1) In blender, place all dressing ingredients. Cover; blend until smooth.

2) On serving platter, alternate slices of orange and cucumber around the edge. Mound bell pepper and jicama in center. Drizzle with dressing. Sprinkle with chili powder and/or cilantro sprigs.

HIGH ALTITUDE (3500-6500 FT.): No change.

Nutrition Information Per Serving:	
Calories: 120	From Fat: 60
Total Fat	7g
Saturated Fat	1g
Trans Fat	0g
Cholesterol	0mg
Sodium	105mg
Total Carbohydrate	12g
Dietary Fiber	4g
Sugars	5g
Protein	1g

Smoked Salmon-Avocado Sushi Salad

PREP TIME: 20 MINUTES (READY IN 1 HOUR)
SERVINGS: 4

e EASY   f LOW FAT

SUSHI RICE

- 1¼ cups water
- 1 cup uncooked sushi rice
- ¼ cup seasoned rice vinegar

DRESSING

- 2 tablespoons less-sodium soy sauce
- 1½ teaspoons seasoned rice vinegar
- ¼ to ½ teaspoon wasabi paste

SALAD

- 2 tablespoons sesame seed, toasted
- 1 avocado, peeled and cut lengthwise into 16 slices
- 1 package (3 oz) thinly sliced salmon lox
- 4 teaspoons chopped pickled ginger slices (from 6-oz jar)

1) In 2-quart saucepan, heat 1¼ cups water and the rice to boiling. Reduce heat to low; cover and simmer 10 to 15 minutes or until tender. Transfer to large bowl, tossing rice with chopsticks or 2 forks to cool slightly. Gradually add ¼ cup vinegar to rice, tossing constantly. Cover bowl with damp towel; cool the rice to room temperature.

2) In small bowl, mix dressing ingredients with wire whisk.

3) Dip hands into cold water; divide rice into 4 equal portions. Form each into oval-shaped patty about ¾ inch thick. Roll edges in sesame seed. Place each patty on serving plate. Sprinkle the top of each rice patty with 1 to 2 teaspoons dressing. Arrange 4 avocado slices over each. Top each with ¼ of the sliced salmon and 1 teaspoon ginger slices. Serve immediately.

HIGH ALTITUDE (3500-6500 FT.): No change.

Nutrition Information Per Serving:	
Calories: 290	From Fat: 80
Total Fat	8g
Saturated Fat	1.5g
Trans Fat	0g
Cholesterol	0mg
Sodium	480mg
Total Carbohydrate	45g
Dietary Fiber	3g
Sugars	6g
Protein	9g

Apple and Celery Salad with Creamy Lemon Dressing

PREP TIME: 15 MINUTES (READY IN 15 MINUTES)
SERVINGS: 20 (1/2 CUP EACH)

DRESSING

- ½ cup mayonnaise or salad dressing
- 3 tablespoons plain yogurt
- 2 tablespoons sugar
- 2 teaspoons grated fresh lemon peel

SALAD

- 2 large Granny Smith apples, cut into 8 wedges, then cut crosswise into bite-size pieces (4½ cups)
- 2 large Gala apples, cut into 8 wedges, then cut crosswise into bite-size pieces (3½ cups)
- 1 tablespoon fresh lemon juice
- 6 medium stalks celery with leaves
- ¾ cup chopped walnuts, toasted

1) In a small bowl, mix the dressing ingredients until blended. Refrigerate until serving time.

2) Place apples in large bowl. Sprinkle with lemon juice; toss until coated.

3) Remove the leaves from celery; chop leaves into ½-inch pieces to measure ½ cup. Cut celery stalks diagonally into ¼- to ½-inch slices to measure 2 cups. Add to bowl with the apples. Refrigerate until serving time.

4) Just before serving, toss apples and celery. Add dressing; toss until coated. Sprinkle with walnuts.

HIGH ALTITUDE (3500-6500 FT.): No change.

Nutrition Information Per Serving:

Calories:	100	From Fat:	70
Total Fat			7g
Saturated Fat			1g
Trans Fat			0g
Cholesterol			0mg
Sodium			45mg
Total Carbohydrate			9g
Dietary Fiber			1g
Sugars			6g
Protein			1g

Shanghai Sliders

PREP TIME: 20 MINUTES (READY IN 35 MINUTES)
SERVINGS: 8 (2 SANDWICHES EACH)

ⓔ EASY

ONION TOPPING

- **4** small yellow onions, thinly sliced (about 2 cups)
- **1** cup Progresso® reduced-sodium chicken broth (from 32-oz carton)
- **1/4** cup dry sherry or apple juice
- **1/4** cup soy sauce
- **1** tablespoon sugar
- **2** slices (1/4 inch) gingerroot

PATTIES

- **1** cup ketchup
- **2** teaspoons roasted red chile paste, if desired
- **1 1/2** lb lean (at least 80%) ground beef
- **1/4** cup finely chopped green onions (4 medium)
- **1** tablespoon finely chopped gingerroot
- **1** teaspoon garlic salt
- **16** turkey buns, split

1) In 10-inch skillet, mix the onion topping ingredients. Heat to boiling over high heat, stirring occasionally. Reduce the heat to medium-low; simmer about 15 minutes or until onions are softened and liquid is reduced by half. Remove gingerroot slices.

2) Meanwhile, in small bowl, mix ketchup and chile paste; set aside. In large bowl, mix beef, green onions, 1 tablespoon gingerroot and the garlic salt with hands just until blended. Divide mixture into 16 equal portions. Using wet hands, shape each portion into patty, about 1/4 inch thick.

3) Heat 12-inch nonstick skillet over medium-high heat. Add patties; cook 3 to 4 minutes on each side, pressing patties down lightly with spatula before turning over, until thoroughly cooked and no longer pink in center.

4) Place patties on bottoms of buns. Top patties with ketchup mixture. Using slotted spoon or fork, remove onion slices from the cooking liquid; place on top of ketchup mixture. Top with tops of buns.

HIGH ALTITUDE (3500-6500 FT.): No change.

Nutrition Information Per Serving:		
Calories: 350	**From Fat:**	110
Total Fat		12g
Saturated Fat		4g
Trans Fat		1g
Cholesterol		55mg
Sodium		1250mg
Total Carbohydrate		38g
Dietary Fiber		2g
Sugars		13g
Protein		21g

Garden Bounty Fontina Salad

PREP TIME: 25 MINUTES (READY IN 25 MINUTES)
SERVINGS: 8 (1-1/4 CUPS EACH)

SALAD

4 cups torn arugula

1½ cups cherry tomatoes, cut in half

6 oz fontina cheese, cubed

2 small zucchini, cut in half lengthwise, then sliced

2 ears fresh sweet corn, cooked, corn cut off, ears discarded

1 small cucumber, peeled, seeded, diced

½ cup walnut halves, toasted

DRESSING

¼ cup olive oil

2 tablespoons sherry vinegar

2 teaspoons Dijon mustard

¼ teaspoon salt

⅛ teaspoon coarse ground black pepper

1) In 3-quart bowl, layer salad ingredients in the order listed. In small jar with tight-fitting lid, shake dressing ingredients.

2) Pour dressing over salad; toss gently to coat. Serve immediately. Or, cover and refrigerate salad and dressing separately up to 4 hours; toss salad with dressing just before serving.

HIGH ALTITUDE (3500-6500 FT.): No change.

Nutrition Information Per Serving:

Calories:	240	From Fat:	160
Total Fat			18g
Saturated Fat			5g
Trans Fat			0g
Cholesterol			25mg
Sodium			290mg
Total Carbohydrate			11g
Dietary Fiber			2g
Sugars			3g
Protein			8g

Cannellini Bean and Tuna Salad

PREP TIME:	15 MINUTES (READY IN 15 MINUTES)	
SERVINGS:	8 (1 CUP EACH)	⊖ EASY

DRESSING

- ¼ cup olive oil
- ½ cup tarragon vinegar
- 2 tablespoons chopped fresh parsley
- 1 teaspoon sugar
- 1 teaspoon ground mustard
- 1 teaspoon dried thyme leaves
- ½ teaspoon dried oregano leaves
- ½ teaspoon garlic powder
- ½ teaspoon salt

SALAD

- 4 cups Green Giant® frozen broccoli cuts
- 2 cans (19 oz each) cannellini beans, drained
- 2 cans (6 oz each) tuna in water, drained, flaked
- Lettuce, if desired
- ½ cup shredded carrot

1) In small jar with tight-fitting lid, mix the dressing ingredients. Cover and shake well.

2) Cook broccoli as directed on the package until crisp-tender; rinse with cold water to cool.

3) In large bowl, mix broccoli, beans and tuna. Add dressing; toss gently to coat. Serve in lettuce-lined bowl. Sprinkle with carrot.

HIGH ALTITUDE (3500-6500 FT.): No change.

Nutrition Information Per Serving:

Calories:	290	From Fat:	70
Total Fat			8g
Saturated Fat			1g
Trans Fat			0g
Cholesterol			10mg
Sodium			630mg
Total Carbohydrate			34g
Dietary Fiber			9g
Sugars			3g
Protein			22g

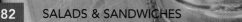

Roasted Red Pepper Potato Salad

PREP TIME: 30 MINUTES (READY IN 1 HOUR)
SERVINGS: 16 (1/2 CUP EACH)

3 lb small red potatoes (about 24)

¾ cup mayonnaise or salad dressing

¼ cup zesty Italian dressing

½ teaspoon salt

¼ teaspoon pepper

8 medium green onions, sliced (½ cup)

1 garlic clove, finely chopped

1 jar (7 oz) roasted red bell peppers, drained, chopped

1) Place potatoes in 4-quart saucepan or Dutch oven. Add enough cold water to cover 1 inch over potatoes. Heat to boiling. Reduce heat to medium; simmer uncovered 15 to 20 minutes or until the potatoes are fork-tender.

2) Drain potatoes; rinse with cold water. Place in single layer in 15x10x1-inch pan; refrigerate until cooled, about 30 minutes.

3) Cut cooled potatoes into eighths (bite-size wedges). In large serving bowl, mix remaining ingredients. Gently fold in potatoes. Serve immediately, or cover and refrigerate until serving time.

HIGH ALTITUDE (3500-6500 FT.): No change.

Nutrition Information Per Serving:

Calories:	160	From Fat:	80
Total Fat			9g
Saturated Fat			1.5g
Trans Fat			0g
Cholesterol			0mg
Sodium			200mg
Total Carbohydrate			17g
Dietary Fiber			2g
Sugars			3g
Protein			1g

Mexican Sloppy Joes

PREP TIME: 25 MINUTES (READY IN 40 MINUTES)
SERVINGS: 8 SANDWICHES

1) Heat oven to 375°F. Spray cookie sheet with cooking spray. Unroll both cans of dough on work surface (if using crescent rolls, pinch the seams to seal); press into two 12x8-inch rectangles. Cut into total of 8 rectangles.

2) In 10-inch skillet, cook beef over medium-high heat 5 to 7 minutes, stirring frequently, until thoroughly cooked. Stir in taco seasoning mix and salsa; simmer 5 minutes. Spoon about ¼ cup meat mixture in center of 1 dough rectangle. Sprinkle with 2 tablespoons cheese. Fold rectangle over to form triangle; press edges with fork to seal. Place on cookie sheet. Brush with egg; sprinkle with cornmeal. Repeat with remaining dough and filling.

3) Bake 10 to 15 minutes or until deep golden brown.

HIGH ALTITUDE (3500-6500 FT.): Bake 12 to 17 minutes.

2 cans (8 oz each) Pillsbury® refrigerated crescent dinner rolls or 2 cans (8 oz each) Pillsbury® Crescent Recipe Creations™ refrigerated flaky dough sheet

½ lb lean (at least 80%) ground beef

2 tablespoons Old El Paso® taco seasoning mix (from 1-oz package)

1 cup Old El Paso® Thick 'n Chunky salsa

1 cup shredded Cheddar-Jack with jalapeño peppers cheese blend (4 oz)

1 egg, beaten

1 tablespoon cornmeal

Nutrition Information Per Serving:

Calories:	310	From Fat:	150
Total Fat			16g
Saturated Fat			7g
Trans Fat			0g
Cholesterol			55mg
Sodium			1060mg
Total Carbohydrate			30g
Dietary Fiber			0g
Sugars			6g
Protein			12g

Layered Tortellini Pesto Chicken Salad

PREP TIME: 40 MINUTES (READY IN 2 HOURS 40 MINUTES)
SERVINGS: 8 (1-1/2 CUPS EACH)

1 package (9 oz) refrigerated cheese-filled tortellini

1 cup Green Giant® frozen sweet peas (from 1-lb bag)

5 cups torn romaine lettuce

1½ cups julienne (matchstick-cut) carrots

2 cups chopped or strips grilled chicken

1 medium red bell pepper, cut into strips

½ cup reduced-fat mayonnaise or salad dressing

½ cup basil pesto

¼ cup buttermilk

2 tablespoons chopped fresh parsley or basil leaves

1) Cook tortellini as directed on package, adding peas during last 4 minutes of cook time. Drain; rinse immediately with cold water. Pat with paper towels to remove moisture.

2) In 3- or 4-quart clear bowl, layer the lettuce, carrots, grilled chicken, peas, tortellini and bell pepper.

3) In small bowl, mix mayonnaise, pesto and buttermilk. Spread over peppers; sprinkle with fresh parsley. Cover and refrigerate at least 2 hours until chilled or overnight. Stir just before serving.

HIGH ALTITUDE (3500-6500 FT.): No change.

Nutrition Information Per Serving:

Calories:	330	From Fat:	160
Total Fat			18g
Saturated Fat			4g
Trans Fat			0g
Cholesterol			50mg
Sodium			440mg
Total Carbohydrate			24g
Dietary Fiber			3g
Sugars			5g
Protein			17g

Roasted Beets and Nectarine Salad

PREP TIME: 10 MINUTES (READY IN 1 HOUR 45 MINUTES)
SERVINGS: 4 (1 CUP EACH)

e EASY

SALAD

- 4 medium beets (about 1 lb)
- 4 cups mixed spring greens
- 2 nectarines, sliced
- $1/4$ cup crumbled chèvre (goat) cheese or Brie cheese (1 oz)
- 2 tablespoons walnuts, toasted

DRESSING

- 3 tablespoons extra-virgin olive oil
- 2 tablespoons orange juice
- 2 tablespoons finely chopped onion
- 1 teaspoon Dijon mustard
- $1/4$ teaspoon salt

1) Heat oven to 425°F. Remove greens from beets, leaving about $1/2$ inch of stem. Do not trim or cut root. Wash beets well. Tightly wrap beets in double layer of foil, and roast on cookie sheet 1 to $1^{1}/4$ hours or until tender. When beets are cool enough to handle, peel them, discarding stems and root ends, then cut them into $1/2$-inch-wide wedges.

2) In small bowl, mix dressing ingredients with wire whisk.

3) In large bowl, toss half the dressing with the mixed greens. Divide evenly among 4 salad plates. Arrange beets, nectarines, cheese and walnuts over each salad. Drizzle remaining dressing over each salad. Serve immediately.

HIGH ALTITUDE (3500-6500 FT.): No change.

Nutrition Information Per Serving:		
Calories: 240	From Fat:	140
Total Fat		16g
Saturated Fat		4g
Trans Fat		0g
Cholesterol		10mg
Sodium		280mg
Total Carbohydrate		19g
Dietary Fiber		5g
Sugars		12g
Protein		6g

Fruited Jicama Salad

PREP TIME: 20 MINUTES (READY IN 20 MINUTES)
SERVINGS: 4 (1 CUP EACH)

🅔 EASY   🅕 LOW FAT

DRESSING

- 2 tablespoons fresh lime juice
- 1 tablespoon honey
- 2 teaspoons water
- 1/2 teaspoon poppy seed
- 1/2 teaspoon grated orange peel

SALAD

- 1 cup peeled jicama strips (1 1/2 x 1/4 x 1/4 inch)
- 1 seedless orange, peeled, sectioned
- 1 medium apple, unpeeled, thinly sliced
- 1 can (8 oz) pineapple chunks in juice, drained

  Lettuce leaves, if desired

1) In small jar with tight-fitting lid, shake the dressing ingredients. Set aside.

2) In medium bowl, mix all salad ingredients except lettuce. Pour dressing over salad; toss lightly to coat. Cover and refrigerate until serving time.

3) Serve the salad on lettuce-lined salad plates if desired.

HIGH ALTITUDE (3500-6500 FT.): No change.

Nutrition Information Per Serving:

Calories:	160	From Fat:	120
Total Fat			13g
Saturated Fat			6g
Trans Fat			0g
Cholesterol			25mg
Sodium			210mg
Total Carbohydrate			9g
Dietary Fiber			0g
Sugars			0g
Protein			3g

Bacon-Ranch Potato Salad

PREP TIME: 15 MINUTES (READY IN 30 MINUTES)
SERVINGS: 9 (ABOUT 3/4 CUP EACH)

🅔 EASY

- 1 1/2 lb small red potatoes (about 10), quartered
- 1/2 teaspoon salt
- 1 cup grape tomatoes, cut in half
- 1/2 cup chopped celery
- 1/4 cup chopped fresh chives or green onions
- 1/4 cup cooked crumbled bacon or 6 slices packaged precooked bacon (from 2.2-oz package), chopped
- 1/2 cup ranch dressing

Nutrition Information Per Serving:

Calories:	140	From Fat:	70
Total Fat			8g
Saturated Fat			1.5g
Trans Fat			0g
Cholesterol			5mg
Sodium			300mg
Total Carbohydrate			15g
Dietary Fiber			2g
Sugars			2g
Protein			2g

1) In Dutch oven or 5-quart saucepan, place potatoes and salt. Add water just to cover. Heat to boiling; reduce heat to low. Cover; simmer 10 to 15 minutes or until tender. Drain; rinse with cold water to cool. Drain well. Cool slightly.

2) Place potatoes in large bowl. Add grape tomatoes, celery, chives and bacon. Stir in the ranch dressing. Serve salad warm, or cover and refrigerate until ready to serve.

HIGH ALTITUDE (3500-6500 FT.): No change.

Napa Cabbage Slaw

PREP TIME: 40 MINUTES (READY IN 2 HOURS 40 MINUTES)
SERVINGS: 21 (1/2 CUP EACH)

LOW FAT

SLAW

½ medium head Chinese (napa) cabbage, chopped (about 8 cups)

1 large red bell pepper, coarsely chopped

1 large green bell pepper, coarsely chopped

1 small jicama, peeled, julienned (matchstick-cut) 1x¼x¼ inch (2 cups)

3 tablespoons sliced fresh chives

DRESSING

3 tablespoons rice vinegar

3 tablespoons honey

2 tablespoons olive oil

1 teaspoon grated lemon peel

1 to 2 tablespoons fresh lemon juice

¼ teaspoon salt

¼ teaspoon freshly ground black pepper

1 tablespoon grated gingerroot, if desired

1) In 3-quart clear bowl, mix the slaw ingredients. In small jar with tight-fitting lid, mix dressing ingredients. Cover; shake well. Pour over slaw. Stir and serve immediately, or cover and refrigerate up to 2 hours before serving.

HIGH ALTITUDE (3500-6500 FT.): No change.

Nutrition Information Per Serving:

Calories:	40	From Fat:	15
Total Fat			1.5g
Saturated Fat			0g
Trans Fat			0g
Cholesterol			0mg
Sodium			45mg
Total Carbohydrate			6g
Dietary Fiber			1g
Sugars			3g
Protein			0g

Turkey and Rice Salad

PREP TIME: 25 MINUTES (READY IN 1 HOUR 20 MINUTES)
SERVINGS: 6

SALAD

1 box (10 oz) Green Giant® frozen white and wild rice (with green beans)

6 large tomatoes

2 cups diced cooked turkey

1/2 cup sliced celery

1/2 medium red or green bell pepper, chopped

1/4 cup chopped green onions (4 medium)

DRESSING

1/4 cup mayonnaise or salad dressing

2 tablespoons balsamic vinegar

1/4 teaspoon salt

1/4 teaspoon pepper

1) Cook rice as directed on box. Refrigerate 10 minutes to cool.

2) Meanwhile, cut thin slices from the tops of tomatoes. Gently squeeze out and discard seeds. Using teaspoon, remove pulp from tomatoes, leaving 1/4-inch shell. Drain upside down on paper towels. Refrigerate until serving time.

3) In medium bowl, mix rice, turkey, celery, bell pepper and onions. In small bowl, mix the dressing ingredients. Pour dressing over salad; stir gently to coat. Cover; refrigerate until thoroughly chilled, at least 45 minutes.

4) Just before serving, spoon salad into tomato shells. If desired, garnish with additional chopped green onions.

HIGH ALTITUDE (3500-6500 FT.): No change.

Nutrition Information Per Serving:	
Calories: 240	From Fat: 110
Total Fat	12g
Saturated Fat	2g
Trans Fat	0g
Cholesterol	45mg
Sodium	420mg
Total Carbohydrate	18g
Dietary Fiber	3g
Sugars	7g
Protein	1g

Refreshing Ginger Fruit Salad

PREP TIME: 20 MINUTES (READY IN 1 HOUR 20 MINUTES)
SERVINGS: 8 (1/2 CUP EACH)

e EASY   **f** LOW FAT

- 1/3 cup ginger ale
- 1 tablespoon honey or light brown sugar
- 1/2 teaspoon grated lime peel
- 2 teaspoons fresh lime juice
- 2 nectarines, halved, pitted and sliced
- 1/2 cup seedless green grapes, halved
- 1/2 cup seedless red grapes, halved
- 1/2 cup fresh raspberries
- 1/2 cup fresh blackberries

1) In large bowl, mix ginger ale, honey, lime peel and lime juice.

2) Add remaining ingredients; stir gently to combine. Cover; refrigerate at least 1 hour before serving.

HIGH ALTITUDE (3500-6500 FT.): No change.

Nutrition Information Per Serving:

Calories: 70	From Fat: 40
Total Fat	4.5g
Saturated Fat	1g
Trans Fat	0.5g
Cholesterol	0mg
Sodium	90mg
Total Carbohydrate	6g
Dietary Fiber	0g
Sugars	2g
Protein	1g

Taco Lettuce Cups

PREP TIME: 30 MINUTES (READY IN 30 MINUTES)
SERVINGS: 4 (2 LETTUCE CUPS EACH)

1 lb lean (at least 80%) ground beef

1 package (1 oz) Old El Paso® taco seasoning mix

2/3 cup water

1 cup Old El Paso® Thick 'n Chunky salsa

1 cup Green Giant® Niblets® frozen whole kernel corn

1 cup shredded Mexican cheese blend (4 oz)

8 leaves Bibb lettuce

2 cups coarsely crushed tortilla chips (about 3 oz)

1/2 cup sour cream, if desired

1) In 10-inch skillet, cook beef over medium-high heat 5 to 7 minutes, stirring occasionally, until thoroughly cooked; drain. Stir in taco seasoning mix and water. Reduce heat to medium. Cook uncovered 2 to 4 minutes, stirring occasionally, until most of liquid is absorbed.

2) Stir the salsa and corn into the beef mixture. Cook over medium heat 3 to 4 minutes, stirring occasionally, until thoroughly heated. Stir in 1/2 cup of the Mexican cheese blend.

3) Spoon about 1/2 cup beef mixture into each lettuce leaf; place 2 lettuce cups on each of 4 individual plates. Top each lettuce cup with about 1 tablespoon remaining cheese, 1/4 cup crushed chips and 1 tablespoon sour cream.

HIGH ALTITUDE (3500-6500 FT.): No change.

Nutrition Information Per Serving:		
Calories: 490	From Fat:	250
Total Fat		28g
Saturated Fat		11g
Trans Fat		1.5g
Cholesterol		100mg
Sodium		1630mg
Total Carbohydrate		32g
Dietary Fiber		2g
Sugars		5g
Protein		29g

tip

If your lettuce leaves are large enough, encourage the kids to wrap the lettuce around the filling and eat the cups with their fingers.

Grilled Margarita Chicken Salad

PREP TIME: 35 MINUTES (READY IN 35 MINUTES)
SERVINGS: 4

SALAD

- 4 boneless skinless chicken breasts (about 1¼ lb)
- 1 teaspoon ground cumin
- ½ teaspoon salt
- ¼ teaspoon pepper
- 1 bag (12 oz) ready-to-eat salad greens
- 1 avocado, pitted, peeled and cubed
- 1 mango, seed removed, peeled and cubed
- 1 cup halved fresh strawberries

VINAIGRETTE

- ¼ cup vegetable oil
- ¼ cup frozen limeade concentrate
- ¼ cup tequila or water
- 2 tablespoons chopped fresh cilantro
- ½ teaspoon salt

1) Heat gas or charcoal grill. Sprinkle the chicken with cumin, ½ teaspoon salt and the pepper.

2) Carefully brush oil on grill rack. Place chicken on grill over medium heat. Cover grill; cook 15 to 20 minutes, turning once, until juice of chicken is clear when center of thickest part is cut (170°F).

3) Meanwhile, in large bowl, mix remaining salad ingredients.

4) In jar with tight-fitting lid, place vinaigrette ingredients; shake well. Pour half of vinaigrette over salad; toss well. Divide salad among individual plates.

5) Cut chicken into slices; arrange on salads. Drizzle the remaining vinaigrette over salads.

HIGH ALTITUDE (3500-6500 FT.): Cook over medium-low heat.

Nutrition Information Per Serving:	
Calories: 500	From Fat: 220
Total Fat	24g
Saturated Fat	4g
Trans Fat	0g
Cholesterol	85mg
Sodium	700mg
Total Carbohydrate	29g
Dietary Fiber	6g
Sugars	17g
Protein	33g

Brie, Lettuce and Tomato Salad

PREP TIME:	15 MINUTES (READY IN 15 MINUTES)	
SERVINGS:	4 (ABOUT 1 CUP EACH)	EASY

DRESSING

3 tablespoons extra-virgin olive oil

1 tablespoon red wine vinegar

1 tablespoon finely chopped shallots

1 teaspoon Dijon mustard

¼ teaspoon salt

¼ teaspoon pepper

SALAD

4 cups packed arugula or mixed greens (about 5 oz)

2 medium tomatoes, sliced

3 oz Brie cheese, cut into bite-size strips

1) In small bowl, mix dressing ingredients with wire whisk.

2) In large bowl, toss arugula with half of the dressing. Arrange sliced tomatoes on medium platter. Place arugula and Brie around tomatoes; drizzle with remaining dressing. Serve immediately.

HIGH ALTITUDE (3500-6500 FT.): No change.

Nutrition Information Per Serving:

Calories:	180	From Fat:	150
Total Fat			16g
Saturated Fat			5g
Trans Fat			0g
Cholesterol			20mg
Sodium			320mg
Total Carbohydrate			4g
Dietary Fiber			1g
Sugars			2g
Protein			5g

Chicken Louis Sandwiches

PREP TIME: 15 MINUTES (READY IN 15 MINUTES)
SERVINGS: 6

😊 EASY   🥗 LOW FAT

2 tablespoons mayonnaise or salad dressing

¼ cup chili sauce

1 teaspoon lemon juice

1½ teaspoons seafood seasoning (from 6-oz container)

1½ cups chopped cooked chicken breast

1 medium stalk celery, sliced (½ cup)

2 tablespoons diced red bell pepper

6 croissants, split

1 cup shredded iceberg lettuce

Nutrition Information Per Serving:

Calories: 160	From Fat: 120
Total Fat	13g
Saturated Fat	6g
Trans Fat	0g
Cholesterol	25mg
Sodium	210mg
Total Carbohydrate	9g
Dietary Fiber	0g
Sugars	0g
Protein	3g

1) In large bowl, mix the mayonnaise, chili sauce, lemon juice and seafood seasoning. Stir in chicken, celery and bell pepper.

2) Spoon the chicken mixture onto the bottoms of buns. Top with lettuce and tops of buns.

HIGH ALTITUDE (3500-6500 FT.): No change.

Escarole-Pear Salad

PREP TIME: 15 MINUTES (READY IN 15 MINUTES)
SERVINGS: 6

😊 EASY   🥗 LOW FAT

DRESSING

3 tablespoons cider vinegar

3 tablespoons raspberry jam

1 tablespoon vegetable oil

SALAD

3 cups torn escarole or leaf lettuce

2 small pears, cored

1 tablespoon chopped hazelnuts (filberts)

Nutrition Information Per Serving:

Calories: 90	From Fat: 30
Total Fat	3g
Saturated Fat	0g
Trans Fat	0g
Cholesterol	0mg
Sodium	5mg
Total Carbohydrate	15g
Dietary Fiber	2g
Sugars	10g
Protein	0g

1) In small jar with tight-fitting lid, shake dressing ingredients. Set aside. Arrange escarole on 6 individual salad plates. Thinly slice pears; arrange slices over lettuce. Sprinkle hazelnuts over salads; drizzle with dressing. Serve immediately.

HIGH ALTITUDE (3500-6500 FT.): No change.

Italian Bean and Tuna Salad

PREP TIME: 20 MINUTES (READY IN 30 MINUTES)
SERVINGS: 4 (1 CUP EACH)

e EASY   **lf** LOW FAT

1 can (19 or 15 oz) Progresso® cannellini beans or 1 can (16 oz) navy beans, drained, rinsed

1 can (6 oz) white tuna in water, drained, flaked

1 cup fresh or frozen cut (1-inch) green beans, cooked, rinsed with cold water

1 cup chopped celery

1/2 cup chopped red bell pepper

3 tablespoons chopped fresh chives

2 tablespoons chopped fresh parsley

1/2 cup reduced-calorie or fat-free Italian dressing

1/2 teaspoon dried oregano leaves

Lettuce leaves, if desired

1) In medium bowl, mix all ingredients except lettuce. Refrigerate 10 minutes to blend flavors.

2) Just before serving, place the lettuce in serving bowl; spoon the salad on the lettuce.

HIGH ALTITUDE (3500-6500 FT.): No change.

Nutrition Information Per Serving:

Calories:	270	From Fat:	60
Total Fat		6g	
Saturated Fat		1g	
Trans Fat		0g	
Cholesterol		10mg	
Sodium		530mg	
Total Carbohydrate		33g	
Dietary Fiber		8g	
Sugars		4g	
Protein		20g	

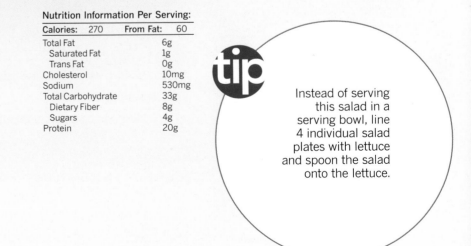

tip

Instead of serving this salad in a serving bowl, line 4 individual salad plates with lettuce and spoon the salad onto the lettuce.

Buffalo Shrimp Salad

PREP TIME: 15 MINUTES (READY IN 35 MINUTES)
SERVINGS: 8

E EASY

2 lb uncooked deveined peeled large shrimp, tail shells removed

1/2 cup buffalo wing sauce

2 bags (10 oz each) torn mixed salad greens (such as romaine lettuce and radicchio)

2 medium stalks celery, sliced (1 cup)

1 1/2 cups seasoned croutons

1 cup blue cheese dressing

1) Heat gas or charcoal grill. Thread shrimp onto eight 12-inch metal skewers. Brush with wing sauce, covering all sides of shrimp. Let stand 10 minutes to marinate.

2) Place shrimp on grill over medium heat. Cover grill; cook 5 to 7 minutes or until shrimp turn pink.

3) In large bowl, place salad greens, celery, croutons and dressing; toss gently. Divide salad among individual serving plates. Top each salad with grilled shrimp.

HIGH ALTITUDE (3500-6500 FT.): No change.

Nutrition Information Per Serving:	
Calories: 290	From Fat: 170
Total Fat	19g
Saturated Fat	3g
Trans Fat	0g
Cholesterol	170mg
Sodium	1110mg
Total Carbohydrate	10g
Dietary Fiber	2g
Sugars	2g
Protein	19g

Grilled Chicken Garden Salad

PREP TIME: 35 MINUTES (READY IN 1 HOUR 5 MINUTES)
SERVINGS: 6

1 lb   fresh asparagus spears

2   tablespoons olive or canola oil

2   teaspoons finely chopped garlic

1½   teaspoons dried rosemary leaves

1   teaspoon seasoned salt

6   boneless skinless chicken breasts
(4 to 5 oz each)

1   bag (5 oz) ready-to-eat spring mix
salad greens

1   pint (2 cups) grape tomatoes,
cut in half

1   cup thinly sliced red onion

½   cup refrigerated reduced-fat
honey Dijon dressing

1) Snap or cut off tough ends of asparagus spears; place spears in shallow glass dish. Drizzle with 1 teaspoon of the oil; turn to coat. Cover; refrigerate until grilling time.

2) In small bowl, mix remaining oil, the garlic, rosemary and seasoned salt. Rub both sides of each chicken breast with oil mixture; place in another shallow dish. Cover; refrigerate 30 minutes to marinate.

3) Heat gas or charcoal grill. Place chicken on grill over medium heat. Cover grill; cook chicken 15 to 20 minutes, turning once or twice and adding asparagus after 7 minutes, until juice of chicken is clear when center of thickest part is cut (170°F). Cook asparagus 6 to 8 minutes, turning frequently, until crisp-tender.

4) Cut the asparagus into 1-inch pieces. In large bowl, toss asparagus, salad greens, tomatoes and onion. Pour dressing over salad; toss to coat. Cut chicken into strips; serve over salad.

HIGH ALTITUDE (3500-6500 FT.): Cook over medium-low heat.

Nutrition Information Per Serving:		
Calories: 260	From Fat:	100
Total Fat		11g
Saturated Fat		2g
Trans Fat		0g
Cholesterol		70mg
Sodium		500mg
Total Carbohydrate		12g
Dietary Fiber		2g
Sugars		7g
Protein		27g

Pizza Bread Salad

PREP TIME: 15 MINUTES (READY IN 15 MINUTES)
SERVINGS: 8 (1 CUP EACH)

 EASY

½   cup fat-free Italian dressing

1   tablespoon chopped fresh or
1 teaspoon dried basil leaves

1   bag (10 oz) hearts of romaine
lettuce, torn into bite-size pieces

1   (8-inch) prebaked Italian pizza crust
(from 10-oz package), cut into 1-inch
pieces

25   slices turkey pepperoni (2 oz),
chopped

1   large tomato, coarsely chopped (1 cup)

1   piece (4 oz) mozzarella cheese, cut into ½-inch cubes

1) In small bowl, mix the Italian dressing and basil; set aside. In large bowl, toss the remaining ingredients. Pour the dressing over the salad mixture; toss to coat well. Serve immediately.

HIGH ALTITUDE (3500-6500 FT.): No change.

Nutrition Information Per Serving:		
Calories: 330	From Fat:	150
Total Fat		16g
Saturated Fat		6g
Trans Fat		0g
Cholesterol		90mg
Sodium		1990mg
Total Carbohydrate		15g
Dietary Fiber		1g
Sugars		3g
Protein		30g

Sloppy BBQ Joes

PREP TIME: 30 MINUTES (READY IN 30 MINUTES)
SERVINGS: 6 (2 SANDWICHES EACH)

 EASY

1 lb lean (at least 80%) ground beef

1 small onion, chopped (about 1/3 cup)

1 cup barbecue sauce

1 can (15 oz) spicy chili beans, undrained

12 sandwich buns, split

3/4 cup shredded Cheddar cheese (3 oz)

1) In 10-inch nonstick skillet, cook beef and onion over medium-high heat 5 to 7 minutes, stirring occasionally, until beef is thoroughly cooked; drain.

2) Stir in barbecue sauce and chili beans. Heat to boiling. Reduce heat to low; simmer uncovered 10 to 15 minutes, stirring occasionally, until mixture is slightly thickened.

3) Spoon mixture onto bottoms of buns; sprinkle with Cheddar cheese. Top with tops of buns.

HIGH ALTITUDE (3500-6500 FT.): No change.

Nutrition Information Per Serving:	
Calories: 18	From Fat: 7
Total Fat	18g
Saturated Fat	7g
Trans Fat	1.5g
Cholesterol	60mg
Sodium	1490mg
Total Carbohydrate	73g
Dietary Fiber	5g
Sugars	22g
Protein	28g

tip

To make these ahead, cook the barbecue mixture and let it cool for 30 minutes. Refrigerate it for up to 4 days. To reheat, bring it to a boil, stirring occasionally.

Chicken Niçoise Salad Sandwiches

PREP TIME: 45 MINUTES (READY IN 45 MINUTES)
SERVINGS: 8

3 cups shredded deli rotisserie chicken (from 2- to 2½-lb chicken)

½ cup refrigerated cooked diced potatoes with onions (from 20-oz bag)

½ cup chopped fresh green beans

½ cup quartered cherry tomatoes

¼ cup chopped kalamata olives

2 tablespoons mayonnaise or salad dressing

4 hard-cooked eggs, diced

¾ cup balsamic vinaigrette dressing

8 unsliced bolillo or small hoagie rolls

2 cups chopped romaine lettuce

1) In medium bowl, gently mix all ingredients except ½ cup of the dressing, the rolls and romaine lettuce. Season with salt and pepper to taste.

2) Cut slit in the top of each roll, being careful not to cut all the way through. If necessary, remove excess bread from interior of each to allow room for filling.

3) Stuff each roll with ¼ cup romaine lettuce and rounded ½ cup chicken salad mixture. Drizzle each sandwich with 1 tablespoon dressing.

HIGH ALTITUDE (3500-6500 FT.): No change.

Nutrition Information Per Serving:	
Calories: 430 From Fat: 170	
Total Fat	19g
Saturated Fat	3.5g
Trans Fat	0.5g
Cholesterol	150mg
Sodium	900mg
Total Carbohydrate	39g
Dietary Fiber	2g
Sugars	8g
Protein	24g

tip

Any crusty roll can be used for this sandwich. To hold 1/2 cup of the filling, choose a roll that is about 6 to 7 inches long.

Pomegranate and Almond Salad

PREP TIME: 20 MINUTES (READY IN 20 MINUTES)
SERVINGS: 16 (1 CUP EACH)

e EASY

1 cup sliced almonds

$1/3$ cup olive or vegetable oil

2 tablespoons fresh lime juice

1 tablespoon sugar

$1/4$ teaspoon salt

$1/8$ teaspoon coarsely ground pepper

1 garlic clove, finely chopped

2 bags (5 oz each) sweet baby lettuces or butter and red leaf lettuce (about 12 cups)

1 pomegranate, seeded ($3/4$ cup seeds)

1) Sprinkle almonds in ungreased heavy skillet. Cook over medium heat 5 to 7 minutes, stirring frequently until almonds begin to brown, then stirring constantly until light brown. Remove from skillet; set aside.

2) Meanwhile, in small bowl, beat oil, lime juice, sugar, salt, pepper and garlic with wire whisk until smooth.

3) In large serving bowl, mix the lettuces and pomegranate seeds. Add dressing; toss to coat. Sprinkle with almonds; toss gently.

HIGH ALTITUDE (3500-6500 FT.): No change.

Nutrition Information Per Serving:

Calories:	90	From Fat:	70
Total Fat			7g
Saturated Fat			1g
Trans Fat			0g
Cholesterol			0mg
Sodium			40mg
Total Carbohydrate			4g
Dietary Fiber			1g
Sugars			2g
Protein			1g

Side Dishes & More

Rely on this chapter for everything from special holiday breads to quick veggies for weeknights.

STEAMED VEGETABLES
WITH CHILE-LIME BUTTER
PG. 117

RICE WITH PASTA
PG. 121

CRESCENT ROLLS
WITH FRESH HERBS
PG. 103

MAPLE-GLAZED
CARROTS WITH PECANS
PG. 104

Cranberry-Cornmeal Muffins

PREP TIME: 15 MINUTES (READY IN 35 MINUTES)
SERVINGS: 12 MUFFINS

e EASY

1 cup all-purpose flour

3/4 cup cornmeal

1/2 cup sugar

1 1/2 teaspoons baking powder

1/4 teaspoon salt

1/2 cup sweetened dried cranberries

1 egg

3/4 cup milk

1/3 cup vegetable oil

1/2 cup coarsely chopped pecans

1) Heat oven to 400°F. Line 12 regular-size muffin cups with paper baking cups.

2) In large bowl, mix flour, cornmeal, sugar, baking powder and salt. In small bowl, mix 2 tablespoons flour mixture and the cranberries; set aside.

3) In medium bowl, beat egg with wire whisk until blended. Beat in milk and oil.

4) Make a well in center of dry ingredients. Add the egg mixture to dry ingredients; stir just until dry ingredients are moistened (batter will be thin). Stir in cranberries and pecans. Divide batter evenly among muffin cups.

5) Bake 15 to 18 minutes or until lightly browned and toothpick inserted in center comes out clean. Cool 1 minute; remove from pan to cooling rack. Serve warm or at room temperature.

HIGH ALTITUDE (3500-6500 FT.): Bake 17 to 20 minutes.

Nutrition Information Per Serving:		
Calories: 230	From Fat:	90
Total Fat		10g
Saturated Fat		1.5g
Trans Fat		0g
Cholesterol		20mg
Sodium		125mg
Total Carbohydrate		30g
Dietary Fiber		1g
Sugars		13g
Protein		3g

Crescent Rolls with Fresh Herbs

PREP TIME: 25 MINUTES (READY IN 40 MINUTES)
SERVINGS: 16 ROLLS

4 teaspoons finely chopped fresh parsley

4 teaspoons finely chopped fresh thyme leaves

4 teaspoons finely chopped fresh basil leaves

4 teaspoons finely chopped fresh oregano leaves

2 cans (8 oz each) Pillsbury® refrigerated crescent dinner rolls

1 egg

1 teaspoon water

16 small leaves fresh herbs, if desired

1) Heat oven to 375°F. In small bowl, mix all chopped herbs. Separate dough into 16 triangles. Sprinkle each with 1 teaspoon herb mixture; press lightly into dough. Roll up each triangle, starting at shortest side and rolling to opposite point. On ungreased cookie sheets, place rolls point sides down; curve each into crescent shape.

2) In small bowl, beat egg and water until blended. Brush egg mixture over tops of rolls. Place 1 herb leaf on top of each roll; brush egg mixture over top of leaf.

3) Bake 10 to 12 minutes or until golden brown. Serve warm.

HIGH ALTITUDE (3500-6500 FT.): No change.

Nutrition Information Per Serving:		
Calories: 110	From Fat: 60	
Total Fat		6g
Saturated Fat		2g
Trans Fat		1.5g
Cholesterol		15mg
Sodium		220mg
Total Carbohydrate		11g
Dietary Fiber		0g
Sugars		2g
Protein		2g

Maple-Glazed Carrots with Pecans

PREP TIME: 10 MINUTES (READY IN 10 MINUTES)
SERVINGS: 12 (1/2 CUP EACH)

 EASY

¼ cup chicken broth

¼ teaspoon salt

2 lb ready-to-eat baby-cut carrots

¼ cup real maple or maple-flavored syrup

2 tablespoons butter or margarine

¼ cup coarsely chopped pecans

Nutrition Information Per Serving:	
Calories: 90	From Fat: 35
Total Fat	4g
Saturated Fat	1.5g
Trans Fat	0g
Cholesterol	5mg
Sodium	135mg
Total Carbohydrate	12g
Dietary Fiber	2g
Sugars	8g
Protein	1g

1) In 12-inch skillet, heat chicken broth and salt to boiling over high heat. Add carrots; reduce heat to medium. Cover; cook 10 to 12 minutes or just until crisp-tender. Drain if necessary.

2) Add syrup and butter to carrots in saucepan. Cook over medium-high heat 3 to 4 minutes, stirring frequently, until carrots are glazed. Sprinkle with pecans.

HIGH ALTITUDE (3500-6500 FT.): In Step 1, reduce heat to medium-low. Cover; cook 14 to 16 minutes. In Step 2, cook 4 to 5 minutes.

Cauliflower and Broccoli with Fresh Herb Butter

PREP TIME: 15 MINUTES (READY IN 15 MINUTES)
SERVINGS: 8 (1/2 CUP EACH)

 EASY

3 tablespoons butter or margarine, softened

3 tablespoons finely sliced fresh chives

1½ teaspoons chopped fresh or ½ teaspoon dried thyme leaves

1 teaspoon grated lemon peel

¼ teaspoon salt

¼ teaspoon pepper

3 cups fresh cauliflower florets (about 1 lb)

3 cups fresh broccoli florets (7 oz)

Nutrition Information Per Serving:	
Calories: 70	From Fat: 40
Total Fat	4.5g
Saturated Fat	3g
Trans Fat	0g
Cholesterol	10mg
Sodium	125mg
Total Carbohydrate	4g
Dietary Fiber	2g
Sugars	2g
Protein	1g

1) In 4-quart saucepan, heat 2 quarts water to boiling over high heat. Meanwhile, in small bowl, stir together butter, chives, thyme, lemon peel, salt and pepper until blended; set aside.

2) Add cauliflower to boiling water in saucepan; cook 2 minutes. Add broccoli; cook 2 to 3 minutes longer or until vegetables are crisp-tender. Drain; return to saucepan.

3) Add the butter mixture to the cauliflower and broccoli in the saucepan; toss to coat.

HIGH ALTITUDE (3500-6500 FT.): No change.

Cornbread and Sausage Dressing

PREP TIME: 40 MINUTES (READY IN 1 HOUR 50 MINUTES)
SERVINGS: 24 (1/2 CUP EACH)

2 pouches (6.5 oz each) Betty Crocker® cornbread and muffin mix

²/₃ cup milk

¹/₄ cup butter or margarine, melted

2 eggs

3 medium stalks celery, chopped (1¹/₂ cups)

1 large onion, finely chopped (1 cup)

4 garlic cloves, finely chopped

1 lb bulk hot pork sausage

¹/₄ teaspoon crushed red pepper flakes

1 jalapeño chile, seeded, finely chopped

2 cups Green Giant® Valley Fresh Steamers™ Niblets® frozen corn, thawed

1¹/₂ teaspoons chopped fresh or ¹/₂ teaspoon dried sage leaves

1¹/₂ teaspoons chopped fresh or ¹/₂ teaspoon dried thyme leaves

1 teaspoon salt

¹/₂ teaspoon pepper

1³/₄ to 2 cups Progresso® chicken broth (from 32-oz carton)

1) Heat oven to 400°F. Spray 15x10x1-inch pan with cooking spray. In large bowl, stir muffin mixes, milk, butter and eggs just until moistened (batter will be lumpy). Spread batter in pan. Bake 10 to 12 minutes or until golden brown. Cool in pan 10 minutes. While still in pan, cut warm cornbread into ¹/₂-inch cubes. Fluff cubes. Bake 10 minutes. Stir cubes; bake 10 to 15 minutes longer or until golden brown on top.

2) Meanwhile, in 10-inch skillet, cook celery, onion, garlic and sausage over medium-high heat 7 to 10 minutes, stirring frequently, until sausage is until no longer pink; drain if desired. Stir pepper flakes and jalapeño chile into sausage mixture.

3) In another large bowl, place the cornbread cubes, sausage mixture and remaining ingredients. Stir gently, adding enough broth to moisten bread cubes but not make mixture mushy.

4) Spoon dressing into ungreased 13x9-inch (3-quart) glass baking dish. Cover with foil; bake 25 to 30 minutes or until hot in center.

HIGH ALTITUDE (3500-6500 FT.): Use 2 cups chicken broth. In Step 1, after stirring cubes, bake 7 minutes; stir again and bake 3 to 8 minutes longer.

Nutrition Information Per Serving:

Calories:	130	From Fat:	50
Total Fat			6g
Saturated Fat			2.5g
Trans Fat			0g
Cholesterol			30mg
Sodium			370mg
Total Carbohydrate			16g
Dietary Fiber			0g
Sugars			4g
Protein			4g

Roasted Green Beans with Roasted Garlic Aioli

PREP TIME: 10 MINUTES (READY IN 1 HOUR 15 MINUTES)
SERVINGS: 24 (ABOUT 1 OZ BEANS AND 1-1/2 TEASPOONS AIOLI EACH)

ⓔ EASY

AIOLI

- 1 medium head garlic
- 1 teaspoon olive or vegetable oil
- $^1/_2$ teaspoon coarse sea salt
- $^2/_3$ cup mayonnaise or salad dressing

GREEN BEANS

- 2 bags (12 oz each) fresh whole green beans
- 1 tablespoon olive or vegetable oil
- 1 teaspoon coarse sea salt

1) Heat oven to 400°F. Cut crosswise slice from top of garlic head, removing tops of cloves (discard top). Place garlic head on 7-inch square sheet of foil. Drizzle 1 teaspoon oil over cut cloves; sprinkle with $^1/_4$ teaspoon of the salt; wrap foil around garlic.

2) Roast garlic 35 to 40 minutes or until garlic is soft and golden brown. Cool 10 minutes or until cool enough to handle.

3) Squeeze roasted cloves from skins. Place each clove in garlic press; press garlic into small bowl. Add mayonnaise and remaining $^1/_4$ teaspoon salt; mix thoroughly. Cover; refrigerate until ready to serve.

4) Place green beans in ungreased 15x10x1-inch pan. Drizzle 1 tablespoon oil over beans; toss lightly to coat. Sprinkle with $^1/_2$ teaspoon of the salt.

5) Roast beans 12 to 15 minutes, stirring halfway through roasting time, until lightly browned. Transfer beans to a serving platter. Sprinkle with remaining $^1/_2$ teaspoon salt. Serve beans hot or cold with aioli and small tongs.

HIGH ALTITUDE (3500-6500 FT.): No change.

Nutrition Information Per Serving:		
Calories: 60	From Fat:	50
Total Fat		6g
Saturated Fat		1g
Trans Fat		0g
Cholesterol		0mg
Sodium		180mg
Total Carbohydrate		3g
Dietary Fiber		0g
Sugars		0g
Protein		0g

A garlic press acts as a mini ricer and is perfect for obtaining a smooth texture from the roasted cloves in this recipe.

Brown Butter Snap Peas and New Potatoes

PREP TIME: 10 MINUTES (READY IN 30 MINUTES)
SERVINGS: 12 (1/2 CUP EACH)

e EASY   **f** LOW FAT

1 lb small new potatoes, cut into
$^1/_4$-inch-thick slices

1$^1/_2$ cups Green Giant® Select® frozen
sugar snap peas

3 tablespoons butter (do not use
margarine or low-fat spread)

3 tablespoons water

2 tablespoons lemon juice

$^1/_4$ teaspoon chicken bouillon granules

1 teaspoon chopped fresh or
freeze-dried chives

1) In 4-quart saucepan, heat 1 cup water to boiling. Add potatoes. Cover; cook over medium heat 10 to 12 minutes or until almost tender.

2) Add sugar snap peas to potatoes. Cover; cook 5 to 8 minutes or until peas are hot and potatoes are tender. Drain; return to the saucepan.

3) Meanwhile, in 1-quart saucepan, cook butter over medium heat, stirring frequently, until it begins to brown. Stir in 3 tablespoons water, the lemon juice and bouillon; cook about 2 minutes, stirring occasionally, until hot. Stir in chives.

4) Pour browned butter mixture over cooked vegetables; stir gently to coat. If desired, season to taste with salt.

HIGH ALTITUDE (3500-6500 FT.): No change.

Nutrition Information Per Serving:		
Calories: 70	From Fat:	25
Total Fat		3g
Saturated Fat		2g
Trans Fat		0g
Cholesterol		10mg
Sodium		40mg
Total Carbohydrate		8g
Dietary Fiber		1g
Sugars		0g
Protein		1g

Pinto Beans and Bacon

PREP TIME: 35 MINUTES (READY IN 35 MINUTES)
SERVINGS: 8 (1/2 CUP EACH)

3/4 lb mesquite-flavored bacon, cut into 1-inch pieces

1 cup chopped onions

2 garlic cloves, crushed

3 cans (15.5 oz each) pinto beans, drained, rinsed

1 can (12 oz) beer or beef broth

1 teaspoon ground cumin

1/2 teaspoon coarsely ground black pepper

1/4 teaspoon salt

1) In 4-quart saucepan or Dutch oven, cook bacon over medium-high heat until crisp. Drain on paper towels. Reserve 2 tablespoons drippings in saucepan.

2) Stir in onions and garlic; cook over medium-high heat 5 to 8 minutes or until onion is softened.

3) Add remaining ingredients except bacon; mix well. Reduce heat to medium; cook 18 to 20 minutes, stirring occasionally, until slightly thickened. Stir in all but 1/4 cup bacon. Crumble remaining bacon and sprinkle on top of beans. Serve immediately.

HIGH ALTITUDE (3500-6500 FT.): In Step 3, add up to 2 tablespoons water if beans get too dry.

Nutrition Information Per Serving:

Calories: 220	From Fat: 50
Total Fat	6g
Saturated Fat	2g
Trans Fat	0g
Cholesterol	15mg
Sodium	530mg
Total Carbohydrate	28g
Dietary Fiber	9g
Sugars	1g
Protein	14g

Green Beans with Tomatoes and Cotija

PREP TIME: 20 MINUTES (READY IN 20 MINUTES)
SERVINGS: 8 (2/3 CUP EACH)

e EASY

1 lb fresh green beans, trimmed

1 tablespoon olive oil

1 medium onion, sliced

2 garlic cloves, finely chopped

1 can (14.5 oz) diced tomatoes, undrained

1 teaspoon chopped fresh or 1/2 teaspoon dried oregano leaves

1/8 teaspoon crushed red pepper flakes, if desired

1/3 cup crumbled Cotija cheese

1/4 cup sliced almonds

1) In Dutch oven, place 2 cups water. Cover tightly; heat to boiling. Place green beans in steamer basket in Dutch oven. Reduce heat to medium-low; cook 8 to 10 minutes or until crisp-tender. Drain thoroughly.

2) Meanwhile, in 10-inch skillet, heat oil over medium heat. Cook onion and garlic in oil 3 to 4 minutes, stirring frequently, until onion is crisp-tender. Stir in the tomatoes, oregano and pepper flakes. Heat to boiling. Reduce heat; simmer uncovered about 5 minutes, stirring occasionally, until thickened and most of liquid is evaporated.

3) Spoon drained beans onto a serving platter; top with the tomato mixture. Sprinkle with cheese and almonds; serve warm.

HIGH ALTITUDE (3500-6500 FT.): No change.

Nutrition Information Per Serving:

Calories:	80	From Fat:	35
Total Fat			3.5g
Saturated Fat			0.5g
Trans Fat			0g
Cholesterol			0mg
Sodium			125mg
Total Carbohydrate			9g
Dietary Fiber			3g
Sugars			4g
Protein			3g

Grilled Corn-on-the-Cob with Herb Butter

PREP TIME: 40 MINUTES (READY IN 40 MINUTES)
SERVINGS: 8

e EASY

1/2 cup butter, softened

1/3 cup chopped fresh chives

2 tablespoons chopped fresh basil leaves

2 tablespoons chopped fresh oregano leaves

8 medium ears fresh sweet corn with husks

1) In small bowl, mix butter, chives, basil and oregano. Cover and refrigerate until serving time.

2) Heat gas or charcoal grill. Remove all but innermost husks from corn. Fold back inner husks and remove corn silk. Rewrap inner husks around corn. Place corn on grill over medium heat. Cover grill; cook 10 to 15 minutes or until corn is tender and husks are slightly brown. Serve immediately with herb butter.

HIGH ALTITUDE (3500-6500 FT.): No change.

Nutrition Information Per Serving:

Calories:	230	From Fat:	120
Total Fat			13g
Saturated Fat			8g
Trans Fat			0g
Cholesterol			30mg
Sodium			100mg
Total Carbohydrate			25g
Dietary Fiber			4g
Sugars			3g
Protein			3g

Easy Grilled Baked Potatoes

PREP TIME: 15 MINUTES (READY IN 30 MINUTES)
SERVINGS: 4

e) EASY

CHEESY BUTTER
- ¼ cup butter, softened
- ½ cup shredded Cheddar-American cheese blend (2 oz)
- 2 tablespoons chopped fresh parsley

POTATOES
- 4 medium baking or russet potatoes
- 1 tablespoon butter, melted
- ½ teaspoon seasoned salt
- ½ teaspoon garlic-pepper blend

1) Heat gas or charcoal grill. In small bowl, mix cheesy butter ingredients until blended. Refrigerate until serving time.

2) Pierce potatoes to allow steam to escape. Brush outside of potatoes with melted butter; sprinkle with seasoned salt. Place potatoes on microwavable plate or in shallow microwavable dish. Microwave on High 6 to 8 minutes, turning once, until fork-tender.

3) Place potatoes on grill over medium heat. Cover grill; cook 8 to 12 minutes, turning occasionally, until crisp and browned.

4) Cut large X in top of each baked potato; press sides slightly to fluff. Top each with cheesy butter; sprinkle with garlic-pepper blend.

HIGH ALTITUDE (3500-6500 FT.): In Step 3, grill over medium-low heat.

Nutrition Information Per Serving:		
Calories: 360	From Fat: 170	
Total Fat		19g
Saturated Fat		12g
Trans Fat		0.5g
Cholesterol		55mg
Sodium		380mg
Total Carbohydrate		37g
Dietary Fiber		4g
Sugars		2g
Protein		8g

Spicy Chipotle Twists

PREP TIME: 10 MINUTES (READY IN 30 MINUTES)
SERVINGS: 16 TWISTS

e) EASY

- ½ cup finely shredded Cheddar cheese (2 oz)
- 1 teaspoon chili powder
- ¼ to ½ teaspoon chipotle chili powder
- 2 cans (8 oz each) Pillsbury® refrigerated crescent dinner rolls

1) Heat oven to 375°F. Lightly grease cookie sheets with cooking spray or shortening. In small bowl, gently toss the Cheddar cheese and both chili powders.

2) On floured cutting board, unroll 1 can of crescent dough into 12x8-inch rectangle; press the perforations to seal. Sprinkle evenly with the cheese mixture to within ½ inch of edges. Unroll remaining can of dough; place over cheese mixture. Seal perforations. With rolling pin, lightly roll dough to press layers together.

3) Cut crosswise through both layers of dough into 16 strips. Holding each end of dough strip, gently twist strip; place on cookie sheets.

4) Bake 10 to 15 minutes or until golden brown. Remove twists from cookie sheets to cooling rack; cool 5 minutes. Serve warm.

HIGH ALTITUDE (3500-6500 FT.): No change.

Nutrition Information Per Serving:		
Calories: 120	From Fat: 60	
Total Fat		7g
Saturated Fat		3g
Trans Fat		1.5g
Cholesterol		0mg
Sodium		240mg
Total Carbohydrate		11g
Dietary Fiber		0g
Sugars		2g
Protein		3g

Asiago Cheese and Onion Braid

PREP TIME: 25 MINUTES (READY IN 45 MINUTES)
SERVINGS: 12

2 tablespoons butter or margarine

1 large sweet onion, cut in half, thinly sliced (about 2 cups)

1 tablespoon packed brown sugar

1 teaspoon dried thyme leaves

1 can (13.8 oz) Pillsbury® refrigerated classic pizza crust

1 cup shredded Asiago cheese (4 oz)

1 egg white, beaten

$1/2$ teaspoon poppy seed

1) Heat oven to 425°F. Spray large cookie sheet with cooking spray.

2) In 10-inch skillet, melt butter over medium heat. Add onion; cook about 15 minutes, stirring occasionally, until onion is golden brown. Stir in brown sugar and thyme. Cook 1 to 2 minutes, stirring occasionally, until sugar is dissolved. Remove from heat.

3) Unroll pizza dough; place on cookie sheet. Starting at center, roll or press dough into 15x10-inch rectangle. Sprinkle cheese down the center third of dough. Spoon onion mixture evenly over cheese.

4) With scissors or sharp knife, make cuts 1 inch apart on both long sides of dough to within $1/2$ inch of filling. Alternately cross strips diagonally over filling; turn ends under and press to seal. Brush egg white over top. Sprinkle with poppy seed.

5) Bake 11 to 15 minutes or until crust is golden brown. Let stand 5 minutes before serving. Remove from cookie sheet; cut crosswise into slices.

HIGH ALTITUDE (3500-6500 FT.): No change.

Nutrition Information Per Serving:

Calories:	160	From Fat:	60
Total Fat			7g
Saturated Fat			4g
Trans Fat			0g
Cholesterol			15mg
Sodium			360mg
Total Carbohydrate			19g
Dietary Fiber			0g
Sugars			4g
Protein			5g

Green Poblano Rice

PREP TIME: 20 MINUTES (READY IN 55 MINUTES)
SERVINGS: 10 (1/2 CUP EACH)

EASY   LOW FAT

4 poblano chiles

1/3 cup chopped fresh cilantro

4 cups reduced-sodium chicken broth

1/2 teaspoon chicken bouillon granules

2 tablespoons olive oil

1/4 cup finely chopped onion

2 garlic cloves, finely chopped

2 cups uncooked converted white rice

1/3 cup finely chopped parsley

1/2 teaspoon salt, if desired

Nutrition Information Per Serving:

Calories:	180	From Fat:	30
Total Fat			3g
Saturated Fat			0g
Trans Fat			0g
Cholesterol			0mg
Sodium			730mg
Total Carbohydrate			33g
Dietary Fiber			1g
Sugars			0g
Protein			5g

1) Place whole chiles over open flame of gas stove, turning them from time to time, until skin is blistered and lightly charred. (Or brush oil on chile surface and place under broiler, turning carefully with tongs until blistered.) Place roasted chiles in food-storage plastic bag for about 10 minutes to loosen skins. Remove skin of each by running your hands down the chile. Make a vertical slit on one side of roasted and peeled chile, open down one side, and carefully remove seeds and stems.

2) In blender, place the roasted chiles, cilantro, 2 cups of the broth and the bouillon granules. Cover; blend about 45 seconds or until smooth. Strain; discard solids. Set aside.

3) In 12-inch skillet, heat oil over medium-high heat. Add the onion and garlic; cook and stir 1 minute. Add rice; cook about 5 minutes, stirring occasionally, until rice is light golden.

4) Stir in the strained chile liquid. Stir in remaining 2 cups broth, half of the parsley and the salt. Reduce heat to low. Cover; cook 20 to 25 minutes or until rice is almost tender. Stir in remaining parsley.

5) Increase heat to medium. Uncover; cook about 3 minutes or until liquid is absorbed. Add salt to taste. Let stand 5 minutes before serving.

HIGH ALTITUDE (3500-6500 FT.): No change.

Corn with Fresh Herbs

| PREP TIME: | 15 MINUTES (READY IN 15 MINUTES) |
| SERVINGS: | 10 (1/2 CUP EACH) |

e EASY

3 bags (12 oz each) Green Giant®
  Valley Fresh Steamers™ Niblets®
  frozen corn

3 tablespoons butter or margarine

1 tablespoon chopped fresh parsley

1 tablespoon chopped fresh chives

1 tablespoon chopped fresh thyme
  leaves

1/4 teaspoon salt

Nutrition Information Per Serving:		
Calories: 110	From Fat:	35
Total Fat		4g
Saturated Fat		2.5g
Trans Fat		0g
Cholesterol		10mg
Sodium		85mg
Total Carbohydrate		17g
Dietary Fiber		2g
Sugars		3g
Protein		2g

1) Place corn in colander or strainer. Hold under cold running water in sink until thawed; drain well.

2) In 12-inch skillet, heat butter over medium-high heat until foamy. Add corn and remaining ingredients; cook 3 to 5 minutes, stirring frequently, until corn is thoroughly heated.

HIGH ALTITUDE (3500-6500 FT.): No change.

Perfect Mashed Potatoes

| PREP TIME: | 15 MINUTES (READY IN 35 MINUTES) |
| SERVINGS: | 8 (1/2 CUP EACH) |

e EASY   f LOW FAT

4 medium russet or Idaho baking
  potatoes (about 1 1/2 lb)

3/4 teaspoon salt

1 to 2 tablespoons butter or
  margarine, if desired

Dash pepper

1/4 to 1/3 cup hot milk

Nutrition Information Per Serving:		
Calories: 50	From Fat:	0
Total Fat		0g
Saturated Fat		0g
Trans Fat		0g
Cholesterol		0mg
Sodium		230mg
Total Carbohydrate		12g
Dietary Fiber		0g
Sugars		0g
Protein		1g

1) Wash and peel the potatoes; cut into quarters. Place potatoes in 3-quart saucepan; add enough water to cover. Add 1/2 teaspoon of the salt. Heat to boiling. Reduce heat to medium-low; cover loosely and boil gently 15 to 20 minutes or until potatoes break apart easily when pierced with fork.

2) Drain potatoes well; return to saucepan. Shake saucepan gently over low heat 1 to 2 minutes to evaporate any excess moisture.

3) With potato masher, mash potatoes until no lumps remain. Add the butter, remaining 1/4 teaspoon salt and the pepper; continue mashing, gradually adding enough milk until potatoes are smooth and creamy. Serve immediately.

HIGH ALTITUDE (3500-6500 FT.): No change.

tip

Use a swivel-type vegetable peeler to easily remove only the thin brown peel from the potatoes.

Twice-Baked Sweet Potato Casserole with Bacon

PREP TIME: 15 MINUTES (READY IN 2 HOURS 10 MINUTES)
SERVINGS: 18 (1/2 CUP EACH)

e EASY *f* LOW FAT

- 6 lb dark-orange sweet potatoes (9 large or 12 medium)
- 8 oz bacon (8 to 10 slices)
- 1/4 cup Progresso® panko crispy bread crumbs or Progresso® plain bread crumbs
- 1 tablespoon butter or margarine, melted
- 1/2 cup sour cream
- 1/4 cup butter or margarine, softened
- 2 medium green onions, chopped (2 tablespoons)
- 1/2 teaspoon salt
- 1/4 teaspoon pepper

1) Heat oven to 350°F. Line 15x10x1-inch pan with foil; spray 13x9-inch (3-quart) glass baking dish with cooking spray. Pierce sweet potatoes several times with fork. Place in pan. Bake about 1 hour 15 minutes or until tender. Cool 10 minutes. When potatoes are cool enough to handle, peel potatoes and cut out any eyes or dark spots.

2) Meanwhile, cook bacon as desired until crisp; chop. In small bowl, mix bread crumbs and 1 tablespoon butter; set aside.

3) In large bowl, mash potatoes with potato masher. Stir in chopped bacon, sour cream, 1/4 cup butter, the onions, salt and pepper until well blended. Spread mixture in baking dish, or form individual servings in dish with 1/2-cup ice cream scoop or measuring cup. Sprinkle crumb mixture evenly over top.

4) Bake 20 to 30 minutes or until thoroughly heated and bread crumbs just begin to brown.

HIGH ALTITUDE (3500-6500 FT.): In Step 1, bake potatoes 1 hour 15 minutes to 1 hour 30 minutes. In Step 4, bake casserole 30 to 40 minutes.

Nutrition Information Per Serving:		
Calories: 150	From Fat:	60
Total Fat		6g
Saturated Fat		3.5g
Trans Fat		0g
Cholesterol		15mg
Sodium		210mg
Total Carbohydrate		21g
Dietary Fiber		3g
Sugars		6g
Protein		3g

Baked Potato Pizza

PREP TIME: 15 MINUTES (READY IN 30 MINUTES)
SERVINGS: 8

e EASY

1 can (11 oz) Pillsbury® refrigerated thin pizza crust

6 slices (1 oz each) provolone cheese

2 cups cubed unpeeled baked potato (about 1 large)

2 tablespoons olive oil

2 tablespoons ranch dressing and seasoning mix (from 1-oz milk recipe package)

8 strips crisply cooked bacon, chopped

1 cup shredded mild Cheddar cheese (4 oz)

¼ cup sliced green onions (4 medium), if desired

Sour cream, if desired

1) Heat oven to 400°F. Spray or grease 15x10-inch or larger dark or nonstick cookie sheet. Unroll dough on cookie sheet; starting at center, press dough into 15x10-inch rectangle.

2) Arrange the provolone cheese slices on dough. In medium bowl, mix potato, olive oil and ranch dressing mix. Spoon evenly over cheese. Sprinkle with bacon and Cheddar cheese.

3) Bake 13 to 16 minutes or until crust is golden brown and cheese is melted. Sprinkle with onions. Serve with sour cream.

HIGH ALTITUDE (3500-6500 FT.): Bake 2 to 4 minutes longer.

Nutrition Information Per Serving:	
Calories: 360	From Fat: 180
Total Fat	20g
Saturated Fat	9g
Trans Fat	0g
Cholesterol	40mg
Sodium	980mg
Total Carbohydrate	28g
Dietary Fiber	1g
Sugars	4g
Protein	16g

Steamed Vegetables with Chile-Lime Butter

PREP TIME: 20 MINUTES (READY IN 20 MINUTES)
SERVINGS: 6 (1/2 CUP EACH)

EASY

2 tablespoons butter or margarine

1 small garlic clove, finely chopped

1 teaspoon grated lime peel

1 teaspoon finely chopped serrano or jalapeño chile

1/2 teaspoon salt

1 tablespoon fresh lime juice

3 cups cut-up fresh vegetables, such as broccoli florets, cauliflower florets and/or sliced carrots

1) In 1-quart saucepan, melt butter over low heat. Add garlic; cook and stir about 20 seconds. Add lime peel, chile, salt and lime juice; mix well. Set butter mixture aside.

2) In 4-quart saucepan, place steamer basket. Add 1 cup water; heat to boiling.

3) Add cut-up vegetables to basket; cover and cook 4 to 5 minutes or until crisp-tender.

4) To serve, place vegetables in serving bowl. Add butter mixture; toss gently to coat.

HIGH ALTITUDE (3500-6500 FT.): No change.

Nutrition Information Per Serving:		
Calories: 60	From Fat:	35
Total Fat		4g
Saturated Fat		2.5g
Trans Fat		0g
Cholesterol		10mg
Sodium		240mg
Total Carbohydrate		3g
Dietary Fiber		1g
Sugars		0g
Protein		1g

Baked Butternut Squash with Apples

PREP TIME: 20 MINUTES (READY IN 1 HOUR)
SERVINGS: 12 (1/2 CUP EACH)

EASY

2 tablespoons butter or margarine

$1/2$ teaspoon ground cinnamon

$1/4$ teaspoon ground nutmeg

$1^1/2$ lb butternut squash, peeled, seeded and cut into $1/2$-inch cubes (about 5 cups)

2 to 3 large Granny Smith apples, cored, cut into $1/2$-inch cubes (4 cups)

$1/4$ cup real maple or maple-flavored syrup

1 tablespoon balsamic vinegar

$1/4$ cup chopped pecans, toasted

1) Heat oven to 375°F. Place the butter in 13x9-inch (3-quart) glass baking dish; heat in oven 5 to 7 minutes or until butter is melted.

2) Stir cinnamon and nutmeg into melted butter. Add squash; toss to coat. Cover with foil; bake 20 minutes. Meanwhile, in large bowl, mix apples, syrup and vinegar.

3) Pour apple mixture over the squash. Cover; bake 10 minutes. Stir; bake 5 to 10 minutes longer or until squash is tender. Stir before serving and sprinkle with pecans.

HIGH ALTITUDE (3500-6500 FT.): In Step 3, stir and bake 10 to 15 minutes longer.

Nutrition Information Per Serving:	
Calories: 100	From Fat: 35
Total Fat	3.5g
Saturated Fat	1.5g
Trans Fat	0g
Cholesterol	5mg
Sodium	15mg
Total Carbohydrate	17g
Dietary Fiber	1g
Sugars	11g
Protein	1g

Spicy Gazpacho

PREP TIME: 15 MINUTES (READY IN 15 MINUTES)
SERVINGS: 7 (1 CUP EACH)

e EASY   **f** LOW FAT

2 medium tomatoes, chopped

1 small cucumber, chopped

1 small onion, chopped

$\frac{1}{2}$ green bell pepper, chopped

1 garlic clove, finely chopped

1 tablespoon wine vinegar or lemon juice

1 to 2 dashes red pepper sauce

$\frac{1}{4}$ teaspoon salt

1 can (24 oz) spicy hot vegetable juice cocktail or tomato juice (3 cups), chilled

1) In large bowl, mix all ingredients. Cover; refrigerate until serving time. Cover and refrigerate any remaining gazpacho.

HIGH ALTITUDE (3500-6500 FT.): No change.

Nutrition Information Per Serving:		
Calories: 40	From Fat:	0
Total Fat		0g
Saturated Fat		0g
Trans Fat		0g
Cholesterol		0mg
Sodium		370mg
Total Carbohydrate		8g
Dietary Fiber		1g
Sugars		5g
Protein		1g

Cilantro Corn

PREP TIME: 25 MINUTES (READY IN 25 MINUTES)
SERVINGS: 5

e EASY

2 tablespoons butter or margarine

3 serrano chiles, seeded, finely chopped

$\frac{1}{2}$ cup finely chopped onion

2 teaspoons finely chopped garlic

1 bag (12 oz) Green Giant® Valley Fresh Steamers™ Niblets® frozen corn, thawed

1 cup water

$\frac{1}{4}$ cup chopped fresh cilantro or 3 tablespoons dried epazote or 1 tablespoon fresh epazote

$\frac{1}{2}$ teaspoon salt

2 tablespoons fresh cilantro leaves

2 to 3 teaspoons fresh lime juice

1) In 2-quart saucepan, heat butter over medium heat until melted. Stir in chiles, onion and garlic; cook and stir until onion is transparent.

2) Stir in corn, water, chopped cilantro and salt. Cover and cook over low heat until corn is tender; drain. Serve hot with cilantro leaves and lime juice.

HIGH ALTITUDE (3500-6500 FT.): No change.

Nutrition Information Per Serving:		
Calories: 110	From Fat:	45
Total Fat		5g
Saturated Fat		3g
Trans Fat		0g
Cholesterol		10mg
Sodium		270mg
Total Carbohydrate		14g
Dietary Fiber		2g
Sugars		3g
Protein		2g

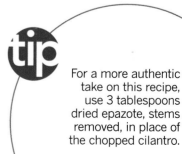

tip

For a more authentic take on this recipe, use 3 tablespoons dried epazote, stems removed, in place of the chopped cilantro.

Lettuce Bundles

PREP TIME: 30 MINUTES (READY IN 30 MINUTES)
SERVINGS: 24 (1 BUNDLE AND 1 TEASPOON SAUCE EACH)

e EASY   **(f)** LOW FAT

½ cup orange juice

2 tablespoons sugar

1 teaspoon cornstarch

⅛ teaspoon crushed red pepper flakes

1 tablespoon cider vinegar

½ teaspoon grated orange peel

2 heads butterhead (Boston or Bibb) lettuce, separated into 24 medium leaves (or 12 large leaves, cut in half)

1 large red bell pepper, cut into thin 2-inch-long strips (about 1½ cups)

½ English cucumber, cut into julienne (matchstick-cut) strips (1 cup)

1 cup julienne (matchstick-cut) carrots

1) In 2-quart saucepan, stir orange juice, sugar, cornstarch and red pepper flakes with wire whisk until cornstarch is completely dissolved. Heat to boiling over medium-high heat, stirring frequently. Boil 1 minute, stirring frequently. Remove from heat; stir in vinegar and orange peel. Cool completely, about 15 minutes.

2) Meanwhile, on the center of each lettuce leaf, place equal amounts of bell pepper, cucumber and carrots; roll up, leaving ends open. Secure with toothpick; place on serving platter. Serve lettuce bundles with the sauce.

HIGH ALTITUDE (3500-6500 FT.): In Step 1, boil 2 minutes.

Nutrition Information Per Serving:		
Calories: 15	From Fat:	0
Total Fat		0g
Saturated Fat		0g
Trans Fat		0g
Cholesterol		0mg
Sodium		0mg
Total Carbohydrate		3g
Dietary Fiber		0g
Sugars		2g
Protein		0g

Rice with Pasta

PREP TIME: 30 MINUTES (READY IN 30 MINUTES)
SERVINGS: 16 (1/2 CUP EACH)

e EASY   **lf** LOW FAT

2 tablespoons olive oil

1 package (7 oz) fideo pasta or vermicelli or angel hair pasta, broken into 1-inch lengths

½ cup finely chopped onion

1 garlic clove, finely chopped

2 cups converted long grain white rice

4 cups chicken broth

1 teaspoon salt

Fresh cilantro leaves, if desired

1) In 12-inch skillet, heat oil over medium-high heat. Stir in pasta; cook and stir 3 to 5 minutes or until golden brown. Stir in onion and garlic; cook 2 to 3 minutes, stirring constantly, until tender.

2) Stir in rice; cook 30 to 60 seconds or until light golden brown. Stir in chicken broth and salt. Reduce heat to low; cover and cook 20 to 25 minutes or until rice is tender and liquid is absorbed. Garnish with cilantro leaves.

HIGH ALTITUDE (3500-6500 FT.): Use 4-1/4 cups chicken broth. In Step 2, stir in rice and cook 2 to 3 minutes, stirring constantly until golden.

Nutrition Information Per Serving:		
Calories: 170	From Fat:	25
Total Fat		2.5g
Saturated Fat		0g
Trans Fat		0g
Cholesterol		0mg
Sodium		720mg
Total Carbohydrate		32g
Dietary Fiber		1g
Sugars		0g
Protein		5g

Garden-Style Red Rice

PREP TIME: 10 MINUTES (READY IN 40 MINUTES)
SERVINGS: 8 (1 CUP EACH)

e EASY

1 can (14.5 oz) fire-roasted crushed tomatoes, undrained

4 cups chicken broth

1 teaspoon tomato bouillon granules with chicken flavor

2 garlic cloves, finely chopped (about 1 teaspoon)

2 tablespoons vegetable oil

1/2 cup finely chopped onion

2 cups uncooked converted white rice

2 large parsley sprigs

2 whole serrano chiles

1 teaspoon salt

1 bag (12 oz) Green Giant® Valley Fresh Steamers™ frozen mixed vegetables

1) In blender, place tomatoes, 1 cup of the broth, the bouillon and garlic. Cover; blend on low speed 20 to 30 seconds or until smooth.

2) In 4-quart Dutch oven, heat oil over medium-high heat. Cook onion in oil until tender, stirring constantly. Stir in rice; cook 1 to 2 minutes, stirring constantly, just until rice begins to turn golden.

3) Carefully stir in tomato mixture. Cook about 1 minute or until mixture starts to bubble. Stir in remaining broth, parsley sprigs, chiles and salt. Return mixture to boiling.

4) Cover and cook over low heat 20 minutes, stirring occasionally. Stir in the frozen vegetables; cook 8 to 10 minutes, stirring frequently, until vegetables are tender and liquid is absorbed. Remove parsley sprigs.

HIGH ALTITUDE (3500-6500 FT.): In Step 4, cover and cook over medium-low heat 25 minutes.

Nutrition Information Per Serving:

Calories: 270	From Fat: 40
Total Fat	4.5g
Saturated Fat	1g
Trans Fat	0g
Cholesterol	0mg
Sodium	1610mg
Total Carbohydrate	49g
Dietary Fiber	3g
Sugars	4g
Protein	8g

Rice with Pasta

PREP TIME: 30 MINUTES (READY IN 30 MINUTES)
SERVINGS: 16 (1/2 CUP EACH)

e EASY   **f** LOW FAT

2 tablespoons olive oil

1 package (7 oz) fideo pasta or vermicelli or angel hair pasta, broken into 1-inch lengths

1/2 cup finely chopped onion

1 garlic clove, finely chopped

2 cups converted long grain white rice

4 cups chicken broth

1 teaspoon salt

Fresh cilantro leaves, if desired

1) In 12-inch skillet, heat oil over medium-high heat. Stir in pasta; cook and stir 3 to 5 minutes or until golden brown. Stir in onion and garlic; cook 2 to 3 minutes, stirring constantly, until tender.

2) Stir in rice; cook 30 to 60 seconds or until light golden brown. Stir in chicken broth and salt. Reduce heat to low; cover and cook 20 to 25 minutes or until rice is tender and liquid is absorbed. Garnish with cilantro leaves.

HIGH ALTITUDE (3500-6500 FT.): Use 4-1/4 cups chicken broth. In Step 2, stir in rice and cook 2 to 3 minutes, stirring constantly until golden.

Nutrition Information Per Serving:

Calories:	170	From Fat:	25
Total Fat			2.5g
Saturated Fat			0g
Trans Fat			0g
Cholesterol			0mg
Sodium			720mg
Total Carbohydrate			32g
Dietary Fiber			1g
Sugars			0g
Protein			5g

Grilled Zucchini and Tomatoes

PREP TIME: 20 MINUTES (READY IN 20 MINUTES)
SERVINGS: 4

e EASY

3 tablespoons olive oil

1/8 teaspoon ground cumin

4 small zucchini (5x1 inch), cut in half lengthwise

4 medium plum (Roma) tomatoes, cut in half lengthwise, seeded

2 teaspoons chopped fresh thyme leaves

1 teaspoon finely chopped fresh rosemary leaves

1/4 teaspoon kosher (coarse) salt

1) Heat gas or charcoal grill. In large bowl, mix olive oil and cumin. Add zucchini and tomatoes; sprinkle with thyme, rosemary and salt. Toss gently to coat.

2) Place vegetables, cut sides up, on grill over medium-high heat. Cover grill; cook 5 minutes. Turn vegetables over; cook 5 minutes longer or until crisp-tender.

HIGH ALTITUDE (3500-6500 FT.): No change.

Nutrition Information Per Serving:

Calories:	130	From Fat:	90
Total Fat			10g
Saturated Fat			1.5g
Trans Fat			0g
Cholesterol			0mg
Sodium			85mg
Total Carbohydrate			6g
Dietary Fiber			2g
Sugars			3g
Protein			2g

tip

For an extra-special presentation, serve the vegetables on an elegant platter and garnish with fresh rosemary sprigs.

Grilled Balsamic Vegetables

PREP TIME: 25 MINUTES (READY IN 25 MINUTES)
SERVINGS: 7 (1 CUP EACH)

- 1 small eggplant (about ³/₄ lb), cut into 1-inch pieces
- 1 medium red bell pepper, cut into strips
- 1 yellow summer squash, cut diagonally into ¹/₂-inch slices
- ¹/₂ medium red onion, cut into ¹/₂-inch wedges
- ¹/₂ cup balsamic dressing
- 2 tablespoons finely shredded Parmesan cheese
- 3 tablespoons sliced fresh basil leaves

Nutrition Information Per Serving:	
Calories: 120	From Fat: 80
Total Fat	9g
Saturated Fat	1.5g
Trans Fat	0g
Cholesterol	0mg
Sodium	160mg
Total Carbohydrate	8g
Dietary Fiber	2g
Sugars	4g
Protein	2g

1) In large nonmetal dish or resealable food-storage plastic bag, mix the vegetables and dressing; turn to coat.

2) Heat gas or charcoal grill. Remove vegetables from the marinade. Place vegetables in grill basket (grill "wok"). Place on grill over medium-high heat. Cover grill; cook 10 to 15 minutes, stirring occasionally, until crisp-tender. Sprinkle with cheese and basil.

HIGH ALTITUDE (3500-6500 FT.): No change.

Broccoli and Tomatoes

PREP TIME: 10 MINUTES (READY IN 10 MINUTES)
SERVINGS: 6 (3/4 CUP EACH)

🄴 EASY   🄵 LOW FAT

- ¹/₂ cup water
- 4 cups bite-sized pieces fresh broccoli
- 1 pint (2 cups) cherry tomatoes, halved
- ¹/₂ teaspoon dried dill weed
- ¹/₄ teaspoon lemon-pepper seasoning

Nutrition Information Per Serving:	
Calories: 40	From Fat: 0
Total Fat	0g
Saturated Fat	0g
Trans Fat	0g
Cholesterol	0mg
Sodium	35mg
Total Carbohydrate	6g
Dietary Fiber	2g
Sugars	3g
Protein	2g

1) In 4-quart saucepan, heat water to boiling. Add broccoli; return to boiling.

2) Reduce heat; simmer over medium-low heat 4 to 6 minutes or until the broccoli is crisp-tender. Add tomatoes; cook 1 minute. Drain; toss with dill and lemon-pepper seasoning.

HIGH ALTITUDE (3500-6500 FT.): No change.

Garden-Style Red Rice

PREP TIME: 10 MINUTES (READY IN 40 MINUTES)
SERVINGS: 8 (1 CUP EACH)

EASY

1 can (14.5 oz) fire-roasted crushed tomatoes, undrained

4 cups chicken broth

1 teaspoon tomato bouillon granules with chicken flavor

2 garlic cloves, finely chopped (about 1 teaspoon)

2 tablespoons vegetable oil

½ cup finely chopped onion

2 cups uncooked converted white rice

2 large parsley sprigs

2 whole serrano chiles

1 teaspoon salt

1 bag (12 oz) Green Giant® Valley Fresh Steamers™ frozen mixed vegetables

1) In blender, place tomatoes, 1 cup of the broth, the bouillon and garlic. Cover; blend on low speed 20 to 30 seconds or until smooth.

2) In 4-quart Dutch oven, heat oil over medium-high heat. Cook onion in oil until tender, stirring constantly. Stir in rice; cook 1 to 2 minutes, stirring constantly, just until rice begins to turn golden.

3) Carefully stir in tomato mixture. Cook about 1 minute or until mixture starts to bubble. Stir in remaining broth, parsley sprigs, chiles and salt. Return mixture to boiling.

4) Cover and cook over low heat 20 minutes, stirring occasionally. Stir in the frozen vegetables; cook 8 to 10 minutes, stirring frequently, until vegetables are tender and liquid is absorbed. Remove parsley sprigs.

HIGH ALTITUDE (3500-6500 FT.): In Step 4, cover and cook over medium-low heat 25 minutes.

Nutrition Information Per Serving:	
Calories: 270	From Fat: 40
Total Fat	4.5g
Saturated Fat	1g
Trans Fat	0g
Cholesterol	0mg
Sodium	1610mg
Total Carbohydrate	49g
Dietary Fiber	3g
Sugars	4g
Protein	8g

Green Beans with Colored Peppers

PREP TIME: 30 MINUTES (READY IN 30 MINUTES)
SERVINGS: 18 (1/2 CUP EACH)

 EASY   LOW FAT

1 bag (22 oz) Green Giant® SELECT® frozen whole green beans

1 tablespoon lemon juice

2 teaspoons Dijon mustard

1 tablespoon chopped fresh or 1 teaspoon dried basil leaves

2 teaspoons chopped fresh or 3/4 teaspoon dried thyme leaves

1 tablespoon olive or vegetable oil

1 medium red bell pepper, cut into strips

1 medium yellow bell pepper, cut into strips

1/2 teaspoon salt

Freshly ground black pepper, if desired

1) In 12-inch skillet, cook green beans on stovetop as directed on the bag. Drain; place beans on plate and loosely cover to keep warm.

2) Meanwhile, in small bowl, mix lemon juice, mustard, basil and thyme; set aside.

3) Add oil to the same skillet; heat over medium-high heat. Add bell peppers; cook 6 to 8 minutes, stirring frequently, just until tender.

4) Add green beans and lemon mixture to peppers; toss to coat. Sprinkle with salt; cook 2 to 3 minutes, stirring frequently. Serve sprinkled with freshly ground black pepper.

HIGH ALTITUDE (3500-6500 FT.): No change.

Nutrition Information Per Serving:		
Calories: 20	From Fat:	10
Total Fat		1g
Saturated Fat		0g
Trans Fat		0g
Cholesterol		0mg
Sodium		80mg
Total Carbohydrate		3g
Dietary Fiber		1g
Sugars		1g
Protein		0g

LEMON AND HERB
ROAST TURKEY BREAST
PG. 147

Main Dishes

Savory entrees of beef, chicken, seafood, pork and more—you get them all in this extra-big chapter!

GROUND BEEF- AND CORN-TOPPED POTATO SKINS PG. 168

FETTUCCINE WITH CHICKEN AND HERBED VEGETABLES PG. 155

CHICKEN BRUSCHETTA PG. 158

Spring Asparagus and Turkey Pie

PREP TIME: 35 MINUTES (READY IN 1 HOUR 10 MINUTES)
SERVINGS: 6

3 tablespoons butter or margarine

1/4 cup chopped onion

2 tablespoons all-purpose flour

1 cup half-and-half

1/4 teaspoon salt

1/8 teaspoon pepper

2 cups cubed cooked turkey or chicken

1 box (9 oz) Green Giant® frozen asparagus cuts, thawed, drained

1/2 cup sliced fresh mushrooms

3 tablespoons dry white wine or chicken broth

1 can (8 oz) Pillsbury® refrigerated crescent dinner rolls

1) Heat oven to 350°F. In 2-quart saucepan, melt the butter over medium heat. Cook onion in butter, stirring occasionally, until tender. Stir in the flour; cook until mixture is smooth and bubbly. Gradually add the half-and-half, salt and pepper. Heat to boiling, stirring constantly, until thick. Remove from the heat; stir in the turkey, asparagus, mushrooms and wine.

2) Separate dough into 8 triangles. Place dough in ungreased 9-inch pie plate in spoke pattern, with the narrow tips overlapping rim of plate about 3 inches (see photo). Press dough in side and bottom to form crust. Spoon turkey mixture evenly over dough. Bring the tips of dough over filling to meet in the center; do not overlap. Bake 25 to 30 minutes or until golden brown. Garnish as desired.

HIGH ALTITUDE (3500-6500 FT.): Bake 28 to 33 minutes.

Nutrition Information Per Serving:	
Calories: 360	From Fat: 200
Total Fat	22g
Saturated Fat	10g
Trans Fat	2.5g
Cholesterol	70mg
Sodium	490mg
Total Carbohydrate	21g
Dietary Fiber	1g
Sugars	5g
Protein	18g

Lean Pasta Primavera

PREP TIME:	1 HOUR (READY IN 1 HOUR)		LOW FAT
SERVINGS:	6 (1-1/2 CUPS EACH)		

16 oz refrigerated fettuccine or 12 oz uncooked fettuccine

2½ cups fat-free (skim) milk

3 tablespoons cornstarch

1 tablespoon chopped fresh basil or 1 teaspoon dried basil leaves

½ teaspoon salt

¼ teaspoon pepper

1 cup light ricotta cheese

⅓ cup shredded Parmesan cheese

⅓ cup chicken broth

4 garlic cloves, finely chopped

2 cups sliced fresh mushrooms (about 5 oz)

2 cups broccoli florets

6 medium green onions, cut into 1-inch pieces

2 cups halved fresh snow pea pods

1 cup halved cherry tomatoes

1) Cook and drain fettuccine as directed on package; cover to keep warm.

2) Meanwhile, in 2-quart saucepan, heat milk, cornstarch, basil, salt and pepper to boiling over medium-high heat, stirring constantly with wire whisk. Reduce heat to medium; simmer 2 to 5 minutes, stirring constantly, until sauce thickens. Remove from heat.

3) In blender or food processor, place ½ cup of the sauce, the ricotta cheese and ¼ cup of the Parmesan cheese. Cover; blend on medium-low speed until smooth. Return mixture to remaining sauce in saucepan; stir well.

4) In nonstick 8-quart Dutch oven or stockpot, heat broth to boiling over medium-high heat. Add garlic; cook 2 minutes, stirring occasionally. Add mushrooms, broccoli and onions; cover and cook 4 minutes. Add pea pods and tomatoes; cook 1 minute longer. Add sauce and cooked fettuccine; heat until hot. Transfer to serving platter; sprinkle with the remaining Parmesan cheese.

HIGH ALTITUDE (3500-6500 FT.): Increase milk to 3 cups. Increase chicken broth to 1/2 cup. Use small broccoli florets. In Step 2, heat to boiling over medium heat, stirring constantly to avoid scorching.

Nutrition Information Per Serving:		
Calories: 360	From Fat:	50
Total Fat		5g
Saturated Fat		2g
Trans Fat		0g
Cholesterol		55mg
Sodium		690mg
Total Carbohydrate		56g
Dietary Fiber		4g
Sugars		12g
Protein		21g

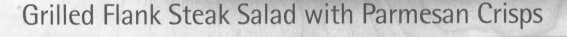

Grilled Flank Steak Salad with Parmesan Crisps

PREP TIME: 45 MINUTES (READY IN 2 HOURS 35 MINUTES)
SERVINGS: 4 (4 OZ STEAK, 6 TO 7 ASPARAGUS SPEARS, 1-1/2 CUPS SALAD AND 3 CRISPS EACH)

STEAK AND SALAD

- 1 lb beef flank steak
- 1/2 cup balsamic vinaigrette dressing or Italian dressing
- 1/4 teaspoon cracked black pepper
- 1 lb fresh asparagus spears, trimmed
- 1/4 teaspoon salt
- 1/8 teaspoon pepper
- 6 cups torn romaine lettuce
- 1/2 cup thinly sliced radishes

  Additional 1/4 cup dressing

PARMESAN CRISPS

- 6 tablespoons finely shredded Parmesan cheese

1) In large nonmetal dish or resealable food-storage plastic bag, place steak and 1/2 cup dressing; turn to coat. Cover dish or seal bag; refrigerate at least 2 hours or overnight to marinate.

2) Heat oven to 350°F. Spray large cookie sheet with cooking spray. To make the Parmesan Crisps, spoon heaping teaspoonfuls Parmesan cheese in 12 mounds on cookie sheet. Spread each mound into 2-inch circle. Bake 6 to 8 minutes or until light brown. Carefully remove from pan to cooling rack. (Crisps may be made up to 2 days ahead and kept between layers of waxed paper in airtight container at room temperature.)

3) Heat gas or charcoal grill. Remove steak from marinade; reserve marinade. Sprinkle steak with cracked black pepper. Place steak on grill over medium heat. Cover grill; cook 15 to 18 minutes or until desired doneness, turning halfway through grilling. Let stand 5 minutes.

4) Meanwhile, toss asparagus with reserved marinade. Place asparagus in grill basket (grill "wok"); discard any remaining marinade. Place asparagus on grill. Cover grill; cook 6 to 8 minutes, turning occasionally, until tender. Season asparagus with salt and pepper.

5) In large bowl, toss lettuce, radishes and the additional 1/4 cup dressing. Divide lettuce mixture among 4 dinner plates. Cut steak across grain into thin slices. Divide steak slices and asparagus evenly among plates. Serve with Crisps.

HIGH ALTITUDE (3500-6500 FT.): No change.

Nutrition Information Per Serving:	
Calories: 440	From Fat: 260
Total Fat	29g
Saturated Fat	6g
Trans Fat	0g
Cholesterol	90mg
Sodium	700mg
Total Carbohydrate	6g
Dietary Fiber	3g
Sugars	3g
Protein	39g

Layered Mac 'n Cheese with Ground Beef

PREP TIME: 30 MINUTES (READY IN 1 HOUR)
SERVINGS: 6 (1-1/2 CUPS EACH)

2 cups uncooked elbow macaroni (8 oz)

1 lb lean (at least 80%) ground beef

1 teaspoon salt

$\frac{1}{8}$ teaspoon pepper

2 tablespoons butter or margarine

2 tablespoons all-purpose flour

2 cups milk

$\frac{1}{2}$ cup Progresso® chicken broth (from 32-oz carton)

3 cups shredded Cheddar cheese (12 oz)

1 cup soft bread crumbs (about 2 slices bread)

1) Heat oven to 350°F. Spray 2-quart casserole with cooking spray. Cook and drain macaroni as directed on package.

2) Meanwhile, in 10-inch skillet, cook beef, $\frac{1}{2}$ teaspoon of the salt and the pepper over medium-high heat 5 to 7 minutes, stirring occasionally, until beef is thoroughly cooked; drain if desired.

3) In 2-quart saucepan, melt butter over medium heat. Stir in the flour; cook 1 minute, stirring constantly, until bubbly. Stir in milk; cook 5 to 6 minutes, stirring constantly, until mixture thickens slightly. Stir in broth and remaining $\frac{1}{2}$ teaspoon salt. Remove from heat; stir in cheese. Fold in macaroni.

4) Spoon $\frac{1}{3}$ of the macaroni mixture (about 1$\frac{1}{3}$ cups) into casserole; top with half of the beef (about 1$\frac{1}{2}$ cups). Layer with another $\frac{1}{3}$ of macaroni mixture, remaining beef and remaining macaroni mixture. Top with bread crumbs. Bake uncovered 25 to 30 minutes or until bread crumbs are golden brown.

HIGH ALTITUDE (3500-6500 FT.): Bake 30 to 35 minutes.

Nutrition Information Per Serving:

Calories:	630	From Fat:	310
Total Fat			34g
Saturated Fat			19g
Trans Fat			1.5g
Cholesterol			125mg
Sodium			1130mg
Total Carbohydrate			43g
Dietary Fiber			2g
Sugars			6g
Protein			37g

Cashew Chicken and Broccoli

PREP TIME: 40 MINUTES (READY IN 45 MINUTES)
SERVINGS: 4

1 cup uncooked regular long-grain white rice

3 tablespoons soy sauce

2 teaspoons grated gingerroot

1 teaspoon sugar

1 teaspoon sesame oil, if desired

1 lb boneless skinless chicken breasts, cut into bite-size pieces

3/4 cup Progresso® chicken broth (from 32-oz carton)

1 1/2 teaspoons cornstarch

1 tablespoon vegetable oil

3 cups fresh broccoli florets

2 green onions, sliced (2 tablespoons)

1 cup salted roasted cashews

1) Cook the rice in water as directed on the package.

2) Meanwhile, in large bowl, mix soy sauce, gingerroot, sugar and sesame oil. Stir in chicken until coated; let stand 15 minutes to marinate.

3) In small bowl, stir 1/4 cup of the broth and the cornstarch until cornstarch is dissolved; set aside.

4) In 12-inch skillet, heat vegetable oil over high heat. Remove chicken from marinade and add to heated oil in skillet; reserve any remaining marinade. Cook chicken about 3 minutes, stirring frequently, until no longer pink in center.

5) Stir broccoli and remaining 1/2 cup broth into chicken in skillet; cover and cook 1 minute. Stir in onions and cashews.

6) Stir reserved marinade into cornstarch mixture. Stir into chicken mixture; cook and stir 1 to 2 minutes or until sauce thickens slightly. Serve over rice.

HIGH ALTITUDE (3500-6500 FT.): In Step 4, cook chicken about 5 minutes.

Nutrition Information Per Serving:		
Calories: 590	From Fat: 210	
Total Fat		23g
Saturated Fat		4.5g
Trans Fat		0g
Cholesterol		70mg
Sodium		1590mg
Total Carbohydrate		58g
Dietary Fiber		3g
Sugars		4g
Protein		37g

Chicken 'n Bacon Ranch Pizza

PREP TIME: 20 MINUTES (READY IN 35 MINUTES)
SERVINGS: 8

EASY

1 can (11 oz) Pillsbury® refrigerated thin pizza crust

1/2 cup ranch dressing

2 packages (6 oz each) refrigerated cooked Italian-style chicken breast strips, chopped

4 slices crisply cooked bacon, coarsely chopped

1/4 cup chopped onion

1 large plum (Roma) tomato, seeded, chopped

1 cup shredded Cheddar cheese (4 oz)

1 cup shredded mozzarella cheese (4 oz)

Nutrition Information Per Serving:	
Calories: 360	From Fat: 190
Total Fat	21g
Saturated Fat	8g
Trans Fat	0g
Cholesterol	60mg
Sodium	990mg
Total Carbohydrate	21g
Dietary Fiber	1g
Sugars	3g
Protein	21g

1) Heat oven to 400°F. Spray or grease 15x10-inch or larger dark or nonstick cookie sheet. Unroll dough on cookie sheet; starting at center, press dough into 15x10-inch rectangle.

2) Spread ranch dressing evenly over dough. Top with remaining ingredients. Bake 13 to 16 minutes or until crust is golden brown and cheese is melted.

HIGH ALTITUDE (3500-6500 FT.): Bake 2 to 4 minutes longer.

Lemon-Garlic Chicken

PREP TIME: 1 HOUR 5 MINUTES (READY IN 2 HOURS 5 MINUTES)
SERVINGS: 4

3/4 cup water

1/3 cup olive or vegetable oil

Grated fresh peel from 1 lemon (about 2 tablespoons)

1/4 cup fresh lemon juice

1 tablespoon garlic-pepper blend

1 teaspoon salt

4 garlic cloves, finely chopped

1 cut-up whole chicken (3 to 3 1/2 lb)

1) In 1-gallon resealable heavy-duty plastic food-storage bag, mix all ingredients except chicken. Add chicken; seal bag and turn to coat with the marinade. Refrigerate at least 1 hour but no longer than 24 hours, turning bag occasionally, to marinate.

2) Heat gas or charcoal grill. Remove the chicken from marinade; discard marinade.

3) Place chicken, skin sides up, on grill over medium heat. Cover grill; cook 15 minutes. Turn chicken. Cover grill; cook 20 to 40 minutes longer, turning occasionally, until juice of chicken is clear when thickest piece is cut to bone (170°F for breasts; 180°F for thighs and drumsticks).

HIGH ALTITUDE (3500-6500 FT.): Cook over low heat 25 to 45 minutes, turning occasionally.

Nutrition Information Per Serving:	
Calories: 380	From Fat: 220
Total Fat	24g
Saturated Fat	6g
Trans Fat	0.5g
Cholesterol	130mg
Sodium	270mg
Total Carbohydrate	0g
Dietary Fiber	0g
Sugars	0g
Protein	40g

Spicy Beef 'n Corn Casserole

PREP TIME: 35 MINUTES (READY IN 1 HOUR 5 MINUTES)
SERVINGS: 6 (1-1/4 CUPS EACH)

1/2 cup uncooked regular long-grain white rice

1 1/3 cups water

1 lb lean (at least 80%) ground beef

1/2 cup chopped onion (1 medium)

1/4 cup chopped green bell pepper

1/4 cup chopped celery

1 can (15.5 oz) red beans, drained

1 can (14.5 oz) diced tomatoes, undrained

1/2 cup Green Giant® Valley Fresh Steamers™ Niblets® frozen corn

1 tablespoon Worcestershire sauce

1/2 teaspoon ground red pepper (cayenne)

1 can (8 oz) Pillsbury® refrigerated crescent dinner rolls or 1 can (8 oz) Pillsbury® Crescent Recipe Creations™ refrigerated flaky dough sheet

1) Heat oven to 375°F. Cook rice in water as directed on the package, omitting butter and salt.

2) Meanwhile, in 12-inch skillet, cook beef, onion, green bell pepper and celery over medium-high heat 6 to 8 minutes, stirring occasionally, until beef is thoroughly cooked; drain. Stir in cooked rice, red beans, tomatoes, corn, Worcestershire sauce and red pepper. Simmer 3 to 5 minutes, stirring occasionally, until hot. Spoon mixture into 2-quart casserole.

3) Open can of dough; do not unroll. With serrated knife, cut dough into 1-inch slices. Cut each slice in half; place cut side down around edge of casserole.

4) Bake 25 to 30 minutes or until bubbly and golden brown.

HIGH ALTITUDE (3500-6500 FT.): No change.

Nutrition Information Per Serving:		
Calories: 430	From Fat:	140
Total Fat		15g
Saturated Fat		6g
Trans Fat		0.5g
Cholesterol		45mg
Sodium		610mg
Total Carbohydrate		51g
Dietary Fiber		5g
Sugars		7g
Protein		23g

Chicken Saltimbocca

PREP TIME: 30 MINUTES (READY IN 30 MINUTES)
SERVINGS: 4

4 boneless skinless chicken breasts (about 6 oz each)

1/3 cup all-purpose flour

2 tablespoons grated Parmesan cheese

1 teaspoon Italian seasoning

1/2 teaspoon salt

2 tablespoons olive or vegetable oil

4 slices prosciutto (about 3 oz)

4 slices (1 oz each) mozzarella cheese

1 teaspoon chopped fresh sage leaves

3/4 cup Progresso® chicken broth (from 32-oz carton)

1 tablespoon butter or margarine

1) Between pieces of plastic wrap or waxed paper, place each chicken breast smooth side down; gently pound with the flat side of meat mallet or rolling pin until 1/4 inch thick. In shallow dish, mix flour, Parmesan cheese, Italian seasoning and salt. Coat chicken with flour mixture; shake off excess flour.

2) In 12-inch nonstick skillet, heat oil over medium-high heat. Add chicken; cook about 8 minutes, turning once, until browned on outside and no longer pink in center. Top each chicken breast with 1 slice prosciutto and 1 slice mozzarella cheese. Cover skillet tightly; cook 1 to 2 minutes or until cheese is melted. Sprinkle sage over chicken. Remove chicken from skillet to serving platter; cover loosely with tent of foil, being careful not to let foil touch cheese.

3) Increase heat to high. Add broth to skillet. Heat to boiling, scraping up any browned bits from bottom of skillet. Boil about 3 minutes or until broth is reduced to about 1/4 cup. Remove from heat; beat in butter. Spoon over chicken.

HIGH ALTITUDE (3500-6500 FT.): No change.

Nutrition Information Per Serving:	
Calories: 460	From Fat: 220
Total Fat	24g
Saturated Fat	9g
Trans Fat	0g
Cholesterol	140mg
Sodium	1130mg
Total Carbohydrate	9g
Dietary Fiber	0g
Sugars	0g
Protein	52g

Grilled Salmon Paella Packets

PREP TIME: 1 HOUR 15 MINUTES (READY IN 1 HOUR 30 MINUTES)
SERVINGS: 8

³/₄ teaspoon saffron threads, if desired

4 large green onions, finely chopped (¹/₃ cup)

4 large garlic cloves, finely chopped

3 tablespoons fresh lemon juice

3 tablespoons extra-virgin olive oil

1 tablespoon sweet smoky Spanish paprika or any sweet paprika

2 teaspoons salt

¹/₂ teaspoon freshly ground black pepper

8 skinless salmon fillets (5 oz each)

1 can (14 oz) chicken broth

8 servings cooked instant brown rice

1 package (12 oz) fully cooked linguiça or andouille sausage links

4 medium plum (Roma) tomatoes, seeded, chopped

2 medium red bell peppers, diced ¹/₄ inch

1 cup lightly packed fresh Italian (flat-leaf) parsley, chopped

1) Soak saffron in 2 teaspoons hot water; set aside 30 minutes.

2) To make salmon marinade, in small bowl, mix green onions, garlic, lemon juice, 2 tablespoons of the oil, the paprika, salt and pepper. In 13x9-inch (3-quart) glass baking dish, arrange salmon; spoon marinade over salmon, turning to evenly coat. Cover; refrigerate 20 minutes.

3) Cut 8 (18x12-inch) sheets of heavy-duty foil. Grease with remaining 1 tablespoon oil.

4) Add water to broth to measure amount of water called for on rice package for 8 servings. Make 8 servings rice as directed on package, using broth and water mixture for the water.

5) Meanwhile, cut sausages in half lengthwise. Cut crosswise into thin slices; stir into rice along with tomatoes, bell peppers and saffron threads with soaking liquid. Use fork to mix ingredients and separate saffron.

6) Mound generous 1 cup rice mixture on center of each piece of foil. Top with 1 salmon fillet, and drizzle with a spoonful of the marinade. Spoon any remaining marinade over fillets. Bring up long sides of foil together so edges meet. Seal edges, making tight ¹/₂-inch fold; fold again, allowing space for heat circulation and expansion. Fold other sides to seal.

7) Heat gas or charcoal grill. Place packets on grill over low heat, allowing space around packets for circulation. Cover grill; cook 10 minutes for salmon that is opaque with a deeper pink center, or about 15 minutes until fish flakes easily with fork. Place packets on plates. Carefully unfold foil away from face. Sprinkle each serving with parsley.

HIGH ALTITUDE (3500-6500 FT.): No change.

Nutrition Information Per Serving:

Calories:	620	From Fat:	240
Total Fat			27g
Saturated Fat			7g
Trans Fat			0g
Cholesterol			115mg
Sodium			1430mg
Total Carbohydrate			49g
Dietary Fiber			4g
Sugars			3g
Protein			44g

Barbecue Chicken Kabobs

PREP TIME: 45 MINUTES (READY IN 45 MINUTES)
SERVINGS: 4

½ cup barbecue sauce

¼ cup orange marmalade

1 lb boneless skinless chicken breasts, cut into ¾-inch pieces

½ medium red onion, cut into 1-inch chunks

1 medium red bell pepper, cut into 1-inch chunks

2 tablespoons olive or vegetable oil

1 teaspoon seasoned salt

1) Heat gas or charcoal grill. In small microwavable bowl, mix barbecue sauce and marmalade. Remove ¼ cup of the sauce mixture to small dish; set aside.

2) On each of 4 (11-inch) metal skewers, thread the chicken pieces, leaving ¼-inch space between each piece. On 4 additional skewers, thread onion and bell pepper chunks, leaving ¼-inch space between each piece. Brush the chicken and vegetables with oil; sprinkle with seasoned salt.

3) Place the kabobs on grill over medium heat. Cover grill; cook 10 to 15 minutes, turning the kabobs 2 or 3 times and brushing chicken and vegetables with reserved ¼ cup sauce mixture during last 5 to 8 minutes of grilling, until chicken is no longer pink in center.

4) Microwave remaining barbecue sauce mixture uncovered on High 20 to 30 seconds or until thoroughly heated. Serve sauce with kabobs.

HIGH ALTITUDE (3500-6500 FT.): Cook over medium-low heat.

Nutrition Information Per Serving:

Calories:	320	From Fat:	90
Total Fat			11g
Saturated Fat			2g
Trans Fat			0g
Cholesterol			70mg
Sodium			740mg
Total Carbohydrate			30g
Dietary Fiber			1g
Sugars			22g
Protein			25g

Tangy Bacon-Chicken Grill

PREP TIME: 45 MINUTES (READY IN 45 MINUTES)
SERVINGS: 4

3 slices bacon, cut into ½-inch pieces

¾ cup balsamic vinaigrette dressing

1½ cups ready-to-eat baby-cut carrots

1 medium onion, cut into 8 wedges

1 medium green bell pepper, cut into 8 pieces

1 medium red bell pepper, cut into 8 pieces

8 oz fresh whole green beans, trimmed

4 boneless skinless chicken breasts (4 to 5 oz each)

Nutrition Information Per Serving:	
Calories: 510	From Fat: 310
Total Fat	35g
Saturated Fat	8g
Trans Fat	0g
Cholesterol	100mg
Sodium	590mg
Total Carbohydrate	14g
Dietary Fiber	4g
Sugars	7g
Protein	35g

1) Heat gas or charcoal grill. In 12-inch nonstick skillet, cook bacon, stirring occasionally, until crisp; drain bacon on paper towel. Discard all but 2 tablespoons of the bacon drippings in skillet.

2) Stir dressing into drippings in skillet. Remove from heat. Remove ¼ cup dressing mixture from skillet; reserve.

3) Add carrots, onion, bell peppers and beans to remaining dressing mixture in skillet; stir to coat. With slotted spoon, place vegetables in grill basket (grill "wok"). Reserve dressing mixture in skillet.

4) Place chicken and grill basket on grill over medium heat. Cover grill; cook 15 to 20 minutes, shaking grill basket occasionally, turning chicken once and brushing reserved dressing mixture from skillet over chicken, until vegetables are crisp-tender and juice of chicken is clear when center of thickest part is cut (170°F).

5) To serve, arrange vegetables around chicken. Sprinkle with bacon; drizzle with reserved ¼ cup dressing mixture.

HIGH ALTITUDE (3500-6500 FT.): Cook over medium-low heat.

Rotisserie Chicken Salad with Cherries and Gorgonzola

PREP TIME: 15 MINUTES (READY IN 15 MINUTES)
SERVINGS: 4 (ABOUT 2 CUPS EACH)

 EASY

6 cups fresh baby spinach leaves

2 cups chopped skinned deli rotisserie chicken (from 2- to 2½-lb chicken)

1 cup halved pitted Bing cherries

½ cup crumbled Gorgonzola cheese (2 oz)

¼ cup chopped green onions (4 medium)

½ cup champagne dressing

Nutrition Information Per Serving:	
Calories: 360	From Fat: 230
Total Fat	25g
Saturated Fat	6g
Trans Fat	0g
Cholesterol	70mg
Sodium	1110mg
Total Carbohydrate	10g
Dietary Fiber	2g
Sugars	6g
Protein	24g

1) Place spinach on large platter. Arrange chicken, cherries, cheese and onions evenly over spinach. Drizzle with dressing. Serve immediately.

HIGH ALTITUDE (3500-6500 FT.): No change.

Double Crust Pizza

PREP TIME: 20 MINUTES (READY IN 40 MINUTES)
SERVINGS: 8

🄴 EASY

2 cans (11 oz each) Pillsbury® refrigerated thin pizza crust

½ cup pizza sauce

½ lb bulk Italian sausage

¼ cup chopped onion

½ cup sliced pepperoni

½ cup red bell pepper, cut into 2x½-inch strips

1½ cups shredded Italian cheese blend (6 oz)

¼ teaspoon crushed red pepper flakes, if desired

1 tablespoon olive oil

1) Heat oven to 400°F. Spray or grease 15x10-inch or larger dark or nonstick cookie sheet. Unroll 1 can of dough on cookie sheet; starting at center, press dough into 15x10-inch rectangle.

2) Spread pizza sauce on dough. In 10-inch nonstick skillet, cook the sausage and chopped onion over medium-high heat 5 to 7 minutes, stirring frequently, until sausage is no longer pink; drain. Spoon evenly over sauce. Top with pepperoni, red bell pepper and cheese. Sprinkle with red pepper flakes.

3) Unroll remaining can of dough. Place on cheese, stretching to cover. Brush with olive oil.

4) Bake 15 to 20 minutes or until crust is golden brown.

HIGH ALTITUDE (3500-6500 FT.): Bake 11 to 13 minutes.

Nutrition Information Per Serving:	
Calories: 430	From Fat: 200
Total Fat	22g
Saturated Fat	8g
Trans Fat	0g
Cholesterol	35mg
Sodium	1030mg
Total Carbohydrate	40g
Dietary Fiber	2g
Sugars	6g
Protein	17g

Spinach-Stuffed Chicken Breasts

PREP TIME: 25 MINUTES (READY IN 1 HOUR)
SERVINGS: 4

1 box (9 oz) Green Giant® frozen spinach, thawed, squeezed to drain

2 tablespoons finely chopped sweet onion

$\frac{1}{2}$ cup shredded mozzarella cheese (2 oz)

4 boneless skinless chicken breasts (4 to 5 oz each)

$\frac{1}{2}$ teaspoon garlic salt

$\frac{1}{2}$ cup Progresso® panko crispy bread crumbs

2 tablespoons grated Parmesan cheese

2 tablespoons butter or margarine, melted

1) Heat oven to 375°F. Spray 13x9-inch (3-quart) glass baking dish with cooking spray. In small bowl, mix spinach, onion and mozzarella cheese.

2) Between pieces of plastic wrap or waxed paper, place each chicken breast smooth side down; gently pound with flat side of meat mallet or rolling pin until about $\frac{1}{8}$ inch thick. Sprinkle with garlic salt.

3) Place $\frac{1}{4}$ of the spinach mixture on center of each flattened chicken breast. Fold in sides; fold up top and bottom, overlapping in center.

4) On shallow plate, mix bread crumbs and Parmesan cheese. Roll chicken in melted butter, then coat with bread crumb mixture. Place seam sides down in baking dish.

5) Bake 30 to 35 minutes, turning chicken breasts over after 15 minutes, until light golden brown.

HIGH ALTITUDE (3500-6500 FT.): Heat oven to 400°F.

tip The chicken breasts may be stuffed up to 24 hours in advance. Cover them tightly and refrigerate them until cooking time. Wait to roll them in butter and the bread crumb mixture until you're ready to bake.

Nutrition Information Per Serving:

Calories:	350	From Fat:	140
Total Fat			16g
Saturated Fat			7g
Trans Fat			0g
Cholesterol			110mg
Sodium			440mg
Total Carbohydrate			13g
Dietary Fiber			1g
Sugars			1g
Protein			39g

Crescent-Topped Cheeseburger Casserole

PREP TIME: 20 MINUTES (READY IN 50 MINUTES)
SERVINGS: 6

1 lb lean (at least 80%) ground beef

1/4 cup chopped onion

1/4 cup chopped dill pickles

1/2 cup water

1/2 cup ketchup

1 tablespoon yellow mustard

1/8 teaspoon pepper

1 1/2 cups shredded American cheese (6 oz)

1 can (8 oz) Pillsbury® refrigerated crescent dinner rolls or 1 can (8 oz) Pillsbury® Crescent Recipe Creations™ refrigerated flaky dough sheet

1 egg, beaten

1 tablespoon sesame seed

1) Heat oven to 375°F. In 10-inch nonstick skillet, cook the beef and onion over medium-high heat 5 to 7 minutes, stirring frequently, until thoroughly cooked; drain. Stir in pickles, water, ketchup, mustard and pepper.

2) Spoon beef mixture into ungreased 11x7-inch (2-quart) glass baking dish. Sprinkle with cheese.

3) Unroll dough (if using crescent rolls, pinch the seams to seal); press into 12x8-inch rectangle. Cut into 6 squares; place on top of cheese. Brush with egg; sprinkle with sesame seed. Bake 25 to 30 minutes or until deep golden brown.

HIGH ALTITUDE (3500-6500 FT.): Bake 27 to 32 minutes.

Nutrition Information Per Serving:	
Calories: 410	From Fat: 230
Total Fat	25g
Saturated Fat	12g
Trans Fat	1g
Cholesterol	110mg
Sodium	1070mg
Total Carbohydrate	23g
Dietary Fiber	0g
Sugars	8g
Protein	23g

Chicken–Broccoli au Gratin

KIBBY JACKSON | GRAY, GEORGIA

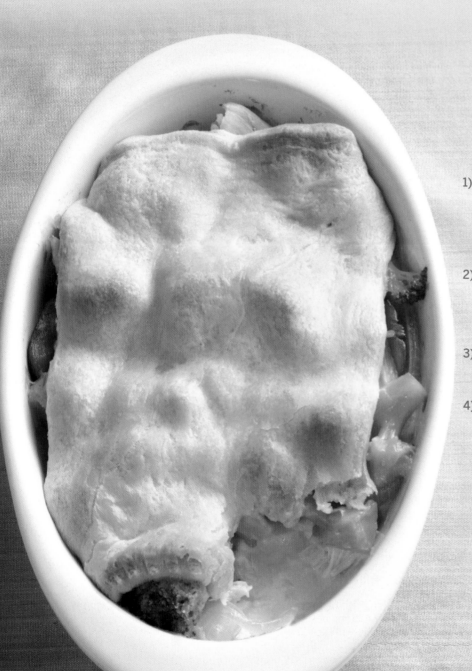

Bake-Off®   BAKE-OFF® CONTEST 42, 2006

PREP TIME: 20 MINUTES (READY IN 45 MINUTES)
SERVINGS: 2

e EASY

1 tablespoon olive oil

1 cup sliced fresh mushrooms

1 small onion, sliced ($\frac{1}{2}$ cup)

1 box (10 oz) Green Giant® frozen broccoli and zesty cheese sauce

$\frac{2}{3}$ cup ricotta cheese

1 cup chopped cooked chicken

1 can (4 oz) Pillsbury® refrigerated crescent dinner rolls (4 rolls)

1) Heat oven to 375°F. In 10-inch skillet, heat oil over medium-high heat. Add the mushrooms and onion; cook 5 to 7 minutes, stirring frequently, until tender. Meanwhile, microwave broccoli and cheese sauce as directed on box.

2) Spread $\frac{1}{3}$ cup ricotta cheese in bottom of each of 2 ungreased 2-cup au gratin dishes or individual casseroles. Top each evenly with chicken, mushroom mixture and broccoli with cheese sauce.

3) Unroll dough; separate into 2 rectangles. Place 1 rectangle over top of each dish, tucking corners into dish as needed.

4) Place the dishes on cookie sheet. Bake 20 to 25 minutes or until tops are golden brown and edges are bubbly.

HIGH ALTITUDE (3500-6500 FT.): For either au gratin dishes or glass baking dish—In Step 1, cook the mushrooms and onion 5 minutes, stirring frequently. Add chicken to mixture; cook and stir 2 minutes longer. In Step 4, bake 23 to 28 minutes.

Nutrition Information Per Serving:

Calories:	610	From Fat:	300
Total Fat			33g
Saturated Fat			11g
Trans Fat			3.5g
Cholesterol			85mg
Sodium			1210mg
Total Carbohydrate			40g
Dietary Fiber			2g
Sugars			12g
Protein			37g

Sage- and Oregano-Rubbed Turkey with Honey-Lemon Glaze

PREP TIME: 20 MINUTES (READY IN 4 HOURS 20 MINUTES)
SERVINGS: 12

 EASY

TURKEY

1 whole turkey (12 lb), thawed if frozen

3 teaspoons dried rubbed sage

3 teaspoons dried oregano leaves

1 teaspoon salt

1 teaspoon pepper

2 tablespoons olive or vegetable oil

GLAZE

¼ cup honey

2 tablespoons lemon juice

1 tablespoon butter or margarine

1) Move oven rack to lowest position. Heat oven to 325°F. Remove and discard neck and giblets from turkey. Rinse turkey inside and out with cold water; pat dry with paper towels. Fasten neck skin to back of turkey with skewer. Fold wings across back of turkey so the tips are touching. In shallow roasting pan, place turkey, breast side up.

2) In small bowl, mix sage, oregano, salt, pepper and oil. Rub herb mixture over turkey. Refasten drumsticks with metal piece or tuck under skin at the tail. (Drumsticks can also be tied together with cotton string.) Insert ovenproof meat thermometer so tip is in thickest part of inside thigh and does not touch bone.

3) Roast uncovered 1 hour. When turkey begins to turn golden brown, place tent of heavy-duty foil over turkey. Roast 2 hours 15 minutes longer.

4) In 1-quart saucepan, heat the glaze ingredients over low heat, stirring occasionally, until honey and butter are melted.

5) Cut the band of skin or remove tie holding legs to allow inside of thighs to cook thoroughly. Brush turkey with glaze; roast uncovered 10 minutes. Brush with glaze; roast uncovered 10 to 20 minutes longer. Turkey is done when thermometer reads 180°F and drumsticks move easily when lifted or twisted.

6) Place the turkey on warm platter; cover with foil to keep warm. Let stand 15 minutes for easier carving.

HIGH ALTITUDE (3500-6500 FT.): No change.

Nutrition Information Per Serving:		
Calories: 540	From Fat:	280
Total Fat		32g
Saturated Fat		9g
Trans Fat		1g
Cholesterol		185mg
Sodium		370mg
Total Carbohydrate		6g
Dietary Fiber		0g
Sugars		6g
Protein		57g

Chicken Fajita Crescent Braid

PREP TIME: 25 MINUTES (READY IN 50 MINUTES)
SERVINGS: 6

- 1 can (8 oz) Pillsbury® refrigerated crescent dinner rolls or 1 can (8 oz) Pillsbury® Crescent Recipe Creations™ refrigerated flaky dough sheet

- 1 tablespoon vegetable oil

- 2 small boneless skinless chicken breasts, cut into 1x$\frac{1}{2}$x$\frac{1}{2}$-inch strips

- 1 teaspoon chili powder

- $\frac{1}{4}$ teaspoon salt

- 1 garlic clove, finely chopped

- 1 small onion, thinly sliced

- $\frac{1}{2}$ cup green or red bell pepper strips (2x1x$\frac{1}{4}$ inch)

- $\frac{1}{4}$ cup Old El Paso® Thick 'n Chunky salsa

- 2 cups shredded Cheddar-Monterey Jack cheese blend (8 oz)

- 1 egg white, beaten

1) Heat oven to 375°F. Spray large cookie sheet with cooking spray. Unroll dough onto cookie sheet (if using crescent rolls, pinch the seams to seal); press to 8x12 inches.

2) In 10-inch skillet, heat oil over medium-high heat. Add the chicken; stir in chili powder, salt and garlic; cook 3 to 5 minutes, stirring occasionally, until lightly browned. Add onion and bell pepper strips; cook 2 to 3 minutes longer or until the chicken is no longer pink in center and the vegetables are crisp-tender.

3) Spoon chicken mixture in 4-inch strip lengthwise down center of dough. Top with salsa; sprinkle with cheese. With kitchen scissors or sharp knife, make cuts 1 inch apart on long sides of dough within $\frac{1}{2}$ inch of filling. Alternately cross strips over filling; press edges to seal. Brush with egg white.

4) Bake 20 to 25 minutes or until deep golden brown. Cool 5 minutes. Cut crosswise into slices.

HIGH ALTITUDE (3500-6500 FT.): No change.

Nutrition Information Per Serving:		
Calories: 360	From Fat: 200	
Total Fat		22g
Saturated Fat		11g
Trans Fat		0g
Cholesterol		65mg
Sodium		750mg
Total Carbohydrate		20g
Dietary Fiber		0g
Sugars		5g
Protein		21g

Mini Burger Kabobs

PREP TIME: 20 MINUTES (READY IN 20 MINUTES)
SERVINGS: 4 (3 PATTIES AND 1/4 CUP SAUCE EACH)

⊖ EASY

1 lb lean (at least 80%) ground beef

1 medium onion, finely chopped (1/2 cup)

3 tablespoons Progresso® plain bread crumbs

3 tablespoons grated Parmesan cheese

1 garlic clove, finely chopped

1/2 teaspoon salt

1/4 teaspoon pepper

1 cup tomato sauce

Nutrition Information Per Serving:		
Calories: 260	From Fat:	130
Total Fat		14g
Saturated Fat		6g
Trans Fat		1g
Cholesterol		75mg
Sodium		800mg
Total Carbohydrate		10g
Dietary Fiber		1g
Sugars		4g
Protein		23g

1) Heat gas or charcoal grill. In large bowl, mix all ingredients except tomato sauce. Shape mixture into 12 (2-inch) meatballs, then flatten slightly to 3/4-inch-thick patties. On each of 4 (9-inch) metal skewers, thread 3 patties lengthwise, leaving 1-inch space between each.

2) Carefully brush grill rack with oil. Place kabobs on grill over medium-high heat. Cover grill; cook about 10 minutes, turning occasionally, until browned on outside and no longer pink in center.

3) In 1-quart saucepan, heat tomato sauce over medium-high heat, stirring occasionally, until simmering. Serve over kabobs.

HIGH ALTITUDE (3500-6500 FT.): Cook over medium heat.

Rustic Chicken Pizza

PREP TIME: 20 MINUTES (READY IN 40 MINUTES)
SERVINGS: 8

⊖ EASY

1 can (13.8 oz) Pillsbury® refrigerated classic pizza crust

1/4 cup ranch dressing

2 tablespoons freshly grated Parmesan cheese

2 cups chopped deli rotisserie chicken (from 2- to 2 1/2-lb chicken)

1 box (9 oz) Green Giant® frozen spinach, thawed, squeezed to drain

1 jar (7.5 oz) marinated artichoke hearts, drained, coarsely chopped

1 1/2 cups shredded Asiago cheese (about 4 1/2 oz)

3 plum (Roma) tomatoes, sliced

1) Heat oven to 400°F. Lightly spray 12-inch pizza pan with cooking spray. Unroll dough; place in pan. Starting at the center, press out dough with hands to edge of pan.

2) Bake crust about 6 minutes or until crust begins to dry. Meanwhile, in small bowl, mix dressing and Parmesan cheese.

3) Remove partially baked crust from oven. Spread dressing mixture over crust. Top with chicken, spinach and artichokes. Sprinkle with Asiago cheese. Top with plum tomatoes.

4) Bake 15 to 20 minutes longer or until cheese is melted and crust is golden brown. Cut into wedges.

HIGH ALTITUDE (3500-6500 FT.): No change.

Nutrition Information Per Serving:		
Calories: 330	From Fat:	140
Total Fat		15g
Saturated Fat		6g
Trans Fat		0g
Cholesterol		50mg
Sodium		870mg
Total Carbohydrate		28g
Dietary Fiber		2g
Sugars		5g
Protein		20g

Chicken Pot Pies with Biscuits

PREP TIME: 40 MINUTES (READY IN 1 HOUR 10 MINUTES)
SERVINGS: 8

1 tablespoon butter or margarine

1 cup chopped onions (2 medium)

1/4 cup all-purpose flour

2 teaspoons chicken bouillon granules

1 teaspoon dried thyme leaves

1/4 teaspoon pepper

2 cups Progresso® chicken broth (from 32-oz carton)

1 cup milk

2 large baking potatoes, peeled, cubed (about 3 cups)

1 cup julienne (matchstick-cut) carrots

1 bag (12 oz) Green Giant® Valley Fresh Steamers™ frozen cut green beans

1 can (16.3 oz) Pillsbury® Grands!® Flaky Layers refrigerated buttermilk or original biscuits

2 1/2 cups cubed cooked chicken

1) Heat oven to 350°F. In 4-quart saucepan, melt butter over medium-high heat. Add onions; cook 2 to 3 minutes, stirring frequently, until tender. Stir in flour, bouillon, thyme and pepper until well blended. Gradually stir in broth and milk, cooking and stirring until bubbly and slightly thickened.

2) Stir in potatoes, carrots and green beans. Heat to boiling, stirring occasionally. Cook 8 to 10 minutes, stirring frequently, until vegetables are crisp-tender.

3) Meanwhile, separate the dough into 8 biscuits. Using rolling pin, roll each biscuit into a 4-inch round. Cut each round into 6 equal wedges; set aside.

4) Stir chicken into vegetable mixture; return to boiling. Remove from heat. Into each of 8 ungreased 10-oz custard cups or ramekins, spoon about 1 cup mixture. Place 6 biscuit wedges around edge of each, overlapping slightly and leaving hole in center for steam to escape.

5) Bake 20 to 25 minutes or until vegetables are tender and biscuits are golden brown. Let stand 5 minutes before serving.

HIGH ALTITUDE (3500-6500 FT.): In Step 2, cook 10 to 12 minutes.

Nutrition Information Per Serving:		
Calories: 310	From Fat:	110
Total Fat		12g
Saturated Fat		4.5g
Trans Fat		1.5g
Cholesterol		70mg
Sodium		700mg
Total Carbohydrate		31g
Dietary Fiber		3g
Sugars		6g
Protein		19g

Lemon and Herb Roast Turkey Breast

PREP TIME: 15 MINUTES (READY IN 3 HOURS 5 MINUTES)
SERVINGS: 8

e EASY

1 lemon

2 garlic cloves, finely chopped

2 tablespoons finely chopped fresh parsley

1/2 teaspoon salt

1/2 teaspoon dried sage leaves

1/2 teaspoon dried marjoram leaves

1/4 teaspoon pepper

1 tablespoon olive or vegetable oil

1 bone-in skin-on whole turkey breast (5 to 5 1/2 lb), thawed if frozen

1) Heat oven to 325°F. Spray 13x9-inch pan and 16x12-inch sheet of heavy-duty foil with cooking spray. Grate peel from lemon. Cut lemon into quarters; set aside. In small bowl, mix lemon peel, garlic, parsley, salt, sage, marjoram, pepper and oil.

2) Loosen skin covering turkey breast and pull away from breast meat, leaving skin attached at neck. If necessary, use sharp knife to loosen. Rub herb mixture evenly over turkey breast meat. Replace skin over breast, tucking under bottom of breast. Rub any remaining mixture over skin. Place turkey, skin side up, in pan. Place lemon quarters in neck opening.

3) Cover the pan with foil, sprayed side down. Roast 1 hour. Uncover pan; insert ovenproof meat thermometer so the tip is in the thickest part of breast and does not touch bone. Roast uncovered 1 hour 15 minutes to 1 hour 45 minutes longer or until thermometer reads 170°F. Let stand 5 minutes for easier carving. Remove and discard lemon from neck opening before slicing turkey.

HIGH ALTITUDE (3500-6500 FT.): No change.

Nutrition Information Per Serving:

Calories: 370	From Fat: 150
Total Fat	16g
Saturated Fat	4.5g
Trans Fat	0g
Cholesterol	145mg
Sodium	270mg
Total Carbohydrate	1g
Dietary Fiber	0g
Sugars	0g
Protein	53g

Parmesan-Ranch-Chicken Packets

PREP TIME: 45 MINUTES (READY IN 45 MINUTES)
SERVINGS: 4

4 boneless skinless chicken breasts
(4 to 5 oz each)

1/2 teaspoon salt-free garlic-herb blend

1/2 cup reduced-fat ranch dressing

1/4 cup water

2 cups quartered small red potatoes

1 cup ready-to-eat baby-cut carrots,
cut in half lengthwise

1/4 lb fresh green beans, trimmed

1/3 cup finely shredded Parmesan
cheese

1) Heat gas or charcoal grill. Cut 4
(18x12-inch) sheets of heavy-duty foil;
spray with cooking spray. Sprinkle
chicken with garlic-herb blend; place
1 breast on each sheet of foil. Drizzle
1 tablespoon of the ranch dressing over
each breast.

2) In medium bowl, mix remaining 1/4 cup
dressing and the water. Stir in potatoes,
carrots and green beans. Divide the
vegetables among chicken breasts. Sprinkle with cheese.

3) Bring up 2 sides of foil so edges meet. Seal edges, making tight 1/2-inch
fold; fold again, allowing space for heat circulation and expansion. Fold
other sides to seal.

4) Place packets on grill over medium heat. Cover grill; cook 10 minutes.
Rotate packets 1/2 turn; cook 5 to 15 minutes longer or until vegetables
are tender and juice of chicken is clear when center of thickest part is
cut (170°F).

5) To serve, cut large X across top of each packet; carefully fold back foil to
allow steam to escape.

HIGH ALTITUDE (3500-6500 FT.): Cook packets over medium-low heat 20 to 25 minutes, turning
packets over every 5 minutes.

Nutrition Information Per Serving:	
Calories: 320	From Fat: 100
Total Fat	12g
Saturated Fat	3g
Trans Fat	0g
Cholesterol	80mg
Sodium	530mg
Total Carbohydrate	23g
Dietary Fiber	4g
Sugars	4g
Protein	30g

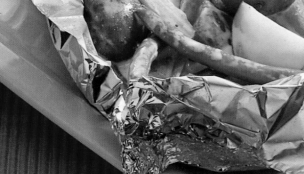

Potato and Ground Beef Gratin

PREP TIME: 35 MINUTES (READY IN 1 HOUR 45 MINUTES)
SERVINGS: 6 (1-1/2 CUPS EACH)

1 lb lean (at least 80%) ground beef

1 teaspoon salt

1/2 teaspoon pepper

3 tablespoons butter or margarine

1 small onion, chopped (1/4 cup)

3 tablespoons all-purpose flour

2 teaspoons chopped fresh thyme leaves

3 cups milk

3 cups shredded mild Cheddar cheese (12 oz)

6 medium white potatoes (2 1/2 lb), peeled, thinly sliced (6 cups)

Paprika, if desired

1) Heat oven to 375°F. Spray 13x9-inch (3-quart) glass baking dish with cooking spray.

2) In 10-inch skillet, cook beef, salt and pepper over medium-high heat 5 to 7 minutes, stirring frequently, until beef is thoroughly cooked; drain.

3) Meanwhile, in 3-quart saucepan, melt butter over medium-low heat. Add onion; cook about 2 minutes, stirring occasionally, until tender. Stir in flour. Cook 1 to 2 minutes, stirring constantly, until bubbly; remove from heat. Stir in thyme.

4) Stir milk into onion mixture. Heat to boiling, stirring constantly. Boil and stir 1 minute; remove from heat. Stir in 2 cups of the cheese until melted.

5) Spread half of the potatoes in baking dish. Top with beef; spread remaining potatoes over beef. Pour cheese sauce over potatoes.

6) Cover with foil; bake 45 minutes. Sprinkle remaining 1 cup cheese and the paprika over potatoes. Bake uncovered 15 to 20 minutes longer or until top is brown and bubbly and potatoes are tender. Let stand 5 minutes before serving.

HIGH ALTITUDE (3500-6500 FT.): No change.

Nutrition Information Per Serving:	
Calories: 640	From Fat: 320
Total Fat	36g
Saturated Fat	20g
Trans Fat	1.5g
Cholesterol	130mg
Sodium	880mg
Total Carbohydrate	45g
Dietary Fiber	4g
Sugars	9g
Protein	35g

Ground Beef Curry

PREP TIME: 50 MINUTES (READY IN 50 MINUTES)
SERVINGS: 6 (1 CUP RICE AND 3/4 CUP BEEF MIXTURE)

(f) LOW FAT

1½ cups uncooked regular long-grain white rice

1 lb lean (at least 80%) ground beef

1 small onion, chopped (¼ cup)

1 garlic clove, finely chopped

2 tablespoons grated gingerroot (about 3 inches)

1 tablespoon tomato paste

1 teaspoon salt

2 teaspoons ground cumin

2 teaspoons chili powder

1 teaspoon garam masala

2 cans (14.5 oz each) diced tomatoes, undrained

3 tablespoons chopped fresh cilantro

1) Cook rice in water as directed on package.

2) Meanwhile, in 12-inch skillet, cook beef, onion, garlic and gingerroot over medium-high heat 5 to 7 minutes, stirring occasionally, until beef is thoroughly cooked; drain if desired.

3) Stir remaining ingredients except cilantro into the beef mixture. Reduce the heat to medium. Simmer uncovered 8 to 10 minutes, stirring occasionally, until slightly thickened.

4) Serve beef mixture over rice. Garnish with cilantro.

HIGH ALTITUDE (3500-6500 FT.): No change.

Nutrition Information Per Serving:	
Calories: 360	From Fat: 80
Total Fat	9g
Saturated Fat	3.5g
Trans Fat	0.5g
Cholesterol	45mg
Sodium	1200mg
Total Carbohydrate	50g
Dietary Fiber	3g
Sugars	4g
Protein	18g

Ground Beef Pot Pie

PREP TIME: 20 MINUTES (READY IN 1 HOUR 5 MINUTES)
SERVINGS: 6

(e) EASY

1) Heat oven to 450°F. Bake bottom pie crust as directed on box for Two-Crust Pie, using 9-inch glass pie plate.

2) In 12-inch skillet, cook beef, onion, garlic salt and pepper over medium-high heat 5 to 7 minutes, stirring frequently, until beef is thoroughly cooked; drain.

3) Stir cornstarch into beef mixture until well mixed. Stir in potatoes, carrots and gravy. Cook 5 to 6 minutes over medium-high heat, stirring constantly, until mixture is hot. Spoon mixture into crust-lined pie plate. Top with second crust; seal edge and flute. Cut slits in several places in top crust; cover edge of crust with 3-inch strip of foil.

4) Bake 35 to 40 minutes or until the crust is golden brown. Cool 5 minutes before serving.

HIGH ALTITUDE (3500-6500 FT.): No change.

Nutrition Information Per Serving:	
Calories: 590	From Fat: 260
Total Fat	29g
Saturated Fat	11g
Trans Fat	0.5g
Cholesterol	60mg
Sodium	850mg
Total Carbohydrate	66g
Dietary Fiber	3g
Sugars	3g
Protein	17g

1 box (15 oz) Pillsbury® refrigerated pie crusts, softened as directed on box

1 lb lean (at least 80%) ground beef

1 medium onion, chopped (½ cup)

1 teaspoon garlic salt

½ teaspoon pepper

3 tablespoons cornstarch

3 cups frozen southern-style diced hash brown potatoes (from 32-oz bag), thawed

3 medium carrots, sliced (1½ cups)

1 jar (12 oz) beef gravy

Chipotle Chicken Salad

PREP TIME: 30 MINUTES (READY IN 50 MINUTES)
SERVINGS: 4 (1-1/2 CUPS BEAN MIXTURE AND 1 CHICKEN BREAST EACH)

4 boneless skinless chicken breasts

¾ cup bottled chipotle marinade

½ cup Old El Paso® Thick 'n Chunky salsa

¼ cup chopped fresh cilantro

2 tablespoons bottled chipotle marinade

2 tablespoons olive oil

Grated peel of 1 medium lime (2 teaspoons)

Juice of 1 medium lime (almost ⅓ cup)

4 cups torn romaine lettuce

1 cup Green Giant® Niblets® frozen corn, cooked, cooled

½ cup chopped red bell pepper

1 can (15 oz) Progresso® black beans, drained, rinsed

Sour cream, if desired

1) In large nonmetal dish or resealable food-storage plastic bag, place chicken and ¾ cup chipotle marinade; turn to coat. Cover dish or seal bag; refrigerate at least 20 minutes or up to 2 hours to marinate.

2) Heat gas or charcoal grill. Remove chicken from marinade; discard marinade. Place chicken on grill over medium heat. Cover grill; cook 10 to 12 minutes, turning halfway through grilling, until chicken is fork-tender and juice is clear when center of thickest part is cut (170°F). Let stand 5 minutes; cut into ½-inch strips.

3) In small bowl, stir together the salsa, cilantro, 2 tablespoons chipotle marinade, the oil, lime peel and lime juice. In large bowl, toss lettuce, corn, bell pepper and beans; toss with salsa mixture.

4) Divide bean mixture among 4 serving plates. Top each with chicken. If desired, serve with sour cream.

HIGH ALTITUDE (3500-6500 FT.): In Step 2, place chicken on grill over medium-low heat. Cover grill; cook 13 to 15 minutes.

Nutrition Information Per Serving:		
Calories: 420	From Fat:	110
Total Fat		12g
Saturated Fat		2g
Trans Fat		0g
Cholesterol		75mg
Sodium		780mg
Total Carbohydrate		43g
Dietary Fiber		12g
Sugars		4g
Protein		36g

Italian-Style Meat Loaf

PREP TIME: 20 MINUTES (READY IN 1 HOUR 35 MINUTES)
SERVINGS: 8

EASY

2 eggs

1 jar (14 oz) tomato pasta sauce

1 cup Progresso® Italian style bread crumbs

1 large onion, finely chopped (1 cup)

2 teaspoons Italian seasoning

1/2 teaspoon salt

2 lb lean (at least 80%) ground beef

1 box (7.2 oz 2 pouches) Betty Crocker® roasted garlic mashed potatoes

2 1/2 cups milk

1 1/2 cups hot water

1/4 cup butter or margarine

1/2 cup grated Parmesan cheese

1) Heat oven to 375°F. Spray 13x9-inch (3-quart) glass baking dish with cooking spray. In large bowl, beat eggs. Stir in pasta sauce, bread crumbs, onion, Italian seasoning, salt and ground beef until well blended. Press mixture in bottom of baking dish.

2) Bake 45 to 55 minutes or until meat thermometer inserted in center of loaf reads 160°F.

3) Meanwhile, make both pouches of mashed potatoes as directed on box, using milk, hot water and butter.

4) Spoon any excess juices from baking dish. Spread mashed potatoes over meat loaf; sprinkle with cheese. Bake 10 to 15 minutes longer or until top begins to brown. Let stand 5 minutes before cutting.

HIGH ALTITUDE (3500-6500 FT.): No change.

Nutrition Information Per Serving:		
Calories: 530	From Fat:	230
Total Fat		26g
Saturated Fat		12g
Trans Fat		1g
Cholesterol		150mg
Sodium		1150mg
Total Carbohydrate		43g
Dietary Fiber		2g
Sugars		11g
Protein		31g

Chicken Florentine Skillet

PREP TIME: 20 MINUTES (READY IN 20 MINUTES)
SERVINGS: 6 (1-1/3 CUPS EACH)

e EASY

3 cups uncooked wagon wheel pasta (8 oz)

1¼ cups half-and-half

2 tablespoons all-purpose flour

1 teaspoon salt

¼ teaspoon ground nutmeg

1 tablespoon butter or margarine

1 package (14 oz) uncooked chicken breast tenders (not breaded), cut into bite-size pieces

1 can (14.5 oz) diced tomatoes, drained

1 cup sliced fresh mushrooms

1 bag (6 oz) fresh baby spinach leaves (about 3½ cups)

1 cup shredded mozzarella cheese (4 oz)

1) Cook and drain the pasta as directed on package. Meanwhile, in small bowl, stir ¼ cup of the half-and-half, the flour, salt and nutmeg until smooth; set aside.

2) In 12-inch nonstick skillet, melt butter over medium-high heat. Add chicken; cook 6 to 8 minutes, stirring occasionally, until browned. Stir in the tomatoes, mushrooms and spinach. Cook about 5 minutes, stirring occasionally, until mushrooms are tender.

3) Reduce heat to low. Stir in the pasta and half-and-half mixture. Cook about 1 minute or until thickened. Stir in remaining 1 cup half-and-half. Sprinkle cheese over top. Cover; let stand 2 to 3 minutes or until cheese is melted.

HIGH ALTITUDE (3500-6500 FT.): In Step 3, reduce heat to medium. Stir in the pasta, half-and-half mixture and 1/4 cup water. Cook 2 to 3 minutes. Stir in remaining 1 cup half-and-half and cheese. Cook about 5 minutes until cheese is melted and mixture is hot.

Nutrition Information Per Serving:	
Calories: 400	From Fat: 120
Total Fat	13g
Saturated Fat	7g
Trans Fat	0g
Cholesterol	65mg
Sodium	880mg
Total Carbohydrate	42g
Dietary Fiber	3g
Sugars	5g
Protein	28g

Thai Beef–Noodle Salad

PREP TIME: 35 MINUTES (READY IN 1 HOUR)
SERVINGS: 6 (1-1/2 CUPS EACH)

1/3 cup soy sauce

2 tablespoons packed brown sugar

2 tablespoons vegetable oil

2 tablespoons lime juice

1 tablespoon fish sauce

1 teaspoon chopped fresh gingerroot

1/2 teaspoon crushed red pepper flakes

1 lb beef flank steak

3.5 oz uncooked rice stick noodles

2 tablespoons peanut butter

1 1/2 cups shredded carrots

1 medium red bell pepper, cut into 1-inch strips

1/2 cup chopped green onions (8 medium)

1/4 cup dry-roasted peanuts, chopped

1) In 1-cup microwavable measuring cup, stir together soy sauce, brown sugar, oil, lime juice, fish sauce, gingerroot and pepper flakes.

2) In large nonmetal dish or resealable food-storage plastic bag, place beef and 3 tablespoons of the soy sauce mixture. (Cover and refrigerate remaining soy sauce mixture for dressing). Turn to coat. Cover dish or seal bag; refrigerate at least 20 minutes or up to 4 hours to marinate.

3) Heat gas or charcoal grill. Remove beef from marinade; discard marinade. Place beef on grill over medium heat. Cover grill; cook 10 to 15 minutes, turning halfway through grilling, until desired doneness. Let beef stand 5 minutes; cut into thin strips. Cut strips into 1- to 1 1/2-inch lengths.

4) Meanwhile, in 2-quart saucepan, heat 6 cups water to boiling. Add rice stick noodles; cook 2 to 3 minutes or just until tender (do not overcook). Rinse in cold water until cool; drain. Cut noodles with kitchen scissors into 3- to 5-inch lengths.

5) Using wire whisk, mix peanut butter into remaining soy sauce mixture to make dressing. If necessary, microwave mixture uncovered on High 15 to 20 seconds to blend in peanut butter.

6) In large bowl, place noodles, beef, carrots, bell pepper and onions. Toss with the dressing until noodles are evenly coated. Sprinkle with peanuts. Serve immediately.

HIGH ALTITUDE (3500-6500 FT.): No change.

Nutrition Information Per Serving:	
Calories: 340	From Fat: 120
Total Fat	14g
Saturated Fat	2.5g
Trans Fat	0g
Cholesterol	55mg
Sodium	1170mg
Total Carbohydrate	27g
Dietary Fiber	3g
Sugars	8g
Protein	27g

Fettuccine with Chicken and Herbed Vegetables

PREP TIME: 30 MINUTES (READY IN 30 MINUTES)
SERVINGS: 6

12 oz uncooked fettuccine

1 tablespoon olive or vegetable oil

1 medium onion, chopped (1/2 cup)

1 1/2 lb boneless skinless chicken breasts, cut into 1-inch pieces

1 small green bell pepper, cut into bite-size strips

2 garlic cloves, finely chopped

1/2 teaspoon salt

1/4 teaspoon pepper

3 small zucchini, cut in half lengthwise, sliced

3 large tomatoes, seeded, chopped (3 cups)

3 tablespoons chopped fresh basil leaves

2 tablespoons chopped fresh oregano leaves

1/2 cup shredded Parmesan cheese (2 oz)

1) Cook fettuccine to desired doneness as directed on package. Drain; cover to keep warm.

2) Meanwhile, in 12-inch nonstick skillet, heat oil over medium-high heat. Add onion; cook 2 to 3 minutes, stirring occasionally, until tender.

3) Stir in chicken, bell pepper, garlic, salt and pepper. Cook 5 to 6 minutes, stirring occasionally, until chicken is browned on outside and no longer pink in center. Stir in zucchini, tomatoes, basil and oregano. Cook 5 to 6 minutes, stirring occasionally, until zucchini is tender.

4) Place fettuccine on serving platter; spoon chicken mixture over top. Sprinkle with cheese. Serve with additional Parmesan cheese if desired.

HIGH ALTITUDE (3500-6500 FT.): In Step 3, decrease heat to medium before stirring in chicken.

Nutrition Information Per Serving:	
Calories: 440	From Fat: 110
Total Fat	12g
Saturated Fat	3.5g
Trans Fat	0g
Cholesterol	120mg
Sodium	670mg
Total Carbohydrate	46g
Dietary Fiber	4g
Sugars	5g
Protein	37g

Tilapia with Green Salsa in Foil

PREP TIME: 10 MINUTES (READY IN 45 MINUTES)
SERVICES: 4

ⓔ EASY

4 tilapia fillets (1½ lb)

1 medium onion, sliced

1 cup green tomatillo salsa

½ cup sliced drained roasted red bell peppers (from a jar)

8 green olives, pitted, sliced

4 teaspoons olive oil

1 jar (15 oz) nopales, drained, rinsed

Black pepper, if desired

4 tablespoons finely chopped cilantro

1) Heat oven to 350°F. Cut 4 (18x18-inch) sheets of heavy-duty foil.

2) Place 1 fillet on center of each sheet. Top each with ¼ each of the onion, salsa, roasted red peppers, olives, olive oil, nopales and black pepper. Wrap packets securely using double-fold seals, leaving a small opening so steam can escape during baking.

3) Bake 30 to 35 minutes or until the fish flakes easily with fork. Sprinkle with cilantro.

HIGH ALTITUDE (3500-6500 FT.): No change.

Nutrition Information Per Serving:		
Calories: 250	From Fat:	70
Total Fat		8g
Saturated Fat		1.5g
Trans Fat		0g
Cholesterol		90mg
Sodium		460mg
Total Carbohydrate		10g
Dietary Fiber		4g
Sugars		4g
Protein		34g

Grilled Salmon Caesar Salad

PREP TIME: 25 MINUTES (READY IN 25 MINUTES)
SERVINGS: 4

1 salmon fillet (1 lb)

½ cup Caesar dressing

1 bag (10 oz) torn romaine lettuce (6 cups)

½ cup Caesar-flavored croutons

¼ cup sliced ripe olives

¼ cup shredded fresh Parmesan cheese (1 oz)

1) Heat gas or charcoal grill. Place salmon, skin side down, on grill over medium heat. Brush the surface of fish with 1 tablespoon of the dressing. Cover grill; cook 9 to 11 minutes, or until fish flakes easily with fork and is opaque.

2) In large bowl, toss lettuce, croutons and olives. Pour remaining dressing over top; toss gently to coat. Spoon salad onto large platter. Remove skin, and flake salmon. Arrange salmon on top of salad. Sprinkle with cheese.

Broiling Directions: To broil salmon, place skin side down on broiler pan; broil with top 4 to 6 inches from heat, using times above as a guide.

HIGH ALTITUDE (3500-6500 FT.): In Step 1, grill salmon over medium-low heat.

Nutrition Information Per Serving:	
Calories: 630	From Fat: 330
Total Fat	36g
Saturated Fat	15g
Trans Fat	0g
Cholesterol	110mg
Sodium	1810mg
Total Carbohydrate	53g
Dietary Fiber	2g
Sugars	10g
Protein	21g

Easy Reuben Sandwich Slices

PREP TIME: 15 MINUTES (READY IN 40 MINUTES)
SERVINGS: 4

EASY

2 cans (8 oz each) Pillsbury® refrigerated crescent dinner rolls or 2 cans (8 oz each) Pillsbury® Crescent Recipe Creations™ refrigerated flaky dough sheet

2 tablespoons Thousand Island dressing

4 oz thinly sliced deli corned beef

4 slices (1 oz each) Swiss cheese

1 cup sauerkraut with caraway seed, well drained (from 14-oz can)

1 tablespoon horseradish mustard

1 egg, beaten

2 teaspoons sesame seed

Nutrition Information Per Serving:	
Calories: 50	From Fat: 25
Total Fat	2.5g
Saturated Fat	1g
Trans Fat	0g
Cholesterol	15mg
Sodium	170mg
Total Carbohydrate	5g
Dietary Fiber	0g
Sugars	0g
Protein	2g

1) Heat oven to 375°F. Onto ungreased cookie sheet, unroll 1 can of dough (if using crescent rolls, pinch the seams to seal). Spread the dressing on the dough to within ½ inch of edges. Top with corned beef, Swiss cheese and sauerkraut.

2) Unroll remaining can of dough on work surface (if using rolls, pinch seams to seal). Spread mustard to within ½ inch of edges. Place mustard side down on sauerkraut. Press edges with fork to seal. Brush with egg. Sprinkle with sesame seed.

3) Bake 20 to 25 minutes or until deep golden brown. Cut the sandwich into slices to serve.

HIGH ALTITUDE (3500-6500 FT.): No change.

Chicken Bruschetta

PREP TIME: 30 MINUTES (READY IN 30 MINUTES)
SERVINGS: 4

TOMATO TOPPING

- 1 large tomato, chopped (1 cup)
- 3 tablespoons chopped fresh basil leaves
- 1 tablespoon olive or vegetable oil
- 1/4 teaspoon salt
- 1/4 teaspoon pepper

CHICKEN

- 4 boneless skinless chicken breasts (4 to 5 oz each)
- 1/2 teaspoon garlic salt
- 1/8 teaspoon pepper
- 1 egg
- 2 tablespoons milk
- 1/4 cup all-purpose flour
- 3/4 cup Progresso® Italian-style bread crumbs
- 2 tablespoons olive or vegetable oil

1) In medium bowl, mix tomato topping ingredients. Cover; refrigerate until serving time.

2) Between pieces of plastic wrap or waxed paper, place each chicken breast smooth side down; gently pound with flat side of meat mallet or rolling pin until 1/4 inch thick. Sprinkle chicken with garlic salt and 1/8 teaspoon pepper.

3) In shallow bowl, beat egg and milk with fork until blended. Spread flour on shallow plate. Spread bread crumbs on another shallow plate. Coat chicken with flour, then dip into egg mixture and coat with bread crumbs.

4) In 12-inch nonstick skillet, heat 2 tablespoons oil over medium-high heat. Reduce heat to medium. Add chicken; cook 10 to 15 minutes, turning once, until crumbs are golden brown and chicken is no longer pink in center. Serve tomato topping over chicken.

HIGH ALTITUDE (3500-6500 FT.): No change.

Nutrition Information Per Serving:	
Calories: 400	From Fat: 160
Total Fat	17g
Saturated Fat	3.5g
Trans Fat	0g
Cholesterol	140mg
Sodium	720mg
Total Carbohydrate	24g
Dietary Fiber	1g
Sugars	3g
Protein	37g

Crescent-Topped Shepherd's Pie

PREP TIME: 25 MINUTES (READY IN 55 MINUTES)
SERVINGS: 4 (1-1/2 CUPS EACH)

1 lb boneless beef sirloin steak, trimmed of fat, cut into $1/2$-inch cubes

1 cup chopped onions

1 cup ready-to-eat baby-cut carrots, cut into $1/4$-inch strips

$1/2$ teaspoon salt

$1/4$ teaspoon pepper

$1/2$ teaspoon Italian seasoning

1 cup sliced fresh mushrooms (3 oz)

$1/2$ cup Green Giant® Valley Fresh Steamers™ frozen sweet peas

1 jar (14 oz) tomato pasta sauce

1 can (8 oz) Pillsbury® refrigerated crescent dinner rolls or 1 can (8 oz) Pillsbury® Crescent Recipe Creations™ refrigerated flaky dough sheet

1 tablespoon butter or margarine, melted

1 tablespoon shredded Parmesan cheese

1) Heat oven to 375°F. Spray 11x7-inch (2-quart) glass baking dish with cooking spray.

2) Heat 12-inch nonstick skillet over medium-high heat. Add beef, onions and carrots to skillet; sprinkle with salt and pepper. Cook 3 to 5 minutes, stirring frequently, until beef is brown.

3) Stir in Italian seasoning, mushrooms, peas and pasta sauce. Heat to boiling. Cook over medium heat 5 minutes, stirring occasionally. Spoon into baking dish.

4) Open can of dough; do not unroll. With serrated knife, cut dough into 1-inch slices. Arrange slices cut side down around edges of casserole. Brush with melted butter; sprinkle with Parmesan cheese.

5) Bake 18 to 23 minutes or until casserole is bubbly and crescent slices on top are golden brown.

HIGH ALTITUDE (3500-6500 FT.): In Step 3, add 1/4 cup water with the pasta sauce. In Step 4, do not sprinkle with Parmesan cheese, but instead, in Step 5, sprinkle with Parmesan cheese the last 5 minutes of bake time.

Nutrition Information Per Serving:

Calories:	540	From Fat:	180
Total Fat			20g
Saturated Fat			8g
Trans Fat			0g
Cholesterol			80mg
Sodium			1350mg
Total Carbohydrate			52g
Dietary Fiber			4g
Sugars			19g
Protein			36g

Magic Potion Meat Sauce for Spaghetti

PREP TIME: 45 MINUTES (READY IN 8 HOURS 45 MINUTES)
SERVINGS: 8

1   lb lean (at least 80%) ground beef

½   lb bulk Italian pork sausage

1   medium onion, chopped (½ cup)

1   medium green bell pepper, chopped (1 cup)

2   garlic cloves, finely chopped

1   cup finely chopped carrots

1   can (28 oz) Progresso® crushed tomatoes, undrained

1   can (8 oz) tomato sauce

1   can (6 oz) tomato paste

1   tablespoon packed brown sugar

3   teaspoons Italian seasoning

½   teaspoon salt

¼   teaspoon pepper

16 oz uncooked spaghetti

Shredded Parmesan cheese, if desired

1) In 12-inch skillet, cook beef and sausage over medium-high heat 5 to 7 minutes, stirring frequently, until the beef is thoroughly cooked and sausage is no longer pink; drain.

2) In 3- to 4-quart slow cooker, mix beef mixture and all remaining ingredients except spaghetti and Parmesan cheese.

3) Cover; cook on Low heat setting 8 to 10 hours.

4) About 20 minutes before serving, cook and drain spaghetti as directed on package. Serve sauce over cooked spaghetti. Sprinkle with shredded Parmesan cheese.

HIGH ALTITUDE (3500-6500 FT.): No change.

Nutrition Information Per Serving:

Calories:	470	From Fat:	110
Total Fat			12g
Saturated Fat			4g
Trans Fat			0g
Cholesterol			45mg
Sodium			1030mg
Total Carbohydrate			66g
Dietary Fiber			6g
Sugars			11g
Protein			24g

Ground Beef and Mushroom Carbonara

PREP TIME: 30 MINUTES (READY IN 30 MINUTES)
SERVINGS: 6 (1-1/2 CUPS EACH)

12 oz uncooked spaghetti

4 slices bacon

1/2 lb lean (at least 80%) ground beef

1 package (8 oz) sliced fresh mushrooms (3 cups)

1 small onion, chopped (1/4 cup)

4 garlic cloves, finely chopped

1/2 teaspoon salt

1/4 teaspoon pepper

1 cup whipping cream

3 pasteurized eggs, beaten

1 cup grated Parmesan cheese

2 tablespoons chopped fresh parsley

1) In 4-quart Dutch oven, cook and drain spaghetti as directed on package. Rinse spaghetti and return to Dutch oven; cover to keep warm.

2) Meanwhile, in 10-inch skillet, cook bacon over medium-high heat 8 to 9 minutes, turning occasionally, until crisp. Remove bacon from skillet, leaving the drippings in skillet. Drain bacon on paper towel. Crumble bacon.

3) In same skillet, cook the beef, mushrooms, onion, garlic, salt and pepper over medium-high heat 5 to 7 minutes, stirring frequently, until beef is thoroughly cooked; drain.

4) Pour whipping cream over the cooked spaghetti in Dutch oven. Cook over medium-high heat 1 to 2 minutes, stirring constantly, until hot.

5) Add beef mixture, bacon and eggs to spaghetti mixture. Reduce heat to medium. Cook 2 to 3 minutes, tossing mixture constantly, until spaghetti is well coated. Stir in cheese. Garnish with parsley.

HIGH ALTITUDE (3500-6500 FT.): No change.

Nutrition Information Per Serving:	
Calories: 610	From Fat: 270
Total Fat	30g
Saturated Fat	15g
Trans Fat	1g
Cholesterol	195mg
Sodium	920mg
Total Carbohydrate	55g
Dietary Fiber	3g
Sugars	4g
Protein	30g

Mega-Meat Pizza

PREP TIME: 25 MINUTES (READY IN 40 MINUTES)
SERVINGS: 8

- 1 can (11 oz) Pillsbury® refrigerated thin pizza crust
- 1/2 lb lean (at least 80%) ground beef
- 1/2 lb bulk Italian sausage
- 1/2 cup pizza sauce
- 1/2 cup sliced pepperoni
- 1 oz thinly sliced deli salami, cut into quarters
- 1/2 cup diced Canadian bacon
- 1 cup shredded Cheddar cheese (4 oz)
- 1 cup shredded mozzarella cheese (4 oz)

1) Heat oven to 400°F. Spray or grease 15x10-inch or larger dark or nonstick cookie sheet. Unroll dough on cookie sheet; starting at center, press out dough into 15x10-inch rectangle.

2) In 10-inch nonstick skillet, cook beef and sausage over medium-high heat 6 to 8 minutes, stirring frequently, until beef is thoroughly cooked and sausage is no longer pink; drain.

3) Spread pizza sauce to within 1/2 inch of edges of dough. Top with cooked drained meat and remaining ingredients.

4) Bake 13 to 16 minutes or until crust is golden brown and cheese is melted.

HIGH ALTITUDE (3500-6500 FT.): Bake 2 to 4 minutes longer.

Nutrition Information Per Serving:

Calories:	390	From Fat:	210
Total Fat			24g
Saturated Fat			10g
Trans Fat			0g
Cholesterol			65mg
Sodium			960mg
Total Carbohydrate			22g
Dietary Fiber			1g
Sugars			4g
Protein			23g

Coffee-Rubbed Steak

PREP TIME: 10 MINUTES (READY IN 20 MINUTES)
SERVINGS: 8

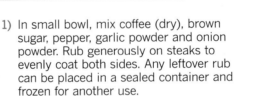 EASY   LOW FAT

1) In small bowl, mix coffee (dry), brown sugar, pepper, garlic powder and onion powder. Rub generously on steaks to evenly coat both sides. Any leftover rub can be placed in a sealed container and frozen for another use.

2) Heat gas or charcoal grill. Place the steaks on grill over medium-high heat. Cover grill; cook 8 to 12 minutes or until desired doneness, turning once. Cut steaks into slices. Season to taste with salt.

HIGH ALTITUDE (3500-6500 FT.): Use medium heat.

Nutrition Information Per Serving:

Calories:	230	From Fat:	50
Total Fat			6g
Saturated Fat			2g
Trans Fat			0g
Cholesterol			100mg
Sodium			50mg
Total Carbohydrate			5g
Dietary Fiber			0g
Sugars			3g
Protein			40g

- 1/4 cup finely ground coffee beans or espresso powder
- 2 tablespoons packed brown sugar
- 2 teaspoons coarse ground black pepper
- 1 teaspoon garlic powder
- 1 teaspoon onion powder
- 2 boneless beef top sirloin steaks, 1 inch thick (1 1/4 to 1 1/2 lb each)

tip
To broil the steaks, place them on a broiler pan. Broil with the tops 4 to 6 inches from the heat, using the times in the recipe as a guide, turning once.

Grilled Meat-Loaf Patties

PREP TIME: 55 MINUTES (READY IN 55 MINUTES)
SERVINGS: 6

½ cup ketchup

1 tablespoon honey

1 teaspoon Worcestershire sauce

1 teaspoon garlic salt

1 teaspoon pepper

1 egg

1 small onion, finely chopped (¼ cup)

¾ cup Progresso® plain bread crumbs

1½ lb lean (at least 80%) ground beef

6 slices bacon

6 slices crusty white bread, if desired

1) Heat gas or charcoal grill for indirect cooking as directed by manufacturer.

2) In small bowl, mix ¼ cup of the ketchup and the honey; set aside. In large bowl, mix remaining ¼ cup ketchup, the Worcestershire sauce, garlic salt, pepper and egg. Stir in onion and plain bread crumbs. Stir in beef until well mixed.

3) Shape the beef mixture into 6 patties, ¾ inch thick and about 3½ inches in diameter. Wrap 1 slice bacon around each patty; secure with toothpick.

4) Carefully spray grill rack with cooking spray. Place patties on unheated side of two-burner gas grill or over drip pan on charcoal grill (medium heat). (If using one-burner gas grill, cook over low heat.) Cover grill; cook 20 to 25 minutes or until slightly pink in center. Using spatula, turn patties over. Brush with the ketchup mixture. Cover grill; cook 5 to 8 minutes longer or until meat thermometer inserted in center of patties reads 160°F and bacon is crisp. Serve on bread.

HIGH ALTITUDE (3500-6500 FT.): No change.

Nutrition Information Per Serving:

Calories:	340	From Fat:	160
Total Fat			18g
Saturated Fat			6g
Trans Fat			1g
Cholesterol			115mg
Sodium			750mg
Total Carbohydrate			20g
Dietary Fiber			1g
Sugars			9g
Protein			26g

Cheese-Stuffed Meatballs and Spaghetti

PREP TIME: 35 MINUTES (READY IN 2 HOURS 5 MINUTES)
SERVINGS: 6

4 sticks (1 oz each) mozzarella string cheese, cut into 18 (³/₄-inch) cubes

¹/₂ cup Progresso® Italian-style bread crumbs

1 jar (48 oz) tomato pasta sauce (any variety)

1¹/₂ lb lean (at least 80%) ground beef

2 tablespoons finely chopped onion

¹/₂ teaspoon salt

¹/₂ teaspoon dried oregano leaves

1 egg

12 oz uncooked spaghetti

²/₃ cup shredded fresh Parmesan cheese

1) Place cheese cubes in small resealable freezer plastic bag; seal bag and freeze at least 1 hour.

2) Heat oven to 375°F. Line 15x10x1-inch pan with foil; spray foil with cooking spray. In large bowl, mix bread crumbs and 3 tablespoons of the pasta sauce. Stir in beef, onion, salt, oregano and egg. Shape mixture into 18 (2-inch) balls. Press 1 cheese cube into center of each ball, sealing it inside. Gently place in pan. Bake 10 minutes.

3) Meanwhile, pour the remaining pasta sauce into 5-quart Dutch oven. Cover; heat to simmering over medium-high heat, stirring frequently. Gently stir in meatballs; reduce heat to medium-low. Cover; simmer about 10 minutes, stirring occasionally, until meatballs are thoroughly cooked and no longer pink in center.

4) Meanwhile, cook and drain spaghetti as directed on package; keep warm. Serve meatballs and sauce over spaghetti. Serve with Parmesan cheese.

HIGH ALTITUDE (3500-6500 FT.): In Step 3, cover and heat the pasta sauce to simmering over medium-low heat. After adding meatballs, cover and simmer 15 to 20 minutes.

Nutrition Information Per Serving:	
Calories: 850	From Fat: 850
Total Fat	30g
Saturated Fat	11g
Trans Fat	1g
Cholesterol	125mg
Sodium	2050mg
Total Carbohydrate	99g
Dietary Fiber	6g
Sugars	25g
Protein	44g

Mediterranean Stuffed Burgers

PREP TIME: 40 MINUTES (READY IN 40 MINUTES)
SERVINGS: 6 SANDWICHES

3 plum (Roma) tomatoes, seeded, chopped

2 tablespoons finely chopped sweet onion

2 teaspoons red wine vinegar

1/2 teaspoon salt

1 tablespoon chopped fresh oregano leaves

1 cup crumbled feta cheese (4 oz)

1 1/2 teaspoons grated fresh lemon peel

1 teaspoon olive or vegetable oil

2 lb lean (at least 80%) ground beef

2 tablespoons garlic-pepper blend

6 burger buns, split

1) Heat gas or charcoal grill. In medium bowl, mix tomatoes, onion, vinegar, salt and 2 teaspoons of the oregano. Let stand at room temperature until burgers are ready to eat.

2) Meanwhile, in small bowl, mix remaining 1 teaspoon oregano, the cheese, lemon peel and oil; set aside.

3) In large bowl, sprinkle the beef with garlic-pepper blend; gently mix until well blended. Shape the mixture into 6 balls. Using end of thumb, make a deep depression in each ball, but do not push all the way through. Spoon about 1 tablespoon cheese mixture into each depression. Gently shape beef around cheese mixture, sealing it inside. Press balls to form patties, 1/4 inch thick and about 5 inches in diameter.

4) Place patties on grill over medium heat. Cover grill; cook 12 to 16 minutes, turning once, until meat thermometer inserted in the center of beef reads 160°F. Place burgers on bottoms of buns; spoon the tomato mixture over burgers. Top with tops of buns.

HIGH ALTITUDE (3500-6500 FT.): Cook over medium-low heat.

Nutrition Information Per Serving:		
Calories: 450	From Fat: 210	
Total Fat		24g
Saturated Fat		10g
Trans Fat		1.5g
Cholesterol		110mg
Sodium		690mg
Total Carbohydrate		25g
Dietary Fiber		2g
Sugars		4g
Protein		33g

Asian Salmon

PREP TIME: 45 MINUTES (READY IN 55 MINUTES)
SERVINGS: 8

2/3 cup teriyaki marinade and sauce

1/4 cup apricot preserves

1/4 cup water

2 tablespoons sesame or canola oil

4 teaspoons grated gingerroot

2 teaspoons Dijon mustard

4 medium garlic cloves, finely chopped (2 1/2 teaspoons)

3 lb salmon fillets

2 medium green onions, thinly sliced (2 tablespoons)

1 tablespoon sesame seed, toasted

1) Heat oven to 425°F. Line 15x10x1-inch pan with foil; spray foil with cooking spray.

2) In 2-quart saucepan, stir together teriyaki sauce, preserves, water, oil, gingerroot, mustard and garlic. Heat to boiling over medium-high heat, stirring occasionally. Reduce heat to low; simmer uncovered 5 minutes, stirring occasionally, until slightly thickened.

3) Rinse salmon fillets; pat dry with paper towels. Place salmon, skin sides down, in pan. Spoon 1/2 cup sauce mixture over salmon.

4) Bake uncovered 20 to 25 minutes, rotating the pan after 10 minutes, until salmon flakes easily with fork.

5) Meanwhile, heat remaining sauce mixture to boiling. Reduce heat to low; simmer uncovered 5 minutes, stirring occasionally, until thickened and reduced to about 1/2 cup.

6) Carefully transfer salmon to serving platter. Drizzle with thickened sauce mixture. Sprinkle with onions and sesame seed.

HIGH ALTITUDE (3500-6500 FT.): In Step 2, add more water, 1 teaspoon at a time, if sauce becomes too thick.

Nutrition Information Per Serving:	
Calories: 280	From Fat: 110
Total Fat	12g
Saturated Fat	3g
Trans Fat	0g
Cholesterol	95mg
Sodium	940mg
Total Carbohydrate	11g
Dietary Fiber	0g
Sugars	8g
Protein	32g

Italian Pork Tenderloin with Roasted Sweet Potatoes

PREP TIME: 15 MINUTES (READY IN 50 MINUTES)
SERVINGS: 6

ⓔ EASY

VEGETABLES

- 2 tablespoons olive or vegetable oil
- 2 teaspoons Italian seasoning
- ½ teaspoon seasoned salt
- 3 garlic cloves, finely chopped (about 1½ teaspoons)
- 3 large dark-orange sweet potatoes (about 2 lb), peeled, cut into 1-inch chunks
- 2 medium yellow onions, cut into 8 wedges each

PORK

- 2 pork tenderloins (about 1 lb each)
- 1 tablespoon olive or vegetable oil
- 2 teaspoons Italian seasoning
- ½ teaspoon seasoned salt
- 2 tablespoons grated Parmesan cheese
- 2 tablespoons chopped fresh parsley, if desired

1) Heat oven to 425°F. In large bowl, mix 2 tablespoons oil, 2 teaspoons Italian seasoning, ½ teaspoon seasoned salt and the garlic. Add sweet potatoes and onion wedges; toss to coat. Spread in 15x10x1-inch pan. Roast uncovered 10 minutes.

2) Meanwhile, brush the pork tenderloins with 1 tablespoon oil. In small bowl, stir together 2 teaspoons Italian seasoning, ½ teaspoon seasoned salt and the Parmesan cheese.

3) Move vegetables to center of pan; place 1 pork tenderloin on each side. Sprinkle seasoning mixture evenly over pork. Insert ovenproof meat thermometer so tip is in thickest part of pork.

4) Roast uncovered 20 to 25 minutes longer or until thermometer reads 155°F. Cover pan with foil; let stand 5 minutes or until thermometer reads 160°F. (Temperature will continue to rise about 5°F, and pork will be easier to carve.)

5) Cut pork into 1-inch-thick slices; arrange on platter with sweet potatoes and onions. Sprinkle with parsley.

HIGH ALTITUDE (3500-6500 FT.): No change.

Nutrition Information Per Serving:	
Calories: 360	From Fat: 120
Total Fat	13g
Saturated Fat	3.5g
Trans Fat	0g
Cholesterol	95mg
Sodium	370mg
Total Carbohydrate	24g
Dietary Fiber	4g
Sugars	8g
Protein	37g

Ground Beef- and Corn-Topped Potato Skins

PREP TIME:	25 MINUTES (READY IN 25 MINUTES)
SERVINGS:	4

e EASY **f** LOW FAT

2 large baking potatoes

1/4 cup chive-and-onion sour cream potato topper (from 12-oz container)

1/2 lb lean (at least 80%) ground beef

1/2 teaspoon salt

1/4 teaspoon pepper

1 cup Green Giant® Niblets® frozen whole kernel corn

1 can (8 oz) tomato sauce

2 green onions, sliced (about 2 tablespoons)

1 plum (Roma) tomato, chopped

Thinly sliced chives, if desired

1) Pierce potatoes with fork; place on microwavable paper towel in microwave oven. Microwave on High 8 to 10 minutes, turning after 4 to 5 minutes, until tender. Let stand about 5 minutes until cool enough to handle.

2) Cut potatoes in half lengthwise. Scoop out about 2 tablespoons of pulp from center of each half; place in medium bowl. Reserve potato shells. Mash pulp with fork. Stir in sour cream; set aside.

3) Meanwhile, in 10-inch skillet, cook beef, salt and pepper over medium-high heat 5 to 7 minutes, stirring frequently, until beef is thoroughly cooked; drain. Stir in corn, tomato sauce, onions and plum tomato. Cook 3 to 4 minutes, stirring occasionally, until hot and bubbly.

4) Spoon beef mixture into potato shells. Top each with about 1/4 cup potato and sour cream mixture. Place on microwavable platter. Microwave uncovered on High 4 to 6 minutes or until thoroughly heated. Serve immediately. Top with chives.

HIGH ALTITUDE (3500-6500 FT.): No change.

Nutrition Information Per Serving:

Calories:	290	From Fat:	90
Total Fat			10g
Saturated Fat			4g
Trans Fat			0.5g
Cholesterol			45mg
Sodium			630mg
Total Carbohydrate			36g
Dietary Fiber			4g
Sugars			6g
Protein			14g

Honey-Glazed Chicken and Carrots

PREP TIME: 30 MINUTES (READY IN 30 MINUTES)
SERVINGS: 4 (1-1/2 CUPS EACH)

1) Cook and drain egg noodles as directed on package.

2) Meanwhile, in 12-inch skillet, heat oil over medium-high heat. Add chicken, bacon, onion and carrots. Cook 8 to 10 minutes, stirring occasionally and turning chicken once, until chicken is browned.

3) Stir in honey, vinegar and thyme. Reduce heat to medium. Cover; cook 5 minutes. Uncover; cook 5 to 8 minutes longer, stirring frequently, until vegetables are tender and juice of chicken is clear when center of thickest part is cut (180°F). Serve over noodles.

HIGH ALTITUDE (3500-6500 FT.): No change.

3 cups uncooked egg noodles (6 oz)

1 tablespoon olive or vegetable oil

1 package (20 oz) boneless skinless chicken thighs (5 or 6 thighs)

2 slices uncooked bacon, cut into ³/₄-inch pieces

1 medium onion, coarsely chopped (1 cup)

2 cups ready-to-eat baby-cut carrots

¹/₂ cup honey

¹/₄ cup red wine vinegar

¹/₂ teaspoon dried thyme leaves

Nutrition Information Per Serving:	
Calories: 630	From Fat: 200
Total Fat	22g
Saturated Fat	6g
Trans Fat	0g
Cholesterol	130mg
Sodium	410mg
Total Carbohydrate	71g
Dietary Fiber	3g
Sugars	39g
Protein	37g

Spaetzle dumplings are a nice substitute for the egg noodles. Look for packages of dried spaetzle near the noodles in your supermarket.

Ground Beef Risotto

PREP TIME: 35 MINUTES (READY IN 35 MINUTES)
SERVINGS: 4 (1-3/4 CUPS EACH)

1 lb lean (at least 80%) ground beef

1 small onion, chopped (¹/₄ cup)

2 garlic cloves, finely chopped

¹/₄ teaspoon pepper

1 cup uncooked Arborio or regular long-grain white rice

3¹/₂ cups Progresso® beef-flavored broth (from 32-oz carton)

¹/₂ cup shredded carrot

¹/₂ cup shredded fresh Parmesan cheese

3 tablespoons chopped fresh chives

1) In 12-inch nonstick skillet, cook beef, onion, garlic and pepper over medium-high heat 5 to 7 minutes, stirring occasionally, until beef is thoroughly cooked; drain if desired. Stir in rice; cook 2 minutes, stirring constantly.

2) Stir in broth; heat to boiling. Reduce heat to medium-low. Cover; simmer 10 minutes.

3) Stir in carrot. Cook uncovered 5 to 7 minutes longer or until liquid is absorbed.

4) Remove skillet from heat. Stir in cheese. Cover; let stand 3 minutes. Sprinkle with the chives.

HIGH ALTITUDE (3500-6500 FT.): In Step 2, cover and simmer 20 minutes.

Nutrition Information Per Serving:	
Calories: 180	From Fat: 15
Total Fat	1.5g
Saturated Fat	0.5g
Trans Fat	0g
Cholesterol	5mg
Sodium	60mg
Total Carbohydrate	37g
Dietary Fiber	4g
Sugars	30g
Protein	4g

Slow Cooker Sensations

Put a hot, hearty dinner on the fast track—let
your slow cooker do most of the work for you!

GINGERED BROCCOLI CHICKEN
PG. 190

ITALIAN MEATBALL HEROES
PG. 181

SPICY CHUNKY BEEF CHILI
PG. 193

FRENCH DIP
SANDWICHES
PG. 183

Chicken with Tomatoes and Artichokes

PREP TIME: 15 MINUTES (READY IN 4 HOURS 45 MINUTES)
SERVINGS: 4

ⓔ EASY   **ⓛⓕ LOW FAT**

4 bone-in chicken breasts (2½ lb)

3 tablespoons fat-free balsamic or Italian vinaigrette dressing

1 teaspoon Italian seasoning

½ teaspoon salt

¼ teaspoon pepper

½ large onion, thinly sliced (1 cup)

¼ cup sliced green olives

4 garlic cloves, finely chopped

1 can (14.5 oz) diced tomatoes, drained

1 can (14 oz) quartered artichokes, drained

2 to 3 tablespoons chopped fresh parsley

1) Spray 3- to 4-quart slow cooker with cooking spray. Remove skin and any fat from the chicken. Brush chicken with the dressing; place in slow cooker. Sprinkle with Italian seasoning, salt and pepper. Top with the remaining ingredients except parsley.

2) Cover and cook on Low heat setting 4 hours 30 minutes to 5 hours 30 minutes.

3) Skim off any fat from the top of mixture in slow cooker. Serve chicken and tomato mixture in shallow bowls; sprinkle with parsley.

Nutrition Information Per Serving:

Calories:	360	From Fat:	80
Total Fat		9g	
Saturated Fat		2g	
Trans Fat		0g	
Cholesterol		125mg	
Sodium		1030mg	
Total Carbohydrate		21g	
Dietary Fiber		9g	
Sugars		6g	
Protein		50g	

Pot Roast with Creamy Dill Sauce

PREP TIME: 30 MINUTES (READY IN 9 HOURS 30 MINUTES)
SERVINGS: 8

POT ROAST

2 tablespoons all-purpose flour

1 teaspoon salt

1/4 teaspoon white pepper

1 boneless beef pot roast (about 2 lb), trimmed of fat

1 cup Progresso® beef-flavored broth (from 32-oz carton)

1 tablespoon Dijon mustard

4 garlic cloves, finely chopped

1/2 teaspoon dried dill weed

1 large onion, cut into 12 wedges

1 bag (16 oz) ready-to-eat baby-cut carrots

4 medium Yukon gold potatoes (about 1 1/4 lb), unpeeled, cut into 1-inch cubes

1/2 teaspoon lemon-pepper seasoning

SAUCE

2 tablespoons all-purpose flour

2 tablespoons water

1 teaspoon dried dill weed

1 cup fat-free sour cream

1) On sheet of waxed paper or in shallow bowl, mix 2 tablespoons flour, the salt and white pepper. Place the beef on flour mixture; turn to coat evenly.

2) Spray 5- to 6-quart slow cooker with cooking spray. Heat 12-inch nonstick skillet over medium-high heat. Add beef to skillet; cook about 5 minutes, turning once, until golden brown on both sides. Place in slow cooker.

3) In small bowl, mix broth, mustard, garlic and dill weed. Pour over beef in slow cooker. Place onion, carrots and potatoes on top of beef. Sprinkle with lemon-pepper seasoning. Cover; cook on Low heat setting 9 to 10 hours.

4) Remove the beef and vegetables from slow cooker; place on large serving platter and cover to keep warm. In small bowl, beat all sauce ingredients except sour cream with wire whisk until smooth.

5) Strain any fat from liquid in slow cooker. Pour liquid into 1-quart saucepan; heat to boiling over high heat. Stir flour mixture into hot liquid; cook 2 to 3 minutes, stirring constantly, until thickened. Remove from heat; stir in sour cream.

6) Cut the beef into 8 serving pieces. Serve the dill sauce with the beef and vegetables.

Nutrition Information Per Serving:		
Calories: 320	From Fat:	110
Total Fat		12g
Saturated Fat		4.5g
Trans Fat		0.5g
Cholesterol		60mg
Sodium		610mg
Total Carbohydrate		28g
Dietary Fiber		4g
Sugars		6g
Protein		22g

Gingered Carrot Soup

PREP TIME: 15 MINUTES (READY IN 8 HOURS 35 MINUTES)
SERVINGS: 9 (1 CUP EACH)

e EASY · f LOW FAT

2 bags (1 lb each) ready-to-eat baby-cut carrots

2 large onions, chopped (about 2 cups)

5¼ cups Progresso® chicken broth (from two 32-oz cartons)

½ teaspoon salt

½ cup whipping cream

½ cup orange juice

3 tablespoons packed brown sugar

2 tablespoons grated gingerroot

¼ teaspoon white pepper

Fresh orange slices, quartered, if desired

Fresh Italian parsley, if desired

1) Spray 4- to 5-quart slow cooker with cooking spray. In slow cooker, mix carrots, onions, broth and salt.

2) Cover; cook on Low heat setting 8 to 10 hours.

3) Pour 4 cups of the soup mixture into blender; add half each of the whipping cream, orange juice, brown sugar, gingerroot and pepper. Cover and blend until smooth; return to slow cooker. Blend remaining soup mixture with the remaining half of ingredients; return to slow cooker.

4) Increase heat setting to High. Cover; cook 15 to 20 minutes longer or until hot. Garnish individual servings with an orange quarter and parsley.

Nutrition Information Per Serving:

Calories:	130	From Fat:	40
Total Fat			4.5g
Saturated Fat			2.5g
Trans Fat			0g
Cholesterol			15mg
Sodium			700mg
Total Carbohydrate			20g
Dietary Fiber			3g
Sugars			13g
Protein			3g

Harvest Pork Stew

PREP TIME: 20 MINUTES (READY IN 8 HOURS 20 MINUTES)
SERVINGS: 8 (1-1/2 CUPS EACH)

EASY

2 lb boneless pork shoulder roast, trimmed of fat, cut into 1-inch pieces

2 medium parsnips (about 12 oz), peeled, chopped (about 2 cups)

1 large red onion, cut into 1-inch pieces (about 3 cups)

1 cup dried apricots (6 oz)

1 cup pitted dried plums (6 oz)

1/4 cup all-purpose flour

1/2 teaspoon salt

1/2 teaspoon pepper

1/4 teaspoon ground cloves

3 1/2 cups Progresso® chicken broth (from 32-oz carton)

1 cup apple cider

2 large Golden Delicious apples (about 1 1/4 lb)

1) Spray 5- to 6-quart slow cooker with cooking spray. In slow cooker, mix pork, parsnips, onion, apricots and plums. Add flour, salt, pepper and cloves; toss until pork, vegetables and fruit are coated. Add broth and cider; mix well. Cover; cook on Low heat setting 7 to 9 hours.

2) Core apples; cut each into large chunks. Stir apples into stew. Cover; cook on Low heat setting 1 hour longer. Stir well before serving.

Nutrition Information Per Serving:

Calories:	440	From Fat:	130
Total Fat			14g
Saturated Fat			5g
Trans Fat			0g
Cholesterol			75mg
Sodium			570mg
Total Carbohydrate			51g
Dietary Fiber			7g
Sugars			33g
Protein			28g

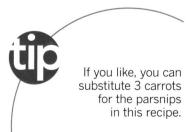

tip

If you like, you can substitute 3 carrots for the parsnips in this recipe.

Chicken Marsala

PREP TIME: 10 MINUTES (READY IN 5 HOURS 25 MINUTES)
SERVINGS: 8

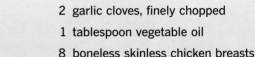 **EASY**   **LOW FAT**

2 garlic cloves, finely chopped

1 tablespoon vegetable oil

8 boneless skinless chicken breasts

1/2 teaspoon salt

1/2 teaspoon pepper

2 jars (6 oz each) Green Giant® sliced mushrooms, drained

1 cup sweet Marsala wine or Progresso® chicken broth (from 32-oz carton)

1/2 cup water

1/4 cup cornstarch

3 tablespoons chopped fresh parsley

1) Spray 4- to 5-quart slow cooker with cooking spray. In slow cooker, place the garlic and oil. Sprinkle chicken with salt and pepper; place in slow cooker over garlic. Place mushrooms over chicken; pour wine over all.

2) Cover; cook on Low heat setting 5 to 6 hours.

3) Remove chicken from slow cooker; place on plate and cover to keep warm. In small bowl, mix water and cornstarch until smooth; stir into liquid in slow cooker. Increase heat setting to High; cover and cook about 10 minutes or until sauce is slightly thickened.

4) Return chicken to slow cooker. Cover; cook on High heat setting 5 minutes longer or until chicken is hot.

5) To serve, spoon mushroom mixture over chicken breasts; sprinkle with parsley.

Nutrition Information Per Serving:		
Calories: 190	From Fat:	50
Total Fat		6g
Saturated Fat		1.5g
Trans Fat		0g
Cholesterol		70mg
Sodium		360mg
Total Carbohydrate		7g
Dietary Fiber		1g
Sugars		1g
Protein		26g

Italian Sausages and Peppers with Rotini

PREP TIME: 15 MINUTES (READY IN 6 HOURS 15 MINUTES)
SERVINGS: 6

EASY

1 package (19.5 oz) turkey Italian sausages, cut into 1-inch pieces

1 cup finely chopped sweet onion

4 garlic cloves, finely chopped (2 teaspoons)

2 medium yellow bell peppers, cut into 1/2-inch pieces

2 medium red bell peppers, cut into 1/2-inch pieces

1 jar (26 oz) tomato pasta sauce

4 1/2 cups uncooked rotini pasta (12 oz)

6 tablespoons shredded Parmesan cheese

Nutrition Information Per Serving:	
Calories: 630	From Fat: 180
Total Fat	20g
Saturated Fat	5g
Trans Fat	0g
Cholesterol	60mg
Sodium	1840mg
Total Carbohydrate	86g
Dietary Fiber	6g
Sugars	18g
Protein	28g

1) Spray 3- to 4-quart slow cooker with cooking spray. In slow cooker, mix all ingredients except pasta and cheese. Cover; cook on Low heat setting 6 to 8 hours.

2) Cook and drain pasta as directed on package. Serve sausage mixture over pasta; sprinkle with Parmesan cheese.

Slow Cooker Barbecued Beans

PREP TIME: 20 MINUTES (READY IN 3 HOURS 20 MINUTES)
SERVINGS: 12 (1/2 CUP EACH)

EASY **LOW FAT**

1/2 lb bacon, cut into 1/2-inch pieces

1 medium onion, chopped (1/2 cup)

1 cup ketchup

1/2 cup packed brown sugar

1/4 cup mild-flavor (light) molasses

1 tablespoon cider vinegar

1 teaspoon ground mustard

2 cans (15.5 oz each) great northern beans, drained, rinsed

2 cans (15 oz each) black beans, drained, 1/2 cup liquid reserved

Nutrition Information Per Serving:	
Calories: 290	From Fat: 25
Total Fat	3g
Saturated Fat	1g
Trans Fat	0g
Cholesterol	5mg
Sodium	590mg
Total Carbohydrate	51g
Dietary Fiber	10g
Sugars	18g
Protein	13g

1) In 10-inch skillet, cook the bacon and onion over medium heat, stirring occasionally, until bacon is crisp and onions are tender; drain.

2) In 3 1/2- to 4-quart slow cooker, mix the bacon, onions and remaining ingredients, including reserved liquid. Cover; cook on Low heat setting 3 to 4 hours.

Green Chile Pulled-Pork Burritos

PREP TIME: 10 MINUTES (READY IN 8 HOURS 10 MINUTES)
SERVINGS: 14 BURRITOS

ⓔ EASY

1 to 2 tablespoons chipotle chili pepper powder

1 tablespoon vegetable oil

1 teaspoon salt

1 boneless pork loin roast (2½ lb), trimmed of fat

1 poblano chile, chopped

1 jar (16 oz) Old El Paso® Thick 'n Chunky green chile salsa

12 Old El Paso® flour tortillas for burritos (8 inch; from two 11-oz packages)

1 cup guacamole

1 cup sour cream, if desired

1) Spray 4- to 5-quart slow cooker with cooking spray. In small bowl, mix chili pepper powder, oil and salt. Rub mixture over pork; place in slow cooker. Sprinkle with poblano chile. Pour salsa over top.

2) Cover; cook on Low heat setting 8 to 10 hours.

3) Remove the pork from slow cooker; place on cutting board. Shred the pork with 2 forks; return to slow cooker and mix well.

4) Using slotted spoon, spoon about ½ cup pork mixture onto each tortilla; top with about 1 tablespoon each guacamole and sour cream. Fold one side of tortilla up about 1 inch over filling; fold right and left sides over folded end, overlapping. Fold remaining end down.

Nutrition Information Per Serving:

Calories: 280		From Fat: 110
Total Fat		12g
Saturated Fat		3.5g
Trans Fat		1g
Cholesterol		50mg
Sodium		780mg
Total Carbohydrate		21g
Dietary Fiber		1g
Sugars		1g
Protein		21g

Tuscan Pot Roast

PREP TIME: 15 MINUTES (READY IN 8 HOURS 25 MINUTES)
SERVINGS: 8

🅔 EASY   🕕 LOW FAT

1 package (1 oz) dried porcini mushrooms

1 cup hot water

2 garlic cloves, finely chopped

1 tablespoon grated lemon peel

1 teaspoon dried oregano leaves

1/2 teaspoon salt

1 boneless beef rump roast (2 1/2 lb), trimmed of fat

1 can (14.5 oz) diced tomatoes, undrained

1 cup frozen small whole onions (from 1-lb bag), thawed

1/2 cup dry red wine or Progresso® beef-flavored broth (from 32-oz carton)

1) In small bowl, place mushrooms and hot water; let stand 10 minutes.

2) Meanwhile, spray 4- to 5-quart slow cooker with cooking spray. In small bowl, mix garlic, lemon peel, oregano and salt. Rub the mixture over the beef; place in slow cooker.

3) Drain mushrooms; coarsely chop. Top beef with mushrooms, tomatoes, thawed onions and wine. Cover; cook on Low heat setting 8 to 9 hours.

4) Remove beef from slow cooker; place on cutting board. Cover; let stand 10 minutes. Cut beef into 8 serving pieces; serve with tomato mixture.

Nutrition Information Per Serving:		
Calories: 200	From Fat:	40
Total Fat		4.5g
Saturated Fat		1.5g
Trans Fat		0g
Cholesterol		75mg
Sodium		260mg
Total Carbohydrate		7g
Dietary Fiber		1g
Sugars		3g
Protein		31g

Veggie Marinara

PREP TIME: 20 MINUTES (READY IN 4 HOURS 20 MINUTES)
SERVINGS: 8

EASY   **LOW FAT**

1 bag (12 oz) frozen sausage-style soy-protein crumbles, thawed

2 cups sliced fresh mushrooms

1 cup grape tomatoes, cut in half

1 can (28 oz) Progresso® crushed tomatoes, undrained

1 can (6 oz) tomato paste

1/2 cup water

1/4 cup dry red wine or water

2 tablespoons honey

3 garlic cloves, finely chopped (1 1/2 teaspoons)

1 teaspoon dried basil leaves

1 teaspoon crushed red pepper flakes

1/2 teaspoon salt

1/2 teaspoon dried oregano leaves

1/2 teaspoon fennel seed

16 oz uncooked multigrain spaghetti

2 tablespoons shredded Parmesan cheese

1) Spray 3- to 4-quart slow cooker with cooking spray. In slow cooker, mix all ingredients except spaghetti and Parmesan cheese. Cover; cook on Low heat setting 4 to 5 hours.

2) Cook and drain the spaghetti as directed on the package. Serve sauce over spaghetti; sprinkle with cheese.

Nutrition Information Per Serving:

Calories:	350	From Fat:	25
Total Fat			3g
Saturated Fat			0.5g
Trans Fat			0g
Cholesterol			0mg
Sodium			890mg
Total Carbohydrate			60g
Dietary Fiber			7g
Sugars			12g
Protein			19g

Italian Meatball Heroes

PREP TIME: 10 MINUTES (READY IN 6 HOURS 10 MINUTES)
SERVINGS: 12 SANDWICHES

e EASY

- 2 bags (16 oz each) frozen cooked Italian-style meatballs, thawed
- 2 jars (26 oz each) tomato pasta sauce
- 1 jar (8 oz) sliced pepperoncini peppers (Italian peppers), drained
- 12 slices (1 oz each) provolone cheese, cut in half
- 12 hoagie buns, split
- 2 tablespoons chopped fresh basil leaves

1) Spray 3- to 4-quart slow cooker with cooking spray. In slow cooker, gently mix the thawed meatballs, pasta sauce and sliced peppers.

2) Cover; cook on Low heat setting 6 to 8 hours.

3) Place 2 cheese half-slices on the bottom half of each bun. Spoon about 5 meatballs and pasta sauce over the cheese on each. Sprinkle each with about $1/2$ teaspoon basil. Cover with top halves of buns.

Nutrition Information Per Serving:

Calories: 690	From Fat: 240
Total Fat	26g
Saturated Fat	10g
Trans Fat	1.5g
Cholesterol	100mg
Sodium	1750mg
Total Carbohydrate	79g
Dietary Fiber	4g
Sugars	21g
Protein	33g

Grandma's Chicken Noodle Soup

PREP TIME: 15 MINUTES (READY IN 6 HOURS 55 MINUTES)
SERVINGS: 6

ⓔ EASY   ⓕ LOW FAT

3/4 lb boneless skinless chicken thighs, cut into 1-inch pieces

2 medium stalks celery (with leaves), sliced (1¼ cups)

1 large carrot, chopped (¾ cup)

1 medium onion, chopped (½ cup)

1 can (14.5 oz) diced tomatoes, undrained

1¾ cups Progresso® chicken broth (from 32-oz carton)

1 teaspoon dried thyme leaves

1 box (9 oz) Green Giant® frozen baby sweet peas

1 cup frozen home-style egg noodles (from 12-oz bag)

1) Spray 10-inch skillet with cooking spray; heat over medium heat until hot. Add the chicken pieces; cook about 5 minutes, stirring frequently, until browned.

2) Spray 3- to 4-quart slow cooker with cooking spray. In slow cooker, mix chicken and remaining ingredients except peas and noodles. Cover; cook on Low heat setting 6 hours 30 minutes to 7 hours.

3) Stir in the peas and frozen noodles. Cover; cook on Low heat setting about 10 minutes longer or until noodles are tender.

Nutrition Information Per Serving:

Calories:	210	From Fat:	50
Total Fat			5g
Saturated Fat			1.5g
Trans Fat			0g
Cholesterol			60mg
Sodium			430mg
Total Carbohydrate			22g
Dietary Fiber			3g
Sugars			6g
Protein			17g

Brown Lentil Soup

PREP TIME: 15 MINUTES (READY IN 8 HOURS 15 MINUTES)
SERVINGS: 7 (1-1/2 CUPS EACH)

ⓔ EASY   ⓕ LOW FAT

1 bag (1 lb) dried brown lentils, sorted, rinsed

2 medium carrots, chopped (about 1 cup)

1 large onion, chopped (about 1 cup)

3 garlic cloves, finely chopped

2 cartons (32 oz each) Progresso® chicken broth (8 cups)

1 can (6 oz) tomato paste

½ cup dry sherry or Progresso® chicken broth

1½ teaspoons ground cumin

1 teaspoon dried thyme leaves

Nutrition Information Per Serving:

Calories:	280	From Fat:	10
Total Fat			1g
Saturated Fat			0g
Trans Fat			0g
Cholesterol			0mg
Sodium			1180mg
Total Carbohydrate			47g
Dietary Fiber			12g
Sugars			7g
Protein			21g

1) Spray 5- to 6-quart slow cooker with cooking spray. In slow cooker, mix ingredients.

2) Cover and cook on Low heat setting 8 to 10 hours. Stir the soup well before serving.

French Dip Sandwiches

PREP TIME: 15 MINUTES (READY IN 8 HOURS 15 MINUTES)
SERVINGS: 12 SANDWICHES

e EASY

- 1 large sweet onion, sliced
- 1¾ cups Progresso® beef-flavored broth (from 32-oz carton)
- 1 boneless beef rump roast (4 lb), trimmed of fat
- 2 tablespoons balsamic vinegar
- 1 package (0.7 oz) Italian dressing mix
- ½ teaspoon salt
- ¼ teaspoon freshly ground black pepper
- 12 hoagie buns, split
- 1 large green bell pepper, cut into thin strips
- 12 slices (1 oz each) provolone cheese, cut in half

1) Spray 3- to 4-quart slow cooker with cooking spray. In slow cooker, place onion; add broth. Brush all surfaces of beef roast with vinegar. Place on onions. Sprinkle with Italian dressing mix, salt and pepper.

2) Cover; cook on Low heat setting 8 to 10 hours.

3) Remove beef from slow cooker; place on cutting board. Cut beef across grain into thin slices. Return slices to slow cooker; mix well.

4) Spoon beef onto bottoms halves of buns. Top each with bell pepper, cheese and top half of bun. Serve sandwiches with juices from slow cooker.

Nutrition Information Per Serving:

Calories:	550	From Fat:	150
Total Fat		16g	
Saturated Fat		7g	
Trans Fat		1g	
Cholesterol		100mg	
Sodium		1180mg	
Total Carbohydrate		51g	
Dietary Fiber		2g	
Sugars		9g	
Protein		49g	

Rosemary-Mushroom Chicken Soup

PREP TIME: 20 MINUTES (READY IN 8 HOURS 20 MINUTES)
SERVINGS: 8 (1-1/3 CUPS EACH)

e EASY

$2^1/_2$ lb boneless skinless chicken thighs, cut into $1^1/_2$-inch pieces

6 oz fresh portabella mushroom caps, cut in half lengthwise, then sliced crosswise (about 3 cups)

3 cups sliced fresh shiitake mushrooms (about 6 oz)

3 large shallots, sliced (about $1^1/_2$ cups)

2 garlic cloves, finely chopped

$^1/_4$ cup all-purpose flour

1 tablespoon chopped fresh rosemary leaves

$^1/_2$ teaspoon salt

$^1/_4$ teaspoon pepper

1 carton (32 oz) Progresso® chicken broth (4 cups)

3 tablespoons Dijon mustard

1) Spray 4- to 5-quart slow cooker with cooking spray. In slow cooker, mix chicken, portabella and shiitake mushrooms, shallots and garlic. Add flour, rosemary, salt and pepper; toss until chicken and vegetables are coated. Stir in broth and mustard until well mixed.

2) Cover and cook on Low heat setting 8 to 10 hours. Stir the soup well before serving.

Nutrition Information Per Serving:

Calories:	290	From Fat:	110
Total Fat			12g
Saturated Fat			3.5g
Trans Fat			0g
Cholesterol			85mg
Sodium			800mg
Total Carbohydrate			13g
Dietary Fiber			1g
Sugars			2g
Protein			33g

Pot Roast and Vegetables

PREP TIME: 25 MINUTES (READY IN 8 HOURS 25 MINUTES)
SERVINGS: 4   LOW FAT

1 tablespoon all-purpose flour

1/2 teaspoon salt

1/8 teaspoon pepper

1 1/2 lb boneless beef top round steak (1/2 inch thick), cut into 4 equal pieces

4 medium potatoes, peeled, each cut into 6 pieces

4 large carrots, cut into 1-inch pieces

1 medium onion, thinly sliced

1 dried bay leaf

1 3/4 cups Progresso® beef-flavored broth (from 32-oz carton)

1 teaspoon Worcestershire sauce

2 tablespoons cornstarch

Fresh ground pepper, if desired

1) In shallow bowl, mix flour, salt and pepper. Add beef pieces; turn to coat both sides. Spray 10-inch skillet with cooking spray; heat over medium-high heat. Add beef; cook 4 to 6 minutes, turning once, until browned. Remove beef from skillet; cover to keep warm.

2) Spray 3- to 4-quart slow cooker with cooking spray. In slow cooker, mix the potatoes, carrots and onion. Add bay leaf. Place browned beef over vegetables. In small bowl, mix 1 1/2 cups of the broth (reserve and refrigerate remaining broth) and the Worcestershire sauce. Pour over beef. Cover; cook on Low heat setting 8 to 10 hours.

3) With slotted spoon, remove beef and vegetables from slow cooker; place on serving platter. Cover to keep warm.

4) Pour liquid from slow cooker into 2-quart saucepan; discard bay leaf. In small bowl, mix remaining 1/4 cup broth and the cornstarch until smooth. Add to liquid in saucepan. Heat to boiling over medium-high heat, stirring constantly. Boil and stir 1 minute. Serve sauce with beef and vegetables. Sprinkle with pepper.

Nutrition Information Per Serving:

Calories:	420	From Fat:	50
Total Fat			6g
Saturated Fat			2g
Trans Fat			0g
Cholesterol			90mg
Sodium			790mg
Total Carbohydrate			52g
Dietary Fiber			7g
Sugars			7g
Protein			41g

Carolina Pulled-Pork Sandwiches

PREP TIME: 10 MINUTES (READY IN 8 HOURS 10 MINUTES)
SERVINGS: 12 SANDWICHES

🅔 EASY

1 boneless pork shoulder blade roast (3 lb)

1 tablespoon packed brown sugar

1 tablespoon kosher (coarse) salt

1 tablespoon pepper

1 tablespoon paprika

2 cups cider vinegar

1 cup ketchup

2 tablespoons Worcestershire sauce

1 teaspoon red pepper sauce

12 kaiser rolls, split

1 pint (2 cups) coleslaw with sweet-and-sour dressing (from deli)

1) Spray 3- to 4-quart slow cooker with cooking spray. Trim fat from pork; place in slow cooker. In small bowl, mix the brown sugar, salt, pepper and paprika; rub over pork.

2) In medium bowl, mix the remaining ingredients except rolls and coleslaw; pour into slow cooker.

3) Cover; cook on Low heat setting 8 to 9 hours.

4) Remove pork from slow cooker; place on cutting board. Shred pork with 2 forks; return to slow cooker and mix well.

5) Using slotted spoon, spoon about 1/2 cup pork mixture, on the bottom half of each roll. Top each with about 2 tablespoons coleslaw. Cover with top halves of rolls. Pork mixture can be kept warm on Low heat setting up to 2 hours; stir occasionally.

Nutrition Information Per Serving:		
Calories: 440	From Fat:	170
Total Fat		19g
Saturated Fat		6g
Trans Fat		0.5g
Cholesterol		75mg
Sodium		1160mg
Total Carbohydrate		38g
Dietary Fiber		2g
Sugars		11g
Protein		30g

Curried Squash Soup

PREP TIME: 20 MINUTES (READY IN 8 HOURS 35 MINUTES)
SERVINGS: 9 (ABOUT 1 CUP EACH)

e EASY   **f** LOW FAT

1 large butternut squash (about 4 lb), peeled, seeded and cut into 1-inch pieces (about 10 cups)

1 large apple, peeled, cut into 1-inch pieces (about 1¾ cups)

1 large onion, cut into 1-inch pieces (about 2 cups)

2 teaspoons curry powder

½ teaspoon salt

⅛ teaspoon white pepper

3½ cups Progresso® chicken broth (from 32-oz carton)

½ cup canned coconut milk (not cream of coconut)

3 tablespoons packed brown sugar

1 small red apple, unpeeled, coarsely chopped (about 1 cup), if desired

1) Spray 4- to 5- quart slow cooker with cooking spray. In slow cooker, toss squash, apple, onion, curry powder, salt and white pepper. Pour the broth over vegetable mixture.

2) Cover; cook on Low heat setting 8 to 10 hours.

3) Pour about 3 cups of the soup mixture into blender; add coconut milk and brown sugar. Cover and blend until smooth; return to slow cooker. Blend remaining soup mixture, in 2 more batches of 3 cups each, until smooth; return to slow cooker.

4) Increase heat setting to High. Cover; cook 10 to 15 minutes longer or until hot. Serve topped with chopped apple.

Nutrition Information Per Serving:		
Calories: 150	From Fat:	25
Total Fat		3g
Saturated Fat		2.5g
Trans Fat		0g
Cholesterol		0mg
Sodium		470mg
Total Carbohydrate		28g
Dietary Fiber		3g
Sugars		15g
Protein		3g

tip

When selecting butternut squash, look for those that have hard, tough rinds and are heavy for their size. Peeling the squash is easier if you microwave it on High for 3 minutes first.

Sweet Potato and Barley Risotto

PREP TIME: 20 MINUTES (READY IN 4 HOURS 50 MINUTES)
SERVINGS: 6 (1-1/3 CUPS EACH)

EASY **LOW FAT**

1 teaspoon olive or vegetable oil

1$\frac{1}{2}$ cups chopped sweet onions (3 medium)

3 medium garlic cloves, finely chopped

12 oz dark-orange sweet potatoes (about 2 medium), peeled, finely chopped (about 3$\frac{1}{2}$ cups)

1$\frac{1}{4}$ cups uncooked pearl barley

1 teaspoon dried thyme leaves

$\frac{1}{2}$ teaspoon salt

1 carton (32 oz) Progresso® chicken broth (4 cups) or vegetable broth

1 cup frozen shelled edamame (green) soybeans (from 12-oz bag), thawed

2 tablespoons shredded Parmesan cheese

1) In 10-inch nonstick skillet, heat oil over medium heat. Add onion; cook about 5 minutes, stirring occasionally, until translucent. Add garlic; cook, stirring frequently, until softened.

2) Spray 3- to 4-quart slow cooker with cooking spray. In slow cooker, mix sweet potatoes, barley, thyme, salt and 3 cups of the broth. Add onion-garlic mixture.

3) Cover; cook on Low heat setting 4 to 5 hours.

4) In 2-cup microwavable measuring cup, microwave remaining 1 cup broth on High 2 to 3 minutes or until boiling. Stir the thawed edamame and boiling broth into the barley mixture in slow cooker. Increase heat setting to High; cover and cook 25 to 30 minutes longer or until edamame are tender. Serve in shallow bowls; sprinkle with cheese.

Nutrition Information Per Serving:

Calories:	290	From Fat:	30
Total Fat			3.5g
Saturated Fat			1g
Trans Fat			0g
Cholesterol			0mg
Sodium			830mg
Total Carbohydrate			54g
Dietary Fiber			10g
Sugars			8g
Protein			11g

Pork Chops with Apple Chutney

PREP TIME: 20 MINUTES (READY IN 4 HOURS 20 MINUTES)
SERVINGS: 4

e EASY

4 center-cut bone-in pork loin chops,
  1 inch thick (about 2 lb), trimmed
  of fat

¼ teaspoon salt

¼ teaspoon pepper

6 tablespoons packed brown sugar

2 tablespoons cider vinegar

1 teaspoon ground ginger

1 teaspoon ground cinnamon

¼ teaspoon ground red pepper
  (cayenne)

¼ cup sweetened dried cranberries

2 medium baking apples, peeled,
  chopped (2 cups)

1) Spray 3- to 4-quart slow cooker with cooking spray. Sprinkle pork with salt and pepper; place in slow cooker.

2) In small bowl, mix brown sugar, vinegar, ginger, cinnamon, red pepper and cranberries. Spoon over pork in slow cooker; top with apples. Cover; cook on Low heat setting 4 hours to 4 hours 30 minutes.

Nutrition Information Per Serving:

Calories:	560	From Fat:	230
Total Fat		25g	
Saturated Fat		10g	
Trans Fat		0g	
Cholesterol		125mg	
Sodium		1220mg	
Total Carbohydrate		44g	
Dietary Fiber		3g	
Sugars		20g	
Protein		39g	

For variety, try substituting dried cherries or golden raisins for the dried cranberries.

Gingered Broccoli Chicken

PREP TIME: 10 MINUTES (READY IN 6 HOURS 25 MINUTES)
SERVINGS: 6

☺ EASY   🎛 LOW FAT

CHICKEN MIXTURE

6 boneless skinless chicken thighs (about 1¼ lb)

2 tablespoons grated gingerroot

1 medium sweet onion, cut into thin wedges

1 bag (1 lb) frozen sliced peaches, thawed

½ cup teriyaki sauce

½ cup water

5 cups Green Giant® Select® frozen broccoli florets (from 22-oz bag), thawed

¼ cup water

2 tablespoons cornstarch

RICE

3 cups water

3 cups uncooked instant white rice

1) Spray 3- to 4-quart slow cooker with cooking spray. Place chicken in slow cooker; top with gingerroot, onion and thawed peaches. In small bowl, mix teriyaki sauce and ½ cup water; pour over chicken mixture.

2) Cover; cook on Low heat setting 6 to 7 hours.

3) Stir thawed broccoli into chicken mixture. In small bowl, mix ¼ cup water and the cornstarch; stir into chicken mixture. Increase heat setting to High; cover and cook 15 minutes longer or until sauce is slightly thickened.

4) Meanwhile, in 2-quart saucepan, heat 3 cups water to boiling. Stir in rice. Cover; remove from heat. Let stand 5 minutes. Fluff rice with fork. Serve chicken mixture over rice.

Nutrition Information Per Serving:

Calories:	430	From Fat:	80
Total Fat			8g
Saturated Fat			2.5g
Trans Fat			0g
Cholesterol			60mg
Sodium			990mg
Total Carbohydrate			61g
Dietary Fiber			6g
Sugars			8g
Protein			29g

Steak Fajitas with Tomato-Corn Relish

PREP TIME: 30 MINUTES (READY IN 7 HOURS 15 MINUTES)
SERVINGS: 12   **LOW FAT**

FAJITAS

- 1 cup thick and chunky cilantro salsa
- 2 garlic cloves, finely chopped
- 1½ teaspoons chipotle chili pepper powder
- ½ teaspoon salt
- ½ teaspoon ground cumin
- 1¼ to 1½ lb beef flank steak, trimmed of fat
- 1 sweet onion, cut into ¾-inch wedges
- 1 medium red bell pepper, cut into ¾-inch strips
- 1 medium yellow bell pepper, cut into ¾-inch strips
- 12 low-fat flour tortillas (8 inch)

  Fat-free sour cream, if desired

RELISH

- 1 can (11 oz) Green Giant® Niblets® whole kernel sweet corn, drained
- 1 large tomato, chopped (about 1 cup)
- 3 tablespoons finely chopped cilantro
- 1 tablespoon lime juice
- ⅛ teaspoon salt

  Freshly ground black pepper, if desired

1) Spray 3- to 4-quart slow cooker with cooking spray. In slow cooker, mix the salsa, garlic, chili pepper powder, salt and cumin.

2) Cut beef into 3x½x½-inch strips; stir into mixture in slow cooker.

3) Cover; cook on Low heat setting 6 to 7 hours.

4) Add onion and bell peppers to beef in slow cooker. Increase heat setting to High. Cover; cook 30 to 45 minutes longer or until the vegetables are crisp-tender. Meanwhile, in medium bowl, mix relish ingredients; set aside.

5) To serve, wrap the tortillas in damp microwavable paper towels; heat in microwave on High 1 minute to 1 minute 30 seconds or until warm. Spoon about ½ cup beef mixture down center of each warm tortilla; top with relish and sour cream. Fold 2 sides of tortilla over filling toward center.

Nutrition Information Per Serving:		
Calories: 280	From Fat:	25
Total Fat		3g
Saturated Fat		0.5g
Trans Fat		0g
Cholesterol		35mg
Sodium		810mg
Total Carbohydrate		42g
Dietary Fiber		4g
Sugars		3g
Protein		21g

Slow Cooker Garlic Smashed Red Potatoes

PREP TIME: 15 MINUTES (READY IN 3 HOURS 45 MINUTES)
SERVINGS: 14 (1/2 CUP EACH)

e EASY

3 lb small red potatoes (2 to 3 inch)

4 garlic cloves, finely chopped

2 tablespoons olive or vegetable oil

1 teaspoon salt

1/2 cup water

1/2 cup regular or reduced-fat chives-and-onion cream cheese spread (from 8-oz container)

1/4 to 1/2 cup milk

1) Spray 4- to 5-quart slow cooker with cooking spray. Halve or quarter potatoes as necessary to make similar-size pieces. Place in slow cooker. Add garlic, oil, salt and water; mix well to coat all potato pieces.

2) Cover; cook on High heat setting 3 hours 30 minutes to 4 hours 30 minutes or until potatoes are tender.

3) Mash potatoes and garlic using fork or potato masher. Add cream cheese; stir until well blended. Stir in enough milk for soft serving consistency. Serve immediately, or cover and hold in slow cooker on Low heat setting up to 2 hours.

Nutrition Information Per Serving:		
Calories: 120	From Fat:	40
Total Fat		4.5g
Saturated Fat		2g
Trans Fat		0g
Cholesterol		10mg
Sodium		230mg
Total Carbohydrate		18g
Dietary Fiber		2g
Sugars		1g
Protein		2g

Spicy Chunky Beef Chili

PREP TIME: 20 MINUTES (READY IN 9 HOURS 50 MINUTES)
SERVINGS: 7 (1-1/2 CUPS EACH)

e EASY

1 1/2 lb boneless beef chuck roast, trimmed of fat, cut into 1/2-inch cubes

1 lb small red potatoes (about 9), unpeeled, quartered

2 medium carrots, sliced (about 1 cup)

1 large green bell pepper, coarsely chopped (about 1 1/2 cups)

1 large onion, chopped (about 1 cup)

2 large garlic cloves, finely chopped

1 can (15 oz) Progresso® dark red kidney beans, drained, rinsed

1/2 teaspoon salt

3 1/2 cups Progresso® beef-flavored broth (from 32-oz carton)

1 chipotle chile in adobo sauce, finely chopped (from 7-oz can)

1 tablespoon adobo sauce from can of chipotle chiles

3 tablespoons packed brown sugar

1) Spray 4- to 5-quart slow cooker with cooking spray. In slow cooker, mix all ingredients except chiles, adobo sauce and brown sugar.

2) Cover; cook on Low heat setting 9 to 10 hours.

3) Stir in the chopped chiles, adobo sauce and brown sugar. Cover; cook on Low heat setting 30 minutes longer. Stir well before serving.

Nutrition Information Per Serving:

Calories: 330	From Fat: 100
Total Fat	11g
Saturated Fat	4g
Trans Fat	0g
Cholesterol	50mg
Sodium	690mg
Total Carbohydrate	35g
Dietary Fiber	6g
Sugars	10g
Protein	23g

Southwest Artichoke and Spinach Dip

PREP TIME: 10 MINUTES (READY IN 2 HOURS 15 MINUTES)
SERVINGS: 26 (2 TABLESPOONS DIP AND 6 CHIPS EACH)

e EASY

1 can (14 oz) artichoke hearts, drained, coarsely chopped

1 box (9 oz) Green Giant® frozen spinach, thawed, squeezed to drain

1 package (8 oz) cream cheese, cubed, softened

1 can (4.5 oz) Old El Paso® chopped green chiles, undrained

1/2 medium red bell pepper, chopped (about 1/2 cup)

1/2 cup shredded pepper Jack cheese (2 oz)

1 bag (14 oz) round tortilla chips

1) Spray 1- to 1½-quart slow cooker with cooking spray. In medium bowl, mix all ingredients except pepper Jack cheese and tortilla chips; spoon into slow cooker. Cover; cook on Low heat setting 2 to 3 hours.

2) Stir pepper Jack cheese into artichoke mixture. Cover; cook on Low heat setting about 5 minutes longer or until cheese is melted. Serve with chips.

Nutrition Information Per Serving:

Calories: 130	From Fat: 70
Total Fat	7g
Saturated Fat	3g
Trans Fat	0g
Cholesterol	10mg
Sodium	150mg
Total Carbohydrate	12g
Dietary Fiber	2g
Sugars	0g
Protein	2g

Turkey Teriyaki Sandwiches

PREP TIME: 10 MINUTES (READY IN 9 HOURS 15 MINUTES)
SERVINGS: 4 SANDWICHES

e EASY   f LOW FAT

2 bone-in turkey thighs (1½ lb), skin removed

1/2 cup teriyaki baste and glaze (from 12-oz bottle)

2 tablespoons orange marmalade

1/2 teaspoon grated gingerroot

1 garlic clove, finely chopped

1 tablespoon water

2 teaspoons cornstarch

4 kaiser rolls, split

1) Spray 3- to 4-quart slow cooker with cooking spray. Place turkey thighs in slow cooker. In small bowl or measuring cup, mix teriyaki glaze, marmalade, gingerroot and garlic. Spoon mixture over turkey, turning as necessary to coat.

2) Cover; cook on Low heat setting 9 to 10 hours.

3) Remove the turkey from slow cooker; place on a serving platter. Remove and discard bones; shred or cut turkey into pieces.

4) In 2-cup microwavable measuring cup or small microwavable bowl, mix water and cornstarch until smooth. Pour the juices from slow cooker into cornstarch mixture; mix well. Microwave on High 1 to 2 minutes, stirring once halfway through cooking, until mixture boils and thickens slightly. To serve, spoon turkey onto bottom halves of rolls; spoon sauce over turkey. Cover with top halves of rolls.

Nutrition Information Per Serving:

Calories: 370	From Fat: 60
Total Fat	6g
Saturated Fat	1.5g
Trans Fat	0.5g
Cholesterol	105mg
Sodium	1160mg
Total Carbohydrate	46g
Dietary Fiber	1g
Sugars	14g
Protein	33g

Texas Two-Meat Chili

PREP TIME: 25 MINUTES (READY IN 7 HOURS 25 MINUTES)
SERVINGS: 6 (1-1/2 CUPS EACH)

e EASY

1 lb boneless beef chuck steak, cut into 1-inch pieces

1 lb pork tenderloin, cut into 1-inch pieces

1/4 cup all-purpose flour

1 tablespoon vegetable oil

2 cans (10 oz each) tomatoes with green chiles, undrained

1 can (15 to 16 oz) pinto beans, undrained

1 can (12 oz) beer or nonalcoholic beer

1/2 cup chopped red onion

2 tablespoons chili powder

1 teaspoon ground cumin

1/2 teaspoon salt

1/2 teaspoon garlic powder

1/8 teaspoon ground cinnamon

Sliced green onions, if desired

1) In large bowl, mix beef, pork and flour until meats are evenly coated. In 12-inch skillet, heat oil over medium-high heat. Add the meats; cook 8 to 10 minutes, stirring frequently, until browned on all sides (if necessary, cook the meats in batches).

2) Spray 4- to 5-quart slow cooker with cooking spray. In slow cooker, mix the browned meats and remaining ingredients except green onions.

3) Cover; cook on Low heat setting 7 to 9 hours. Before serving, skim off fat; sprinkle with green onions.

Nutrition Information Per Serving:

Calories:	380	From Fat:	130
Total Fat		14g	
Saturated Fat		4.5g	
Trans Fat		0g	
Cholesterol		70mg	
Sodium		520mg	
Total Carbohydrate		27g	
Dietary Fiber		8g	
Sugars		3g	
Protein		35g	

Savory Brisket Stew

PREP TIME: 25 MINUTES (READY IN 8 HOURS 40 MINUTES)
SERVINGS: 14 (1-1/4 CUPS STEW AND 1 CUP NOODLES EACH)

LOW FAT

1 fresh beef brisket (3 lb; not corned beef), cut into 3 pieces lengthwise

1 medium butternut squash (3 lb), peeled, cut into 3/4- to 1-inch cubes (about 8 cups)

1 medium onion, cut into 1/2-inch wedges (1 cup)

1 teaspoon salt

1/2 teaspoon pepper

1 can (28 oz) Progresso® crushed tomatoes, undrained

2 cups Progresso® beef-flavored broth (from 32-oz carton)

1 cup dry red wine or Progresso® beef-flavored broth

14 cups uncooked wide egg noodles (28 oz)

1/4 cup quick-cooking tapioca

1) Spray 5- to 6-quart slow cooker with cooking spray. In slow cooker, arrange the brisket pieces, fat side up. Add remaining ingredients except noodles and tapioca in order listed.

2) Cover; cook on Low heat setting 8 to 10 hours.

3) Cook and drain noodles as directed on package. Meanwhile, remove brisket from cooker and place fat side up on cutting board. If necessary, scrape off any fat from brisket and discard. Using 2 forks, coarsely shred brisket.

4) Stir tapioca into the liquid in slow cooker. Return shredded brisket to slow cooker. Increase heat setting to High. Cover; cook about 15 minutes or until thickened. Serve stew in soup bowls over hot noodles.

Nutrition Information Per Serving:		
Calories: 410	From Fat:	80
Total Fat		9g
Saturated Fat		3g
Trans Fat		0g
Cholesterol		80mg
Sodium		650mg
Total Carbohydrate		51g
Dietary Fiber		3g
Sugars		5g
Protein		29g

Buffalo Chicken Chili

PREP TIME: 15 MINUTES (READY IN 8 HOURS 15 MINUTES)
SERVINGS: 6 (1-1/2 CUPS EACH)

e EASY

2½ lb boneless skinless chicken thighs, cut into 1-inch pieces

1 large onion, chopped (about 1 cup)

2 medium stalks celery, sliced (about 1 cup)

2 medium carrots, chopped (about 1 cup)

1 can (28 oz) Progresso® diced tomatoes, undrained

1 can (15 oz) Progresso® black beans, drained, rinsed

1 cup Progresso® chicken broth (from 32-oz carton)

2 teaspoons chili powder

½ teaspoon salt

¼ cup buffalo wing sauce (from 12-oz jar)

Crumbled blue cheese, if desired

1) Spray 5- to 6-quart slow cooker with cooking spray. In slow cooker, mix all ingredients except buffalo wing sauce and cheese.

2) Cover; cook on Low heat setting 8 to 10 hours.

3) Stir in the buffalo wing sauce. Serve sprinkled with blue cheese.

Nutrition Information Per Serving:

Calories:	430	From Fat:	140
Total Fat			16g
Saturated Fat			5g
Trans Fat			0g
Cholesterol			115mg
Sodium			920mg
Total Carbohydrate			27g
Dietary Fiber			9g
Sugars			6g
Protein			46g

Smothered Swiss Steak

PREP TIME: 15 MINUTES (READY IN 8 HOURS 15 MINUTES)
SERVINGS: 4

ⓔ EASY

2 teaspoons vegetable oil

1½ lb boneless beef top round steak, trimmed of fat

1 teaspoon salt

¼ teaspoon pepper

1 medium onion, halved lengthwise, thinly sliced

1 medium carrot, shredded

1 can (4 oz) mushroom pieces and stems, drained

1 can (10¾ oz) condensed cream of mushroom soup

1 can (8 oz) tomato sauce

1) In 10-inch skillet, heat oil over medium-high heat. Sprinkle the beef with salt and pepper; place in skillet. Cook 4 to 6 minutes, turning once, until well browned.

2) Meanwhile, spray 3- to 4-quart slow cooker with cooking spray. In slow cooker, mix onion, carrot and mushrooms.

3) Cut browned beef into 4 pieces; place in slow cooker over vegetables. In same skillet, mix soup and tomato sauce. Pour over beef.

4) Cover; cook on Low heat setting 8 to 10 hours. Stir the sauce well before serving over beef.

Nutrition Information Per Serving:

Calories:	330	From Fat:	110
Total Fat		12g	
Saturated Fat		3.5g	
Trans Fat		0g	
Cholesterol		95mg	
Sodium		1590mg	
Total Carbohydrate		14g	
Dietary Fiber		2g	
Sugars		6g	
Protein		39g	

Chicken 'n Stuffing Pot Pie

PREP TIME: 10 MINUTES (READY IN 6 HOURS 25 MINUTES)
SERVINGS: 8 (1-3/4 CUPS EACH)

e EASY

8 boneless skinless chicken thighs

6 slices precooked bacon (from 2.2-oz package), crumbled

½ bag (1-lb size) ready-to-eat baby-cut carrots, cut in half lengthwise (about 2 cups)

4 medium red potatoes, each cut into 4 pieces

1 teaspoon dried marjoram leaves

1 jar (12 oz) chicken gravy

1 bag (12 oz) Green Giant® Valley Fresh Steamers™ frozen cut green beans, thawed

6 tablespoons butter or margarine, melted

½ package (14-oz size) herb-seasoned stuffing cubes (about 4⅔ cups)

1) Spray 4- to 5-quart slow cooker with cooking spray. Place chicken in slow cooker. Top with bacon, carrots, potatoes, marjoram and gravy. Cover; cook on Low heat setting 6 to 8 hours.

2) Gently stir the thawed green beans into chicken mixture. In medium bowl, mix melted butter and stuffing; spoon over chicken mixture. Increase heat setting to High; cover and cook 15 minutes longer.

Nutrition Information Per Serving:

Calories:	450	From Fat:	210
Total Fat			24g
Saturated Fat			10g
Trans Fat			1.5g
Cholesterol			75mg
Sodium			990mg
Total Carbohydrate			37g
Dietary Fiber			5g
Sugars			4g
Protein			22g

Beefy Wild Mushroom and Barley Soup

PREP TIME: 15 MINUTES (READY IN 8 HOURS 15 MINUTES)
SERVINGS: 8 (1-1/3 CUPS EACH)

$1^1/_2$ lb boneless beef bottom round steak, trimmed of fat, cut into 1-inch cubes

5 cups sliced assorted fresh wild mushrooms, such as portabella, shiitake, oyster and/or porcini (about 10 oz total)

3 medium carrots, sliced (about $1^1/_2$ cups)

2 leeks, trimmed, cut in half lengthwise, rinsed and sliced crosswise (about $1^1/_2$ cups)

2 large garlic cloves, finely chopped

$^1/_2$ cup uncooked pearl barley

$5^1/_4$ cups Progresso® beef-flavored broth (from two 32-oz cartons)

$^1/_2$ cup dry sherry or Progresso® beef-flavored broth

$^1/_2$ teaspoon dried thyme leaves

$^1/_2$ teaspoon salt

$^1/_4$ teaspoon pepper

1) Spray 5- to 6-quart slow cooker with cooking spray. In slow cooker, mix all ingredients.

2) Cover; cook on Low heat setting 8 to 10 hours. Stir well before serving.

Nutrition Information Per Serving:

Calories:	230	From Fat:	35
Total Fat		4g	
Saturated Fat		1.5g	
Trans Fat		0g	
Cholesterol		65mg	
Sodium		760mg	
Total Carbohydrate		20g	
Dietary Fiber		4g	
Sugars		3g	
Protein		29g	

Pork Chops with Cranberry-Cornbread Stuffing

PREP TIME: 10 MINUTES (READY IN 4 HOURS 10 MINUTES)
SERVINGS: 6

€ EASY

6 boneless pork loin chops, about 1 inch thick (about 2¼ lb)

2 teaspoons seasoned salt

½ bag (16-oz size) cornbread stuffing (3 cups)

½ cup sweetened dried cranberries

½ medium apple, chopped (½ cup)

½ medium onion, chopped (¼ cup)

¼ cup chopped pecans

1 cup plus 2 tablespoons water

¼ cup butter or margarine, melted

½ cup cranberry relish or sauce

Nutrition Information Per Serving:	
Calories: 560	From Fat: 230
Total Fat	25g
Saturated Fat	10g
Trans Fat	0g
Cholesterol	125mg
Sodium	1220mg
Total Carbohydrate	44g
Dietary Fiber	3g
Sugars	20g
Protein	39g

1) Place pork chops in large resealable food-storage plastic bag. Add seasoned salt; shake bag to coat pork.

2) Spray 5- to 6-quart slow cooker with cooking spray. In slow cooker, mix the remaining ingredients except the cranberry relish. Arrange pork chops on stuffing mixture.

3) Cover; cook on Low heat setting 4 to 5 hours. Serve pork and stuffing with cranberry relish.

Turkey Mole Chili

PREP TIME: 15 MINUTES (READY IN 8 HOURS 15 MINUTES)
SERVINGS: 6 (1-1/2 CUPS EACH)

€ EASY

2 packages (20 oz each) lean ground turkey

1 large onion, chopped (about 1 cup)

2 medium carrots, chopped (about 1 cup)

1 can (28 oz) Progresso® diced tomatoes, undrained

1 can (15 oz) Progresso® black beans, drained, rinsed

1 jar (8¼ oz) mole

1¾ cups Progresso® chicken broth (from 32-oz carton)

½ cup sour cream

¼ cup crumbled cotija (white Mexican) cheese

1) In 12-inch nonstick skillet, cook ground turkey over medium-high heat 5 to 7 minutes, stirring frequently, until no longer pink; drain.

2) Spray 4- to 5-quart slow cooker with cooking spray. In slow cooker, mix the turkey and remaining ingredients except sour cream and cheese. Cover; cook on Low heat setting 8 to 10 hours.

3) Stir well before serving. Top each serving with dollop of sour cream and sprinkle of cheese.

Nutrition Information Per Serving:	
Calories: 740	From Fat: 360
Total Fat	40g
Saturated Fat	12g
Trans Fat	1g
Cholesterol	140mg
Sodium	1030mg
Total Carbohydrate	43g
Dietary Fiber	10g
Sugars	12g
Protein	51g

Corned Beef and Cabbage

PREP TIME: 15 MINUTES (READY IN 10 HOURS 50 MINUTES)
SERVINGS: 8

ⓔ EASY

BEEF AND VEGETABLES

- 4 medium red potatoes, unpeeled, cut into 1-inch pieces
- 4 medium carrots, cut into 1-inch pieces
- 1 medium onion, cut into 6 wedges
- 1 corned beef brisket with seasoning packet (2 to 2 1/2 lb)
- 1 can (12 oz) beer or nonalcoholic beer

  Water

- 8 thin cabbage wedges

SAUCE

- 1/4 cup applesauce
- 2 tablespoons Dijon mustard

1) Spray 5- to 6-quart slow cooker with cooking spray. In slow cooker, place potatoes, carrots and onion. Top with corned beef; sprinkle with contents of seasoning packet. Add beer and enough water to just cover corned beef. Cover; cook on Low heat setting 10 to 12 hours.

2) Remove corned beef from slow cooker; place on serving platter and cover to keep warm. Add cabbage wedges to the vegetables and broth in slow cooker. Increase heat setting to High. Cover; cook 30 to 35 minutes longer or until cabbage is crisp-tender.

3) Meanwhile, in small bowl, mix sauce ingredients.

4) To serve, cut corned beef across grain into thin slices. With slotted spoon, remove vegetables from slow cooker. If desired, skim fat from juices in slow cooker. Serve vegetables with juices and corned beef with sauce.

Nutrition Information Per Serving:

Calories: 330	From Fat: 140
Total Fat	16g
Saturated Fat	5g
Trans Fat	0.5g
Cholesterol	80mg
Sodium	1040mg
Total Carbohydrate	30g
Dietary Fiber	5g
Sugars	7g
Protein	18g

White Chicken Chili

PREP TIME: 15 MINUTES (READY IN 6 HOURS 15 MINUTES)
SERVINGS: 6 (1-1/2 CUPS EACH)

e EASY   f LOW FAT

2 lb boneless skinless chicken breasts, cut in half lengthwise, then sliced crosswise

1 large onion, chopped (about 1 cup)

1 large red bell pepper, chopped (about 1$\frac{1}{2}$ cups)

4 medium garlic cloves, finely chopped

1 can (15.25 oz) Green Giant® whole kernel corn, drained

1 can (15 to 16 oz) great northern beans, drained, rinsed

2 jars (8 oz each) green taco sauce

$\frac{1}{2}$ cup Progresso® chicken broth (from 32-oz carton)

$\frac{1}{2}$ teaspoon salt

Fresh cilantro, if desired

1) Spray 3- to 4-quart slow cooker with cooking spray. In slow cooker, mix all ingredients except cilantro.

2) Cover; cook on Low heat setting 6 to 7 hours. Stir well and garnish each serving with cilantro.

Nutrition Information Per Serving:

Calories:	380	From Fat:	50
Total Fat		6g	
Saturated Fat		1.5g	
Trans Fat		0g	
Cholesterol		95mg	
Sodium		1010mg	
Total Carbohydrate		37g	
Dietary Fiber		7g	
Sugars		7g	
Protein		43g	

tip

Green taco sauce is made from green tomatoes and tomatillos, also known as Mexican green tomatoes. They are encased in a papery husk and have a fresh flavor with hints of lemon and herbs.

Southwest Turkey Tacos

PREP TIME: 20 MINUTES (READY IN 6 HOURS 20 MINUTES)
SERVINGS: 12 (2 TACOS EACH)

e EASY   **f** LOW FAT

1 package (20 oz) extra-lean ground turkey

$1/2$ cup chopped onion (1 medium)

1 teaspoon salt

$1/4$ teaspoon pepper

2 cups Old El Paso® Thick 'n Chunky salsa

1 can (15 oz) Progresso® black beans, drained

1 can (11 oz) Green Giant® Mexicorn® whole kernel corn with red and green peppers, drained, rinsed

1 tablespoon chili powder

2 boxes (4.6 oz each) Old El Paso® taco shells (24 shells total)

3 tablespoons finely chopped fresh cilantro

3 cups chopped lettuce

3 medium tomatoes, chopped ($1^1/2$ cups)

1) In 12-inch skillet, place the turkey and onion; sprinkle with salt and pepper. Cook over medium-high heat 4 to 6 minutes, stirring occasionally, until the turkey is no longer pink.

2) Spray 3- to 4-quart slow cooker with cooking spray. In slow cooker, mix the turkey mixture, salsa, beans, corn and chili powder. Cover; cook on Low heat setting 6 to 7 hours.

3) To serve, heat taco shells in oven as directed on boxes. Stir cilantro into turkey mixture. Spoon about $1/4$ cup mixture into each warm taco shell; top with lettuce and tomatoes.

Nutrition Information Per Serving:

Calories:	250	From Fat:	70

Total Fat	8g
Saturated Fat	2g
Trans Fat	1.5g
Cholesterol	30mg
Sodium	750mg
Total Carbohydrate	30g
Dietary Fiber	5g
Sugars	4g
Protein	15g

Chicken Parmesan with Penne Pasta

PREP TIME: 15 MINUTES (READY IN 5 HOURS 25 MINUTES)
SERVINGS: 4

EASY

1 egg

$^1/_3$ cup Progresso® plain bread crumbs

$^1/_3$ cup shredded Parmesan cheese

$^1/_2$ teaspoon Italian seasoning

$^1/_4$ teaspoon salt

$^1/_4$ teaspoon pepper

4 boneless skinless chicken breasts (about 1$^1/_4$ lb)

1 jar (26 oz) tomato pasta sauce

$^1/_2$ cup shredded Italian cheese blend (2 oz)

2$^2/_3$ cups uncooked penne pasta (8 oz)

1) Spray 2- to 3-quart slow cooker with cooking spray. In small shallow bowl, beat the egg until foamy. In separate shallow bowl, mix bread crumbs, Parmesan cheese, Italian seasoning, salt and pepper. Dip the chicken into egg, then coat evenly with bread crumb mixture; place in slow cooker. Spread pasta sauce evenly over chicken. Cover; cook on Low heat setting 5 to 6 hours.

2) Sprinkle Italian cheese blend over top. Cover; cook on Low heat setting 10 minutes longer. Meanwhile, cook and drain pasta as directed on the package. Serve chicken with pasta.

Nutrition Information Per Serving:

Calories:	720	From Fat:	200
Total Fat			22g
Saturated Fat			7g
Trans Fat			0g
Cholesterol			200mg
Sodium			1730mg
Total Carbohydrate			79g
Dietary Fiber			5g
Sugars			20g
Protein			51g

BURRITO GRANDE
PG. 223

Family Fiesta

Spice up dinner with an easy Mexican spread...and turn an ordinary day into a south-of-the-border party!

TOMATILLO SALSA
PG. 233

TOSTADA CHICKEN SALAD
PG. 228

GROUND BEEF FAJITAS
PG. 235

Chicken Ranch Tacos

PREP TIME: 25 MINUTES (READY IN 25 MINUTES)
SERVINGS: 5 (2 TACOS EACH)

1 box (4.7 oz) Old El Paso® Stand 'n Stuff® taco shells (10 shells)

3 cups cut-up deli rotisserie chicken (from 2- to 2½-lb chicken)

1 package (1 oz) Old El Paso® taco seasoning mix

½ cup ranch dressing

1½ cups shredded lettuce

1 medium tomato, chopped (¾ cup)

1 cup shredded Cheddar cheese (4 oz)

¼ cup sliced green onions (4 medium), if desired

Old El Paso® Thick 'n Chunky salsa, if desired

Additional ranch dressing, if desired

1) Heat oven to 325°F. Heat taco shells in oven as directed on box.

2) Meanwhile, in medium microwavable bowl, place chicken. Sprinkle with taco seasoning mix; toss gently to coat. Microwave uncovered on High 2 to 3 minutes or until hot. Stir in ½ cup dressing.

3) Spoon warm chicken mixture into heated taco shells. Top with lettuce, tomato, cheese and onions. Drizzle with salsa and additional dressing.

HIGH ALTITUDE (3500-6500 FT.): No change.

Nutrition Information Per Serving:

Calories:	500	From Fat:	290
Total Fat			32g
Saturated Fat			9g
Trans Fat			2.5g
Cholesterol			105mg
Sodium			1500mg
Total Carbohydrate			23g
Dietary Fiber			2g
Sugars			3g
Protein			31g

tip

Have cooked chicken left over from last night's dinner? Dice it and use it in place of rotisserie chicken in this recipe.

Mexican Chocolate Cake with Caramel Cream Frosting

PREP TIME: 25 MINUTES (READY IN 1 HOUR 45 MINUTES)
SERVINGS: 12

CAKE

- ³/₄ cup hot brewed coffee
- ¹/₂ cup unsweetened baking cocoa
- 3 teaspoons ground cinnamon
- 2 cups all-purpose flour
- 1 teaspoon baking powder
- ³/₄ teaspoon salt
- ¹/₂ teaspoon baking soda
- ³/₄ cup butter or margarine, softened
- 1³/₄ cups sugar
- 3 eggs
- ³/₄ cup buttermilk
- 2 teaspoons vanilla

FROSTING

- 1 can (13.4 oz) dulce de leche (caramelized sweetened condensed milk)
- 1 package (8 oz) cream cheese, softened
- ¹/₂ cup whipping cream

1) Heat oven to 350°F. Spray bottoms and sides of 2 (9-inch) round cake pans with cooking spray. Line bottoms of pans with cooking parchment paper or waxed paper.

2) In medium bowl, beat coffee, cocoa and cinnamon with wire whisk until smooth; set aside to cool slightly. In another medium bowl, mix flour, baking powder, salt and baking soda until well blended; set aside.

3) In large bowl, beat butter and sugar with electric mixer on high speed until creamy. Add eggs, one at a time, beating well after each addition; set aside. Stir buttermilk and vanilla into coffee mixture. Starting with flour mixture, alternately beat flour mixture, ¹/₃ at a time, and coffee mixture, ¹/₃ at a time, into butter mixture on medium speed, scraping the bowl occasionally. When all ingredients have been added, beat 30 to 60 seconds longer or until batter is smooth and well blended. Pour into pans.

4) Bake 32 to 37 minutes or until toothpick inserted near center comes out clean and cake springs back when touched lightly in center. Cool in pans on cooling racks 10 minutes. Remove cakes from pans to cooling racks (leave paper on cakes). Cool completely, about 30 minutes.

5) In large bowl, beat dulce de leche and cream cheese on high speed about 2 minutes or until blended and smooth; scrape side of bowl. Beat in whipping cream until stiff peaks form. On serving plate, place 1 cake, rounded side down; remove the paper liner. Spread ³/₄ cup of the frosting over top to within ¹/₂ inch of edge. Remove paper from other cake. Place cake, rounded side up, on first cake. Frost side and top of cake with remaining frosting. Serve immediately, or refrigerate until serving.

HIGH ALTITUDE (3500-6500 FT.): No change.

Nutrition Information Per Serving:	
Calories: 530	From Fat: 230
Total Fat	25g
Saturated Fat	15g
Trans Fat	1g
Cholesterol	115mg
Sodium	450mg
Total Carbohydrate	67g
Dietary Fiber	2g
Sugars	46g
Protein	9g

Arroz con Pollo

PREP TIME: 20 MINUTES (READY IN 50 MINUTES)
SERVINGS: 4

EASY

1 tablespoon olive or vegetable oil

4 boneless skinless chicken breasts

1 large onion, coarsely chopped

1 cup uncooked converted or regular long-grain white rice

1 teaspoon ground cumin

1/8 teaspoon saffron threads, crushed

2 cups chicken broth

1/2 cup Old El Paso® Thick 'n Chunky salsa

1 red bell pepper, coarsely chopped

1/2 cup Green Giant® Valley Fresh Steamers™ frozen sweet peas

1) In 12-inch skillet, heat oil over medium-high heat until hot. Add chicken; cook 4 to 5 minutes or until browned, turning once. Remove chicken from skillet; cover to keep warm.

2) Add onion to skillet; cook and stir 3 to 4 minutes or until tender. Add rice, cumin and saffron; stir to mix well. Stir in broth and salsa. Heat to boiling; cook 5 minutes. Return chicken to skillet. Reduce heat; cover and simmer 15 minutes.

3) Stir in bell pepper and peas; cook about 5 minutes longer or until liquid is absorbed, chicken is fork-tender and juice is clear when center of thickest part is cut (170°F).

HIGH ALTITUDE (3500-6500 FT.): No change.

Nutrition Information Per Serving:		
Calories: 420	From Fat:	80
Total Fat		9g
Saturated Fat		2g
Trans Fat		0g
Cholesterol		75mg
Sodium		1390mg
Total Carbohydrate		49g
Dietary Fiber		3g
Sugars		5g
Protein		35g

Mexican Cornbread

PREP TIME: 15 MINUTES (READY IN 1 HOUR 15 MINUTES)
SERVINGS: 12

1½ cups shredded sharp Cheddar cheese (6 oz)

¾ cup buttermilk

⅓ cup vegetable oil

2 eggs, slightly beaten

1 can (8.5 oz) cream-style corn

1 can (4.5 oz) Old El Paso® chopped green chiles

1 cup cornmeal

1 cup all-purpose flour

1 teaspoon baking powder

½ teaspoon baking soda

½ teaspoon salt

1) Heat oven to 375°F. Generously spray 1½-quart casserole with cooking spray. In large bowl, mix cheese, buttermilk, oil, eggs, corn and chiles; blend well.

2) In small bowl, mix cornmeal, flour, baking powder, baking soda and salt. Add to cheese mixture; stir just until dry ingredients are moistened. Pour into casserole.

3) Bake 40 to 50 minutes or until cornbread is deep golden brown and toothpick inserted in center comes out clean. Cool 10 minutes; remove from casserole. Serve warm.

HIGH ALTITUDE (3500-6500 FT.): No change.

Nutrition Information Per Serving:		
Calories: 240	From Fat: 120	
Total Fat		13g
Saturated Fat		4.5g
Trans Fat		0g
Cholesterol		50mg
Sodium		410mg
Total Carbohydrate		23g
Dietary Fiber		1g
Sugars		2g
Protein		7g

tip

To substitute for the buttermilk in this bread recipe, use 2 teaspoons vinegar or lemon juice plus milk to make 3/4 cup.

Chicken and Corn Quesadillas

PREP TIME: 15 MINUTES (READY IN 35 MINUTES)
SERVINGS: 4

e EASY

4 flour tortillas (10 inch)

2 tablespoons butter or margarine, melted

¼ cup sour cream

¼ cup Old El Paso® Thick 'n Chunky salsa

1 cup shredded cooked chicken

1½ cups shredded Mexican-style taco-flavored cheese blend (6 oz)

½ cup Green Giant® Niblets® frozen whole kernel corn, thawed

¼ cup sliced green onions (4 medium)

1) Heat oven to 400°F. Brush one side of each tortilla with butter. Place 2 tortillas, butter sides down, on ungreased large cookie sheet.

2) In small bowl, mix sour cream and salsa. Spread about 3 tablespoons of the sour cream mixture over each tortilla on cookie sheet. Top each with chicken, 2 tablespoons of the cheese, the corn and onions. Sprinkle with remaining cheese. Place remaining tortillas, butter sides up, over filling; press gently.

3) Bake 15 to 18 minutes or until cheese is melted and tops are light golden brown. To serve, cut into wedges. Serve with additional salsa if desired.

HIGH ALTITUDE (3500-6500 FT.): No change.

Nutrition Information Per Serving:	
Calories: 560	From Fat: 280
Total Fat	31g
Saturated Fat	16g
Trans Fat	1.5g
Cholesterol	100mg
Sodium	910mg
Total Carbohydrate	43g
Dietary Fiber	2g
Sugars	4g
Protein	27g

Churros

PREP TIME: 40 MINUTES (READY IN 40 MINUTES)
SERVINGS: 18 CHURROS

Vegetable oil for deep frying

$3/4$ cup water

$1/3$ cup butter or margarine

2 tablespoons sugar

$1/8$ teaspoon salt

$3/4$ cup all-purpose flour

$1/4$ cup cornmeal

1 teaspoon ground cinnamon

3 eggs

$1/4$ cup sugar

$1/4$ teaspoon ground cinnamon

1) In deep fryer or heavy skillet, heat 2 to 3 inches oil to 375°F. In 2-quart saucepan, mix water, butter, 2 tablespoons sugar and the salt. Heat to boiling. Add flour and cornmeal; cook until mixture leaves sides of pan in smooth ball, stirring constantly. Remove from heat. Add 1 teaspoon cinnamon. Add eggs, 1 at a time, beating vigorously by hand after each addition until mixture is smooth.

2) Spoon mixture into decorating bag fitted with large star tip. Pipe 4-inch strips of dough directly into hot oil. Fry 2 to 3 minutes or until golden brown, turning several times. Remove carefully from oil with tongs. (Do not prick surface of churros.) Drain on paper towels.

3) In pie pan or shallow dish, mix $1/4$ cup sugar and $1/4$ teaspoon cinnamon. Roll warm churros in sugar-cinnamon mixture. Serve warm.

HIGH ALTITUDE (3500-6500 FT.): Heat oil to 360°F to 365°F.

Nutrition Information Per Serving:

Calories: 90	From Fat: 40
Total Fat	4.5g
Saturated Fat	2.5g
Trans Fat	0g
Cholesterol	45mg
Sodium	50mg
Total Carbohydrate	10g
Dietary Fiber	0g
Sugars	4g
Protein	1g

Authentic Basic Red Salsa

PREP TIME: 15 MINUTES (READY IN 15 MINUTES)
SERVINGS: 12 (1/4 CUP EACH)

🄴 EASY   🄵 LOW FAT

1) In blender, place all ingredients except vegetable oil and chips. Cover and blend until smooth.

2) In 2-quart saucepan, heat oil over medium-high heat. Add tomato mixture; cook about 5 minutes or until hot. Serve warm or cold with tortilla chips, as desired. Cover and refrigerate any remaining salsa.

HIGH ALTITUDE (3500-6500 FT.): No change.

1 lb plum (Roma) tomatoes (about 6 tomatoes)

1 jalapeño chile, seeded

1 garlic clove, peeled

$1/4$ medium white onion

$1/2$ teaspoon chicken tomato bouillon granules

$1/4$ teaspoon salt

$1/2$ cup chicken broth

1 tablespoon vegetable oil

Tortilla chips, as desired

Nutrition Information Per Serving:

Calories: 20	From Fat: 10
Total Fat	1.5g
Saturated Fat	0g
Trans Fat	0g
Cholesterol	0mg
Sodium	130mg
Total Carbohydrate	1g
Dietary Fiber	0g
Sugars	0g
Protein	0g

Chicken Mini Burritos

PREP TIME: 45 MINUTES (READY IN 45 MINUTES)
SERVINGS: 16 MINI BURRITOS

1 teaspoon vegetable oil

1 tablespoon finely chopped onion

1 garlic clove, finely chopped

2 cups shredded cooked chicken

2 tablespoons chopped jalapeño chiles

1/2 teaspoon ground cumin

3/4 cup salsa verde or green salsa

10 Old El Paso® flour tortillas (6 inch, from 11.5 oz package)

1 cup shredded Mexican-style Cheddar Jack cheese with jalapeño peppers (4 oz)

1 medium plum (Roma) tomato, chopped (about 1/2 cup)

1/3 cup chopped fresh cilantro

1) In 10-inch nonstick skillet, heat oil over medium heat. Add onion and garlic; cook 2 to 3 minutes, stirring occasionally, until crisp-tender. Stir in chicken, jalapeño chiles, cumin and salsa verde; cook 4 to 6 minutes or until hot. Keep warm.

2) Heat tortillas as directed on package. Work with 4 tortillas at a time, covering remaining tortillas with a damp paper towel. Spoon 2 level tablespoons chicken mixture and 1 tablespoon shredded cheese in center of each tortilla. Top with tomato and cilantro. Fold 1/3 of tortilla down over filling; fold sides toward center. Fold remaining side up and turn over. Repeat with remaining tortillas. Serve immediately.

HIGH ALTITUDE (3500-6500 FT.): No change.

Nutrition Information Per Serving:		
Calories: 190	From Fat:	70
Total Fat		7g
Saturated Fat		2.5g
Trans Fat		1g
Cholesterol		20mg
Sodium		430mg
Total Carbohydrate		21g
Dietary Fiber		0g
Sugars		0g
Protein		9g

Tres Leches Cake

PREP TIME: 30 MINUTES (READY IN 4 HOURS)
SERVINGS: 15

CAKE

1 box (1 lb 2.25 oz) yellow cake mix with pudding

1 cup water

1/3 cup vegetable oil

3 eggs

SAUCE

1 cup whipping cream

1/3 cup rum or 1 teaspoon rum extract plus 1/3 cup water

1 can (14 oz) sweetened condensed milk (not evaporated)

1 can (12 oz) evaporated milk

TOPPING

1 cup whipping cream

1/3 cup coconut chips, toasted

1/3 cup chopped macadamia nuts

1) Heat oven to 350°F. Grease 13x9-inch (3-quart) glass baking dish. In large bowl, beat the cake mix, water, oil and eggs with electric mixer on low speed about 30 seconds or until blended. Beat on medium speed 2 minutes, scraping bowl occasionally. Pour batter into baking dish. Bake 25 to 35 minutes or until toothpick inserted in the center comes out clean.

2) Meanwhile, in large bowl, mix sauce ingredients. Using long-tined fork, pierce hot cake in baking dish every 1 to 2 inches. Slowly pour the sauce mixture over cake. Refrigerate cake at least 3 hours to chill. (Cake will absorb most of sauce mixture.)

3) Before serving, in small bowl, beat 1 cup whipping cream until stiff peaks form. Spread over cold cake. Sprinkle with coconut and macadamia nuts. Cover and refrigerate any remaining cake.

HIGH ALTITUDE (3500-6500 FT.): No change.

Nutrition Information Per Serving:	
Calories: 440	From Fat: 220
Total Fat	25g
Saturated Fat	11g
Trans Fat	1g
Cholesterol	90mg
Sodium	310mg
Total Carbohydrate	45g
Dietary Fiber	0g
Sugars	37g
Protein	6g

Southwestern BLT Taco Salad

PREP TIME: 25 MINUTES (READY IN 25 MINUTES)
SERVINGS: 4

1 lb lean (at least 80%) ground beef

1 package (1 oz) Old El Paso® taco seasoning mix

2/3 cup water

1/2 cup southwest ranch sour cream dip

1/2 cup Old El Paso® Thick 'n Chunky salsa

1/2 cup chopped precooked bacon

1 can (2 1/4 oz) sliced ripe olives, drained

4 plum (Roma) tomatoes, each cut into 8 pieces

1 bag (10 oz) ready-to-eat romaine lettuce

1 cup shredded Cheddar cheese (4 oz)

1 cup chili cheese-flavored corn chips

1) In 10-inch skillet, cook ground beef over medium-high heat 5 to 7 minutes, stirring occasionally, until thoroughly cooked; drain. Stir in taco seasoning mix and water. Reduce the heat to medium. Cook uncovered 2 to 4 minutes, stirring occasionally, until most of the liquid is absorbed.

2) In large bowl, mix sour cream dip and salsa. Stir in beef mixture, bacon and olives. Gently fold in tomatoes and lettuce.

3) Divide salad among 4 individual plates. Sprinkle with cheese and chips. Serve immediately.

HIGH ALTITUDE (3500-6500 FT.): No change.

Nutrition Information Per Serving:	
Calories: 520	From Fat: 320
Total Fat	35g
Saturated Fat	15g
Trans Fat	1.5g
Cholesterol	120mg
Sodium	1790mg
Total Carbohydrate	19g
Dietary Fiber	3g
Sugars	6g
Protein	32g

Chipotle Chicken Pizza

PREP TIME: 15 MINUTES (READY IN 25 MINUTES)
SERVINGS: 8

EASY

1 can (11 oz) Pillsbury® refrigerated thin pizza crust

1 cup Old El Paso® Thick 'n Chunky mild salsa

½ to 1 chipotle chile in adobo sauce, finely chopped (from 7-oz can)

1 package (5 oz) refrigerated cooked Southwestern-style chicken breast strips

¼ cup chopped onion

½ cup chopped red bell pepper

½ cup chopped green bell pepper

1½ cups shredded Mexican cheese blend (6 oz)

1) Heat oven to 400°F. Spray or grease 15x10-inch or larger dark or nonstick cookie sheet. Unroll dough on cookie sheet; starting at center, press dough into 15x10-inch rectangle.

2) In small bowl, mix salsa and chipotle chile; spread to within ½ inch of edges of dough.

3) Top with chicken strips, onion and peppers; sprinkle with cheese.

4) Bake 10 to 12 minutes or until crust is golden brown and cheese is melted.

HIGH ALTITUDE (3500-6500 FT.): Bake 2 to 4 minutes longer.

Nutrition Information Per Serving:

Calories:	240	From Fat:	90
Total Fat			11g
Saturated Fat			5g
Trans Fat			0g
Cholesterol			25mg
Sodium			710mg
Total Carbohydrate			24g
Dietary Fiber			1g
Sugars			5g
Protein			11g

Salsa-Lime-Bean Dip

PREP TIME: 10 MINUTES (READY IN 10 MINUTES)
SERVINGS: 10 (3 TABLESPOONS DIP AND 3 CRACKERS EACH)

EASY

1 can (16 oz) Old El Paso® refried beans

¼ cup Old El Paso® Thick 'n Chunky salsa

¼ cup sour cream

1 tablespoon lime juice

½ teaspoon ground cumin

1 medium garlic clove, finely chopped

¼ teaspoon salt

½ cup finely chopped seeded tomato

2 tablespoons chopped fresh cilantro

30 tortilla chips

Nutrition Information Per Serving:

Calories:	110	From Fat:	35
Total Fat			4g
Saturated Fat			1.5g
Trans Fat			0g
Cholesterol			5mg
Sodium			320mg
Total Carbohydrate			14g
Dietary Fiber			3g
Sugars			0g
Protein			3g

1) In medium bowl, stir together beans, salsa, 2 tablespoons of the sour cream, the lime juice, cumin, garlic and salt until well blended. Transfer mixture to shallow serving bowl.

2) Sprinkle tomato evenly over bean mixture. Top with dollops of remaining 2 tablespoons sour cream; sprinkle with cilantro. Serve with chips.

HIGH ALTITUDE (3500-6500 FT.): No change.

Chunky Guacamole

PREP TIME: 15 MINUTES (READY IN 15 MINUTES)
SERVINGS: 16 (2 TABLESPOONS EACH)

e EASY

2 large avocados (about 1 lb), pitted, peeled and cubed

1 tablespoon fresh lime juice

1/2 teaspoon salt

Dash ground red pepper (cayenne)

1 medium tomato, seeded, chopped

1 garlic clove, finely chopped

2 tablespoons finely chopped white onion

1 teaspoon chopped fresh cilantro, if desired

Tortilla chips, as desired

1) In large bowl, coarsely mash avocados, lime juice, salt and ground red pepper using pastry blender or fork.

2) Reserve 2 tablespoons chopped tomato for garnish. Stir remaining tomato, garlic and onion into avocado mixture. Spoon into serving bowl. Sprinkle top with reserved 2 tablespoons tomato and the cilantro. Serve with tortilla chips.

HIGH ALTITUDE (3500-6500 FT.): No change.

Nutrition Information Per Serving:

Calories:	50	From Fat:	40
Total Fat			4.5g
Saturated Fat			0.5g
Trans Fat			0g
Cholesterol			0mg
Sodium			75mg
Total Carbohydrate			3g
Dietary Fiber			2g
Sugars			0g
Protein			0g

Pan-Fried Mushroom and Cheese Flautas

PREP TIME: 30 MINUTES (READY IN 30 MINUTES)
SERVINGS: 4 (2 FLAUTAS EACH)

🄴 EASY

2 tablespoons butter or margarine

1 medium onion, chopped

1 medium red bell pepper, chopped

2 garlic cloves, finely chopped

1 package (8 oz) fresh mushrooms, chopped

1 teaspoon dried oregano leaves

¼ teaspoon salt

8 Old El Paso® flour tortillas (6 inch, from 8.2-oz package)

1½ cups finely shredded pepper Jack cheese (6 oz)

2 tablespoons vegetable oil

Sour cream, if desired

Guacamole, if desired

1) In 10-inch skillet, melt the butter over medium-high heat. Add the onion, bell pepper and garlic; cook and stir 2 minutes. Add mushrooms, oregano and salt; cook and stir 2 to 4 minutes or until onion and bell pepper are tender.

2) With slotted spoon, top each tortilla with the mushroom mixture. Sprinkle each with cheese. Roll up tightly; secure with toothpick.

3) Wipe the skillet clean with paper towel. Add oil to the same skillet; heat over medium heat until hot. Add flautas; cook 4 to 6 minutes, turning occasionally, until filling is hot and tortillas are toasted. Remove toothpicks before serving. Serve with sour cream and guacamole.

HIGH ALTITUDE (3500-6500 FT.): In Step 3, cook flautas 6 to 8 minutes.

Nutrition Information Per Serving:	
Calories: 470	From Fat: 270
Total Fat	30g
Saturated Fat	14g
Trans Fat	2g
Cholesterol	55mg
Sodium	790mg
Total Carbohydrate	33g
Dietary Fiber	3g
Sugars	5g
Protein	17g

Steak Tacos with Avocado Salsa

PREP TIME: 15 MINUTES (READY IN 1 HOUR 35 MINUTES)
SERVINGS: 4 (2 TACOS EACH)

e EASY

2 medium limes

1 tablespoon ground cumin

1/4 teaspoon salt

1/4 teaspoon pepper

2 garlic cloves, finely chopped

1 lb beef flank steak, trimmed of fat

1 cup chopped plum (Roma) tomatoes (about 2 medium)

1/4 cup chopped red onion

1 avocado, pitted, peeled and chopped

1/8 teaspoon salt

8 white corn tortillas (6 inch)

1) Squeeze limes into measuring cup; reserve 1 tablespoon juice for salsa. In heavy-duty resealable food-storage plastic bag, mix remaining lime juice (about 1/4 cup), the cumin, 1/4 teaspoon salt, the pepper and garlic. Add beef; seal bag and turn to coat beef. Refrigerate 1 hour to marinate, turning occasionally.

2) Meanwhile, in medium bowl, mix tomatoes, onion, avocado, reserved 1 tablespoon lime juice and 1/8 teaspoon salt; toss to coat.

3) Set oven control to broil. Remove beef from marinade; discard marinade. Place beef on rack in broiler pan. Broil with top 4 to 6 inches from heat 10 to 15 minutes or until desired doneness, turning once. Let stand 5 minutes. Cut diagonally across grain into very thin slices.

4) Warm tortillas as directed on package. Divide steak strips among tortillas; top each with about 1/4 cup avocado salsa; fold in half.

HIGH ALTITUDE (3500-6500 FT.): No change.

Nutrition Information Per Serving:		
Calories: 380	From Fat:	110
Total Fat		12g
Saturated Fat		2.5g
Trans Fat		0g
Cholesterol		85mg
Sodium		290mg
Total Carbohydrate		32g
Dietary Fiber		7g
Sugars		2g
Protein		37g

Chili Potato Dippers with Cheddar Jalapeño Dip

PREP TIME: 15 MINUTES (READY IN 40 MINUTES)
SERVINGS: 8 (2 TABLESPOONS DIP EACH)

e EASY

CHILI POTATO DIPPERS

- 4 medium russet potatoes
- 2 tablespoons olive or vegetable oil
- 2 teaspoons chili powder
- 1 teaspoon garlic powder

CHEDDAR JALAPEÑO DIP

- 1/3 cup sour cream
- 1/3 cup mayonnaise or salad dressing
- 1/4 cup finely chopped tomato
- 1/4 cup finely shredded sharp Cheddar cheese (1 oz)
- 1 to 2 jalapeño chiles, seeded, finely chopped
- 2 tablespoons sliced green onions

1) Heat oven to 450°F. Line 15x10x1-inch pan with foil; spray foil with cooking spray.

2) Cut potatoes into thin wedges. In large bowl, mix potatoes, oil, chili powder and garlic powder; toss to coat. Place in pan.

3) Bake 25 to 30 minutes or until tender and golden brown, turning once.

4) Meanwhile, in medium bowl, mix all dip ingredients except onions. Sprinkle onions on top of dip.

HIGH ALTITUDE (3500-6500 FT.): No change.

Nutrition Information Per Serving:		
Calories: 220	From Fat:	130
Total Fat		14g
Saturated Fat		3.5g
Trans Fat		0g
Cholesterol		15mg
Sodium		95mg
Total Carbohydrate		20g
Dietary Fiber		2g
Sugars		2g
Protein		3g

Fiesta Chicken Quesadillas

PREP TIME: 20 MINUTES (READY IN 20 MINUTES)
SERVINGS: 2

 EASY

4 fat-free flour tortillas (8 inch)

Cooking spray

1 cup chopped cooked chicken

½ cup thin red bell pepper strips

¼ cup thin green bell pepper strips

½ cup shredded reduced-fat sharp Cheddar cheese (2 oz)

1 tablespoon sliced green onion (1 medium)

½ cup Old El Paso® Thick 'n Chunky salsa

Nutrition Information Per Serving:	
Calories: 550	From Fat: 110
Total Fat	12g
Saturated Fat	4g
Trans Fat	0g
Cholesterol	65mg
Sodium	1710mg
Total Carbohydrate	73g
Dietary Fiber	7g
Sugars	4g
Protein	37g

1) Heat oven to 450°F. Line 15x10x1-inch pan with foil. Spray both sides of each tortilla lightly with cooking spray. Place 2 tortillas on foil-lined pan. Sprinkle each with half of the chicken, bell pepper strips, cheese and green onion. Top with remaining 2 tortillas.

2) Bake 3 to 5 minutes or until light brown and crisp. Cut into wedges; serve with salsa.

HIGH ALTITUDE (3500-6500 FT.): No change.

Crepas de Cajeta

PREP TIME: 35 MINUTES (READY IN 35 MINUTES)
SERVINGS: 6 (2 CREPES EACH)

 EASY

1 cup original all-purpose baking mix

¾ cup milk

2 eggs

1½ cups cajeta (goat milk candy spread), from 23.3-oz jar

½ cup chopped pecans

Powdered sugar, if desired

Nutrition Information Per Serving:	
Calories: 320	From Fat: 200
Total Fat	22g
Saturated Fat	9g
Trans Fat	1g
Cholesterol	100mg
Sodium	460mg
Total Carbohydrate	17g
Dietary Fiber	1g
Sugars	4g
Protein	13g

1) In medium bowl, stir baking mix, milk and eggs with wire whisk or fork until blended.

2) Heat 8-inch nonstick skillet over medium heat. For each crepe, pour 2 tablespoons batter into skillet; rotate skillet until batter covers bottom. Cook until golden on bottom. Turn; cook other side until golden brown. Stack crepes as removed from skillet, placing waxed paper between each crepe.

3) In small microwavable bowl, microwave cajeta on High about 30 seconds or until thin enough to drizzle.

4) Fold each crepe in half, then in half again. For each serving, top 2 crepes with 2 tablespoons cajeta; sprinkle with pecans and powdered sugar.

HIGH ALTITUDE (3500-6500 FT.): Use 1 cup milk.

Burrito Grande

PREP TIME: 15 MINUTES (READY IN 35 MINUTES)
SERVINGS: 6

⊖ EASY

½ lb bulk chorizo sausage
  or ground beef

1 can (15 oz) spicy chili
  beans, undrained

1 teaspoon ground cumin

4 flour tortillas (10 inch)

2½ cups shredded taco-flavored
  cheese blend (10 oz)

1 cup Old El Paso® mild taco sauce

¾ cup sour cream

Shredded lettuce, if desired

1) Heat oven to 375°F. Spray 15x10x1-inch
   pan with cooking spray.

2) In 10-inch skillet, cook sausage over
   medium-high heat until well browned.
   Drain. Add beans and cumin; mix well.

3) Place tortillas, overlapping, down one
   side of pan. Spoon sausage mixture
   down center of tortillas; sprinkle with
   1½ cups of the cheese. Roll tortillas
   over sausage mixture to create 1 large
   burrito, seam side down. Spoon taco
   sauce over burrito; sprinkle with
   remaining 1 cup cheese and lettuce.

4) Bake 15 to 20 minutes or until hot. To
   serve, cut burrito into slices. Serve with
   sour cream and lettuce.

HIGH ALTITUDE (3500-6500 FT.): In Step 2, add chili
beans and cumin, mix well and cook about 1 minute
or until hot, stirring constantly. In Step 3, do not
spoon taco sauce or cheese over burrito. In Step 4,
bake 15 minutes, then add sauce and cheese over
burrito and bake 5 to 10 minutes longer.

Nutrition Information Per Serving:

Calories:	590	From Fat:	340
Total Fat		38g	
Saturated Fat		19g	
Trans Fat		1g	
Cholesterol		95mg	
Sodium		1780mg	
Total Carbohydrate		35g	
Dietary Fiber		4g	
Sugars		6g	
Protein		26g	

Cajeta Gelatin

PREP TIME: 30 MINUTES (READY IN 8 HOURS 15 MINUTES)
SERVINGS: 8

GELATIN

2 envelopes unflavored gelatin

1/2 cup water

1 can (12 oz) evaporated milk

1 3/4 cups cajeta (goat milk candy spread), from 23.3-oz jar

2 tablespoons brandy, if desired

CRÈME ANGLAISE

2 egg yolks

1/4 cup sugar

1 cup whipping cream

1 1/2 teaspoons brandy or 1 teaspoon vanilla

Mint leaves, if desired

1) Spray 8 (6-oz) custard cups with cooking spray. In small microwavable bowl, sprinkle the gelatin on water. Let stand about 2 minutes to soften. Microwave on High 30 to 45 seconds, stirring after 15 seconds, until gelatin is dissolved.

2) In 2-quart saucepan, heat evaporated milk over medium heat until hot. Do not boil. Stir in cajeta until well blended. Stir in the gelatin mixture and 2 tablespoons brandy. Pour into custard cups. Cover with plastic wrap; refrigerate about 8 hours or until set.

3) In small bowl, mix egg yolks and sugar. In 1-quart saucepan, heat whipping cream just to boiling over low heat. Stir small amount of whipping cream into egg yolk mixture; slowly stir mixture into whipping cream in saucepan. Cook over low heat about 10 minutes, stirring constantly, until custard coats a spoon. Do not boil. Remove from the heat. Stir in 1 1/2 teaspoons brandy. Cover surface with waxed paper. Cool 15 minutes. Refrigerate until mixture is cold, at least 4 hours or overnight, until serving time.

4) To unmold, run knife around edge of cups to loosen; turn upside down onto individual dessert plates. Garnish with mint leaves. Serve with crème anglaise. Cover and refrigerate any remaining gelatin.

HIGH ALTITUDE (3500-6500 FT.): No change.

Nutrition Information Per Serving:		
Calories:	280	From Fat: 190
Total Fat		21g
Saturated Fat		14g
Trans Fat		0.5g
Cholesterol		115mg
Sodium		200mg
Total Carbohydrate		10g
Dietary Fiber		0g
Sugars		10g
Protein		11g

Enchiladas Verde

PREP TIME: 10 MINUTES (READY IN 40 MINUTES)
SERVINGS: 4 (2 ENCHILADAS EACH)

e EASY

8 corn tortillas (6 inch)

2 cups shredded cooked chicken

1¾ cups green tomatillo salsa

1 cup crumbled queso quesadilla cheese (4 oz)

¼ cup sour cream

½ cup finely chopped onion

Cilantro leaves, if desired

1) Heat oven to 350°F. Wrap 4 tortillas at a time in microwavable paper towels. Microwave on High 20 to 30 seconds or until they can be folded without cracking.

2) Spoon chicken evenly in center of each tortilla; roll up. Place in ungreased 11x7-inch (2-quart) glass baking dish. Pour salsa over enchiladas. Sprinkle with cheese, sour cream and onion.

3) Bake uncovered 15 to 25 minutes or until thoroughly heated. Sprinkle with cilantro. Let stand 5 minutes before serving.

HIGH ALTITUDE (3500-6500 FT.): Heat oven to 375°F. Increase salsa to 2 cups. Bake 30 to 35 minutes.

Nutrition Information Per Serving:

Calories: 400	From Fat: 160
Total Fat	18g
Saturated Fat	7g
Trans Fat	0g
Cholesterol	80mg
Sodium	480mg
Total Carbohydrate	33g
Dietary Fiber	4g
Sugars	4g
Protein	26g

tip

Queso quesadilla is a soft, mild cheese that melts easily. Look for it in the Hispanic section of your supermarket.

Mexican Chicken Pot Pies in Crescent Bowls

PREP TIME: 20 MINUTES (READY IN 30 MINUTES)
SERVINGS: 4

e EASY

1 can (8 oz) Pillsbury® refrigerated crescent dinner rolls or 1 can (8 oz) Pillsbury® Crescent Recipe Creations™ refrigerated flaky dough sheet

3 tablespoons butter or margarine

½ cup chopped onion

2 tablespoons all-purpose flour

½ teaspoon salt

¼ teaspoon pepper

2 cups chicken broth

2 packages (6 oz each) refrigerated cooked Southwest-flavor chicken breast strips, coarsely chopped

2 cans (15 oz each) black beans, drained, rinsed

1 can (4.5 oz) Old El Paso® chopped green chiles, drained

2 cups Green Giant® Valley Fresh Steamers™ Niblets® frozen corn

½ cup shredded Cheddar-Jack with jalapeño peppers cheese blend (2 oz)

½ cup Old El Paso® Thick 'n Chunky salsa

1) Heat oven to 375°F. Place four 10-oz custard cups upside down on cookie sheet with sides. Spray cups with cooking spray.

2) Unroll dough on work surface (if using crescent rolls, pinch the seams to seal); press into 12x8-inch rectangle. Cut into 4 rectangles. Place 1 dough rectangle over each custard cup, stretching to fit bowl.

3) Bake 12 to 15 minutes or until golden brown. Cool 5 minutes. Remove from custard cups. Place on cooling rack.

4) Meanwhile, in 3-quart saucepan, melt butter over medium heat. Add onion; cook about 2 minutes, stirring occasionally, until tender. Add flour, salt and pepper; stir until well blended. Gradually stir in broth, cook until bubbly and thickened. Stir in chicken, black beans, green chiles and corn. Simmer about 5 minutes or until hot.

5) Spoon about 1½ cups chicken mixture into each crescent bowl. Top with cheese and salsa.

HIGH ALTITUDE (3500-6500 FT.): No change.

Nutrition Information Per Serving:

Calories: 810	From Fat: 240
Total Fat	26g
Saturated Fat	13g
Trans Fat	0g
Cholesterol	65mg
Sodium	2840mg
Total Carbohydrate	105g
Dietary Fiber	25g
Sugars	11g
Protein	38g

Spicy Mexican Cabbage Slaw

PREP TIME: 20 MINUTES (READY IN 1 HOUR 20 MINUTES)
SERVINGS: 8 (1/2 CUP EACH)

DRESSING

- 1/2 cup mayonnaise or salad dressing
- 1 chipotle chile in adobo sauce (from 11-oz can), chopped
- 1 tablespoon lime juice
- 2 teaspoons sugar
- 1/4 teaspoon ground cumin

SALAD

- 3 cups coleslaw mix (from 16-oz bag)
- 1 chayote squash, unpeeled, cut into 2x1/8x1/8-inch strips (1 1/2 cups)
- 1/2 cup julienne (matchstick-cut) red bell pepper strips (2x1/8x1/8 inch)
- 1/4 cup very thin short red onion strips
- 1/4 cup chopped fresh cilantro

1) In small bowl, mix the dressing ingredients. In large bowl, mix the salad ingredients. Add dressing; toss to coat. Cover and refrigerate at least 1 hour before serving to blend flavors.

HIGH ALTITUDE (3500-6500 FT.): No change.

Nutrition Information Per Serving:

Calories: 240	From Fat: 200
Total Fat	22g
Saturated Fat	5g
Trans Fat	1.5g
Cholesterol	75mg
Sodium	700mg
Total Carbohydrate	15g
Dietary Fiber	2g
Sugars	4g
Protein	21g

Mexican Chocolate Flans

PREP TIME: 35 MINUTES (READY IN 2 HOURS 20 MINUTES)
SERVINGS: 6

TOPPING

³/₄ cup sugar

¹/₂ cup water

FLANS

¹/₂ cup milk

¹/₂ cup sugar

¹/₄ cup unsweetened baking cocoa

¹/₂ teaspoon ground cinnamon

1 can (12 oz) evaporated milk

¹/₂ teaspoon vanilla

3 eggs, beaten

Chocolate shavings, if desired

1) Heat oven to 325°F. In heavy 1-quart saucepan, mix topping ingredients. Heat to boiling over medium heat. Cover; boil 1 minute. Uncover; cook until sugar becomes golden brown. Do not stir. Very carefully pour and swirl sugar into 6 (6-oz) custard cups.

2) In 2-quart saucepan, mix ¹/₂ cup milk, the sugar, cocoa and cinnamon. Heat to boiling over medium-high heat, stirring constantly with wire whisk. Continue to boil 1 minute, stirring constantly. Remove from heat. Using wire whisk, beat in evaporated milk, vanilla and eggs. Pour mixture evenly over sugar in custard cups.

3) Place custard cups in 13x9-inch (3-quart) glass baking dish. Place baking dish on center oven rack. Pour hot water into baking dish until it is halfway up sides of custard cups. Bake 50 to 55 minutes or until knife inserted near edge of custard mixture comes out clean. Carefully remove cups from water; cool slightly, about 5 minutes. Refrigerate until well chilled, about 50 minutes.

4) To serve, unmold flans onto individual dessert plates. If desired, top each with chocolate shavings. Cover and refrigerate any remaining flans.

HIGH ALTITUDE (3500-6500 FT.): Heat oven to 350°F. For topping, decrease sugar to 1/2 cup. Do not add water. Heat sugar over medium heat, stirring constantly until caramel colored. (Watch carefully.) Decrease bake time to 45 to 50 minutes.

Nutrition Information Per Serving:	
Calories: 280	From Fat: 70
Total Fat	8g
Saturated Fat	4g
Trans Fat	0g
Cholesterol	115mg
Sodium	65mg
Total Carbohydrate	47g
Dietary Fiber	1g
Sugars	45g
Protein	6g

Tostada Chicken Salad

PREP TIME: 40 MINUTES (READY IN 40 MINUTES)
SERVINGS: 2

1 cup shredded cooked chicken

2 tablespoons chopped fresh cilantro

2 tablespoons sour cream

2 tablespoons mayonnaise or salad dressing

2 teaspoons Old El Paso® taco seasoning mix (from 1-oz package) or Southwest seasoning mix

1 tablespoon chopped green onion (1 medium)

2 tostada shells

3 cups shredded lettuce

¹/₄ cup Old El Paso® Thick 'n Chunky salsa

¹/₂ medium avocado, sliced, if desired

1) In medium bowl, mix chicken, cilantro, sour cream, mayonnaise, seasoning mix and onion.

2) Place 1 tostada shell on each dinner plate. Top each with 1¹/₂ cups shredded lettuce. Top each with half of chicken mixture; drizzle each with 2 tablespoons salsa. Garnish with avocado.

HIGH ALTITUDE (3500-6500 FT.): No change.

Nutrition Information Per Serving:	
Calories: 240	From Fat: 200
Total Fat	22g
Saturated Fat	5g
Trans Fat	1.5g
Cholesterol	75mg
Sodium	700mg
Total Carbohydrate	15g
Dietary Fiber	2g
Sugars	4g
Protein	21g

Tortilla Soup with Baked Tortilla Strips

PREP TIME: 30 MINUTES (READY IN 45 MINUTES)
SERVINGS: 6

6 soft corn tortillas (6 inch)

2 tablespoons vegetable oil

1 small onion, chopped ($1/3$ cup)

2 garlic cloves, finely chopped

1 medium Anaheim, poblano or jalapeño chile, seeded, chopped

1 carton (32 oz) reduced-sodium chicken broth

1 can (14.5 oz) fire-roasted diced tomatoes, undrained

$1/2$ teaspoon salt

$1 1/2$ cups shredded cooked chicken breast

TOPPINGS

Avocado slices

1 cup shredded Oaxaca, Cotija or Manchego cheese

Chopped fresh cilantro

1 lime, cut into wedges

1) Heat oven to 450°F. Brush both sides of tortillas with 1 tablespoon of the oil. Cut tortillas in half; cut halves into $1/4$-inch strips. Place in single layer on cookie sheets. Bake 6 to 8 minutes, stirring once halfway through bake time, until tortilla strips begin to brown; cool. Strips will become crisp when cooled.

2) Meanwhile, in 3-quart saucepan, heat the remaining 1 tablespoon oil over medium-high heat. Cook onion in oil about 2 minutes, stirring frequently. Add the garlic and chile; cook 2 to 3 minutes, stirring frequently, until vegetables are crisp-tender. Stir in the chicken broth, tomatoes and salt. Heat to boiling. Reduce heat; cover and simmer 15 minutes. Add chicken; heat until hot.

3) To serve, divide half of tortilla strips among 6 individual serving bowls; ladle in soup. Top with avocado and cheese; garnish with remaining tortilla strips and cilantro. Serve with lime wedges.

HIGH ALTITUDE (3500-6500 FT.): No change.

Nutrition Information Per Serving:		
Calories: 20	From Fat:	10
Total Fat		1g
Saturated Fat		0g
Trans Fat		0g
Cholesterol		0mg
Sodium		75mg
Total Carbohydrate		2g
Dietary Fiber		0g
Sugars		0g
Protein		0g

tip

You can substitute another cheese for the Oaxaca—try Chihuahua (Mexican melting cheese) or mozzarella.

Easy Chicken-Rice Burritos

PREP TIME: 20 MINUTES (READY IN 50 MINUTES)
SERVINGS: 4 (2 BURRITOS EACH)

ⓔ EASY

2 cups Old El Paso® Thick 'n Chunky salsa

1 cup water

1 cup uncooked instant white rice

1½ cups shredded deli rotisserie chicken (from 2- to 2½-lb chicken)

1 cup shredded Cheddar cheese (4 oz)

½ teaspoon garlic powder

1 package (11.5 oz) Old El Paso® flour tortillas for burritos (eight 8-inch tortillas)

Shredded lettuce, if desired

Chopped tomatoes, if desired

1) Heat oven to 375°F. In 2-quart saucepan, heat salsa and water to boiling. Stir in rice. Cover; remove from heat. Let stand 5 minutes.

2) Stir chicken, cheese and garlic powder into rice mixture. Spoon ½ cup chicken-rice mixture onto center of each tortilla. Fold bottom ⅓ of tortilla over filling; fold in sides toward center, leaving top open. Place seam side down in ungreased 13x9-inch (3-quart) glass baking dish.

3) Cover tightly with foil; bake 20 to 30 minutes or until thoroughly heated. Garnish with lettuce and tomatoes.

HIGH ALTITUDE (3500-6500 FT.): No change.

Nutrition Information Per Serving:		
Calories: 610	From Fat:	190
Total Fat		22g
Saturated Fat		9g
Trans Fat		2.5g
Cholesterol		75mg
Sodium		1960mg
Total Carbohydrate		73g
Dietary Fiber		0g
Sugars		4g
Protein		29g

Fish Tacos with Creamy Avocado Topping

PREP TIME: 30 MINUTES (READY IN 30 MINUTES)
SERVINGS: 6 (2 TACOS EACH)

 EASY

1 avocado, pitted, peeled and diced

2 tablespoons chopped fresh cilantro

1/3 cup ranch dressing

1 package (4.6 oz) Old El Paso® taco shells (12 shells)

1 tablespoon vegetable oil

1 1/2 teaspoons lemon-pepper seasoning

1 teaspoon chili powder

1/4 teaspoon salt

1 1/2 lb halibut, skin removed, cut into 1-inch pieces

1 cup shredded lettuce or mixed salad greens

1 small tomato, diced

1) Heat gas or charcoal grill. In medium bowl, mix avocado, cilantro and dressing. Set aside. Heat taco shells as directed on package.

2) In large bowl, mix oil, lemon-pepper seasoning, chili powder and salt. Add halibut; toss gently to coat. Place halibut in grill basket. Place basket on grill over medium heat. Cover grill; cook 5 to 10 minutes or until fish flakes easily with fork, rearranging twice. Fill taco shells with fish, lettuce, avocado mixture and tomato.

HIGH ALTITUDE (3500-6500 FT.): No change.

Nutrition Information Per Serving:

Calories:	300	From Fat:	160
Total Fat			18g
Saturated Fat			3g
Trans Fat			1.5g
Cholesterol			50mg
Sodium			560mg
Total Carbohydrate			17g
Dietary Fiber			3g
Sugars			0g
Protein			18g

Spicy Mole Poblano

PREP TIME: 30 MINUTES (READY IN 1 HOUR 15 MINUTES)
SERVINGS: 12 (1 CUP EACH)

¼ cup olive oil

1 slice (4 inches long) French baguette, cut in half lengthwise

2 whole garlic cloves, peeled

1 jar (8.25 oz) mole sauce

3 cans (14 oz each) chicken broth

1 can (14 oz) diced tomatoes, undrained

1½ lb small red potatoes, peeled (about 12 small potatoes)

1 jar (15 oz) nopales, drained, rinsed

1 deli rotisserie chicken (2 to 2½ lb), shredded (about 3 cups)

3 cups converted long-grain white rice

6 cups water

Salt to taste, if desired

2 tablespoons sesame seed

1) In 4-quart Dutch oven, heat 2 tablespoons of the oil over medium-high heat. Add bread halves; cook until golden brown on one side. Turn; cook until golden brown on the other side. Stir in garlic. Cook 2 to 3 minutes, stirring constantly, until garlic is light golden brown. Set bread aside.

2) In same Dutch oven, heat remaining 2 tablespoons oil over very low heat.

3) Meanwhile, make mole mixture in 2 batches. In blender, place 1 baguette half, 1 garlic clove, half each of the mole sauce, chicken broth and tomatoes. Cover; blend on high speed about 45 seconds or until smooth. Add mixture to Dutch oven. Repeat with the remaining baguette half, garlic, mole sauce, chicken broth and tomatoes.

4) Stir in potatoes and nopales. Heat to boiling. Stir in chicken. Reduce heat to low; simmer 30 to 45 minutes or until potatoes are tender.

5) Meanwhile, in 3-quart saucepan, heat rice and water to boiling. Reduce heat; cover and simmer 20 minutes. Remove from heat; let stand about 5 minutes or until liquid is absorbed. Fluff rice with fork. Sprinkle mole mixture with salt. Serve mole mixture over rice; sprinkle with sesame seed.

HIGH ALTITUDE (3500-6500 FT.): Cut potatoes into 1-1/2-inch cubes.

Nutrition Information Per Serving:		
Calories: 500	From Fat: 110	
Total Fat	12g	
Saturated Fat	2.5g	
Trans Fat	0g	
Cholesterol	50mg	
Sodium	1180mg	
Total Carbohydrate	71g	
Dietary Fiber	3g	
Sugars	3g	
Protein	26g	

Tomatillo Salsa

PREP TIME: 30 MINUTES (READY IN 30 MINUTES)
SERVINGS: 32 (2 TABLESPOONS EACH)

EASY   **LOW FAT**

1) In 3-quart saucepan, place tomatillos; cover with cold water. Cook over medium heat 10 to 15 minutes or until tender. Drain and discard water.

2) In blender, mix tomatillos and remaining ingredients except oil and tortilla chips. Cover and blend until desired consistency.

3) In 2-quart saucepan, heat oil over medium heat. Add tomatillo mixture. Cook 10 to 15 minutes, stirring constantly, until mixture is thoroughly heated and darker in color. Serve warm or cold with tortilla chips.

HIGH ALTITUDE (3500-6500 FT.): No change.

1 1/2 lb fresh tomatillos, husks removed

2 to 3 serrano chiles, seeded

2 large garlic cloves, peeled

1/2 medium white onion, coarsely chopped

1/4 cup coarsely chopped fresh cilantro

3/4 cup chicken broth

1/2 teaspoon salt

1/2 teaspoon chicken bouillon granules

2 tablespoons vegetable oil

Tortilla chips, as desired

Nutrition Information Per Serving:

Calories:	240	From Fat:	200
Total Fat			22g
Saturated Fat			5g
Trans Fat			1.5g
Cholesterol			75mg
Sodium			700mg
Total Carbohydrate			15g
Dietary Fiber			2g
Sugars			4g
Protein			21g

Black Bean-Chorizo Dip

PREP TIME: 20 MINUTES (READY IN 20 MINUTES)
SERVINGS: 12

EASY

1/4 lb bulk chorizo sausage

1 garlic clove, finely chopped

1 can (19 oz) Progresso® Vegetable Classics hearty black bean soup

1 can (4.5 oz) Old El Paso® chopped green chiles, if desired

2 tablespoons crema (Mexican-style cream) or sour cream

1/3 cup Cotija or fresco-style cheese, crumbled

2 tablespoons cilantro, finely chopped

Tortilla chips, as desired

1) In 2-quart saucepan, cook sausage and garlic over medium heat, stirring frequently, until sausage is no longer pink. Stir in soup and chiles. Reduce heat to medium-low. Cook until hot, stirring occasionally.

2) Spoon dip into medium bowl; top with crema, cheese and cilantro. Serve with chips.

HIGH ALTITUDE (3500-6500 FT.): No change.

Nutrition Information Per Serving:

Calories:	100	From Fat:	50
Total Fat			5g
Saturated Fat			2g
Trans Fat			0g
Cholesterol			15mg
Sodium			500mg
Total Carbohydrate			6g
Dietary Fiber			1g
Sugars			0g
Protein			5g

Salsa Pico de Gallo with Chile

PREP TIME: 10 MINUTES (READY IN 10 MINUTES)
SERVINGS: 12 (1/4 CUP EACH)

e EASY   **lf** LOW FAT

4 medium tomatoes, chopped
   (3 cups)

1 serrano or jalapeño chile, seeded,
   finely chopped

1 tablespoon finely chopped onion

1 tablespoon chopped fresh cilantro

1 teaspoon fresh lime juice

1/2 teaspoon salt

   Tortilla chips, as desired

1) In medium bowl, mix all ingredients
   except tortilla chips until blended. Cover
   and refrigerate until serving time. Serve
   with tortilla chips.

   HIGH ALTITUDE (3500-6500 FT.): No change.

Nutrition Information Per Serving:

Calories:	10	From Fat:	0
Total Fat			0g
Saturated Fat			0g
Trans Fat			0g
Cholesterol			0mg
Sodium			100mg
Total Carbohydrate			2g
Dietary Fiber			0g
Sugars			1g
Protein			0g

Ground Beef Fajitas

PREP TIME: 35 MINUTES (READY IN 35 MINUTES)
SERVINGS: 4

1 lb lean (at least 80%) ground beef

1 teaspoon grated fresh lime peel

1 tablespoon fresh lime juice

1 tablespoon chili powder

1 tablespoon tomato paste

2 garlic cloves, finely chopped

1 medium red bell pepper, cut into strips

1 medium onion, cut into thin wedges

2 teaspoons vegetable oil

4 Old El Paso® flour tortillas for burritos (8 inch, from 11.5-oz package), warmed

1/4 cup sour cream

4 teaspoons chopped fresh cilantro leaves

Guacamole, if desired

1) Heat gas or charcoal grill. In medium bowl, mix the ground beef, lime peel, lime juice, chili powder, tomato paste and garlic. Shape mixture into 4 sausage-shaped rolls, about 6 inches long. Thread 1 beef roll on each of 4 (11-inch) metal skewers; flatten slightly.

2) In another medium bowl, mix bell pepper, onion and oil; place mixture in grill basket (grill "wok").

3) Place skewered beef rolls and grill basket on grill over medium heat. Cover grill; cook 7 to 8 minutes, turning beef rolls after 5 minutes and shaking basket to turn vegetables occasionally, until beef rolls are thoroughly cooked and no longer pink in center and vegetables are crisp-tender.

4) Remove each beef roll from skewer onto center of tortilla. Spoon vegetables over beef rolls. Top with sour cream and cilantro. Serve with guacamole.

HIGH ALTITUDE (3500-6500 FT.): Cook 18 to 20 minutes.

Nutrition Information Per Serving:		
Calories: 410	From Fat: 200	
Total Fat		22g
Saturated Fat		8g
Trans Fat		2g
Cholesterol		80mg
Sodium		410mg
Total Carbohydrate		28g
Dietary Fiber		2g
Sugars		4g
Protein		24g

Potluck Pleasers

Bring the showstopping treat that wows the crowd.
It's easy with the group-size delights in this chapter!

CURRIED CHICKEN PACKETS
PG. 242

STRAWBERRY-HARD
LEMONADE SLUSH
PG. 243

MAKE-AHEAD DAGWOOD
SANDWICHES
PG. 238

LAYERED SUMMER FRUITS
WITH CREAMY LIME DRESSING
PG. 245

Make-Ahead Dagwood Sandwiches

PREP TIME: 40 MINUTES (READY IN 40 MINUTES)
SERVINGS: 12 SANDWICHES

2   loaves herb-flavored or
    cheese-flavored bread, such as
    Focaccia, ciabatta or Asiago cheese
    bread (1 lb each, about 1 inch thick)

1   container (6.5 oz) garlic-and-herbs
    spreadable cheese

1   lb thinly sliced smoked turkey

8   oz sliced provolone cheese

8   oz thinly sliced salami

1/4 cup loosely packed fresh basil leaves

8   slices bacon, cooked

1   sweet onion, thinly sliced, separated
    into rings

3   small plum (Roma) tomatoes, sliced

4   cups lightly packed torn arugula

1/2 cup basil pesto

1) With long serrated knife, cut bread in
   half horizontally. Spread cut side of each
   bread bottom with half of the spreadable
   cheese. Overlapping slices, arrange the
   remaining ingredients except pesto in
   the order listed over each bread bottom.
   Spread cut side of each bread top with
   half of the pesto, and place over arugula.

2) Place each whole bread loaf in a large
   food-storage plastic bag; seal and
   refrigerate topped with cast-iron skillet or other heavy weight up to 24 hours.

3) When ready to serve, cut each loaf into 6 equal sandwiches. Secure the
   sandwiches with toothpicks or small skewers.

HIGH ALTITUDE (3500-6500 FT.): No change.

Nutrition Information Per Serving:		
Calories: 520	From Fat: 270	
Total Fat		30g
Saturated Fat		11g
Trans Fat		0g
Cholesterol		65mg
Sodium		1710mg
Total Carbohydrate		40g
Dietary Fiber		2g
Sugars		3g
Protein		23g

Antipasto Rotini Salad

PREP TIME: 30 MINUTES (READY IN 2 HOURS 30 MINUTES)
SERVINGS: 24 (1/2 CUP EACH)

SALAD

- 3 cups uncooked rotini pasta
- 2 cups fresh broccoli florets
- 4 oz thinly sliced Genoa salami, cut into strips
- 1 can (15 oz) Progresso® dark red kidney beans, drained, rinsed
- 4 medium plum (Roma) tomatoes, cut into thin wedges
- 1 medium green bell pepper, sliced
- 1/2 medium red onion, sliced, rinsed
- 1/2 cup pitted kalamata olives, halved

PARMESAN-PEPPER DRESSING

- 3/4 cup Italian dressing
- 1/2 cup freshly shredded Parmesan cheese (2 oz)
- 1 1/2 teaspoons coarse ground black pepper
- 1/2 teaspoon Worcestershire sauce
- 3 garlic cloves, finely chopped

1) Cook rotini to desired doneness as directed on package, adding broccoli during last 3 minutes of cook time.

2) Drain rotini and broccoli; rinse with cold water until cool. In large bowl, mix cooked rotini and broccoli with remaining salad ingredients.

3) In medium bowl, mix the dressing ingredients. Pour dressing over salad; toss until well mixed. Cover; refrigerate at least 2 hours. Stir before serving.

HIGH ALTITUDE (3500-6500 FT.): No change.

Nutrition Information Per Serving:		
Calories: 120	From Fat:	45
Total Fat		5g
Saturated Fat		1g
Trans Fat		0g
Cholesterol		5mg
Sodium		330mg
Total Carbohydrate		15g
Dietary Fiber		2g
Sugars		2g
Protein		5g

tip

This salad can be made the night before and refrigerated in a covered container. If the salad seems dry, add a little extra Italian dressing.

Herbed Cheese Dip

PREP TIME: 15 MINUTES (READY IN 15 MINUTES)
SERVINGS: 14 (2 TABLESPOONS DIP EACH)

 EASY

1 package (8 oz) $\frac{1}{3}$-less-fat cream cheese (Neufchâtel)

$\frac{1}{2}$ cup plain fat-free yogurt

2 teaspoons milk

$\frac{1}{4}$ cup finely chopped fresh parsley

3 tablespoons finely chopped fresh chives

2 tablespoons finely chopped fresh basil leaves

$\frac{1}{8}$ teaspoon garlic salt

Raw vegetable dippers or crackers, as desired

Fresh basil, if desired

1) In small bowl, beat cream cheese, yogurt and milk with electric mixer on low speed until blended.

2) Fold in parsley, chives, basil and garlic salt. Serve immediately with dippers, or cover and refrigerate until serving time. Garnish with basil.

HIGH ALTITUDE (3500-6500 FT.): No change.

Nutrition Information Per Serving:	
Calories: 50	From Fat: 35
Total Fat	4g
Saturated Fat	2.5g
Trans Fat	0g
Cholesterol	15mg
Sodium	85mg
Total Carbohydrate	2g
Dietary Fiber	0g
Sugars	1g
Protein	2g

Caribbean Shrimp Spread

PREP TIME: 18 MINUTES (READY IN 20 MINUTES)
SERVINGS: 18 (2 TABLESPOONS SPREAD EACH)

 EASY

$\frac{1}{2}$ teaspoon Caribbean jerk seasoning (dry)

1 container (8 oz) whipped cream cheese spread

$\frac{1}{4}$ teaspoon grated lime peel

$\frac{1}{2}$ lb cooked deveined peeled shrimp, tails removed, chopped

4 medium green onions, chopped ($\frac{1}{4}$ cup)

2 tablespoons chopped red bell pepper

2 tablespoons shredded Cheddar cheese

Assorted crackers or cut-up vegetables, as desired

1) Stir seasoning into cream cheese container. Spread mixture on large serving plate or dinner plate.

2) Top with lime peel, shrimp, onions, red bell pepper and cheese.

3) Serve immediately with crackers or vegetables, or cover and refrigerate until serving time.

HIGH ALTITUDE (3500-6500 FT.): No change.

Nutrition Information Per Serving:	
Calories: 50	From Fat: 35
Total Fat	4g
Saturated Fat	2.5g
Trans Fat	0g
Cholesterol	35mg
Sodium	125mg
Total Carbohydrate	0g
Dietary Fiber	0g
Sugars	0g
Protein	3g

Fajita Chicken Wings

PREP TIME: 20 MINUTES (READY IN 5 HOURS)
SERVINGS: 24 APPETIZERS

⊜ EASY

12 chicken wings, tips removed

MARINADE

¼ cup lime juice

2 tablespoons vegetable oil

3 tablespoons chopped fresh cilantro

1 teaspoon ground cumin

½ teaspoon salt

½ teaspoon dried oregano leaves

¼ teaspoon crushed red pepper flakes

1 garlic clove, finely chopped

1) Cut each chicken wing in half; place in large resealable food-storage plastic bag. Add marinade ingredients; seal bag. Turn bag to coat wings. Refrigerate at least 4 hours but no longer than 24 hours, turning bag occasionally.

2) Heat oven to 375°F. Drain chicken wings, reserving marinade. Place chicken on broiler pan.

3) Bake 45 to 60 minutes or until juice of chicken is clear when thickest part is cut to bone (180°F), brushing occasionally with the reserved marinade. Discard any remaining marinade. Serve warm.

HIGH ALTITUDE (3500-6500 FT.): No change.

Nutrition Information Per Serving:		
Calories: 50	From Fat:	35
Total Fat		4g
Saturated Fat		1g
Trans Fat		0g
Cholesterol		15mg
Sodium		40mg
Total Carbohydrate		0g
Dietary Fiber		0g
Sugars		0g
Protein		4g

Curried Chicken Packets

PREP TIME: 50 MINUTES (READY IN 1 HOUR)
SERVINGS: 24 APPETIZERS

DIPPING SAUCE

- 1 cup orange marmalade
- 2 tablespoons soy sauce
- 2 teaspoons Dijon mustard
- 1/2 teaspoon ground ginger

PACKETS

- 1 cup finely chopped cooked chicken
- 1/2 cup finely shredded Monterey Jack cheese (2 oz)
- 1/4 cup golden raisins, chopped
- 1 medium green onion, finely chopped (1 tablespoon)
- 1 tablespoon finely chopped fresh parsley
- 1/2 teaspoon ground ginger
- 1 teaspoon ground curry
- 1 can (16.3 oz) Pillsbury® Grands!® Flaky Layers refrigerated original biscuits
- 1 egg
- 1 teaspoon water
- 1 tablespoon toasted sesame seed, if desired

1) In small bowl, mix the dipping sauce ingredients with wire whisk; set aside.

2) Heat oven to 350°F. Grease 2 cookie sheets with shortening, or spray with cooking spray. In medium bowl, mix chicken, cheese, raisins, onion, parsley, ginger and curry until well blended. Cover and refrigerate.

3) Working with 4 biscuits at a time, evenly split each biscuit between layers into thirds. Refrigerate remaining 4 biscuits. Gently stretch each third of dough. Place 1 tablespoon chicken mixture in center of each; fold 2 sides upward, forming a standing half-moon shape. Pinch edges tightly to seal. Place on cookie sheet, pinched edges up.

4) In small bowl, beat egg and water. Brush tops of each packet with egg, and sprinkle with sesame seed.

5) Bake 12 to 15 minutes or until tops are golden brown and filling is hot. Repeat with remaining dough and filling. Serve warm or cold with sauce.

HIGH ALTITUDE (3500-6500 FT.): No change.

Nutrition Information Per Serving:		
Calories: 30	From Fat:	40
Total Fat		4.5g
Saturated Fat		1.5g
Trans Fat		1g
Cholesterol		15mg
Sodium		290mg
Total Carbohydrate		19g
Dietary Fiber		0g
Sugars		9g
Protein		4g

Strawberry–Hard Lemonade Slush

PREP TIME: 15 MINUTES (READY IN 4 HOURS 15 MINUTES)
SERVINGS: 23 (ABOUT 3/4 CUP EACH)

e EASY   LF LOW FAT

1 box (4-serving size) strawberry-flavored gelatin

1 cup boiling water

2 boxes (10 oz each) frozen strawberries in light syrup, partially thawed

1 quart (4 cups) fresh strawberries, hulled

1 can (12 oz) frozen lemonade concentrate, partially thawed

$\frac{1}{2}$ cup sugar

1 bottle (11.2 oz) hard lemonade 5% alcohol beverage or 1 can (12 oz) lemon-lime carbonated beverage

6 additional bottles (11.2 oz each) hard lemonade 5% alcohol beverage or 1 bottle (2 liters) lemon-lime carbonated beverage or ginger ale, chilled

1) In 13x9-inch (3-quart) glass baking dish, place gelatin; pour boiling water on gelatin; stir until gelatin is dissolved.

2) In food processor, place strawberries in syrup, fresh strawberries, lemonade concentrate and sugar. Cover; process until smooth. Pour into gelatin. Stir in 1 bottle hard lemonade. Freeze 4 to 6 hours or overnight until of slush consistency, stirring after 2 hours.

3) To serve, spoon $\frac{1}{2}$ cup slush mixture into each glass; pour $\frac{1}{3}$ cup hard lemonade over each. Stir and serve.

HIGH ALTITUDE (3500-6500 FT.): No change.

Nutrition Information Per Serving:

Calories:	160	From Fat:	0
Total Fat			0g
Saturated Fat			0g
Trans Fat			0g
Cholesterol			0mg
Sodium			20mg
Total Carbohydrate			31g
Dietary Fiber			1g
Sugars			28g
Protein			0g

Caramelized-Onion Bread Pudding

PREP TIME: 35 MINUTES (READY IN 1 HOUR 15 MINUTES)
SERVINGS: 12

1 tablespoon olive or vegetable oil

2 large sweet onions (such as Maui or Walla Walla), cut into 1/4-inch slices

1 lb rustic whole-grain bread, cut into 3/4-inch cubes (8 cups)

2 small zucchini (8 oz), shredded (3 cups)

2 cups shredded Swiss cheese (8 oz)

4 eggs

2 cups milk

1 teaspoon salt

1 teaspoon dried thyme leaves

1/4 teaspoon pepper

1) Heat oven to 350°F. In 12-inch skillet, heat oil over medium-high heat. Add onions; cook 20 to 25 minutes, stirring occasionally, until onions are brown and caramelized.

2) Meanwhile, spray 13x9-inch (3-quart) glass baking dish with cooking spray. Layer 4 cups of the bread cubes, 1 1/2 cups of the zucchini and 3/4 cup of the cheese in baking dish. Repeat layers once.

3) In large bowl, beat the remaining ingredients with wire whisk until well blended. Pour over bread mixture. Arrange onions on bread mixture.

4) Cover with foil; bake 30 to 40 minutes or until knife inserted in the center comes out clean. Sprinkle remaining 1/2 cup cheese over the top; bake 2 to 3 minutes longer or until cheese is melted.

HIGH ALTITUDE (3500-6500 FT.): In Step 1, cook onions 25 to 30 minutes. In Step 4, cover with foil; bake 40 to 50 minutes.

Nutrition Information Per Serving:

Calories:	240	From Fat:	90
Total Fat			10g
Saturated Fat			5g
Trans Fat			0g
Cholesterol			90mg
Sodium			450mg
Total Carbohydrate			22g
Dietary Fiber			3g
Sugars			8g
Protein			14g

tip

Use large sweet onions to ensure you have enough to cover the top of the pudding.

Layered Summer Fruits with Creamy Lime Dressing

PREP TIME: 40 MINUTES (READY IN 40 MINUTES)
SERVINGS: ABOUT 24 (1/2 CUP EACH)

CREAMY LIME DRESSING

1 package (8 oz) cream cheese, softened

1/2 cup frozen limeade concentrate, thawed

1/4 cup powdered sugar

1 cup whipping cream, whipped

FRUIT

3 cups cut-up cantaloupe

1 quart strawberries, quartered

2 ripe medium mangoes, seed removed, peeled and cut up

2 cups blueberries

2 cups cut-up honeydew melon

Mint leaves, if desired

1) In medium bowl, beat cream cheese, limeade concentrate and powdered sugar with electric mixer on medium-high speed about 3 minutes or until smooth. Fold in whipped cream. Set aside.

2) In 3-quart trifle bowl, layer cantaloupe and strawberries. Spread half the cream cheese mixture over the strawberries. Layer mangoes, blueberries and honeydew over cream cheese mixture. Spread remaining cream cheese mixture on top. Garnish with mint leaves.

3) Serve immediately, or cover and refrigerate up to 2 hours before serving.

HIGH ALTITUDE (3500-6500 FT.): No change.

Nutrition Information Per Serving:

Calories:	130	From Fat:	60
Total Fat		7g	
Saturated Fat		4g	
Trans Fat		0g	
Cholesterol		20mg	
Sodium		40mg	
Total Carbohydrate		15g	
Dietary Fiber		1g	
Sugars		12g	
Protein		1g	

Super-Simple Picnic Potato Salad

PREP TIME: 45 MINUTES (READY IN 5 HOURS 45 MINUTES)
SERVINGS: 16 (1/2 CUP EACH)

- 1 bag (32 oz) frozen southern-style diced hash brown potatoes
- 1/4 cup water
- 2 tablespoons cider vinegar
- 1 tablespoon yellow mustard
- 1 1/2 teaspoons salt
- 1/4 teaspoon pepper
- 5 eggs
- 1 cup mayonnaise or salad dressing
- 1/2 cup chopped celery
- 1/3 cup chopped onion
- Paprika, if desired

1) In ungreased 3-quart microwavable bowl, mix the frozen potatoes and water; spread evenly in bowl. Cover tightly with microwavable plastic wrap. Microwave on High 15 to 20 minutes or until potatoes are hot and tender, stirring once halfway through cooking.

2) Add vinegar, mustard, salt and pepper to hot potatoes; mix well. Spread evenly in bowl. Cover, refrigerate at least 5 hours or until completely cold.

3) Meanwhile, in 2-quart saucepan, place the eggs in single layer. Add enough water to cover the eggs by 1 inch. Heat to boiling. Immediately remove from the heat; cover and let stand 15 minutes. Drain; rinse with cold water. Place eggs in bowl of ice water; let stand 10 minutes. Drain. Peel eggs. Reserve 1 egg for garnish; chop remaining 4 eggs.

4) Stir mayonnaise into cold potato mixture. Add celery, onion and chopped eggs; toss gently to mix. Spoon mixture into large serving bowl. Slice the reserved hard-cooked egg; arrange on top of salad. Sprinkle with paprika. Serve immediately, or cover and refrigerate until serving time.

HIGH ALTITUDE (3500-6500 FT.): In Step 3, add a pinch of salt to the water. After heating the salt water to boiling, boil 5 minutes. Remove from heat, cover and let stand 15 minutes.

Nutrition Information Per Serving:		
Calories: 200	From Fat:	110
Total Fat		13g
Saturated Fat		2g
Trans Fat		0g
Cholesterol		70mg
Sodium		350mg
Total Carbohydrate		17g
Dietary Fiber		2g
Sugars		2g
Protein		3g

Pulled-Beef Sandwiches

PREP TIME: 15 MINUTES (READY IN 8 HOURS 15 MINUTES)
SERVINGS: 12 SANDWICHES

e EASY

1 large onion, chopped (1 cup)

1 cup barbecue sauce

1/2 cup French dressing

1/2 cup condensed beef broth (from 10 1/2-oz can)

1 boneless beef chuck roast (3 1/2 to 4 lb)

12 burger buns, split

1) Spray 3- to 4-quart slow cooker with cooking spray. Mix onion, barbecue sauce, dressing and broth in slow cooker. Add beef; stir to coat. Cover; cook on Low heat setting 8 to 10 hours.

2) Remove beef from slow cooker; skim fat from the sauce. Shred beef with 2 forks; stir beef back into sauce. Using slotted spoon, place 1/2 cup beef mixture onto bottom of each bun. Cover with tops of buns.

HIGH ALTITUDE (3500-6500 FT.): No change.

Nutrition Information Per Serving:

Calories: 420	From Fat: 190
Total Fat	21g
Saturated Fat	6g
Trans Fat	1g
Cholesterol	70mg
Sodium	650mg
Total Carbohydrate	31g
Dietary Fiber	1g
Sugars	10g
Protein	27g

Grilled Chicken Salsa Verde

PREP TIME: 35 MINUTES (READY IN 8 HOURS 50 MINUTES)
SERVINGS: 12

2 tablespoons olive oil

5 large garlic cloves, halved

1 small white onion, quartered, separated

1½ pounds tomatillos (about 13)

3 medium to large jalapeño chiles, seeded

½ cup loosely packed fresh cilantro (10 to 15 sprigs)

2 teaspoons salt

1 teaspoon sugar

1 teaspoon ground cumin

12 boneless skinless chicken breasts (about 4½ lb)

Nutrition Information Per Serving:

Calories:	250	From Fat:	80
Total Fat			8g
Saturated Fat			2g
Trans Fat			0g
Cholesterol			105mg
Sodium			490mg
Total Carbohydrate			5g
Dietary Fiber			1g
Sugars			2g
Protein			38g

1) In 10-inch nonstick skillet, heat oil over medium-high heat until hot. Add garlic and onion; cook about 5 minutes, stirring constantly, until evenly roasted.

2) Remove husks and rinse tomatillos well. Core top stem area of each; cut tomatillos into quarters. In large food processor, place roasted garlic and onion, tomatillos, jalapeño chiles, cilantro, 1 teaspoon of the salt and the sugar. Cover; process about 15 seconds or until almost smooth.

3) Pour 2 cups mixture into small serving bowl; cover and refrigerate to use as salsa. To make marinade, add remaining 1 teaspoon salt and the cumin to remaining mixture in food processor. Cover; process 10 seconds.

4) Place 6 chicken breasts in each of 2 gallon-size resealable freezer plastic bags; divide marinade between bags. Seal bags; shake to evenly distribute marinade and coat chicken. Refrigerate at least 8 hours but no longer than 24 hours; turn bags over at least once while marinating.

5) Take salsa, bags of chicken, tongs, metal spatula and a serving platter to potluck. Salsa should be room temperature when served with grilled chicken.

6) Heat gas or charcoal grill. Carefully brush oil on grill rack. Place chicken on grill over medium heat; discard marinade. Cover grill; cook 12 to 15 minutes or until juice of chicken is clear when center of thickest part is cut (170°F), turning once. Serve each chicken breast with about 2 tablespoons salsa.

HIGH ALTITUDE (3500-6500 FT.): In Step 6, grill over medium-low heat about 15 minutes.

tip
In place of fresh tomatillos, use 3 cans (12 oz each) whole tomatillos. Drain the liquid and reduce the salt to 1 teaspoon total. Salsa made with the canned kind will gelatinize when refrigerated, so stir it well; it loosens up at room temperature.

Peppered Roast Beef Salad

PREP TIME: 40 MINUTES (READY IN 40 MINUTES)
SERVINGS: 8 (1-1/4 CUPS EACH)

DRESSING

- 1/4 cup vegetable oil
- 2 tablespoons white wine tarragon vinegar
- 1 tablespoon Dijon mustard
- 2 teaspoons soy sauce
- 1/4 to 1/2 teaspoon coarse ground black pepper
- 1 garlic clove, finely chopped

SALAD

- 4 cups coarsely chopped Chinese (napa) cabbage
- 1 1/2 cups cherry tomatoes, halved
- 1 cup sliced fresh mushrooms
- 1/2 cup shredded peeled celery root (celeriac)
- 3/4 lb cooked rare roast beef, cut into chunks (about 2 1/3 cups)
- 1 medium green bell pepper, cut into bite-size strips
- 1 medium yellow bell pepper, cut into bite-size strips

1) In small jar with tight-fitting lid, mix dressing ingredients. Cover dressing; shake well.

2) In large bowl, mix salad ingredients. Pour dressing over salad; toss gently to coat. Serve immediately.

HIGH ALTITUDE (3500-6500 FT.): No change.

Nutrition Information Per Serving:

Calories: 190	From Fat: 120
Total Fat	14g
Saturated Fat	3.5g
Trans Fat	0g
Cholesterol	30mg
Sodium	190mg
Total Carbohydrate	5g
Dietary Fiber	1g
Sugars	3g
Protein	12g

Honey-Mustard Coleslaw with Apples

PREP TIME: 15 MINUTES (READY IN 15 MINUTES)
SERVINGS: 12 (3/4 CUP EACH)

⊜ EASY **ⓕ LOW FAT**

- 1 bag (16 oz) coleslaw mix (8 cups)
- 1/2 cup chopped green onions (8 medium)
- 2 medium apples, cored and cut into matchstick pieces
- 1 cup light honey-mustard dressing

Nutrition Information Per Serving:

Calories: 80	From Fat: 25
Total Fat	2.5g
Saturated Fat	0g
Trans Fat	0g
Cholesterol	0mg
Sodium	210mg
Total Carbohydrate	12g
Dietary Fiber	2g
Sugars	8g
Protein	0g

1) In large bowl, toss all ingredients. Serve immediately, or cover and refrigerate up to 24 hours before serving.

HIGH ALTITUDE (3500-6500 FT.): No change.

Bruschetta-Style Tortellini Salad

PREP TIME:	20 MINUTES (READY IN 20 MINUTES)	🌀 EASY
SERVINGS:	10 (1 CUP EACH)	

BRUSCHETTA DRESSING

1 can (14.5 oz) Muir Glen® organic diced tomatoes, drained, juice reserved

¼ cup chopped fresh basil leaves

2 tablespoons extra-virgin olive oil

1 garlic clove, finely chopped

SALAD

1 package (20 oz) refrigerated cheese-filled tortellini

2 cups sliced fresh mushrooms (about 5 oz)

1 cup cubed mozzarella cheese

½ cup chopped red onion

1 can (2¼ oz) sliced ripe olives, drained

½ package (3.5-oz size) sliced pepperoni, cut in half

1) In medium bowl, mix the dressing ingredients. Cook and drain tortellini as directed on package. Rinse with cold water to cool; drain.

2) In large bowl, toss tortellini with dressing, mushrooms, mozzarella cheese, red onion, olives and pepperoni; stir in reserved tomato juice. Cover and refrigerate 1 to 4 hours before serving.

HIGH ALTITUDE (3500-6500 FT.): No change.

Nutrition Information Per Serving:

Calories:	280	From Fat:	100
Total Fat			11g
Saturated Fat			4.5g
Trans Fat			0g
Cholesterol			35mg
Sodium			510mg
Total Carbohydrate			31g
Dietary Fiber			2g
Sugars			4g
Protein			13g

Layered Pizza Salad

PREP TIME: 45 MINUTES (READY IN 2 HOURS 45 MINUTES)
SERVINGS: 10 (ABOUT 1-1/2 CUPS EACH)

1 package (16 oz) uncooked rotini pasta

2 tablespoons salad supreme seasoning

1 medium red bell pepper, chopped

2 plum (Roma) tomatoes, chopped

1 large green bell pepper, chopped

1 package (3.5 oz) sliced pepperoni

8 oz fresh mozzarella ciliegini (cheese balls), drained, halved

3 green onions with tops, sliced (about 1/2 cup)

1/2 cup sliced pimiento-stuffed green olives

1 cup zesty Italian dressing

1/4 cup shredded Parmesan cheese

1) Cook and drain pasta as directed on package. Rinse with cold water to cool; drain.

2) In 3- or 4-quart clear bowl, layer 4 cups pasta, 1 tablespoon of the seasoning, the red bell pepper, tomatoes, green bell pepper, remaining pasta, remaining 1 tablespoon seasoning, the pepperoni, mozzarella, onions and olives.

3) Pour dressing over salad; sprinkle with Parmesan cheese. Refrigerate 2 hours. Stir just before serving.

HIGH ALTITUDE (3500-6500 FT.): No change.

Nutrition Information Per Serving:		
Calories: 420	From Fat:	170
Total Fat		18g
Saturated Fat		6g
Trans Fat		0g
Cholesterol		25mg
Sodium		1200mg
Total Carbohydrate		46g
Dietary Fiber		3g
Sugars		6g
Protein		16g

Pulled-Pork Fajitas

PREP TIME: 20 MINUTES (READY IN 8 HOURS 50 MINUTES)
SERVINGS: 16

e EASY

1 pork boneless loin roast (2$\frac{1}{2}$ lb), trimmed of fat

2 tablespoons fajita seasoning (from 3-oz container)

1 cup Old El Paso® Thick 'n Chunky salsa

1 bag (1 lb) frozen stir-fry bell peppers and onions, thawed

2 packages (11.5 oz each) Old El Paso® flour tortillas for burritos (16 tortillas), warmed

2 cups shredded Mexican-style taco cheese (8 oz)

1 cup sour cream, if desired

1) Place pork in 3- to 4-quart slow cooker. Sprinkle with fajita seasoning. Top with salsa. Cover; cook on Low heat setting 8 to 10 hours.

2) Remove pork from slow cooker; place on cutting board. Shred pork using 2 forks; return pork to slow cooker and mix well. Stir in stir-fry vegetables. Increase heat setting to High. Cover; cook 30 minutes longer or until mixture is hot and vegetables are tender.

3) Using slotted spoon, place $\frac{1}{2}$ cup meat mixture in each warm tortilla. Sprinkle with cheese. Serve with sour cream.

HIGH ALTITUDE (3500-6500 FT.): No change.

Nutrition Information Per Serving:		
Calories: 320	From Fat:	130
Total Fat		14g
Saturated Fat		6g
Trans Fat		1g
Cholesterol		60mg
Sodium		730mg
Total Carbohydrate		24g
Dietary Fiber		0g
Sugars		2g
Protein		22g

Crunchy Asian Chicken Salad

PREP TIME: 25 MINUTES (READY IN 25 MINUTES)
SERVINGS: 10 (1-1/4 CUPS EACH)

3 packages (3 oz each) chicken-flavor ramen noodle soup mix

8 cups shredded Chinese (napa) cabbage (1 medium head)

4 cups cut-up cooked chicken

1 cup shredded carrots

$\frac{1}{2}$ cup chopped red onion

1 cup sesame-ginger dressing

1 tablespoon sugar

1 cup wasabi peas

3 tablespoons sesame seed, toasted

1) In 2-quart saucepan, heat 1½ cups water to boiling over high heat. Break apart noodles before opening soup packages. Stir 2 of the seasoning packets and all of the noodles into boiling water. Cook 2 to 3 minutes, stirring constantly, until noodles are tender; do not drain.

2) In large bowl, toss noodles, cabbage, chicken, carrots and onion. In small bowl, stir together sesame-ginger dressing, sugar and the remaining seasoning packet. Toss dressing with salad.

3) Cover and refrigerate up to 1 hour. Stir in wasabi peas and sesame seed just before serving.

HIGH ALTITUDE (3500-6500 FT.): No change.

Nutrition Information Per Serving:		
Calories: 390	From Fat:	170
Total Fat		19g
Saturated Fat		4g
Trans Fat		1.5g
Cholesterol		50mg
Sodium		850mg
Total Carbohydrate		34g
Dietary Fiber		3g
Sugars		14g
Protein		21g

Sesame-Wheat Berry Salad

PREP TIME: 30 MINUTES (READY IN 2 HOURS)
SERVINGS: 8 (1/2 CUP EACH)

SALAD

1 cup uncooked wheat berries

2½ cups chicken broth

½ cup chopped celery

½ cup chopped seeded cucumber

½ cup shredded carrot

4 medium green onions, sliced (¼ cup)

2 tablespoons sesame seed, toasted

DRESSING

2 tablespoons sugar

2 tablespoons rice vinegar

1 tablespoon vegetable oil

1½ teaspoons sesame oil

1 teaspoon Thai chili garlic paste

½ teaspoon reduced-sodium soy sauce

1) In 2-quart saucepan, heat wheat berries and chicken broth to boiling over high heat; stir. Reduce heat to low; cover and simmer about 1 hour or until wheat is tender. Drain and cool to room temperature, about 20 minutes.

2) Meanwhile, in small jar with tight-fitting lid, mix the dressing ingredients. Cover; shake well.

3) In medium bowl, mix remaining salad ingredients. Pour dressing over salad; toss to coat. If making ahead, add the toasted sesame seed just before serving.

HIGH ALTITUDE (3500-6500 FT.): Cover and simmer wheat berries about 1 hour 10 minutes or until wheat is tender.

Nutrition Information Per Serving:

Calories:	120	From Fat:	45
Total Fat			5g
Saturated Fat			1g
Trans Fat			0g
Cholesterol			0mg
Sodium			360mg
Total Carbohydrate			15g
Dietary Fiber			2g
Sugars			4g
Protein			3g

Confetti Quinoa Salad

PREP TIME: 20 MINUTES (READY IN 1 HOUR)
SERVINGS: 16 (ABOUT 1/2 CUP EACH)

 EASY

1) In 3-quart saucepan, heat quinoa, water and salt to boiling; reduce heat. Cover and simmer 15 to 20 minutes or until quinoa is tender. Cool at least 30 minutes.

2) Cook and drain edamame as directed on bag. Rinse with cold water to cool; drain.

3) In large serving bowl, toss quinoa, edamame and remaining ingredients. Serve immediately, or cover and refrigerate 1 to 2 hours before serving.

HIGH ALTITUDE (3500-6500 FT.): No change.

Nutrition Information Per Serving:

Calories:	120	From Fat:	50
Total Fat			6g
Saturated Fat			1g
Trans Fat			0g
Cholesterol			0mg
Sodium			320mg
Total Carbohydrate			12g
Dietary Fiber			2g
Sugars			4g
Protein			4g

1 cup uncooked quinoa

2 cups water

½ teaspoon salt

1 bag (10 oz) Cascadian Farm® frozen organic shelled edamame

1 cup grape tomatoes, cut in half

¾ cup Italian or Greek vinaigrette dressing

¼ cup chopped red onion

½ cup crumbled feta cheese (2 oz)

¼ cup chopped fresh Italian (flat-leaf) parsley

1 yellow bell pepper, chopped

 If quinoa isn't available, replace it with 3 cups cooked couscous, preferably whole wheat.

Greek-Style Pasta Salad

PREP TIME: 30 MINUTES (READY IN 30 MINUTES)
SERVINGS: 10 (1-1/3 CUPS EACH)

DRESSING

- 2/3 cup extra-virgin olive oil
- 1/4 cup red wine vinegar
- 2 tablespoons grated Parmesan cheese
- 1 teaspoon chopped fresh oregano leaves or 1/4 teaspoon dried oregano leaves
- 1/2 teaspoon salt
- 1/4 teaspoon coarse ground black pepper
- 1 garlic clove, finely chopped

SALAD

- 3 cups uncooked rotini pasta (8 oz)
- 4 oz hard salami slices, quartered
- 1 medium cucumber, seeded, cut into chunks (1 1/4 cups)
- 1 small green bell pepper, cut into thin bite-sized strips
- 1 small red bell pepper, cut into thin bite-sized strips
- 2 medium tomatoes, cut into wedges, then cut in half
- 1/2 cup sliced kalamata or other Greek olives
- 1/4 cup sliced fresh basil leaves or 2 teaspoons dried basil leaves
- 6 oz feta cheese, crumbled (1 1/2 cups)

1) In blender or food processor bowl, place all dressing ingredients. Cover; blend on medium speed about 20 seconds or until smooth; set aside.

2) Cook and drain pasta as directed on package. Rinse with cold water to cool; drain.

3) In 4-quart bowl, place pasta and remaining salad ingredients. Add salad dressing; toss gently. Serve immediately.

HIGH ALTITUDE (3500-6500 FT.): No change.

Nutrition Information Per Serving:

Calories:	340	From Fat:	210
Total Fat			23g
Saturated Fat			6g
Trans Fat			0g
Cholesterol			25mg
Sodium			710mg
Total Carbohydrate			24g
Dietary Fiber			2g
Sugars			3g
Protein			9g

Mediterranean Vegetable Bulgur Salad

PREP TIME: 10 MINUTES (READY IN 45 MINUTES)
SERVINGS: 12 (3/4 CUP EACH)

e EASY   **f** LOW FAT

2 cups boiling water

1½ cups uncooked bulgur

1½ cups water

2 cups fresh broccoli florets

1 cup grape tomatoes

½ cup shredded carrot

1 cup crumbled feta cheese (4 oz)

2 tablespoons chopped fresh parsley

½ teaspoon salt

1 can (15 oz) Progresso® chickpeas
(garbanzo beans), drained

½ cup Greek or Italian dressing

1) In large bowl, pour 2 cups boiling water over bulgur. Let stand 30 minutes. In 2-quart saucepan, heat 1½ cups water to boiling; add the broccoli. Cook 1 minute; drain and rinse in cold water.

2) Stir broccoli and remaining ingredients into bulgur. Serve salad immediately, or cover and refrigerate up to 4 hours before serving.

HIGH ALTITUDE (3500-6500 FT.): No change.

Nutrition Information Per Serving:		
Calories: 190	From Fat:	60
Total Fat		7g
Saturated Fat		2g
Trans Fat		0g
Cholesterol		10mg
Sodium		360mg
Total Carbohydrate		25g
Dietary Fiber		6g
Sugars		3g
Protein		7g

tip

Bulgur is whole wheat that has been cooked, dried and then broken into coarse fragments. You'll find it with the other grains at your grocery store.

Grilled Bell Pepper Panzanella Salad

PREP TIME: 40 MINUTES (READY IN 1 HOUR 10 MINUTES)
SERVINGS: 11 (1 CUP EACH)

6 cups cubes (³/₄ inch) dry French or Italian bread

2 large yellow bell peppers

2 large red bell peppers

1 medium red onion, cut into ¹/₂-inch thick slices

¹/₂ cup sliced kalamata or black olives

¹/₄ cup julienne (matchstick-cut) fresh basil leaves

8 oz fresh mozzarella ciliegini (cheese balls), drained, halved

4 medium plum (Roma) tomatoes, chopped

¹/₂ English (seedless) cucumber, quartered, sliced

³/₄ cup balsamic vinaigrette dressing

1) Place the bread cubes on shallow trays. Let stand to dry out slightly while making salad.

2) Heat gas or charcoal grill. Place bell peppers on grill over medium-high heat. Cover grill; cook 15 to 30 minutes, turning occasionally, until peppers are blackened. Place the roasted peppers in large bowl; cover with plastic wrap. Let stand 15 to 20 minutes. Peel and seed bell peppers. Cut into bite-size strips.

3) Place the red onion slices on grill. Cover grill; cook 3 to 6 minutes, turning once during grilling, until golden on the edges and slightly tender. Cut into ¹/₂-inch pieces.

4) In large bowl, place cubed bread, grilled pepper strips, grilled onions, olives, basil, cheese, tomatoes and cucumber. Drizzle with dressing, tossing to coat. Serve immediately.

HIGH ALTITUDE (3500-6500 FT.): No change.

Nutrition Information Per Serving:

Calories:	230	From Fat:	130
Total Fat			14g
Saturated Fat			4.5g
Trans Fat			0g
Cholesterol			20mg
Sodium			390mg
Total Carbohydrate			18g
Dietary Fiber			2g
Sugars			6g
Protein			7g

Ham and Cheese Pull-Apart Sandwich Loaf

PREP TIME: 15 MINUTES (READY IN 40 MINUTES)
SERVINGS: 6 SANDWICHES

e EASY

1 loaf Italian bread (10 to 12 inches)

3 tablespoons butter or margarine, softened

1 tablespoon spicy brown or country-style Dijon mustard

6 slices (1 oz each) Swiss cheese

3/4 lb thinly sliced fully cooked ham

1) Heat gas or charcoal grill. Spray a 25x18-inch sheet of heavy-duty foil with cooking spray. Without cutting all the way through, cut the loaf of bread into 12 (3/4-inch) slices, cutting to within 1/4 inch of bottom.

2) Stir together butter and mustard. Spread every other slice of bread with slightly less than 2 teaspoons mustard mixture, creating 6 sandwiches. Fold each slice of cheese in half diagonally; tuck each into sandwich. Divide ham evenly among sandwiches, tucking in to fit. Place loaf on center of foil. Seal edges, making tight 1/2-inch fold; fold again, allowing space for heat circulation and expansion.

3) Place foil-wrapped loaf on grill over medium heat. Cover grill; cook 20 to 25 minutes or until cheese is melted and loaf is hot, turning loaf frequently. To serve, open packet carefully to allow steam to escape. Remove foil from loaf; pull apart sandwiches.

HIGH ALTITUDE (3500-6500 FT.): Heat gas or charcoal grill for indirect cooking. For two-burner gas grill, heat one burner to medium; place packet on unheated side. For one-burner gas grill, cook over very low heat. For charcoal grill, move medium coals to edge; place packet in center of grill. Cover grill; cook 20 to 30 minutes, rotating and turning packet over every 5 minutes.

Nutrition Information Per Serving:

Calories:	440	From Fat:	180
Total Fat			20g
Saturated Fat			10g
Trans Fat			1g
Cholesterol			70mg
Sodium			1250mg
Total Carbohydrate			40g
Dietary Fiber			2g
Sugars			0g
Protein			26g

Black-Eyed Pea Salad Bowl

PREP TIME: 25 MINUTES (READY IN 25 MINUTES)
SERVINGS: 8 (1-1/3 CUPS EACH)

2 cans (15 or 15½ oz each)
black-eyed peas, drained, rinsed

8 oz Monterey Jack cheese, cubed

1 medium yellow bell pepper, cut into
1-inch-long julienne strips

1 medium tomato, coarsely chopped

⅓ cup chopped fresh parsley

¼ cup chopped red onion

½ cup reduced-calorie Italian dressing

5 cups torn lettuce

1) In medium bowl, gently mix all ingredients except lettuce. Refrigerate until serving time.

2) Just before serving, in large bowl, place lettuce; spoon salad over lettuce. Stir just to combine.

HIGH ALTITUDE (3500-6500 FT.): No change.

Nutrition Information Per Serving:

Calories:	260	From Fat:	110
Total Fat			12g
Saturated Fat			6g
Trans Fat			0g
Cholesterol			25mg
Sodium			560mg
Total Carbohydrate			23g
Dietary Fiber			5g
Sugars			3g
Protein			14g

tip

Need a little more salad to feed an extra guest? Toss in 8 oz Cheddar cheese cubes in addition to the Monterey Jack.

SCARY SLOW-COOKED CHILI
PG. 264

Cozy Holiday Favorites

When brisk fall and winter days arrive, celebrate
with Halloween, Thanksgiving and Christmas treats.

PUMPKIN PIE
PG. 280

ELEGANT BEEF TENDERLOIN
WITH HERB-DIJON CRUST
PG. 292

ROAST TURKEY
PG. 276

Sinister Pepperoni-Ravioli Supper

PREP TIME: 30 MINUTES (READY IN 30 MINUTES)
SERVINGS: 5

ⓔ EASY

2 packages (9 oz each) refrigerated cheese-filled ravioli

1 jar (26 oz) spaghetti sauce

1 jar (4.5 oz) Green Giant® sliced mushrooms, drained

1 package (3.5 oz) sliced pepperoni, halved (about 1 cup)

1 cup shredded mozzarella cheese (4 oz)

1) Cook and drain ravioli as directed on package; cover to keep warm.

2) Meanwhile, in 4-quart saucepan, heat spaghetti sauce, mushrooms and pepperoni to boiling. Reduce heat to low; simmer 8 to 10 minutes, stirring occasionally, until sauce is slightly thickened.

3) Carefully stir cooked ravioli into sauce mixture. Spoon onto serving platter. Sprinkle with cheese.

HIGH ALTITUDE (3500-6500 FT.): No change.

Nutrition Information Per Serving:

Calories:	660	From Fat:	260
Total Fat			29g
Saturated Fat			13g
Trans Fat			0g
Cholesterol			90mg
Sodium			1670mg
Total Carbohydrate			74g
Dietary Fiber			4g
Sugars			20g
Protein			26g

Mashed Potato Monsters

PREP TIME: 25 MINUTES (READY IN 25 MINUTES)
SERVINGS: 4

e EASY

1 cup milk

¾ cup hot water

2 tablespoons margarine or butter

1 pouch (from 7.2-oz box) Betty Crocker® homestyle creamy butter mashed potatoes

INGREDIENTS FOR FACES, AS LISTED BELOW

Eyes: peas, corn kernels, mushrooms, olive halves

Eyelashes: herbs

Eyebrows: ripe olive slices, zigzag-cut bell pepper

Nose: pickle, sliced radish

Teeth: carrot wedges

Mouth: red bell pepper slice

Ears: corn kernels, broccoli florets

Hair: shredded cheese, broccoli florets, shredded carrots, green onion curls

1) In 2-quart saucepan, heat milk, hot water and margarine to a rapid boil over medium-high heat (watch carefully to avoid boilover).

2) Remove from heat. Stir in 1 pouch potatoes with seasoning just until well blended. Let stand 4 to 5 minutes or until liquid is absorbed.

3) Meanwhile, cut 4 pieces plastic wrap, about 9x12 inches each. Line insides of 4 (6-oz) custard cups with plastic wrap; spray with cooking spray. Divide potatoes evenly among custard cups. Press firmly; turn upside down onto individual serving plates.

4) Remove the plastic wrap from each potato mound; choose from suggested ingredients at left to make faces. Serve immediately.

HIGH ALTITUDE (3500-6500 FT.): No change.

Nutrition Information Per Serving:		
Calories: 180	From Fat:	80
Total Fat		9g
Saturated Fat		3g
Trans Fat		2g
Cholesterol		5mg
Sodium		450mg
Total Carbohydrate		22g
Dietary Fiber		1g
Sugars		4g
Protein		4g

Scary Slow-Cooked Chili

PREP TIME: 20 MINUTES (READY IN 7 HOURS 20 MINUTES)
SERVINGS: 6

e EASY

1 lb lean (at least 80%) ground beef

½ lb bulk Italian pork sausage

1 medium onion, chopped (about ½ cup)

1 can (28 oz) whole tomatoes, undrained, cut up

1 can (15 oz) tomato sauce

2 teaspoons chili powder

1 to 1½ teaspoons ground cumin

1 teaspoon sugar

1 teaspoon dried oregano leaves

1 can (15 oz) spicy chili beans, undrained

1 can (15 oz) Progresso® chickpeas, drained, rinsed

6 slices (1 oz each) American cheese

1) In 10-inch skillet, cook beef, sausage and onion over medium-high heat 5 to 7 minutes, stirring frequently, until beef is thoroughly cooked and sausage is no longer pink; drain.

2) In 3½- to 4-quart slow cooker, mix beef mixture and all remaining ingredients except cheese.

3) Cover; cook on Low heat setting 7 to 8 hours. Use a Halloween-themed cookie cutter to cut out shape from cheese. Top individual servings with cutouts.

HIGH ALTITUDE (3500-6500 FT.): No change.

Nutrition Information Per Serving:		
Calories: 420	From Fat:	150
Total Fat		16g
Saturated Fat		5g
Trans Fat		0.5g
Cholesterol		60mg
Sodium		1260mg
Total Carbohydrate		41g
Dietary Fiber		10g
Sugars		10g
Protein		28g

Globlins

PREP TIME: 35 MINUTES (READY IN 35 MINUTES)
SERVINGS: 12

6 cups Kix® cereal

3 tablespoons butter or margarine

4 cups miniature marshmallows

12 drops green food color

24 orange circus peanut candies
(from two 4-oz bags)

24 candy-coated chocolate candies

Red string licorice, cut into
24 (1-inch) pieces

1) Line 2 cookie sheets with waxed paper. In large bowl, place cereal.

2) In 4-quart saucepan, melt butter over low heat. Add marshmallows; stir until completely melted. Remove from heat. Stir in food color. Pour marshmallow mixture over cereal in bowl, stirring until well coated.

3) For feet, place 2 peanut candies on cookie sheet. Spray inside of $1/2$-cup measuring cup with cooking spray. For body, fill sprayed $1/2$-cup measuring cup with warm cereal mixture; place over feet, releasing cereal mixture and covering back half of feet. Repeat with the remaining peanut candies and cereal mixture to make 12 globlins. Immediately attach chocolate candies for eyes. Insert licorice for antennae.

HIGH ALTITUDE (3500-6500 FT.): No change.

Nutrition Information Per Serving:

Calories:	200	From Fat:	35
Total Fat			3.5g
Saturated Fat			2g
Trans Fat			0g
Cholesterol			10mg
Sodium			130mg
Total Carbohydrate			40g
Dietary Fiber			1g
Sugars			24g
Protein			1g

Boo Brownie Cupcakes

PREP TIME: 20 MINUTES (READY IN 1 HOUR 25 MINUTES)
SERVINGS: 16 CUPCAKES

😊 EASY

1 box (1 lb 6.5 oz) supreme brownie mix with pouch of chocolate-flavor syrup

Water, vegetable oil and eggs called for on brownie box

1/2 cup dark chocolate chips

1/4 cup white vanilla baking chips

Nutrition Information Per Serving:

Calories: 70	From Fat: 70
Total Fat	8g
Saturated Fat	2g
Trans Fat	0g
Cholesterol	25mg
Sodium	150mg
Total Carbohydrate	35g
Dietary Fiber	0g
Sugars	25g
Protein	2g

1) Heat oven to 350°F. Place paper baking cup in each of 16 regular-size muffin cups; spray paper cups with baking spray with flour. Make brownie batter as directed; stir in dark chocolate chips. Divide batter evenly among muffin cups.

2) In small resealable freezer plastic bag, place the vanilla chips; seal the bag. Microwave on High about 20 seconds or until softened. Gently squeeze bag until chips are smooth. If necessary, continue to microwave at 10-second intervals. Cut off a tiny corner of bag. Squeeze bag on top of the unbaked cupcakes to draw ghost shapes.

3) Bake 24 to 26 minutes or until tops appear cracked and dry. Cool in pan 10 minutes. Remove from pan to cooling rack. Cool completely, about 30 minutes.

HIGH ALTITUDE (3500-6500 FT.): Bake 25 to 27 minutes.

Eyes-of-Newt

PREP TIME: 10 MINUTES (READY IN 1 HOUR 10 MINUTES)
SERVINGS: ABOUT 48 APPETIZERS

😊 EASY

2 containers (8 oz each) fresh ciliegini mozzarella cheese (cherry-size balls) (about 2 cups)

12 ready-to-eat baby-cut carrots, cut into 1/2-inch slices

1/4 cup light olive oil

2 tablespoons chopped fresh basil leaves

1 tablespoon white vinegar

1/4 teaspoon salt

1 garlic clove, finely chopped

Nutrition Information Per Serving:

Calories: 40	From Fat: 30
Total Fat	3.5g
Saturated Fat	1.5g
Trans Fat	0g
Cholesterol	10mg
Sodium	55mg
Total Carbohydrate	0g
Dietary Fiber	0g
Sugars	0g
Protein	2g

1) Make small cut in center of each cheese ball; insert carrot slice. In medium bowl, mix remaining ingredients. Stir in stuffed cheese balls.

2) Cover and refrigerate the appetizers 1 to 2 hours to blend the flavors. Stir after 30 minutes.

HIGH ALTITUDE (3500-6500 FT.): No change.

Skewered Worms

PREP TIME: 20 MINUTES (READY IN 2 HOURS 15 MINUTES)
SERVINGS: 8

e EASY

BEEF

- 16 wooden skewers
- ²/₃ cup olive oil
- 1 tablespoon grated lemon peel
- ¹/₃ cup lemon juice
- 1 tablespoon chopped fresh thyme leaves
- ³/₄ teaspoon salt
- 3 garlic cloves, finely chopped
- 2 lb beef flank steak

SPICY SAUCE

- 1 cup ketchup
- 2 garlic cloves, peeled
- 1 canned chipotle chili in adobo sauce

1) In 11x8-inch baking dish, soak the wooden skewers in water at least 30 minutes.

2) Meanwhile, in 1-gallon resealable food-storage plastic bag, mix oil, lemon peel, lemon juice, thyme leaves, salt and garlic. Slice beef across the grain into ¹/₄-inch strips. Place beef in oil mixture. Seal bag; refrigerate 2 to 4 hours to marinate.

3) Meanwhile, in blender or food processor, place sauce ingredients. Cover; blend on high speed until smooth.

4) Thread the beef on the skewers, twirling 2 to 3 beef strips around each skewer to look like worms. Reserve any remaining marinade.

5) Set oven control to broil. Place skewers on broiler pan. Broil with tops 4 to 6 inches from heat 3 minutes. Turn skewers and brush with marinade. (Discard any remaining marinade.) Broil 2 to 3 minutes longer or until desired doneness. Serve with sauce.

HIGH ALTITUDE (3500-6500 FT.): No change.

Nutrition Information Per Serving:		
Calories: 380	From Fat:	210
Total Fat		23g
Saturated Fat		4g
Trans Fat		0g
Cholesterol		85mg
Sodium		630mg
Total Carbohydrate		9g
Dietary Fiber		0g
Sugars		7g
Protein		34g

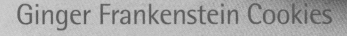

Ginger Frankenstein Cookies

PREP TIME: 1 HOUR (READY IN 2 HOURS 20 MINUTES)
SERVINGS: 3 DOZEN COOKIES

1½ cups sugar

1 cup butter or margarine, softened

3 tablespoons mild-flavor (light) molasses

1 egg

2 tablespoons milk

3¼ cups all-purpose flour

2 teaspoons baking soda

2 teaspoons ground cinnamon

1½ teaspoons ground ginger

½ teaspoon ground cloves

½ teaspoon ground cardamom

1 container (1 lb) vanilla creamy ready-to-spread frosting

5 drops green food color

⅓ cup candy-coated chocolate candies (72 candies)

¾ cup candy corn (72 candies)

1 cup semisweet chocolate chips

1) In large bowl, beat the sugar, butter and molasses with electric mixer on medium speed until well blended. Beat in egg and milk. Stir in flour, baking soda, cinnamon, ginger, cloves and cardamom until dough forms. Divide dough into 2 balls; flatten each ball to make 4-inch disk. Wrap each disk in plastic wrap; refrigerate about 1 hour or until firm, or freeze 15 minutes.

2) Heat oven to 350°F. On floured surface, roll each dough disk into 12x9-inch rectangle. Cut each 12x9-inch rectangle into 3 rows by 6 rows to make 18 smaller rectangles (36 total); place 1 inch apart on ungreased large cookie sheet. Bake 6 to 8 minutes or until set. Immediately remove from cookie sheet to cooling rack. Cool completely, 15 to 20 minutes.

3) In small bowl, stir frosting and food color until well blended. Frost each cookie with slightly less than 1 tablespoon frosting. Add 2 candy-coated candies for eyes and 2 candy corn pieces for neck "bolts."

4) Place chocolate chips in small resealable freezer plastic bag; seal bag. Microwave on High 30 to 45 seconds or until softened. Squeeze bag until mixture is smooth. (If necessary, microwave 30 seconds longer or just until all chips are melted.) Cut small tip from one corner of bag. Squeeze bag to drizzle melted chips on cookies for hair and mouth.

HIGH ALTITUDE (3500-6500 FT.): Bake 8 to 10 minutes. Let cool 1 minute before removing from cookie sheet.

Nutrition Information Per Serving:		
Calories: 220	From Fat: 80	
Total Fat		9g
Saturated Fat		5g
Trans Fat		1g
Cholesterol		20mg
Sodium		140mg
Total Carbohydrate		33g
Dietary Fiber		0g
Sugars		22g
Protein		1g

Crusty Mummy Fingers

PREP TIME: 15 MINUTES (READY IN 35 MINUTES)
SERVINGS: 8

e EASY   **(fF)** LOW FAT

2 lb sweet potatoes, peeled
(about 2 large potatoes)

2 tablespoons water

2 egg whites

1 cup Progresso® Italian-style
bread crumbs

$\frac{1}{4}$ cup grated Parmesan cheese

$\frac{1}{2}$ teaspoon salt

$\frac{1}{2}$ teaspoon pepper

$\frac{1}{4}$ teaspoon ground red pepper
(cayenne)

Cooking spray

1) Heat oven to 450°F. Spray 2 large cookie sheets with cooking spray.

2) Cut potatoes into $\frac{1}{2}$x$\frac{1}{2}$-inch strips. In shallow dish, mix water and egg whites with wire whisk or fork. In another shallow dish, mix bread crumbs, cheese, salt, pepper and red pepper. Working in batches, dip sweet potatoes into egg white mixture; roll in bread crumb mixture. Place potatoes in single layer on cookie sheet. Spray potatoes with cooking spray about 10 seconds.

3) Bake 18 to 20 minutes, turning after 10 minutes, until crisp.

HIGH ALTITUDE (3500-6500 FT.): No change.

Nutrition Information Per Serving:

Calories: 140	From Fat: 15
Total Fat	2g
Saturated Fat	1g
Trans Fat	0g
Cholesterol	0mg
Sodium	480mg
Total Carbohydrate	26g
Dietary Fiber	3g
Sugars	6g
Protein	5g

Halloweenies with Mustard Dip

PREP TIME: 20 MINUTES (READY IN 40 MINUTES)
SERVINGS: 44

EASY

1 can (8 oz) Pillsbury® Crescent Recipe Creations™ refrigerated flaky dough sheet

44 cocktail-size smoked link sausages (from a 1-lb package)

½ cup creamy Dijon mustard

1 tablespoon dried oregano leaves

1) Heat oven to 375°F. Line two 15x10x1-inch pans with cooking parchment paper.

2) On work surface, roll crescent dough sheet out to 14x11-inch rectangle. Cut dough vertically to make two 11x7-inch rectangles. Cut crosswise into total of 44 (7x½-inch) strips. Pat sausages dry with paper towels.

3) Wrap 1 strip of dough around each sausage to look like a little mummy; press firmly at each end to secure. Place on cookie sheet 2 inches apart for even browning.

4) Bake 15 to 20 minutes or until golden brown. Meanwhile, in small bowl, mix mustard and oregano. Serve sausages warm with mustard dip.

HIGH ALTITUDE (3500-6500 FT.): No change.

Nutrition Information Per Serving:	
Calories: 45	From Fat: 35
Total Fat	3.5g
Saturated Fat	1g
Trans Fat	0g
Cholesterol	0mg
Sodium	190mg
Total Carbohydrate	2g
Dietary Fiber	0g
Sugars	0g
Protein	1g

Bubbling Cauldron Cheese Dip with Bat Wing Dippers

PREP TIME: 5 MINUTES (READY IN 10 MINUTES)
SERVINGS: 14

e EASY

- 1 loaf (16 oz) prepared cheese product, cut into cubes
- 1 container (8 oz) reduced-fat chives-and-onion cream cheese
- 1 cup shredded sharp Cheddar cheese (4 oz)
- 1/2 cup milk
- 1 large garlic clove, finely chopped
- 12 oz blue tortilla chips (from two 9-oz bags)

1) In 1½-quart microwavable bowl, mix all ingredients except tortilla chips. Microwave uncovered on High 5 to 8 minutes, stirring every 3 minutes, until cheese is melted and dip is smooth. Serve warm with chips.

HIGH ALTITUDE (3500-6500 FT.): No change.

Nutrition Information Per Serving:

Calories:	300	From Fat:	170
Total Fat			19g
Saturated Fat			9g
Trans Fat			0g
Cholesterol			45mg
Sodium			740mg
Total Carbohydrate			21g
Dietary Fiber			0g
Sugars			5g
Protein			10g

tip

To make this on the stovetop, mix all of the ingredients except the chips in a double boiler. Cook the dip over hot water on medium heat, stirring frequently, until it is melted and smooth.

Chocolate Mocha Mummy Cookies

PREP TIME: 1 HOUR 30 MINUTES (READY IN 1 HOUR 40 MINUTES)
SERVINGS: 20 COOKIES

1 cup butter or margarine, softened

1 cup powdered sugar

1 teaspoon vanilla

1³/₄ cups all-purpose flour

¹/₃ cup unsweetened baking cocoa

1 teaspoon instant coffee granules or crystals

1¹/₄ cups white vanilla baking chips (from 11-oz bag)

¹/₄ cup miniature candy-coated semisweet chocolate baking bits (40 bits)

tip

Instead of using vanilla chips, use a small food-storage plastic bag to pipe prepared frosting on these cookies.

1) Heat oven to 350°F. In large bowl, beat butter, powdered sugar and vanilla with electric mixer on medium speed about 2 minutes or until creamy. On low speed, beat in flour, cocoa and coffee granules 1 to 2 minutes or until well mixed. Divide dough into 2 balls; press each to form disk. Wrap each disk in plastic wrap; freeze 10 minutes.

2) On lightly floured surface, roll 1 dough disk at a time until ¹/₈ inch thick. Cut with 5-inch gingerbread boy cutter. On ungreased cookie sheets, place cutouts 1 inch apart. Reroll and cut any remaining dough. Bake 9 to 10 minutes or until set. Cool 1 minute; remove from cookie sheets to cooling racks. Cool completely, 15 to 20 minutes.

3) Place white baking chips in small resealable freezer plastic bag; seal bag. Microwave on High 30 seconds. Turn bag over; microwave 15 seconds longer until chips are softened. Squeeze bag until mixture is smooth. (If necessary, microwave 10 seconds longer or until chips are completely melted and mixture is smooth.)

4) Cut very small tip from one corner of bag. Squeeze bag to drizzle melted chips over cookies for mummy wrapping. Add 2 baking bits to each cookie for eyes.

HIGH ALTITUDE (3500-6500 FT.): No change.

Nutrition Information Per Serving:		
Calories: 220	From Fat: 120	
Total Fat		13g
Saturated Fat		8g
Trans Fat		0g
Cholesterol		25mg
Sodium		75mg
Total Carbohydrate		23g
Dietary Fiber		1g
Sugars		14g
Protein		2g

Peanut Butter Pumpkin Cookies

PREP TIME: 1 HOUR (READY IN 1 HOUR)
SERVINGS: 28 COOKIES

1 roll (16.5 oz) Pillsbury® refrigerated peanut butter cookies

1 egg yolk

½ cup all-purpose flour

⅓ cup orange decorator sugar crystals

14 twisted butter-flavor pretzel sticks, broken in half

1) Heat oven to 350°F. Spray cookie sheets with cooking spray. In medium bowl, stir cookie dough, egg yolk and flour until well mixed.

2) Pour sugar crystals into small bowl. Shape dough into 28 (1-inch) balls; roll in sugar crystals. Insert 1 pretzel piece into each ball for pumpkin stem. Using toothpick or tip of teaspoon, make lines around sides for pumpkin ridges. Place balls 2 inches apart on cookie sheets.

3) Bake 9 to 11 minutes or just until set in center when touched with fingertip. Cool 2 minutes; remove from the cookie sheets to cooling racks. Cool completely, about 10 minutes.

HIGH ALTITUDE (3500-6500 FT.): No change.

Nutrition Information Per Serving:

Calories: 90	From Fat: 30
Total Fat	3.5g
Saturated Fat	1g
Trans Fat	0.5g
Cholesterol	10mg
Sodium	80mg
Total Carbohydrate	13g
Dietary Fiber	0g
Sugars	8g
Protein	1g

Grilled Ham and Cheese Boo Bites

PREP TIME: 20 MINUTES (READY IN 20 MINUTES)
SERVINGS: 4 SANDWICHES

e EASY

8 slices whole wheat bread

¼ cup chives-and-onion cream cheese spread (from 8-oz container)

8 slices deli ham

4 slices sharp Cheddar cheese

2 tablespoons butter or margarine

Nutrition Information Per Serving:

Calories: 380	From Fat: 190
Total Fat	21g
Saturated Fat	12g
Trans Fat	1g
Cholesterol	75mg
Sodium	1050mg
Total Carbohydrate	25g
Dietary Fiber	4g
Sugars	7g
Protein	22g

1) Use alphabet cookie cutters to cut "BOO" out of 4 slices of bread, or use paring knife to cut jack-o'-lantern eyes, nose and mouth in 4 slices of bread; set aside. On the remaining 4 slices of bread, spread 1 tablespoon of the cream cheese; top with 2 slices ham and 1 slice cheese. Top each with cut bread slice.

2) In 12-inch nonstick skillet, melt 1 tablespoon of the butter over medium-high heat. Place 2 sandwiches cut side down in skillet; cook 1 to 2 minutes or until cut side is light brown and cheese is beginning to melt. Turn sandwich, reduce heat to medium-low; cook 3 to 4 minutes longer or until light brown and cheese is melted. Repeat with remaining 1 tablespoon butter and 2 sandwiches. Serve immediately.

HIGH ALTITUDE (3500-6500 FT.): No change.

Ghoulish Chicken-Ramen Brew

PREP TIME: 30 MINUTES (READY IN 45 MINUTES)
SERVINGS: 6

1 tablespoon olive oil

1 cup ready-to-eat baby-cut carrots, cut into 1/4-inch slices

1 cup sliced (1/4 inch) celery (2 medium stalks)

1 medium onion, chopped (1/2 cup)

2 garlic cloves, finely chopped

2 cups cut-up deli rotisserie chicken (from 2- to 2 1/2-lb chicken)

6 cups water

1 package (3 oz) chicken-flavor ramen noodle soup mix

1/4 teaspoon salt

1/4 teaspoon pepper

1) In 5-quart Dutch oven, heat oil over medium heat. Add carrots, celery, onion and garlic; cook 3 to 4 minutes, stirring frequently, until tender.

2) Stir in the chicken, water, contents of seasoning packet from soup mix, salt and pepper. Heat to boiling over high heat. Reduce heat to medium; simmer uncovered 10 to 15 minutes.

3) Break apart noodles, stir into soup; simmer uncovered about 3 minutes longer or until noodles are tender.

HIGH ALTITUDE (3500-6500 FT.): No change.

Nutrition Information Per Serving:		
Calories: 160	From Fat:	90
Total Fat		10g
Saturated Fat		2.5g
Trans Fat		1.5g
Cholesterol		25mg
Sodium		360mg
Total Carbohydrate		14g
Dietary Fiber		0g
Sugars		3g
Protein		4g

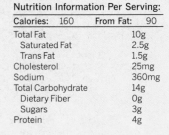

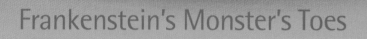

Frankenstein's Monster's Toes

PREP TIME: 1 HOUR 10 MINUTES (READY IN 2 HOURS 10 MINUTES)
SERVINGS: 36 COOKIES

1 pouch (1 lb 1.5 oz) sugar cookie mix

¼ cup all-purpose flour

⅓ cup butter or margarine, melted

1 egg

½ teaspoon almond extract

7 drops green food color

36 whole blanched almonds

½ teaspoon red food color

1) In large bowl, stir cookie mix, flour, melted butter, egg, almond extract and green food color until soft dough forms. Cover; refrigerate 1 hour.

2) Meanwhile, place almonds and red food color in resealable food-storage plastic bag; shake bag until almonds are evenly coated with food color. Place on paper plate or waxed paper to dry. Set aside.

3) Heat oven to 375°F. For each cookie, roll heaping teaspoonful of the cookie dough into 2½-inch toe shape. On ungreased cookie sheets, place shapes 2 inches apart.

4) Press almond, colored side up, into one end of each "toe" to look like a toenail. About 1 inch from each end of each "toe," squeeze dough slightly; with knife, gently make lines in dough to look like knuckles.

5) Bake 6 to 8 minutes or until set. (Cookies should not brown along edges.) Cool 1 minute; remove from the cookie sheets to cooling racks. Cool completely, about 15 minutes.

HIGH ALTITUDE (3500-6500 FT.): No change.

Nutrition Information Per Serving:		
Calories: 80	From Fat: 35	
Total Fat		3.5g
Saturated Fat		1.5g
Trans Fat		0.5g
Cholesterol		10mg
Sodium		55mg
Total Carbohydrate		11g
Dietary Fiber		0g
Sugars		6g
Protein		1g

Roast Turkey

PREP TIME: 25 MINUTES (READY IN 6 HOURS 15 MINUTES)
SERVINGS: 14 TO 18

Bread Stuffing (page 277)

1 whole turkey (14 to 18 lb), thawed if frozen

½ teaspoon salt

3 tablespoons butter or margarine, melted

Nutrition Information Per Serving:

Calories: 580	From Fat: 310
Total Fat	34g
Saturated Fat	11g
Trans Fat	1g
Cholesterol	200mg
Sodium	550mg
Total Carbohydrate	9g
Dietary Fiber	0g
Sugars	1g
Protein	58g

1) Move oven rack to lowest position. Heat oven to 325°F. Make the Bread Stuffing; set aside. (Stuff turkey just before roasting.)

2) Remove and discard neck and giblets from turkey. Rinse turkey inside and out with cold water; pat dry with paper towels. Sprinkle cavity of turkey with salt.

3) Spoon stuffing loosely into neck cavity; turn wings back to hold neck skin in place, or fasten neck skin to back with skewers. Spoon stuffing into body cavity; refasten drumsticks with metal piece or tuck under the skin at tail. (Drumsticks can also be tied together with cotton string.)

4) Place the turkey, breast side up, in roasting pan. Insert ovenproof meat thermometer so tip is in thickest part of inside thigh and does not touch bone. Brush butter over turkey. Do not add water or cover turkey.

5) Roast uncovered 4 hours to 4 hours 30 minutes or until thermometer reads 180°F and drumsticks move easily when lifted or twisted. Thermometer inserted in center of stuffing should read 165°F. If necessary, cover turkey breast with tent of heavy-duty foil during last 1 hour 30 minutes to 2 hours of baking to prevent excessive browning.

6) Let turkey stand 15 to 20 minutes for easier carving. Remove skewers. Remove stuffing; place in serving bowl.

HIGH ALTITUDE (3500-6500 FT.): No change.

Bread Stuffing

PREP TIME: 20 MINUTES (READY IN 60 MINUTES)
SERVINGS: 18 (1/2 CUP EACH)

1/4 cup butter or margarine

1 medium onion, chopped (1/2 cup)

2 medium stalks celery, chopped (1 cup)

8 cups dry bread cubes (about 11 slices bread)

2 tablespoons finely chopped fresh parsley, if desired

2 tablespoons poultry seasoning or dried sage leaves

1 teaspoon salt

1/4 teaspoon pepper

About 1/2 cup Progresso® chicken broth (from 32-oz carton) or water

1) In 10-inch skillet, melt butter over medium-high heat. Add onion and celery; cook, stirring occasionally, until tender.

2) In large bowl, mix bread cubes, parsley, poultry seasoning, salt and pepper. Add broth and butter-onion mixture, stirring until the desired moistness is reached (stuffing will become a little more moist during roasting because it absorbs juices from turkey).

3) Use to stuff one 14- to 18-pound turkey. After stuffing tukey, place any remaining stuffing in 1- or 2-quart casserole that's been sprayed with cooking spray; cover and refrigerate. Bake stuffing in casserole with turkey for last 35 to 40 minutes of roasting time or until thoroughly heated.

HIGH ALTITUDE (3500-6500 FT.): No change.

Nutrition Information Per Serving:		
Calories: 70	From Fat:	30
Total Fat		3g
Saturated Fat		2g
Trans Fat		0g
Cholesterol		5mg
Sodium		280mg
Total Carbohydrate		9g
Dietary Fiber		0g
Sugars		1g
Protein		1g

tip

Day-old soft bread cubes can be substituted for the dry bread cubes. Decrease the broth to about 1/4 cup.

Maple-Glazed Turkey with Wild Rice Stuffing

PREP TIME: 1 HOUR 10 MINUTES (READY IN 6 HOURS 55 MINUTES)
SERVINGS: 16 TO 18

STUFFING

¼ cup butter or margarine

2 cups chopped onions (4 medium)

3 garlic cloves, finely chopped

1½ cups uncooked wild rice

3 tablespoons chopped fresh thyme leaves

5 to 6 cups Progresso® chicken broth (from two 32-oz cartons)

1½ cups uncooked long-grain brown rice

2 cups sliced celery (about 4 medium stalks)

2 cups shredded carrots (about 3 medium)

6 slices bacon (½ lb), cooked, crumbled

1 teaspoon salt

½ teaspoon pepper

TURKEY

1 whole turkey (16 to 18 lb), thawed if frozen

1 tablespoon vegetable oil

½ teaspoon salt

½ teaspoon pepper

GLAZE

1½ teaspoons finely grated orange peel

½ cup orange juice

¼ cup maple-flavored syrup

2 tablespoons cider vinegar

½ teaspoon ground mustard

¼ teaspoon salt

Nutrition Information Per Serving:

Calories:	700	From Fat:	310
Total Fat			34g
Saturated Fat			10g
Trans Fat			1g
Cholesterol			195mg
Sodium			810mg
Total Carbohydrate			35g
Dietary Fiber			4g
Sugars			6g
Protein			63g

1) In 4-quart Dutch oven, melt butter over medium-high heat. Add onions and garlic; cook 5 minutes, stirring occasionally. Stir in wild rice, thyme and 5 cups of the broth. Heat to boiling over high heat, stirring occasionally. Reduce the heat to low. Cover; simmer 10 minutes. Stir in brown rice and celery. Cover; simmer 40 to 50 minutes longer or until the rice is tender and the liquid is absorbed, adding more broth by ¼ cupfuls if necessary to prevent scorching.

2) Stir in carrots, bacon, 1 teaspoon salt and ½ teaspoon pepper. Remove from heat. Cover; let stand 10 minutes. Uncover; cool 30 minutes before stuffing turkey. (Stuff turkey just before roasting.)

3) Move oven rack to lowest position. Heat oven to 325°F. Remove and discard neck and giblets from turkey. Rinse turkey inside and out with cold water; pat dry with paper towels. Spoon stuffing loosely into neck cavity; turn wings back to hold neck skin in place, or fasten neck skin to back with skewers.

4) Spoon stuffing into body cavity; refasten drumsticks with metal piece or tuck under skin at tail. (Drumsticks can also be tied together with cotton string.) Place any remaining stuffing in 2-quart casserole that's been sprayed with cooking spray; cover and refrigerate.

5) Place turkey, breast side up, in roasting pan. Insert ovenproof meat thermometer so tip is in thickest part of inside thigh and does not touch bone. Brush with oil to prevent skin from drying. Sprinkle with ½ teaspoon salt and ½ teaspoon pepper. Place tent of heavy-duty foil loosely over turkey. Roast turkey 1 hour 30 minutes. Remove foil; roast 1 hour 30 minutes to 2 hours longer or until thermometer reads 160°F.

6) Meanwhile, in 2-quart saucepan, stir together the glaze ingredients. Heat to boiling over medium-high heat, stirring frequently. Reduce the heat to medium-low; gently boil uncovered 20 to 30 minutes, stirring occasionally, until mixture is reduced to ½ cup. Remove from heat.

7) Remove stuffing in casserole from refrigerator; uncover and set aside. When thermometer reads 160°F, brush turkey with ½ of glaze; roast 20 minutes. Brush with remaining glaze; roast 15 to 30 minutes longer or until thermometer reads 180°F and drumsticks move easily when lifted or twisted. Cover loosely with foil; let stand 15 to 20 minutes for easier carving.

8) Meanwhile, increase oven temperature to 375°F. Bake uncovered casserole with stuffing 15 to 20 minutes or until thoroughly heated. Place turkey on serving platter. Remove skewers. Remove stuffing from turkey; place in serving bowl.

HIGH ALTITUDE (3500-6500 FT.): In Step 1, increase broth to 5-1/2 cups. After stirring in rice and celery, cover; simmer 60 to 70 minutes. In Step 9, bake casserole with stuffing uncovered 35 to 40 minutes, stirring halfway through bake time.

Savory Turkey Gravy

PREP TIME: 15 MINUTES (READY IN 15 MINUTES)
SERVINGS: 22 (1/4 CUP EACH)

EASY

Drippings from roasted turkey

$2/3$ cup all-purpose flour

$2 1/3$ cups Progresso® chicken broth
(from 32-oz carton)

Water

1) Remove turkey from roasting pan. Place strainer over small bowl. Pour drippings (turkey juices and fat) from pan into strainer. Skim $2/3$ cup fat from top of drippings; place fat in 3-quart saucepan. Discard any remaining fat (or if there is not enough fat, add enough melted butter to the fat to measure $2/3$ cup). Reserve remaining drippings.

2) With wire whisk, stir flour into fat in saucepan. Cook over medium heat 1 to 2 minutes, stirring constantly, until mixture is smooth and bubbly. Remove from heat.

3) Measure reserved drippings together with broth; add enough water to equal 5 cups liquid. Gradually stir broth mixture into flour mixture. Heat to boiling over high heat (5 to 6 minutes), stirring constantly. Boil and stir 1 minute.

HIGH ALTITUDE (3500-6500 FT.): In Step 3, boil and stir 2 to 3 minutes.

Nutrition Information Per Serving:	
Calories: 80	From Fat: 60
Total Fat	7g
Saturated Fat	2g
Trans Fat	0g
Cholesterol	5mg
Sodium	260mg
Total Carbohydrate	3g
Dietary Fiber	0g
Sugars	0g
Protein	1g

Pumpkin Pie

PREP TIME: 25 MINUTES (READY IN 4 HOURS)
SERVINGS: 8

CRUST

1 Pillsbury® refrigerated pie crust (from 15-oz box), softened as directed on box

FILLING

3/4 cup sugar

1 1/2 teaspoons pumpkin pie spice

1/2 teaspoon salt

1 can (15 oz) pumpkin (not pumpkin pie mix)

1 can (12 oz) evaporated milk

2 eggs, beaten

1) Heat oven to 425°F. Place pie crust in 9-inch glass pie plate as directed on box for One-Crust Filled Pie.

2) In large bowl, beat filling ingredients with hand beater or wire whisk until well blended. Pour into crust-lined plate. Cover crust edge with strips of foil to prevent excessive browning.

3) Bake 15 minutes. Reduce the oven temperature to 350°F; bake 40 to 50 minutes longer or until knife inserted near center comes out clean. Cool 30 minutes. Refrigerate at least 2 hours before serving. Store covered in refrigerator.

HIGH ALTITUDE (3500-6500 FT.): No change.

Nutrition Information Per Serving:		
Calories: 290	From Fat:	110
Total Fat		12g
Saturated Fat		5g
Trans Fat		0g
Cholesterol		70mg
Sodium		320mg
Total Carbohydrate		41g
Dietary Fiber		1g
Sugars		25g
Protein		5g

tip

To add a little maple flavor to the pie, substitute 1/2 cup maple-flavored syrup for 1/2 cup of the evaporated milk.

Roasted Harvest Vegetables

PREP TIME: 25 MINUTES (READY IN 1 HOUR 10 MINUTES)
SERVINGS: 8 (3/4 CUP EACH)

4 medium carrots (about 10 oz), cut into 1-inch pieces (2 cups)

4 medium parsnips (about 1 lb), peeled, cut into $^1/_2$-inch slices (3$^1/_2$ cups)

$^1/_4$ cup olive or vegetable oil

4 teaspoons chopped fresh or 1$^1/_2$ teaspoons dried thyme leaves

1 teaspoon salt

$^1/_4$ teaspoon pepper

2 lb butternut squash, peeled, seeded and cut into 1$^1/_2$-inch chunks (6$^1/_2$ cups)

   Fresh thyme sprigs, if desired

1) Heat oven to 425°F. In large bowl, place the carrots, parsnips, and half each of the oil, chopped thyme, salt and pepper; toss to the coat vegetables. In an ungreased 15x10x1-inch pan, spread mixture in a single layer. Bake 15 minutes.

2) Meanwhile, in same large bowl, toss squash with remaining oil, chopped thyme, salt and pepper. Add to pan; stir to combine vegetables.

3) Bake 35 to 40 minutes longer, turning vegetables twice with pancake turner, until vegetables are tender. Spoon into serving bowl or on platter; garnish with thyme sprigs.

HIGH ALTITUDE (3500-6500 FT.): To assure doneness, cut top, stem-ends of parsnips in half lengthwise, then into 1/2-inch slices.

Nutrition Information Per Serving:		
Calories: 150	From Fat:	60
Total Fat		7g
Saturated Fat		1g
Trans Fat		0g
Cholesterol		0mg
Sodium		320mg
Total Carbohydrate		20g
Dietary Fiber		4g
Sugars		7g
Protein		1g

Sweet Orange Cream Topping

PREP TIME: 10 MINUTES (READY IN 10 MINUTES)
SERVINGS: 8 (1/4 CUP EACH)

⊖ EASY

1 cup whipping cream

2 tablespoons powdered sugar

¼ cup orange juice

½ teaspoon grated fresh orange peel

Additional grated fresh orange peel
or orange twists, if desired

1) In large bowl, beat whipping cream and powdered sugar with electric mixer on medium speed about 1 minute or until cream begins to thicken, then on high speed until stiff peaks form.

2) Fold in orange juice and ½ teaspoon orange peel. Refrigerate until ready to serve. Garnish with additional orange peel.

HIGH ALTITUDE (3500-6500 FT.): No change.

Nutrition Information Per Serving:

Calories:	100	From Fat:	80
Total Fat			9g
Saturated Fat			6g
Trans Fat			0g
Cholesterol			35mg
Sodium			10mg
Total Carbohydrate			4g
Dietary Fiber			0g
Sugars			3g
Protein			0g

Caramel-Apple Cream Topping

PREP TIME: 5 MINUTES (READY IN 5 MINUTES)
SERVINGS: 8 (1/4 CUP EACH)

⊖ EASY

1 cup whipping cream

¼ cup caramel topping

1 tablespoon packed brown sugar

½ teaspoon apple pie spice

Additional caramel ice cream
topping, if desired

1) In large bowl, beat whipping cream with electric mixer on medium speed about 1 minute or until cream begins to thicken, then on high speed until soft peaks form.

2) Gradually beat in ¼ cup caramel topping, the brown sugar and apple pie spice, scraping bowl once, until blended and stiff peaks form. Refrigerate until ready to serve. Garnish with additional caramel topping.

HIGH ALTITUDE (3500-6500 FT.): No change.

Nutrition Information Per Serving:

Calories:	120	From Fat:	80
Total Fat			9g
Saturated Fat			6g
Trans Fat			0g
Cholesterol			35mg
Sodium			45mg
Total Carbohydrate			9g
Dietary Fiber			0g
Sugars			8g
Protein			0g

tip

When whipping
cream, it's a good
idea to chill the
bowl and beaters
in the fridge first.

Cinnamon-Maple Cream Topping

PREP TIME: 5 MINUTES (READY IN 5 MINUTES)
SERVINGS: 8 (1/4 CUP EACH)

🅔 EASY

1 cup whipping cream

1/4 cup real maple or maple-flavored syrup

1/2 teaspoon ground cinnamon

Pecan halves or additional ground cinnamon, if desired

1) In large bowl, beat whipping cream with electric mixer on medium speed about 1 minute or until cream begins to thicken, then on high speed until soft peaks form.

2) Gradually beat in syrup and 1/2 teaspoon cinnamon, scraping bowl once, until blended and stiff peaks form. Refrigerate until ready to serve. Garnish with pecans.

HIGH ALTITUDE (3500-6500 FT.): No change.

Nutrition Information Per Serving:

Calories:	120	From Fat:	80
Total Fat			9g
Saturated Fat			6g
Trans Fat			0g
Cholesterol			35mg
Sodium			10mg
Total Carbohydrate			8g
Dietary Fiber			0g
Sugars			7g
Protein			0g

Pizza Pinwheels

PREP TIME:	20 MINUTES (READY IN 35 MINUTES)
SERVINGS:	24 (1 APPETIZER AND 1 TEASPOON SAUCE EACH)

🅔 EASY

1 can (8 oz) Pillsbury® refrigerated
crescent dinner rolls

2 tablespoons grated Parmesan
cheese

1/3 cup finely chopped pepperoni (about
1 1/2 oz)

2 tablespoons finely chopped green
bell pepper

1/2 cup shredded Italian cheese blend
(2 oz)

1/2 cup pizza sauce

1) Heat oven to 350°F. Spray cookie sheet
with cooking spray. Unroll dough and
separate into 4 rectangles; firmly press
perforations to seal.

2) Sprinkle Parmesan cheese, pepperoni,
bell pepper and Italian cheese blend
over each rectangle.

3) Starting with one short side, roll up each
rectangle; press the edge to seal. With
serrated knife, cut each roll into 6 slices; place the rolls cut sides down on
cookie sheet.

4) Bake 13 to 17 minutes or until edges are golden brown. Meanwhile, heat
pizza sauce. Immediately remove pinwheels from cookie sheet. Serve warm
with warm pizza sauce for dipping.

HIGH ALTITUDE (3500-6500 FT.): No change.

Nutrition Information Per Serving:			
Calories:	60	From Fat:	30
Total Fat			3.5g
Saturated Fat			1.5g
Trans Fat			0.5g
Cholesterol			0mg
Sodium			160mg
Total Carbohydrate			4g
Dietary Fiber			0g
Sugars			1g
Protein			2g

Athenian-Style Bruschetta

PREP TIME: 20 MINUTES (READY IN 20 MINUTES)
SERVINGS: 30 APPETIZERS

🅔 EASY   🅕 LOW FAT

1 loaf (18 inch) baguette French bread (8 oz), cut into 1/2-inch-thick slices (about 30)

3 tablespoons olive oil

1/2 cup finely chopped red bell pepper

1/2 cup finely chopped yellow bell pepper

3 tablespoons finely chopped red onion

2 garlic cloves, finely chopped

1/2 teaspoon salt

1/2 teaspoon chopped fresh oregano leaves

1/2 teaspoon chopped fresh thyme leaves

1/4 cup reduced-fat balsamic vinaigrette

20 pitted kalamata olives, finely chopped (1/3 cup)

1/4 cup crumbled feta cheese (1 oz)

3 tablespoons finely chopped fresh parsley, if desired

1) Heat oven to 375°F. In 15x10-inch pan with sides, place bread slices in single layer. Using pastry brush, lightly brush tops of slices with about 2 tablespoons of the oil. Bake 8 to 10 minutes or until lightly browned and crisp.

2) Meanwhile, in 10-inch nonstick skillet, heat remaining 1 tablespoon oil over medium-high heat 1 to 2 minutes or until hot. Add the bell peppers, onion, garlic, salt, oregano and thyme. Cook 3 to 5 minutes, stirring occasionally, until vegetables are crisp-tender.

3) Transfer vegetables to medium bowl. Add vinaigrette and olives; stir until vegetables are coated.

4) Top each bread slice with 1 teaspoon vegetable mixture. Sprinkle with the cheese and parsley.

HIGH ALTITUDE (3500-6500 FT.): No change.

Nutrition Information Per Serving:	
Calories: 45	From Fat: 20
Total Fat	2g
Saturated Fat	0g
Trans Fat	0g
Cholesterol	0mg
Sodium	130mg
Total Carbohydrate	5g
Dietary Fiber	0g
Sugars	1g
Protein	1g

Bourbon-Glazed Ham

PREP TIME: 15 MINUTES (READY IN 2 HOURS 50 MINUTES)
SERVINGS: 16

e EASY   **f** LOW FAT

1 fully cooked smoked bone-in half ham (9 to 10 lb)

1 teaspoon whole cloves

1 cup packed dark brown sugar

2 tablespoons ground mustard

1/4 cup bourbon or apple juice

Nutrition Information Per Serving:

Calories:	250	From Fat:	70
Total Fat			8g
Saturated Fat			2.5g
Trans Fat			0g
Cholesterol			75mg
Sodium			1660mg
Total Carbohydrate			16g
Dietary Fiber			0g
Sugars			13g
Protein			29g

1) Heat oven to 325°F. Spray shallow roasting pan or 15x10x1-inch pan with cooking spray. Place ham, fat side up, on rack in shallow pan. Score the outside of ham in diamond pattern; insert cloves into diamond shapes. (To make inserting cloves easier, use small paring knife or toothpick to make small holes before inserting the cloves.) Insert ovenproof meat thermometer in thickest part of ham. Bake 1 hour.

2) In small bowl, stir together brown sugar, mustard and bourbon. Brush 1/2 of brown sugar mixture evenly over ham.

3) Bake 30 minutes. Brush with remaining brown sugar mixture. Bake 40 to 50 minutes longer or until thermometer reads 140°F. If pan drippings start to burn, add up to 1/4 cup water to pan.

4) Remove ham from oven; cover with foil and let stand 10 to 15 minutes for easier carving.

HIGH ALTITUDE (3500-6500 FT.): No change.

Cinnamon Snack Mix

PREP TIME: 15 MINUTES (READY IN 1 HOUR)
SERVINGS: 24 (ABOUT 1/2 CUP EACH)

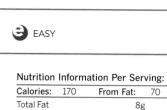 EASY

4 cups Honey Nut Chex® cereal

3 cups vanilla Yogurt Burst™ Cheerios® cereal

2 cups Cinnamon Toast Crunch® cereal

1½ cups raisins

1 cup pecan halves

½ cup butter or margarine

¼ cup honey

1 teaspoon grated orange peel

½ teaspoon ground cinnamon

1) Heat oven to 350°F. In large bowl, mix cereals, raisins and pecans.

2) In 2-cup microwavable measuring cup, microwave butter uncovered on High 30 seconds to 1 minute or until melted; stir in honey, orange peel and cinnamon. Pour over the cereal mixture, tossing to coat evenly. Spread evenly in ungreased broiler pan or 15x10x1-inch pan.

3) Bake 11 to 13 minutes or until mixture is glazed, stirring once during bake time. Spread on foil to cool completely, about 30 minutes. Store in tightly covered container.

HIGH ALTITUDE (3500-6500 FT.): Bake 16 to 18 minutes, stirring every 5 minutes.

Nutrition Information Per Serving:

Calories:	170	From Fat:	70
Total Fat			8g
Saturated Fat			3g
Trans Fat			0g
Cholesterol			10mg
Sodium			130mg
Total Carbohydrate			24g
Dietary Fiber			1g
Sugars			13g
Protein			1g

Apple and Blue Cheese Tart

PREP TIME: 15 MINUTES (READY IN 55 MINUTES)
SERVINGS: 12

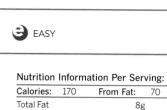 EASY

1 Pillsbury® refrigerated pie crust (from 15-oz box), softened as directed on box

3 tablespoons butter or margarine

2 medium shallots, finely chopped (about ⅓ cup)

1 medium apple, peeled, cut into ¼-inch slices (about 1 cup)

¼ cup chopped pistachio nuts

2 tablespoons sweetened dried cranberries

¼ cup crumbled blue cheese (1 oz)

1 teaspoon chopped fresh thyme leaves

1 red pearl onion, halved, if desired

1) Heat oven to 450°F. Make pie crust as directed on box for One-Crust Baked Shell using 9-inch tart pan with removable bottom. Bake 8 to 10 minutes or until lightly browned.

2) Meanwhile, in 8-inch skillet, melt butter over medium heat. Add shallots; cook 2 to 4 minutes, stirring occasionally, until tender. Remove from heat.

3) Arrange apple slices in concentric circles in single layer in crust. Spread butter mixture over apples.

4) Bake 15 to 20 minutes. Sprinkle nuts, cranberries, cheese and thyme over apples. Bake about 3 minutes longer or until the crust is golden brown. Cool on cooling rack 10 minutes. Serve warm or at room temperature. Garnish with onion.

HIGH ALTITUDE (3500-6500 FT.): Cut apples into thin slices.

Nutrition Information Per Serving:

Calories:	120	From Fat:	80
Total Fat			8g
Saturated Fat			3.5g
Trans Fat			0g
Cholesterol			10mg
Sodium			110mg
Total Carbohydrate			11g
Dietary Fiber			0g
Sugars			2g
Protein			1g

Warm Southwest Salsa with Tortilla Chips

PREP TIME: 20 MINUTES (READY IN 30 MINUTES)
SERVINGS: 20 (1/4 CUP SALSA AND 4 CHIPS EACH)

 EASY

2 cans (10 oz each) petite diced tomatoes with lime juice and cilantro, drained

1 can (15 oz) Progresso® black beans, drained, rinsed

1 cup Green Giant® Valley Fresh Steamers™ Niblets® frozen corn

1/2 cup finely chopped green bell pepper

2 medium tomatillos, husks removed, rinsed and finely chopped (about 1/2 cup)

1 jalapeño chile, seeded, finely chopped

1 garlic clove, finely chopped

1 teaspoon chili powder

1/2 teaspoon ground cumin

1/2 cup shredded Mexican cheese blend (2 oz)

2 tablespoons chopped fresh cilantro, if desired

12 oz yellow tortilla chips

1) Lightly spray 1½-quart round microwavable casserole with cooking spray. In large bowl, mix all ingredients except cheese, cilantro and tortilla chips. Spoon into casserole. Sprinkle cheese evenly over top.

2) Microwave uncovered on High 5 to 7 minutes or until warm. Sprinkle with cilantro. Place casserole on large round platter; surround with tortilla chips. Serve immediately. (Salsa will be saucy; serve with slotted spoon.)

HIGH ALTITUDE (3500-6500 FT.): No change.

Nutrition Information Per Serving:		
Calories: 140	From Fat:	50
Total Fat		5g
Saturated Fat		1g
Trans Fat		0g
Cholesterol		0mg
Sodium		160mg
Total Carbohydrate		19g
Dietary Fiber		3g
Sugars		2g
Protein		3g

Asian Chicken Tenders with Zesty Lemon Sauce

PREP TIME: 15 MINUTES (READY IN 50 MINUTES)
SERVINGS: 12 (2 CHICKEN STRIPS AND 2 TEASPOONS SAUCE EACH)

e EASY   **LF** LOW FAT

3 boneless skinless chicken breasts
   (about 1 lb)

2 tablespoons soy sauce

1 tablespoon honey

1/2 teaspoon ground ginger

1/4 teaspoon garlic powder

1 cup Progresso® panko crispy
   bread crumbs

1/2 cup sweet-and-sour sauce

1/2 teaspoon grated lemon peel

1) Cut each chicken breast across grain
   into 8 (1/2-inch-thick) slices. In medium
   bowl, mix soy sauce, honey, ginger and
   garlic powder. Add chicken; stir gently
   until coated. Let stand 20 minutes
   to marinate.

2) Heat oven to 400°F. Line 15x10x1-inch
   pan with foil; spray foil with cooking
   spray. Place bread crumbs in shallow
   dish. Drain off any remaining soy sauce
   mixture from chicken. Toss chicken
   pieces in bread crumbs to coat; arrange
   in single layer in pan.

3) Bake 5 minutes. Turn chicken; bake 5 to
   7 minutes longer or until golden brown
   and crisp.

4) In a small bowl, stir together the
   sweet-and-sour sauce and lemon peel.
   Serve chicken with sauce for dipping.

HIGH ALTITUDE (3500-6500 FT.): No change.

Nutrition Information Per Serving:

Calories:	100	From Fat:	20
Total Fat		2.5g	
Saturated Fat		0g	
Trans Fat		0g	
Cholesterol		25mg	
Sodium		230mg	
Total Carbohydrate		11g	
Dietary Fiber		0g	
Sugars		4g	
Protein		9g	

Peppermint-Bark Hearts

PREP TIME: 20 MINUTES (READY IN 50 MINUTES)
SERVINGS: 9 CANDY HEARTS

e EASY

18 peppermint candy canes (2 1/2 inch), unwrapped

5 oz vanilla-flavored candy coating (almond bark), chopped

2 teaspoons crushed peppermint candy canes

1) Line cookie sheet with waxed paper. Arrange candy canes on waxed paper in groups of 2 with ends touching to form heart shapes.

2) In 2-cup microwavable measuring cup, microwave candy coating uncovered on Medium (50%) 2 to 3 minutes, stirring once halfway through cooking time, until softened. Stir until melted and smooth.

3) Spoon or pipe candy coating into the centers of hearts to fill spaces. Sprinkle with crushed candy. Cool 30 minutes or until set.

HIGH ALTITUDE (3500-6500 FT.): No change.

Nutrition Information Per Serving:

Calories:	120	From Fat:	45
Total Fat			5g
Saturated Fat			3g
Trans Fat			0g
Cholesterol			0mg
Sodium			15mg
Total Carbohydrate			17g
Dietary Fiber			0g
Sugars			17g
Protein			1g

Christmas Tree Vegetable Platter

PREP TIME: 25 MINUTES (READY IN 1 HOUR 25 MINUTES)
SERVINGS: 8 (ABOUT 1-1/2 TABLESPOONS DIP AND 1/2 CUP VEGETABLES EACH)

CREAMY HERB DIP

- ½ cup sour cream or crème fraîche
- ¼ cup mayonnaise or salad dressing
- 3 tablespoons fresh chopped parsley
- 3 tablespoons finely chopped fresh chives
- ½ teaspoon Worcestershire sauce
- ¼ teaspoon salt
- ¼ teaspoon freshly ground black pepper
- 1 small garlic clove, finely chopped

VEGETABLE PLATTER

- 3 cups fresh broccoli florets
- 14 grape tomatoes
- ½ yellow bell pepper, cut into strips
- 1½ cups fresh cauliflower florets
- ¾ oz (about 40) pretzel sticks (from 15-oz bag)

1) In small bowl, stir together dip ingredients. Cover; refrigerate at least 1 hour to blend flavors.

2) Rinse and thoroughly dry vegetables. Trim broccoli and cauliflower floret stems.

3) Arrange broccoli on serving platter to form tree shape and tomatoes to form garland. Arrange bell pepper to form star and cauliflower to form snow (see photo). If desired, cover and refrigerate up to 4 hours.

4) Just before serving, arrange pretzels at bottom of tree to form trunk. Serve with dip.

HIGH ALTITUDE (3500-6500 FT.): No change.

Nutrition Information Per Serving:	
Calories: 130	From Fat: 80
Total Fat	9g
Saturated Fat	2.5g
Trans Fat	0g
Cholesterol	10mg
Sodium	220mg
Total Carbohydrate	11g
Dietary Fiber	2g
Sugars	3g
Protein	3g

tip
Use mini star or heart-shaped cookie cutters to cut shapes from yellow and red bell peppers or thick slices of cheese. Top the tree platter with a star cutout, and trim the veggie tree with heart shapes.

Elegant Beef Tenderloin with Herb-Dijon Crust

PREP TIME: 15 MINUTES (READY IN 1 HOUR 15 MINUTES)
SERVINGS: 8

ⓔ EASY **⑪ LOW FAT**

¼ cup chopped fresh parsley

¼ cup chopped fresh basil leaves

¼ cup chopped fresh thyme leaves

¼ cup chopped fresh oregano leaves

3 garlic cloves, finely chopped

2 lb beef tenderloin, trimmed

¾ teaspoon salt

¼ teaspoon freshly ground black pepper

3 tablespoons Dijon mustard

1) Heat oven to 400°F. In small bowl, mix parsley, basil, thyme, oregano and garlic; set aside.

2) Spray the bottom of roasting pan with cooking spray. Place beef in pan; sprinkle with salt and pepper. Spread mustard evenly over beef; pat the parsley mixture over the mustard. Insert ovenproof meat thermometer so the tip is in the center of thickest part of beef.

3) Bake uncovered 35 to 45 minutes or until thermometer reads at least 140°F (for medium-rare doneness).

4) Place beef on cutting board. Cover loosely with foil; let stand 15 minutes or until thermometer reads 145°F. (Temperature will continue to rise about 5°F, and beef will be easier to carve.) Cut beef into ½-inch-thick slices.

HIGH ALTITUDE (3500-6500 FT.): No change.

Nutrition Information Per Serving:		
Calories: 180	From Fat:	70
Total Fat		8g
Saturated Fat		3g
Trans Fat		0g
Cholesterol		45mg
Sodium		400mg
Total Carbohydrate		2g
Dietary Fiber		0g
Sugars		0g
Protein		25g

Mini Bacon-Wrapped Sausages

PREP TIME: 40 MINUTES (READY IN 1 HOUR)
SERVINGS: 40 APPETIZERS

1 lb bacon (14 slices)

1 package (1 lb) cocktail-size smoked link sausages (40 sausages)

¾ cup ketchup

½ cup granulated sugar

½ cup packed brown sugar

1 tablespoon white vinegar

¼ teaspoon onion salt

¼ teaspoon garlic powder

¼ teaspoon pepper

1) Set oven control to broil. Spray 13x9-inch (3-quart) glass baking dish with cooking spray. Spray broiler rack and pan with cooking spray. Cut each bacon slice crosswise into 3 pieces. Wrap each bacon piece around 1 sausage, securing with a toothpick; place on rack in pan.

2) Broil with tops about 6 inches from heat 12 to 16 minutes, turning once, until bacon is crisp.

3) Meanwhile, in 1-quart saucepan, mix remaining ingredients. Cook over medium heat about 5 minutes, stirring frequently, until sugar is dissolved and mixture is bubbly.

4) Heat oven to 350°F. Transfer sausages from broiler pan to baking dish. Pour sauce over sausages; turn to coat with sauce. Bake about 20 minutes or until hot and bubbly. Serve hot.

HIGH ALTITUDE (3500-6500 FT.): No change.

Nutrition Information Per Serving:		
Calories: 80	From Fat:	45
Total Fat		5g
Saturated Fat		1.5g
Trans Fat		0g
Cholesterol		10mg
Sodium		250mg
Total Carbohydrate		6g
Dietary Fiber		0g
Sugars		6g
Protein		2g

Cookies, Bars &Candies

What's not to love? Indulge in decadent
brownies, toffee, shortbread and more!

DULCE DE LECHE BARS
PG. 310

CHOCOLATE-COCONUT
THUMBPRINT COOKIES
PG. 299

CREAMY LIME SQUARES
PG. 297

CARAMEL APPLE STREUSEL BARS
PG. 302

Midnight Espresso Crinkles

PREP TIME: 1 HOUR 40 MINUTES (READY IN 1 HOUR 40 MINUTES)
SERVINGS: 3 DOZEN COOKIES

6 oz unsweetened baking chocolate, cut into small pieces

3/4 cup butter or margarine, softened

1/4 cup vegetable oil

1 cup granulated sugar

1 cup packed brown sugar

2 eggs

2 tablespoons instant coffee or espresso coffee granules

2 tablespoons water

1 teaspoon vanilla

2 cups all-purpose flour

2 teaspoons baking powder

1/2 teaspoon salt

1/2 cup dark chocolate chips (from 12-oz bag)

1/4 cup decorator sugar crystals

1) In small microwavable bowl, microwave baking chocolate uncovered on High 1 minute. Stir; microwave 1 minute longer, stirring every 15 seconds, until melted and smooth.

2) In large bowl, beat butter, oil, granulated sugar and brown sugar with electric mixer on medium speed, scraping bowl occasionally, until light and fluffy. Beat in melted chocolate and eggs until well blended.

3) In small bowl, dissolve coffee granules in water. Add coffee mixture and vanilla to batter; beat until well blended. On low speed, beat in flour, baking powder and salt. Stir in chocolate chips. Cover with plastic wrap; refrigerate 30 minutes for easier handling.

4) Heat oven to 350°F. Place sugar crystals in small bowl. Shape dough by rounded tablespoonfuls into 1½-inch balls; dip tops of balls in sugar. On ungreased cookie sheets, place balls, sugar sides up, 3 inches apart.

5) Bake 11 to 13 minutes or until tops look dry (do not overbake). Cool 5 minutes; remove from cookie sheets to cooling racks.

HIGH ALTITUDE (3500-6500 FT.): No change.

Nutrition Information Per Serving:		
Calories: 170	From Fat: 80	
Total Fat		9g
Saturated Fat		4.5g
Trans Fat		0g
Cholesterol		20mg
Sodium		95mg
Total Carbohydrate		21g
Dietary Fiber		1g
Sugars		14g
Protein		2g

Creamy Lime Squares

PREP TIME: 30 MINUTES (READY IN 2 HOURS 30 MINUTES)
SERVINGS: 24

2 cups all-purpose flour

1/2 cup powdered sugar

1 cup cold butter or margarine

3/4 cup frozen (thawed) limeade concentrate (from 12-oz can)

2 containers (6 oz each) Yoplait® Thick & Creamy key lime pie yogurt

1 box (4-serving size) French vanilla instant pudding and pie filling mix

1 1/2 teaspoons grated lime peel

1 container (8 oz) frozen whipped topping, thawed

1 to 4 drops green food color

Extra whipped topping, if desired

Lime slices, if desired

Fresh mint leaves, if desired

Nutrition Information Per Serving:		
Calories: 200	From Fat:	90
Total Fat	10g	
Saturated Fat	6g	
Trans Fat	0g	
Cholesterol	20mg	
Sodium	125mg	
Total Carbohydrate	25g	
Dietary Fiber	0g	
Sugars	13g	
Protein	2g	

1) Heat oven to 350°F. In large bowl, mix flour and powdered sugar. With pastry blender, cut in butter until mixture looks like fine crumbs. In bottom of ungreased 13x9-inch pan, press mixture evenly. Bake 20 to 30 minutes or until light golden brown. Cool completely, about 40 minutes.

2) In large bowl, mix limeade and yogurt with wire whisk until blended. Beat in pudding mix until well blended. Let stand 5 minutes to thicken. Stir lime peel into yogurt mixture. Gently stir in whipped topping and food color until desired green color.

3) Pour yogurt mixture over cooled crust; spread evenly. Refrigerate at least 2 hours before serving.

4) For squares, cut into 6 rows by 4 rows. Serve each square topped with extra whipped topping, lime slice and fresh mint leaf.

HIGH ALTITUDE (3500-6500 FT.): Bake 23 to 28 minutes.

tip

This treat needs to be refrigerated for at least two hours, so it's a great dessert to make the night before an event.

Triple-Nut Toffee

PREP TIME: 40 MINUTES (READY IN 1 HOUR 10 MINUTES)
SERVINGS: 3 DOZEN PIECES

⅓ cup chopped pecans

⅓ cup slivered almonds

⅓ cup cashew halves and pieces

½ packed brown sugar

½ cup granulated sugar

1 cup butter or margarine

¼ cup water

½ cup semisweet chocolate chips

1) Heat oven to 350°F. Line 15x10x1-inch pan with foil. Spread nuts in pan. Bake uncovered 6 to 10 minutes, stirring occasionally, until light brown. Pour into small bowl; set aside. Set aside pan with foil to use in Step 3.

2) Meanwhile, in heavy 2-quart saucepan, cook sugars, butter and water over medium-high heat 4 to 6 minutes, stirring constantly with wooden spoon, until mixture comes to a full boil. Boil 20 to 25 minutes, stirring frequently, until candy thermometer reaches 300°F or a small amount of the mixture dropped into ice water forms a hard brittle strand.

3) Stir in ½ cup of the nuts; immediately pour toffee into same foil-lined pan. Quickly spread mixture to ¼-inch thickness with rubber spatula. Sprinkle with chocolate chips; let stand about 1 minute or until chips are completely softened. Spread softened chocolate evenly over toffee. Sprinkle with remaining nuts.

4) Refrigerate about 30 minutes or until chocolate is firm. Break into pieces. Store in tightly covered container.

HIGH ALTITUDE (3500-6500 FT.): In Step 2, after mixture comes to a full boil, reduce heat to low and boil 20 to 25 minutes, stirring constantly, until candy thermometer reads 294°F to 296°F.

Nutrition Information Per Serving:		
Calories: 100	From Fat:	70
Total Fat		8g
Saturated Fat		4g
Trans Fat		0g
Cholesterol		15mg
Sodium		40mg
Total Carbohydrate		8g
Dietary Fiber		0g
Sugars		7g
Protein		0g

Peanut Butter-Cereal Bars

PREP TIME: 20 MINUTES (READY IN 35 MINUTES)
SERVINGS: 24 BARS

EASY

3 cups Corn Chex® cereal

2 cups Total® Honey Clusters® cereal

2 cups Honey Nut Cheerios® cereal

¾ cup creamy peanut butter

½ cup corn syrup

2 tablespoons butter or margarine

20 large marshmallows

1) Spray 13x9-inch pan with cooking spray. In large bowl, mix cereals; set aside.

2) In 2-quart saucepan, cook remaining ingredients over low heat, stirring constantly, until marshmallows are melted. Pour over cereal mixture; mix well.

3) Using sprayed rubber scraper, press mixture into pan. Cool slightly. For bars, cut into 6 rows by 4 rows.

HIGH ALTITUDE (3500-6500 FT.): No change.

Nutrition Information Per Serving:

Calories: 150	From Fat: 50
Total Fat	5g
Saturated Fat	1.5g
Trans Fat	0g
Cholesterol	0mg
Sodium	140mg
Total Carbohydrate	22g
Dietary Fiber	1g
Sugars	10g
Protein	3g

Chocolate-Coconut Thumbprint Cookies

PREP TIME: 20 MINUTES (READY IN 1 HOUR)
SERVINGS: 3 DOZEN COOKIES

EASY

1 roll (16.5 oz) Pillsbury® refrigerated sugar cookies

4 oz sweet baking chocolate, melted, cooled 10 minutes

2 tablespoons all-purpose flour

½ cup flaked coconut

½ cup coconut pecan ready-to-spread frosting

2 oz sweet baking chocolate

½ teaspoon vegetable oil

1) Heat oven to 350°F. In large bowl, break up cookie dough. Using hands, stir or knead in 4 oz chocolate and the flour until well blended. Divide dough in half; cover and refrigerate one half until ready to use.

2) Shape remaining half into 18 balls. Place coconut in shallow dish; dip half of each ball in coconut to coat. On ungreased large cookie sheet, place balls coconut sides up 1 inch apart. Repeat with remaining half of dough.

3) Bake 7 to 9 minutes or until the edges are set and the centers are almost set. Immediately make indentation in center of each cookie with the end of a wooden spoon. Fill each indentation with ½ teaspoon frosting. Cool 2 minutes on cookie sheet; remove from cookie sheet to cooling rack. Cool until set, about 30 minutes.

4) In small microwavable bowl, microwave 2 oz chocolate and the oil uncovered on High about 1 minute 30 seconds or until chocolate can be stirred completely melted; drizzle over cookies.

HIGH ALTITUDE (3500-6500 FT.): Bake 9 to 11 minutes.

Nutrition Information Per Serving:

Calories: 110	From Fat: 50
Total Fat	5g
Saturated Fat	2g
Trans Fat	1g
Cholesterol	0mg
Sodium	50mg
Total Carbohydrate	14g
Dietary Fiber	0g
Sugars	9g
Protein	0g

Chocolate Caramel-Cashew Bars

PREP TIME: 20 MINUTES (READY IN 1 HOUR 35 MINUTES)
SERVINGS: 16 BARS

EASY

BASE

- ⅓ cup butter or margarine
- 2 oz bittersweet baking chocolate, chopped
- 1 cup all-purpose flour
- ½ cup granulated sugar
- ⅓ cup packed brown sugar
- ¼ teaspoon baking soda
- 1 egg, slightly beaten
- 1 tablespoon milk

FILLING AND TOPPING

- ¼ cup hot caramel topping (from 12-oz jar)
- 6 caramels, unwrapped, cut into quarters
- ⅓ cup cashew pieces
- 1 bar (1.55 oz) milk chocolate candy, broken into pieces

1) Heat oven to 350°F. In a small microwavable bowl, microwave butter and bittersweet chocolate uncovered on Medium (50%) 1 minute, stirring after 30 seconds. Microwave 30 seconds longer or until butter and chocolate are melted and can be stirred smooth. Set aside to cool slightly.

2) In medium bowl, stir together the flour, granulated sugar, brown sugar and baking soda. Stir in egg, milk and cooled chocolate mixture until well blended. In ungreased 8-inch square pan, press half of dough. Bake 8 minutes.

3) Meanwhile, in 1-quart saucepan, cook caramel topping and caramels over medium-low heat, stirring constantly, until caramels are melted.

4) Remove pan from oven. Carefully pour caramel mixture over partially baked base to within ½ inch of sides of pan. Sprinkle with cashews. Crumble remaining dough into small pieces and sprinkle over filling (some of filling will show). Bake 12 to 15 minutes longer or just until edges are set (do not overbake).

5) In small microwavable bowl, microwave chocolate candy bar pieces uncovered on High 30 seconds or until melted. Drizzle chocolate diagonally over baked bars. Cool completely, at least 1 hour. For bars, cut into 4 rows by 4 rows.

HIGH ALTITUDE (3500-6500 FT.): Add 1 tablespoon more flour to ingredients in Step 2.

Nutrition Information Per Serving:	
Calories: 190	From Fat: 80
Total Fat	9g
Saturated Fat	4.5g
Trans Fat	0g
Cholesterol	25mg
Sodium	90mg
Total Carbohydrate	27g
Dietary Fiber	1g
Sugars	17g
Protein	2g

tip

Try making these bars with hot fudge topping instead of the hot caramel topping next time.

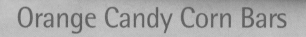

Orange Candy Corn Bars

PREP TIME: 15 MINUTES (READY IN 2 HOURS)
SERVINGS: 32 BARS

e EASY

BARS
- ³/₄ cup butter or margarine, melted, cooled slightly
- 1³/₄ cups granulated sugar
- 1 tablespoon grated orange peel
- 4 eggs
- 1³/₄ cups all-purpose flour
- 1 teaspoon baking powder
- 4 drops yellow food color
- 3 drops red food color

FROSTING
- ¹/₂ cup butter, softened (do not use margarine)
- 1³/₄ cups powdered sugar
- 1 to 2 tablespoons milk
- 1 teaspoon vanilla
- ¹/₈ teaspoon salt

DECORATION
- ¹/₃ cup candy corn (32 candies)

1) Heat oven to 325°F. Line bottom and sides of 9-inch square pan with foil, extending foil 2 inches on 2 opposite sides of pan; spray foil with cooking spray.

2) In medium bowl, beat melted ³/₄ cup butter, the granulated sugar and orange peel with wooden spoon until blended. Beat in eggs, one at a time. Stir in flour and baking powder just until mixed. Stir in yellow food color until well mixed. Spread 1¹/₂ cups yellow batter in pan. Place pan in freezer about 15 minutes or until batter is slightly firm to the touch.

3) Meanwhile, add red food color to remaining cake batter in bowl until well mixed. Spread over chilled yellow batter.

4) Bake 47 to 53 minutes or until toothpick inserted in center comes out clean. Cool completely, about 45 minutes.

5) In medium bowl, beat ¹/₂ cup softened butter with electric mixer on medium speed until light and fluffy. Beat in powdered sugar until well blended. Beat in milk, vanilla and salt until smooth and spreadable. Spread frosting over bars. To serve, remove bars from pan, using foil to lift. Remove foil. Cut into 4 rows by 4 rows; cut each square diagonally in half. Top each triangle with 1 candy corn.

HIGH ALTITUDE (3500-6500 FT.): Decrease butter in bars to 1/2 cup. Decrease sugar in bars to 1-1/2 cups. In Step 2, do not place pan in freezer.

Nutrition Information Per Serving:		
Calories: 130	From Fat:	70
Total Fat		8g
Saturated Fat		5g
Trans Fat		0g
Cholesterol		45mg
Sodium		85mg
Total Carbohydrate		13g
Dietary Fiber		0g
Sugars		8g
Protein		1g

Spicy Straw Stacks

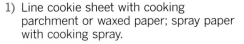

PREP TIME: 20 MINUTES (READY IN 20 MINUTES)
SERVINGS: ABOUT 20 (2-INCH) PIECES

EASY

1/2 cup butter or margarine

1/2 cup sugar

1/4 cup dark corn syrup

1/2 teaspoon ground red pepper (cayenne)

1/2 teaspoon black pepper

1 can (11.5 oz) mixed nuts

1 cup chow mein noodles

1/4 teaspoon kosher (coarse) salt, if desired

1) Line cookie sheet with cooking parchment or waxed paper; spray paper with cooking spray.

2) In 10-inch nonstick skillet, melt butter over medium heat. Stir in sugar, corn syrup and peppers. Cook 4 to 5 minutes, stirring often, until sugar melts and glaze begins to thicken. (Mixture will look foamy.)

3) Remove from heat; stir in nuts and chow mein noodles. Immediately drop in stacks of about 2 tablespoons each onto cookie sheet. Sprinkle with salt. Cool completely.

HIGH ALTITUDE (3500-6500 FT.): No change.

Nutrition Information Per Serving:	
Calories: 190	From Fat: 130
Total Fat	15g
Saturated Fat	4.5g
Trans Fat	0g
Cholesterol	10mg
Sodium	115mg
Total Carbohydrate	13g
Dietary Fiber	1g
Sugars	7g
Protein	3g

Caramel Apple Streusel Bars

PREP TIME: 20 MINUTES (READY IN 45 MINUTES)
SERVINGS: 8

EASY

1 can (8 oz) Pillsbury® refrigerated crescent dinner rolls or 1 can (8 oz) Pillsbury® Crescent Recipe Creations™ refrigerated flaky dough sheet

3 cups chopped peeled cooking apples (2 large)

1/2 cup caramel topping

1/4 cup all-purpose flour

3/4 cup packed brown sugar

1/2 cup all-purpose flour

1/2 cup quick-cooking oats

1/2 teaspoon ground cinnamon

1/2 cup butter or margarine, softened

1/2 cup chopped pecans

1) Heat oven to 375°F. Spray 13x9-inch (3-quart) glass baking dish with cooking spray. Unroll dough (if using crescent rolls, pinch seams to seal); press in bottom and 1/2 inch up sides of pan. Sprinkle apples over the dough.

2) In 1-quart saucepan, heat caramel topping and 1/4 cup flour to boiling over medium heat, stirring constantly. Boil 1 minute, stirring constantly, until thickened. Drizzle over apples.

3) In medium bowl, mix brown sugar, flour, oats and cinnamon. With pastry blender, cut in butter until mixture looks like fine crumbs. Stir in pecans. Sprinkle evenly over apples.

4) Bake 18 to 22 minutes or until top is golden brown and apples are tender.

HIGH ALTITUDE (3500-6500 FT.): Bake 22 to 26 minutes.

Nutrition Information Per Serving:	
Calories: 470	From Fat: 190
Total Fat	21g
Saturated Fat	10g
Trans Fat	0g
Cholesterol	30mg
Sodium	390mg
Total Carbohydrate	65g
Dietary Fiber	2g
Sugars	37g
Protein	4g

Maple-Nut Cookies with Maple Icing

PREP TIME: 1 HOUR 25 MINUTES (READY IN 1 HOUR 25 MINUTES)
SERVINGS: 3-1/2 DOZEN COOKIES

COOKIES

- 3/4 cup pecan halves
- 1 cup butter or margarine, softened
- 1/2 cup packed brown sugar
- 1/2 teaspoon maple flavor
- 1 egg
- 2 cups all-purpose flour
- 1 tablespoon granulated sugar

ICING

- 3/4 cup powdered sugar
- 1 tablespoon milk
- 1 teaspoon maple flavor

1) Heat oven to 350°F. In 8-inch square pan, bake pecans 6 to 8 minutes, stirring occasionally, until light brown. Spread nuts on cutting board; cool 5 minutes. Finely chop.

2) In large bowl, beat butter and brown sugar with electric mixer on medium speed, scraping bowl occasionally, until fluffy. Beat in 1/2 teaspoon maple flavor and the egg until well blended. Stir in flour and chopped toasted pecans.

3) Shape cookie dough into 1-inch balls. On ungreased cookie sheets, place balls 2 inches apart. Flatten in crisscross pattern with a fork dipped in granulated sugar.

4) Bake 11 to 14 minutes or until edges just begin to brown. Cool 1 minute; remove from cookie sheets to cooling racks. Cool completely, about 10 minutes. In small bowl, mix the icing ingredients until smooth; drizzle over cookies.

HIGH ALTITUDE (3500-6500 FT.): No change.

Nutrition Information Per Serving:	
Calories: 100	From Fat: 50
Total Fat	6g
Saturated Fat	3g
Trans Fat	0g
Cholesterol	15mg
Sodium	35mg
Total Carbohydrate	10g
Dietary Fiber	0g
Sugars	5g
Protein	1g

Orange-Spice Pumpkin Bars with Browned Butter Frosting

PREP TIME: 20 MINUTES (READY IN 2 HOURS 5 MINUTES)
SERVINGS: 48 BARS

e EASY

BARS

2 cups all-purpose flour

1½ cups granulated sugar

2 teaspoons baking powder

1 teaspoon baking soda

2 teaspoons pumpkin pie spice

2 teaspoons grated orange peel

¼ teaspoon salt

½ cup vegetable oil

½ cup orange juice

1 cup canned pumpkin (not pumpkin pie mix)

2 eggs

FROSTING

⅓ cup butter (do not use margarine)

2 cups powdered sugar

½ teaspoon vanilla

2 to 4 tablespoons milk

Nutrition Information Per Serving:		
Calories: 100	From Fat: 35	
Total Fat		4g
Saturated Fat		1g
Trans Fat		0g
Cholesterol		10mg
Sodium		70mg
Total Carbohydrate		16g
Dietary Fiber		0g
Sugars		12g
Protein		1g

1) Heat oven to 350°F. Grease the bottom and sides of 15x10x1-inch pan with shortening; lightly flour (or spray with baking spray with flour).

2) In large bowl, beat bar ingredients with electric mixer on low speed, scraping bowl occasionally, until moistened. Beat on medium speed 2 minutes, scraping bowl occasionally. Spread batter evenly in pan.

3) Bake 23 to 27 minutes or until toothpick inserted in center comes out clean. Cool completely, about 1 hour.

4) In 2-quart saucepan, heat butter over medium heat, stirring constantly, until light golden brown. Remove from heat. Stir in the powdered sugar, vanilla and enough milk until frosting is smooth and spreadable. Immediately spread frosting over the cooled bars. Refrigerate about 15 minutes or until set. For bars, cut into 8 rows by 6 rows.

HIGH ALTITUDE (3500-6500 FT.): No change.

tip

To make your own pumpkin pie spice, mix 1-1/2 teaspoons ground cinnamon, 1/4 teaspoon ground ginger, 1/4 teaspoon ground nutmeg and 1/8 teaspoon ground cloves.

Chocolate Truffle-Topped Caramel Bars

PREP TIME: 55 MINUTES (READY IN 3 HOURS 55 MINUTES)
SERVINGS: 75 BARS

CHOCOLATE TRUFFLE TOPPING

1/3 cup whipping cream

3 tablespoons butter or margarine

1 tablespoon light corn syrup

1 bag (12 oz) dark chocolate chips (2 cups)

CRUST

1 cup all-purpose flour

1/2 cup packed brown sugar

1/2 cup cold butter or margarine

1 cup quick-cooking or old-fashioned oats

1 cup chopped pecans

CARAMEL LAYER

1 cup butter or margarine

1 cup packed brown sugar

1/4 cup light corn syrup

1/4 teaspoon salt

1 can (14 oz) sweetened condensed milk (not evaporated)

1) Heat oven to 350°F. In 1-quart saucepan, heat whipping cream, 3 tablespoons butter and 1 tablespoon corn syrup to a full boil over medium heat; turn off the heat. Add the dark chocolate chips; let stand 5 minutes without stirring. After 5 minutes, stir slowly with wire whisk until chocolate chips are melted and mixture is smooth and glossy; set aside.

2) In large bowl, stir together flour and 1/2 cup brown sugar. Cut in 1/2 cup cold butter, using pastry blender (or pulling 2 table knives through mixture in opposite directions), until mixture looks like coarse crumbs. Stir in oats and chopped pecans. Press mixture into ungreased 15x10x1-inch pan. Bake 15 to 20 minutes or until crust is golden brown.

3) Meanwhile, in 2-quart saucepan, heat 1 cup butter, 1 cup brown sugar, 1/4 cup corn syrup, the salt and condensed milk to boiling over medium heat, stirring constantly. Continue boiling 5 minutes, stirring constantly. Pour over crust; spread evenly. Cool slightly, about 10 minutes.

4) Pour chocolate truffle topping over caramel layer; spread evenly. Cool 1 hour at room temperature; refrigerate at least 2 hours before serving. For bars, cut into 15 rows by 5 rows. Cover and refrigerate any remaining bars.

HIGH ALTITUDE (3500-6500 FT.): No change.

Nutrition Information Per Serving:		
Calories: 120	From Fat:	70
Total Fat		7g
Saturated Fat		4g
Trans Fat		0g
Cholesterol		15mg
Sodium		50mg
Total Carbohydrate		13g
Dietary Fiber		0g
Sugars		10g
Protein		1g

Ginger Shortbread Cookies

PREP TIME: 25 MINUTES (READY IN 2 HOURS)
SERVINGS: 4 DOZEN COOKIES

1 cup butter, softened (do not use margarine)

1/2 cup packed brown sugar

2 1/4 cups all-purpose flour

1 teaspoon ground ginger

1/2 teaspoon ground nutmeg

1/3 cup finely chopped crystallized ginger

4 oz bittersweet baking chocolate, chopped

1) Heat oven to 350°F. Line bottom and sides of 13x9-inch pan with foil, extending foil 2 inches on 2 opposite sides of pan.

2) In large bowl, beat butter and brown sugar with electric mixer on medium speed, scraping bowl occasionally, until fluffy. On low speed, beat in flour, ground ginger and nutmeg until crumbly. Stir in crystallized ginger. Press dough firmly in pan. Prick surface generously with fork.

3) Bake 18 to 22 minutes or until light golden brown and set. Cool 10 minutes. Remove from pan by lifting foil. To make 24 squares, cut into 6 rows by 4 rows by pressing down with a long knife (do not use sawing motion). Cut each square diagonally in half to make triangles. Cool completely, about 1 hour.

4) In small microwavable bowl, microwave baking chocolate uncovered on High 1 minute. Stir; microwave 30 seconds longer, stirring every 15 seconds, until completely melted. Dip one short, flat edge of each triangular cookie in the chocolate; if necessary, shake off any excess chocolate. Place on waxed paper; let stand until chocolate is set before storing between layers of waxed paper in loosely covered container.

HIGH ALTITUDE (3500-6500 FT.): No change.

Nutrition Information Per Serving:		
Calories: 80	From Fat:	45
Total Fat		5g
Saturated Fat		3g
Trans Fat		0g
Cholesterol		10mg
Sodium		30mg
Total Carbohydrate		8g
Dietary Fiber		0g
Sugars		2g
Protein		1g

Pumpkin Patch Rocky Road Brownies

PREP TIME: 25 MINUTES (READY IN 2 HOURS 25 MINUTES)
SERVINGS: 24 BARS

1 box (18.3 oz) fudge brownie mix

Water, vegetable oil and eggs called for on brownie mix box

1 cup peanuts

3 cups miniature marshmallows

1/2 cup milk chocolate chips

1/3 cup whipped vanilla ready-to-spread frosting (from 12-oz container)

8 drops green food color

24 small pumpkin-shaped candies

1) Heat oven to 350°F. Spray or grease bottom only of 13x9-inch pan. Make brownie batter as directed on box—except stir in peanuts. Spread in pan.

2) Bake 24 to 26 minutes or until toothpick inserted 2 inches from side of pan comes out almost clean. Immediately sprinkle warm brownies with marshmallows and chocolate chips.

3) Bake about 3 minutes longer or until marshmallows are puffed. Cool 30 minutes.

4) In small microwavable bowl, microwave the vanilla frosting uncovered on High 15 seconds; stir in the green food color. Drizzle over bars. Cool completely, about 1 hour. Cut into 6 rows by 4 rows. Top each bar with 1 candy.

HIGH ALTITUDE (3500-6500 FT.): Follow High Altitude brownie directions for 13x9-inch pan.

Nutrition Information Per Serving:	
Calories: 280	From Fat: 110
Total Fat	12g
Saturated Fat	2g
Trans Fat	0g
Cholesterol	20mg
Sodium	115mg
Total Carbohydrate	41g
Dietary Fiber	1g
Sugars	31g
Protein	3g

Chocolate-Peanut Butter-Oatmeal Munchies

PREP TIME: 40 MINUTES (READY IN 40 MINUTES)
SERVINGS: 20 LARGE COOKIES

2/3 cup peanut butter

1/2 cup quick-cooking oats

2 tablespoons vegetable oil

1 egg

1 roll (16.5 oz) Pillsbury® refrigerated chocolate chip cookies

1/4 cup miniature candy-coated chocolate baking bits

1/4 cup sweetened dried cranberries

1/4 cup chopped salted peanuts

Nutrition Information Per Serving:	
Calories: 220	From Fat: 120
Total Fat	13g
Saturated Fat	3.5g
Trans Fat	1g
Cholesterol	15mg
Sodium	120mg
Total Carbohydrate	20g
Dietary Fiber	2g
Sugars	12g
Protein	4g

1) Heat oven to 350°F. In large bowl, stir together peanut butter, oats, oil and egg. Break up cookie dough; add to peanut butter mixture. Add remaining ingredients; stir until well mixed.

2) On ungreased cookie sheets, drop dough by heaping tablespoonfuls about 2 inches apart. Press with fingers to flatten slightly.

3) Bake 13 to 15 minutes or until golden brown and edges are just set (tops will not look done). Do not overbake. Cool 1 minute; remove from cookie sheets to cooling racks.

HIGH ALTITUDE (3500-6500 FT.): Bake 12 to 14 minutes.

Cranberry-Apple Butter Bars

PREP TIME: 20 MINUTES (READY IN 2 HOURS 20 MINUTES)
SERVINGS: 32 BARS

e EASY

FILLING

- 1 bag (12 oz) fresh or frozen cranberries
- 1 cup granulated sugar
- 1 teaspoon grated orange peel
- ¼ cup orange juice
- ½ cup apple butter
- 2 tablespoons butter or margarine

BASE AND TOPPING

- ¾ cup butter or margarine, softened
- 1 cup packed brown sugar
- 1½ cups all-purpose flour
- 1 teaspoon salt
- ½ teaspoon baking soda
- 1¼ cups quick-cooking oats

Nutrition Information Per Serving:		
Calories: 150	From Fat:	50
Total Fat		5g
Saturated Fat		3g
Trans Fat		0g
Cholesterol		15mg
Sodium		130mg
Total Carbohydrate		23g
Dietary Fiber		1g
Sugars		16g
Protein		1g

1) Heat oven to 400°F. Spray 13x9-inch pan with cooking spray.

2) In 4-quart saucepan, mix cranberries, granulated sugar, orange peel and orange juice. Heat to boiling over high heat, stirring constantly. Cook over high heat 6 to 8 minutes, stirring frequently, until cranberries pop and lose their round shape and mixture thickens. Stir in apple butter and 2 tablespoons butter; remove from heat.

3) In large bowl, beat ¾ cup butter and the brown sugar with electric mixer on medium speed, scraping the bowl occasionally, until fluffy. Stir in flour, salt, baking soda and oats. Press 3 cups oat mixture in pan.

4) Spread cranberry filling over base. Crumble remaining 2 cups oat mixture over filling; press lightly.

5) Bake 25 to 30 minutes or until golden brown. Cool completely, about 1 hour 30 minutes. For bars, cut into 8 rows by 4 rows.

HIGH ALTITUDE (3500-6500 FT.): In Step 2, cook over medium-high to medium heat 6 to 8 minutes.

Apple-Cinnamon Bars

PREP TIME: 15 MINUTES (READY IN 1 HOUR 50 MINUTES)
SERVINGS: 32 BARS

e EASY

BARS

- ½ cup butter or margarine, softened
- ½ cup granulated sugar
- ½ cup packed brown sugar
- ½ cup apple butter
- 2 eggs
- 1 teaspoon vanilla
- 1¾ cups all-purpose flour
- ½ teaspoon baking soda
- ½ teaspoon salt
- 1 cup finely chopped peeled apple (1 medium)
- 1 cup cinnamon-flavored baking chips (from 10-oz bag)

GLAZE

- 1 cup powdered sugar
- 2 tablespoons milk

1) Heat oven to 350°F. Spray 13x9-inch pan with cooking spray.

2) In large bowl, beat butter, granulated sugar and brown sugar with electric mixer on medium speed until light and fluffy. Add apple butter, eggs and vanilla; beat until well blended.

3) On low speed, beat in flour, baking soda and salt until well blended. Stir in apple and cinnamon chips. Spread batter in pan.

4) Bake 28 to 32 minutes or until edges begin to pull away from sides of pan and top is evenly browned. Cool in pan on cooling rack at least 1 hour.

5) In small bowl, mix glaze ingredients until thin enough to drizzle. Drizzle glaze over bars. For bars, cut into 8 rows by 4 rows.

HIGH ALTITUDE (3500-6500 FT.): Decrease butter to 1/3 cup and granulated sugar to 1/4 cup. Add 1/4 cup water with the apple butter, eggs and vanilla.

Nutrition Information Per Serving:	
Calories: 150	From Fat: 50
Total Fat	5g
Saturated Fat	3g
Trans Fat	0g
Cholesterol	20mg
Sodium	100mg
Total Carbohydrate	23g
Dietary Fiber	0g
Sugars	17g
Protein	1g

Dulce de Leche Bars

PREP TIME: 30 MINUTES (READY IN 2 HOURS 55 MINUTES)
SERVINGS: 48 BARS

2 rolls (16.5 oz each) Pillsbury® refrigerated sugar cookies

1¾ cups quick-cooking or old-fashioned oats

⅔ cup packed brown sugar

2 teaspoons vanilla

1 bag (14 oz) caramels, unwrapped, or 1 bag (11 oz) caramel bits

½ cup butter or margarine

1 can (14 oz) sweetened condensed milk (not evaporated)

3 tablespoons caramel topping

Nutrition Information Per Serving:

Calories:	190	From Fat:	70
Total Fat			7g
Saturated Fat			3g
Trans Fat			1g
Cholesterol			15mg
Sodium			115mg
Total Carbohydrate			29g
Dietary Fiber			0g
Sugars			19g
Protein			2g

1) Heat oven to 350°F. In large bowl, break up 1 roll of cookie dough. Stir or knead in ¾ cup of the oats, ⅓ cup of the brown sugar and 1 teaspoon of the vanilla until well blended. With floured fingers, press mixture evenly in bottom of ungreased 13x9-inch pan to form crust.

2) Bake 13 to 18 minutes or until light golden brown.

3) Meanwhile, in same bowl, break up remaining roll of cookie dough. Stir or knead in remaining 1 cup oats, ⅓ cup brown sugar and 1 teaspoon vanilla until well blended; set aside. In 2-quart heavy saucepan, heat caramels, butter and condensed milk over medium-low heat, stirring frequently, until caramels are melted and mixture is smooth.

4) Spread caramel mixture evenly over crust. Crumble remaining dough mixture evenly over caramel. Bake 20 to 25 minutes longer or until light golden brown. Cool 1 hour. Run knife around sides of pan to loosen bars. Refrigerate until firm, about 1 hour.

5) With small spoon, drizzle caramel topping over bars. For bars, cut into 8 rows by 6 rows. Cover and refrigerate any remaining bars.

HIGH ALTITUDE (3500-6500 FT.): No change.

Brown Sugar-Oatmeal Cookies

PREP TIME: 55 MINUTES (READY IN 55 MINUTES)
SERVINGS: 4 DOZEN COOKIES

1¾ cups packed brown sugar

1 cup butter or margarine, softened

1 teaspoon vanilla

2 eggs

1 cup all-purpose flour

1 cup whole wheat flour

1 teaspoon baking powder

3 cups old-fashioned oats

1) Heat oven to 350°F. In large bowl, beat brown sugar and butter with electric mixer on medium speed, scraping bowl occasionally, until light and fluffy. Beat in vanilla and eggs until well blended.

2) On low speed, beat in all-purpose flour, whole wheat flour and baking powder, scraping bowl occasionally, until well combined. Stir in oats.

3) On ungreased cookie sheets, drop dough by heaping tablespoonfuls 2 inches apart. Flatten cookies to about ½-inch thickness.

4) Bake 12 to 14 minutes or until light golden brown. Cool 1 minute; remove from cookie sheets to cooling racks.

HIGH ALTITUDE (3500-6500 FT.): Heat oven to 375°F.

Nutrition Information Per Serving:

Calories:	110	From Fat:	40
Total Fat			4.5g
Saturated Fat			2.5g
Trans Fat			0g
Cholesterol			20mg
Sodium			45mg
Total Carbohydrate			15g
Dietary Fiber			1g
Sugars			8g
Protein			1g

Caramel-Chocolate Layered Fudge

PREP TIME: 30 MINUTES (READY IN 2 HOURS 30 MINUTES)
SERVINGS: 8 DOZEN PIECES

CARAMEL FUDGE LAYER

- 2 cups packed dark brown sugar
- 1/4 cup butter (do not use margarine)
- 3/4 cup evaporated milk (1/2 of 12-oz can)
- 2 cups miniature marshmallows
- 1 bag (12 oz) white vanilla baking chips (2 cups)
- 1 teaspoon vanilla
- 1 cup chopped walnuts

CHOCOLATE FUDGE LAYER

- 2 cups granulated sugar
- 1/4 cup butter (do not use margarine)
- 3/4 cup evaporated milk (remaining 1/2 of 12-oz can)
- 2 cups miniature marshmallows
- 1 bag (12 oz) semisweet chocolate chips (2 cups)
- 1 teaspoon vanilla
- 8 oz walnut halves or pieces (about 1 1/2 cups)

1) Line 13x9-inch pan with foil, extending foil over sides of pan; spray foil with cooking spray.

2) For Caramel Fudge Layer, in heavy 3-quart saucepan, cook brown sugar, 1/4 cup butter and 3/4 cup evaporated milk over medium-high heat, stirring constantly, until sugar is dissolved. Heat to boiling, stirring constantly. Reduce heat to low; boil gently without stirring 5 minutes. Remove saucepan from heat. Stir in 2 cups marshmallows, the vanilla chips and 1 teaspoon vanilla; stir until marshmallows and vanilla chips are melted and mixture is smooth. Stir in chopped walnuts. Quickly spread mixture in the pan. Refrigerate 30 minutes before preparing the Chocolate Fudge Layer.

3) For Chocolate Fudge Layer, in heavy 3-quart saucepan, cook granulated sugar, 1/4 cup butter and 3/4 cup evaporated milk over medium-high heat, stirring constantly, until sugar is dissolved. Heat to boiling, stirring constantly. Reduce heat to low; boil gently without stirring 5 minutes. Remove saucepan from heat. Stir in 2 cups marshmallows, the chocolate chips and 1 teaspoon vanilla; stir until marshmallows and chips are melted and mixture is smooth. Beat 30 seconds with spoon until glossy. Quickly spread mixture on top of caramel fudge layer. Sprinkle walnut halves and pieces over fudge; press gently into fudge. Cover; refrigerate 1 hour 30 minutes.

4) Remove fudge from pan by lifting the foil; remove foil from sides of fudge. With long knife, cut fudge into 12 rows by 8 rows. Store in tightly covered container in refrigerator.

HIGH ALTITUDE (3500-6500 FT.): For Caramel Fudge Layer, no change. For Chocolate Fudge Layer, boil gently without stirring 6 minutes. Beat 1 minute with spoon until glossy.

Nutrition Information Per Serving:		
Calories: 120	From Fat:	50
Total Fat		6g
Saturated Fat		2.5g
Trans Fat		0g
Cholesterol		0mg
Sodium		20mg
Total Carbohydrate		16g
Dietary Fiber		0g
Sugars		14g
Protein		1g

tip

To make this treat ahead, prepare and cool the fudge as directed. Place it in an airtight container or resealable freezer plastic bag and freeze. Thaw the fudge at room temperature.

PEAR-RUM CRISP
PG. 331

Delectable Desserts

Skip dessert? Not when you have irresistible recipes for golden pies, fruit tarts, layer cakes and more!

PEAR-WALNUT CRUMBLE PIE
PG. 335

PEACH DUMPLINGS WITH
FUZZY NAVEL SAUCE
PG. 323

SWEET POTATO PUDDING CUPS
PG. 330

Raspberry-Lemon Cream Pie with Almond Crust

PREP TIME: 25 MINUTES (READY IN 3 HOURS 20 MINUTES)
SERVINGS: 8

1 package (7 oz) almond paste

1 tablespoon cornstarch

1 egg white

1 box (15 oz) Pillsbury® refrigerated pie crusts, softened as directed on box

1 can (14 oz) sweetened condensed milk (not evaporated)

Grated peel of 2 medium lemons (about 2 tablespoons)

Juice of 2 medium lemons (about $1/3$ cup)

3 egg yolks

$1/2$ cup raspberry jelly or jam

$3/4$ cup whipping cream

1 tablespoon powdered sugar

$1/4$ teaspoon vanilla

$1/4$ cup sliced almonds

Fresh raspberries, if desired

1) Heat oven to 400°F. In food processor or medium bowl, crumble almond paste; add the cornstarch and egg white. Cover; process with food processor, or beat with electric mixer until smooth.

2) In ungreased 9-inch glass pie plate, unroll 1 pie crust. Press the crust firmly against side and bottom. Spread almond mixture over crust. Unroll the second pie crust over filling by starting at 1 edge of pie and unrolling to opposite edge. Press pie crusts together in bottom of pie plate. Seal edges; flute. Cover outer edge with foil; fit second pie plate inside first pie plate on top of crust. Bake 10 minutes. Remove top pie plate; gently prick crust surface over filling about 15 times with fork. Leave foil on outer edge. Bake uncovered about 15 minutes longer or until top crust begins to brown.

3) Meanwhile, in medium bowl, mix condensed milk, lemon peel, lemon juice and egg yolks with wire whisk. Pour over hot crust. Reduce oven temperature to 350°F. Bake 25 to 30 minutes longer or until filling is set and bottom crust is golden brown. Remove foil; cool completely, about $2\frac{1}{2}$ hours.

4) Spread jam over filling. In chilled deep small bowl, beat whipping cream, powdered sugar and vanilla with electric mixer on high speed until stiff peaks form. Spread over jam. Garnish with almonds and raspberries.

HIGH ALTITUDE (3500-6500 FT.): No change.

Nutrition Information Per Serving:		
Calories: 680	From Fat: 310	
Total Fat		35g
Saturated Fat		13g
Trans Fat		0g
Cholesterol		125mg
Sodium		310mg
Total Carbohydrate		84g
Dietary Fiber		2g
Sugars		49g
Protein		9g

Chocolate-Hazelnut Pudding Cake

PREP TIME: 20 MINUTES (READY IN 1 HOUR 25 MINUTES)
SERVINGS: 9

e EASY

CAKE

- 1 cup all-purpose flour
- 3/4 cup granulated sugar
- 1/3 cup (2 oz) hazelnuts (filberts), ground
- 2 tablespoons unsweetened baking cocoa
- 2 teaspoons baking powder
- 1/2 cup milk
- 1/4 cup hazelnut-flavored liqueur or coffee syrup
- 2 tablespoons vegetable oil
- 1 cup packed brown sugar
- 1/4 cup unsweetened baking cocoa
- 1 3/4 cups boiling water

HAZELNUT WHIPPED CREAM

- 3/4 cup whipping cream
- 1 tablespoon powdered sugar
- 1 tablespoon hazelnut-flavored liqueur

Nutrition Information Per Serving:	
Calories: 350	From Fat: 100
Total Fat	11g
Saturated Fat	5g
Trans Fat	0g
Cholesterol	25mg
Sodium	130mg
Total Carbohydrate	60g
Dietary Fiber	1g
Sugars	47g
Protein	3g

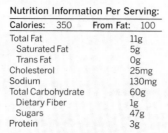

1) Heat oven to 350°F. Grease 8-inch square (2-quart) glass baking dish with cooking spray or shortening. In medium bowl, stir together flour, granulated sugar, hazelnuts, 2 tablespoons cocoa and the baking powder. Stir in milk, 1/4 cup liqueur and the oil. Spread batter in pan.

2) Sprinkle batter with brown sugar and 1/4 cup cocoa. Pour boiling water over batter.

3) Bake 40 to 45 minutes or until center is set. Cool 20 minutes before serving.

4) Meanwhile, in chilled small bowl, beat cream ingredients with electric mixer on high speed until stiff peaks form.

5) To serve, spoon warm pudding cake into individual dessert bowls; spoon pudding over cake. Top with whipped cream.

HIGH ALTITUDE (3500-6500 FT.): Bake 50 to 55 minutes.

tip

Through the years, pudding cakes have also been referred to as upside-down pudding, cake-top pudding, sponge pudding and sponge custard.

Pistachio and White Chocolate Mousse Tartlets

PREP TIME: 15 MINUTES (READY IN 1 HOUR 15 MINUTES)
SERVINGS: 30 TARTLETS

e EASY

1 cup whipping cream

4 oz white chocolate baking bars, coarsely chopped

2 tablespoons orange-flavored liqueur

2 packages (2.1 oz each) frozen mini fillo shells (30 shells total), thawed

1/4 cup finely chopped pistachio nuts

30 fresh raspberries (about 6 oz)

1) In 1-quart saucepan, heat whipping cream just to boiling. Place white chocolate in small metal bowl. Pour hot cream over chocolate; stir until smooth. Stir in liqueur. Refrigerate about 1 hour, stirring occasionally, until very cold.

2) In large bowl, beat cold chocolate mixture with electric mixer on medium speed about 1 minute or until mixture begins to thicken, then on high speed until stiff peaks form. (If mixture will not beat into stiff peaks, it is not cold enough.) Continue with recipe, or store in refrigerator up to 4 hours before making tartlets.

3) Just before serving, spoon mousse into gallon-size food-storage plastic bag; seal bag. Cut 1/2-inch tip off bottom corner of bag; evenly pipe mousse into each fillo shell. Sprinkle each tartlet with nuts and garnish with 1 raspberry. Store covered in refrigerator.

HIGH ALTITUDE (3500-6500 FT.): No change.

Nutrition Information Per Serving:

Calories:	70	From Fat:	45
Total Fat			5g
Saturated Fat			2.5g
Trans Fat			0g
Cholesterol			10mg
Sodium			20mg
Total Carbohydrate			5g
Dietary Fiber			0g
Sugars			3g
Protein			0g

Cream Cheese-Apple Danish Tart

PREP TIME: 25 MINUTES (READY IN 5 HOURS 30 MINUTES)
SERVINGS: 8

TART

1 Pillsbury® refrigerated pie crust (from 15-oz box), softened as directed on box

2 medium apples, peeled, diced (about 2½ cups)

⅓ cup packed brown sugar

2 teaspoons all-purpose flour

1 teaspoon lemon juice

½ teaspoon ground cinnamon

1 package (8 oz) cream cheese, softened

⅓ cup powdered sugar

½ teaspoon vanilla

1 egg

GLAZE

½ cup powdered sugar

1 to 2 teaspoons milk

1) Heat oven to 375°F. Heat cookie sheet on bottom rack of oven. Meanwhile, place pie crust in 9- or 10-inch tart pan with removable bottom as directed on box for One-Crust Filled Pie. Press in bottom and up side of pan. Trim edge if necessary.

2) In medium microwavable bowl, mix apples, brown sugar, flour, lemon juice and cinnamon. Microwave uncovered on High 2 minutes; stir. Microwave 1 to 2 minutes longer, stirring once, until apples are slightly soft.

3) In another medium bowl, beat cream cheese, ⅓ cup powdered sugar, the vanilla and egg with electric mixer on medium speed until creamy. Spread over bottom of crust. Top evenly with apple mixture (apples will not cover top completely).

4) Place tart pan on heated cookie sheet on bottom rack in oven. Bake 30 to 35 minutes or until filling is set, apples are tender and crust is light golden brown. Cool on cooling rack about 30 minutes. Refrigerate at least 4 hours or overnight.

5) Just before serving, in small bowl, mix ½ cup powdered sugar and 1 teaspoon milk. Stir in additional milk, ½ teaspoon at a time, until thin enough to drizzle. Drizzle glaze over tart. Remove side of pan; cut into wedges. Store covered in refrigerator.

HIGH ALTITUDE (3500-6500 FT.): In Step 2, microwave 4 to 6 minutes, stirring every 2 minutes.

Nutrition Information Per Serving:		
Calories: 340	From Fat: 160	
Total Fat		18g
Saturated Fat		9g
Trans Fat		0g
Cholesterol		60mg
Sodium		210mg
Total Carbohydrate		41g
Dietary Fiber		0g
Sugars		25g
Protein		3g

Rhubarb Crunch Pie

PREP TIME: 25 MINUTES (READY IN 3 HOURS 25 MINUTES)
SERVINGS: 8

5 cups sliced fresh rhubarb

¾ cup sugar

3 tablespoons quick-cooking tapioca

1 to 2 teaspoons grated orange peel

1 Pillsbury® refrigerated pie crust (from 15-oz box), softened as directed on box

½ cup all-purpose flour

½ cup sugar

6 tablespoons cold butter or margarine

1) Heat oven to 400°F. In large bowl, mix rhubarb, ¾ cup sugar, the tapioca and orange peel; let stand 15 minutes.

2) Place pie crust in 9-inch glass pie plate as directed on box for One-Crust Filled Pie.

3) To make topping, in small bowl, mix flour and ½ cup sugar. Cut in butter, using pastry blender (or pulling 2 table knives through mixture in opposite directions), until mixture looks like coarse crumbs.

4) Spoon rhubarb mixture into crust-lined pie plate; sprinkle with topping. Cover crust edge with strips of foil to prevent excessive browning. Place foil or cookie sheet on oven rack in lowest position to catch any spills.

5) Bake 15 minutes. Reduce oven temperature to 375°F. Bake 30 minutes longer. Remove foil; bake 15 to 20 minutes longer or until browned and bubbly. Cool 3 hours before serving.

HIGH ALTITUDE (3500-6500 FT.): Bake 50 to 55 minutes. Cover edge of crust with strips of foil after first 30 minutes of baking.

Nutrition Information Per Serving:

Calories:	370	From Fat:	140
Total Fat			16g
Saturated Fat			8g
Trans Fat			0g
Cholesterol			25mg
Sodium			170mg
Total Carbohydrate			55g
Dietary Fiber			0g
Sugars			32g
Protein			1g

Pumpkin Mousse

PREP TIME: 10 MINUTES (READY IN 10 MINUTES)
SERVINGS: 8 (1/2 CUP EACH)

e EASY

1½ cups whipping cream

1 package (3 oz) cream cheese, softened

¾ cup packed brown sugar

1 teaspoon pumpkin pie spice

¼ teaspoon salt

1 can (15 oz) pumpkin (not pumpkin pie mix)

1 pouch (2 bars) Nature Valley® pecan crunch crunchy granola bars (from 8.9-oz box)

8 candy pumpkins, if desired

1) In large bowl, beat whipping cream with electric mixer on high speed until soft peaks form; refrigerate.

2) In medium bowl, beat cream cheese, brown sugar, pumpkin pie spice and salt with electric mixer on medium speed about 2 minutes, scraping the bowl occasionally, until smooth and creamy. On low speed, beat in pumpkin, scraping the bowl occasionally.

3) Using rubber spatula, gently fold 2 cups of the whipped cream into pumpkin mixture. Spoon mousse into 8 individual dessert dishes.

4) To serve, spoon dollop of remaining whipped cream onto each serving. Coarsely crush granola bars; sprinkle over each serving. Garnish with candy pumpkins.

HIGH ALTITUDE (3500-6500 FT.): No change.

Nutrition Information Per Serving:

Calories:	140	From Fat:	15
Total Fat			2g
Saturated Fat			0g
Trans Fat			0g
Cholesterol			0mg
Sodium			40mg
Total Carbohydrate			28g
Dietary Fiber			4g
Sugars			21g
Protein			3g

Sour Cream-Apple Pie

PREP TIME: 30 MINUTES (READY IN 3 HOURS 30 MINUTES)
SERVINGS: 8

CRUST

1 Pillsbury® refrigerated pie crust (from 15-oz box), softened as directed on box

FILLING

1¼ cups sour cream

¾ cup granulated sugar

¼ cup all-purpose flour

¼ teaspoon salt

2 teaspoons vanilla

1 egg

6 cups sliced (¼ inch) peeled baking apples (about 6 medium)

TOPPING

½ cup all-purpose flour

½ cup chopped walnuts

¼ cup granulated sugar

¼ cup packed light brown sugar

½ teaspoon ground cinnamon

Dash salt

3 tablespoons cold butter or margarine

1) Heat oven to 400°F. Place pie crust in 9-inch glass pie plate as directed on box for One-Crust Filled Pie.

2) In large bowl, beat all filling ingredients except apples with wire whisk until well blended. Stir in apples. Pour into the crust-lined pie plate. Cover crust edge with strips of foil to prevent excessive browning.

3) Bake 15 minutes. Reduce the oven temperature to 350°F; bake 30 minutes longer.

4) Meanwhile, in medium bowl, mix all topping ingredients except butter. Cut in butter, using pastry blender or fork, until mixture looks like coarse crumbs; refrigerate until ready to use.

5) Sprinkle topping over pie; bake 20 to 25 minutes longer or until topping is golden brown. Cool completely on cooling rack, about 2 hours, before serving. Store covered in refrigerator.

HIGH ALTITUDE (3500-6500 FT.): In Step 4, bake 25 to 30 minutes.

Nutrition Information Per Serving:		
Calories: 500	From Fat: 220	
Total Fat		24g
Saturated Fat		10g
Trans Fat		0g
Cholesterol		65mg
Sodium		260mg
Total Carbohydrate		67g
Dietary Fiber		2g
Sugars		42g
Protein		4g

tip

The best baking apples are slightly tart. Popular choices are Granny Smith, Braeburn, Cortland, Northern Spy and Rome Beauty.

Spiced Chocolate Chip-Pecan Pie

PREP TIME: 20 MINUTES (READY IN 1 HOUR 30 MINUTES)
SERVINGS: 8

e EASY

CRUST

1 Pillsbury® refrigerated pie crust (from 15-oz box), softened as directed on box

FILLING AND TOPPING

3/4 cup light corn syrup

1/2 cup sugar

3 tablespoons butter or margarine, melted

1 teaspoon ground cinnamon

1/4 teaspoon ground nutmeg

1 teaspoon vanilla

3 eggs

1 cup coarsely chopped pecans

1 cup semisweet chocolate chips (6 oz)

1 teaspoon shortening

Whipped cream, if desired

Nutrition Information Per Serving:		
Calories: 550	From Fat: 270	
Total Fat		30g
Saturated Fat		11g
Trans Fat		0g
Cholesterol		95mg
Sodium		190mg
Total Carbohydrate		66g
Dietary Fiber		2g
Sugars		37g
Protein		4g

1) Heat oven to 325°F. Place pie crust in 9-inch glass pie plate as directed on box for One-Crust Filled Pie.

2) In large bowl, beat corn syrup, sugar, butter, cinnamon, nutmeg, vanilla and eggs with wire whisk. Stir in pecans and 3/4 cup of the chocolate chips. Spread evenly in crust-lined plate. Cover crust edge with strips of foil to prevent excessive browning.

3) Bake 30 minutes. Remove foil; bake 15 to 25 minutes longer or until pie is deep golden brown and filling is set. Cool 15 minutes.

4) In small microwavable bowl, microwave remaining 1/4 cup chocolate chips and the shortening uncovered on High 1 minute; stir until smooth. Drizzle chocolate over top of pie. Serve pie warm or cool. Top each serving with whipped cream. Store covered in refrigerator.

HIGH ALTITUDE (3500-6500 FT.): No change.

Pumpkin Truffle Pound Cake with Browned Butter Icing

PREP TIME: 25 MINUTES (READY IN 2 HOURS 45 MINUTES)
SERVINGS: 16

CAKE

- $2/3$ cup (from 14-oz can) sweetened condensed milk (not evaporated)
- 1 cup semisweet chocolate chips (6 oz)
- 3 cups all-purpose flour
- 2 teaspoons baking powder
- 1 teaspoon baking soda
- 4 teaspoons pumpkin pie spice
- $1/4$ teaspoon salt
- $1\frac{1}{2}$ cups butter or margarine, softened
- 1 cup granulated sugar
- $1/2$ cup packed brown sugar
- 6 eggs
- 1 cup canned pumpkin (not pumpkin pie mix)

ICING

- $1/4$ cup butter (do not use margarine)
- 1 cup powdered sugar
- 1 teaspoon vanilla
- 1 to 2 tablespoons milk

1) Heat oven to 350°F. Grease 12-cup fluted tube cake pan with shortening; lightly flour (or spray with baking spray with flour). In 1-quart saucepan, heat the condensed milk and chocolate chips over medium-low heat, stirring occasionally, until chocolate is melted. Remove from heat; set aside.

2) In medium bowl, mix the flour, baking powder, baking soda, pumpkin pie spice and salt until blended; set aside.

3) In large bowl, beat $1\frac{1}{2}$ cups butter, the granulated sugar and brown sugar with electric mixer on medium speed about 2 minutes or until well blended. Add eggs, one at a time, beating well after each addition. On low speed, beat in flour mixture in 3 additions alternately with pumpkin until well blended (batter will be thick).

4) Spoon $2/3$ of batter (about 5 cups) into pan, bringing batter up about 1 inch on tube and on outside edge of pan. Stir chocolate mixture; spoon into center of batter, being careful not to touch sides of pan. Spoon remaining cake batter (about 2 cups) over filling; smooth top.

5) Bake 55 to 65 minutes or until toothpick inserted in center of cake comes out clean and center of crack is dry to touch. Cool cake in pan 15 minutes. Remove from pan to cooling rack. Cool completely, about 1 hour.

6) Place cooled cake on serving plate. In 1-quart saucepan, heat $1/4$ cup butter over medium heat, stirring occasionally, until golden brown. Pour browned butter into medium bowl; stir in powdered sugar, vanilla and milk, 1 tablespoon at a time, until spreadable (mixture will thicken as it cools). Let stand 1 to 2 minutes or until slightly cool; stir. Drizzle over cake.

HIGH ALTITUDE (3500-6500 FT.): Heat oven to 375°F. Bake 50 to 60 minutes.

Nutrition Information Per Serving:	
Calories: 510	From Fat: 240
Total Fat	27g
Saturated Fat	16g
Trans Fat	1g
Cholesterol	135mg
Sodium	360mg
Total Carbohydrate	60g
Dietary Fiber	2g
Sugars	40g
Protein	6g

Apple-Ginger Tart with Cider-Bourbon Sauce

PREP TIME: 25 MINUTES (READY IN 1 HOUR 45 MINUTES)
SERVINGS: 8

CRUST

1 Pillsbury® refrigerated pie crust (from 15-oz box), softened as directed on box

FILLING

1/2 cup packed brown sugar

2 tablespoons finely chopped crystallized ginger

2 tablespoons cornstarch

1 teaspoon ground cinnamon

4 medium cooking apples, peeled, thinly sliced (about 4 cups)

SAUCE

1 1/4 cups apple cider

2 tablespoons butter or margarine

2 tablespoons packed brown sugar

1 tablespoon cornstarch

2 tablespoons bourbon or water, if desired

1) Heat oven to 450°F. Place cookie sheet in oven while oven preheats. Place pie crust in 9-inch tart pan with removable bottom as directed on box for One-Crust Filled Pie. Bake on preheated cookie sheet 7 minutes.

2) Meanwhile, in large bowl, mix 1/2 cup brown sugar, the ginger, cornstarch and cinnamon until blended. Add apples; toss until evenly coated.

3) In crust-lined plate, arrange apples in concentric circles, overlapping slices and using all of apples, beginning at outer edge and working toward center.

4) Cover top of tart with foil; place on preheated cookie sheet. Bake 40 minutes. Remove foil; bake 8 to 10 minutes longer or until apples are tender and crust is golden brown. Place tart pan on cooling rack; cool 30 minutes while making sauce.

5) Meanwhile, in 1-quart saucepan, heat cider to boiling over high heat. Boil 4 to 6 minutes, stirring occasionally, until reduced to 1 cup. Stir in butter and 2 tablespoons brown sugar; continue boiling 2 minutes, stirring occasionally. In small bowl, stir cornstarch into bourbon until dissolved. Stir bourbon mixture into sauce; boil 1 minute, stirring constantly.

6) To serve dessert, cut the cooled tart into wedges; serve wedges with the warm sauce.

HIGH ALTITUDE (3500-6500 FT.): Heat oven to 425°F. Cut apples into very thin slices. In Step 4, bake covered on cookie sheet 45 minutes. Remove foil; bake 8 to 10 minutes longer.

Nutrition Information Per Serving:		
Calories: 280	From Fat:	90
Total Fat		10g
Saturated Fat		4.5g
Trans Fat		0g
Cholesterol		10mg
Sodium		140mg
Total Carbohydrate		46g
Dietary Fiber		1g
Sugars		26g
Protein		0g

Peach Dumplings with Fuzzy Navel Sauce

PREP TIME: 25 MINUTES (READY IN 1 HOUR 10 MINUTES)
SERVINGS: 4

DUMPLINGS

¼ cup sugar

1 tablespoon all-purpose flour

½ teaspoon ground cinnamon

2 tablespoons butter or margarine, melted

1 Pillsbury® refrigerated pie crust (from 15-oz box), softened as directed on box

2 large fresh peaches, peeled, cut in half and pitted

1 egg white, slightly beaten

2 teaspoons sugar

SAUCE

2 tablespoons sugar

2 teaspoons cornstarch

¾ cup peach nectar

2 tablespoons peach-flavored schnapps or additional peach nectar

1 teaspoon grated orange peel

SERVE WITH

2 cups vanilla ice cream

1) Heat oven to 400°F. Line 15x10x1-inch pan with foil; spray foil with cooking spray. In small bowl, stir together ¼ cup sugar, the flour, cinnamon and butter; set aside.

2) Remove pie crust from pouch; unroll on lightly floured work surface. Roll into 13-inch circle. Cut crust into quarters.

3) Place 1 peach half, cut side up, on each crust quarter. Spoon sugar mixture evenly onto peach halves. Brush crust edges with beaten egg white. Bring sides of each crust quarter up over peach; press edges to seal, making 3 seams. Place dumplings, seam sides up, in pan. Brush crusts with egg white; sprinkle with 2 teaspoons sugar. Make small slits in top of each dumpling to allow steam to escape.

4) Bake 25 to 30 minutes or until golden brown. Cool at least 15 minutes before serving.

5) Meanwhile, in 1-quart saucepan, stir together 2 tablespoons sugar and the cornstarch. Stir in nectar. Heat to boiling, stirring constantly; boil and stir 1 to 2 minutes or until thickened. Stir in schnapps and orange peel.

6) To serve, place dumplings in individual dessert dishes. Top each with ½ cup ice cream. Serve sauce over ice cream and dumplings.

HIGH ALTITUDE (3500-6500 FT.): No change.

Nutrition Information Per Serving:	
Calories: 600	From Fat: 250
Total Fat	28g
Saturated Fat	14g
Trans Fat	0.5g
Cholesterol	55mg
Sodium	340mg
Total Carbohydrate	82g
Dietary Fiber	2g
Sugars	47g
Protein	4g

White Chocolate Raspberry Dessert Cups

PREP TIME: 25 MINUTES (READY IN 45 MINUTES)
SERVINGS: 8

1 can (8 oz) Pillsbury® refrigerated crescent dinner rolls or 1 can (8 oz) Pillsbury® Crescent Recipe Creations™ refrigerated flaky dough sheet

¼ cup blanched slivered almonds, toasted

¼ cup white vanilla baking chips

1 tablespoon butter or margarine

1 tablespoon sugar

¼ teaspoon almond extract

2 eggs

¼ cup flaked coconut

½ cup fresh or frozen (thawed) raspberries (about 24 raspberries)

DRIZZLE

¼ cup white vanilla baking chips

½ teaspoon vegetable oil

1) Heat oven to 350°F. Unroll dough on work surface (if using crescent rolls, pinch seams to seal); press or roll out dough into 16x8-inch rectangle. Cut into 8 (4-inch) squares. Press 1 square in bottom and up side of each of 8 ungreased regular-size muffin cups.

2) In food processor with metal blade, place almonds and ¼ cup white vanilla baking chips. Cover and process using quick on-and-off motions until coarsely chopped. Add butter, sugar, almond extract, eggs and coconut; process until well blended.

3) Place 2 raspberries in center of each dough-lined muffin cup (reserve remaining berries for garnish). Spoon about 2 tablespoons almond mixture onto raspberries in each.

4) Bake 16 to 20 minutes or until golden brown. Cool 5 minutes. Remove from muffin cups.

5) In small microwavable bowl, microwave drizzle ingredients uncovered on High 30 to 60 seconds, stirring every 15 seconds, until melted. Drizzle onto cups; top each with 1 raspberry. Serve warm.

HIGH ALTITUDE (3500-6500 FT.): No change.

Nutrition Information Per Serving:		
Calories: 270	From Fat: 140	
Total Fat		16g
Saturated Fat		7g
Trans Fat		1.5g
Cholesterol		55mg
Sodium		280mg
Total Carbohydrate		25g
Dietary Fiber		1g
Sugars		14g
Protein		5g

tip

To toast almonds, heat the oven to 350°F. Spread the almonds in an ungreased shallow pan. Bake uncovered 8 to 10 minutes, stirring occasionally, until golden brown.

Apple-Raspberry Pie

PREP TIME: 25 MINUTES (READY IN 2 HOURS 20 MINUTES)
SERVINGS: 6

1 box (15 oz) Pillsbury® refrigerated pie crusts, softened as directed on box

5 cups sliced peeled cooking or baking apples (3 large)

¾ cup granulated sugar

¼ cup cornstarch

1 teaspoon grated orange peel

1 container (6 oz) fresh raspberries (about 1 cup)

1 tablespoon cold butter or margarine, cut into small pieces

1 teaspoon granulated sugar

1) Heat oven to 400°F. Make pie crusts as directed on box for Two-Crust Pie using 9-inch glass pie plate.

2) In large bowl, place apples, ¾ cup sugar, the cornstarch and orange peel; toss to coat apples. Spoon ½ of apple mixture into crust-lined pie plate. Sprinkle evenly with raspberries. Top with remaining apple mixture. Dot with butter. Top with second crust; seal edges and flute.

3) Lightly brush crust with water; sprinkle with 1 teaspoon sugar. Cut slits in several places in top crust. Cover crust edge with strips of foil to prevent excessive browning.

4) Place pie on middle oven rack; place sheet of foil on rack below pie in case of spillover. Bake 45 to 55 minutes or until deep golden brown. Cool at least 1 hour before serving.

HIGH ALTITUDE (3500-6500 FT.): Bake 50 to 60 minutes.

Nutrition Information Per Serving:	
Calories: 510	From Fat: 190
Total Fat	21g
Saturated Fat	8g
Trans Fat	0g
Cholesterol	15mg
Sodium	310mg
Total Carbohydrate	80g
Dietary Fiber	3g
Sugars	36g
Protein	0g

Chocolate-Filled Pillows with Chocolate Sauce

PREP TIME: 20 MINUTES (READY IN 40 MINUTES)
SERVINGS: 6

EASY

PILLOWS

1 can (8 oz) Pillsbury® refrigerated crescent dinner rolls or 1 can (8 oz) Pillsbury® Crescent Recipe Creations™ refrigerated flaky dough sheet

18 milk chocolate candy drops

1 tablespoon whipping cream

1 teaspoon sugar

CHOCOLATE SAUCE

½ cup whipping cream

¾ cup milk chocolate chips

Nutrition Information Per Serving:	
Calories: 360	From Fat: 200
Total Fat	22g
Saturated Fat	11g
Trans Fat	0g
Cholesterol	30mg
Sodium	330mg
Total Carbohydrate	36g
Dietary Fiber	1g
Sugars	21g
Protein	5g

1) Heat oven to 375°F. Spray large cookie sheet with cooking spray. Unroll dough on work surface (if using crescent rolls, pinch seams to seal); press dough into 12x8-inch rectangle. Cut into 6 squares. Place on cookie sheet.

2) Place 3 chocolate candy drops in the center of each dough square. Bring 4 corners of dough to center of the candies; twist firmly. Pinch edges to seal. Brush the tops with 1 tablespoon whipping cream; sprinkle with sugar. Bake 14 to 19 minutes or until deep golden brown.

3) Meanwhile, in 1-quart saucepan, heat sauce ingredients over low heat 1 to 2 minutes or until melted and smooth. Spoon 2 tablespoons sauce onto each serving plate. Top each with 1 pillow; drizzle with remaining sauce.

HIGH ALTITUDE (3500-6500 FT.): No change.

Honey Gingerbread Cakes with Caramel Apple Topping

PREP TIME: 35 MINUTES (READY IN 45 MINUTES)
SERVINGS: 12

CAKES

1³/4 cups all-purpose flour

1/2 cup packed brown sugar

1 teaspoon baking soda

2 teaspoons ground ginger

1 teaspoon ground cinnamon

1/2 teaspoon salt

1/4 teaspoon ground cloves

1/2 cup butter or margarine, melted

1/2 cup boiling water

1/4 cup honey

1/4 cup molasses

1 egg, slightly beaten

TOPPING

1/4 cup butter or margarine

1 cup packed brown sugar

5 medium cooking or baking apples, peeled, finely chopped (about 5 cups)

Dash salt

1/2 cup whipping cream

1/2 teaspoon vanilla

1) Heat oven to 350°F. Place paper baking cup in each of 12 regular-size muffin cups. In large bowl, stir together flour, 1/2 cup brown sugar, the baking soda, ginger, cinnamon, 1/2 teaspoon salt and the cloves. With spoon or wire whisk, stir in remaining cake ingredients until well blended. Divide batter evenly among muffin cups.

2) Bake 20 to 25 minutes or until toothpick inserted in center comes out clean. Cool in pan on cooling rack 10 minutes. Remove from pan; carefully remove paper baking cups from cakes.

3) Meanwhile, in 10-inch skillet, melt 1/4 cup butter over medium-high heat. Stir in 1 cup brown sugar, the apples and dash of salt; cook 4 to 5 minutes, stirring frequently, until brown sugar is dissolved and mixture boils. Boil 10 minutes, stirring frequently, until apples are tender and syrup thickens. Stir in whipping cream. Return to boiling; boil 3 minutes, stirring constantly, until mixture thickens and apples look glazed. Remove from heat; stir in vanilla.

4) To serve, cut cakes in half horizontally. Place bottom halves on small dessert plates; spoon a heaping tablespoon topping over each bottom half. Add tops of cakes; spoon a heaping tablespoon topping on top of each, letting topping run down sides and onto plates.

HIGH ALTITUDE (3500-6500 FT.): Heat oven to 375°F. Increase flour to 2 cups. Decrease brown sugar in cake to 1/3 cup.

Nutrition Information Per Serving:		
Calories: 360	From Fat: 230	
Total Fat		26g
Saturated Fat		13g
Trans Fat		1.5g
Cholesterol		330mg
Sodium		420mg
Total Carbohydrate		14g
Dietary Fiber		0g
Sugars		5g
Protein		18g

Cranberry-Apple Napoleons

PREP TIME: 30 MINUTES (READY IN 30 MINUTES)
SERVINGS: 4

CRUST

1 Pillsbury® refrigerated pie crust (from 15-oz box), softened as directed on box

1 tablespoon butter or margarine, melted

2 teaspoons granulated sugar

FILLING

2 tablespoons butter or margarine

2 large apples, peeled, cored, sliced

1/4 cup sweetened dried cranberries

1/4 cup packed brown sugar

1/2 teaspoon ground cinnamon

TOPPING

1 cup vanilla ice cream

2 tablespoons caramel topping

2 tablespoons toasted chopped pecans

1) Heat oven to 425°F. Unroll pie crust on work surface; brush with melted butter. Sprinkle with granulated sugar; cut into 8 wedges. Place on ungreased large cookie sheet. Bake 8 to 10 minutes or until golden brown. Remove from cookie sheet.

2) Meanwhile, in 10-inch skillet, melt 2 tablespoons butter over medium-high heat. Add apples, cranberries, brown sugar and cinnamon; cook 3 to 4 minutes, stirring frequently, until apples are tender and mixture is slightly thickened.

3) Place 1 pie crust wedge on serving plate. Top with about 1/2 cup apple mixture; top with another crust wedge. Top with ice cream. Drizzle with caramel topping and sprinkle with toasted pecans.

HIGH ALTITUDE (3500-6500 FT.): Thinly slice apples.

Nutrition Information Per Serving:	
Calories: 580	From Fat: 260
Total Fat	29g
Saturated Fat	13g
Trans Fat	0g
Cholesterol	45mg
Sodium	350mg
Total Carbohydrate	77g
Dietary Fiber	2g
Sugars	43g
Protein	2g

Berry-Peach Cobbler

PREP TIME: 20 MINUTES (READY IN 1 HOUR 5 MINUTES)
SERVINGS: 8

EASY

BISCUITS

1¼ cups all-purpose flour

⅓ cup sugar

1½ teaspoons baking powder

½ teaspoon salt

¼ teaspoon ground nutmeg

¼ cup cold butter or margarine, cut into pieces

½ cup milk

1 teaspoon decorator sugar crystals, if desired

FRUIT MIXTURE

¾ cup sugar

2 tablespoons all-purpose flour

1 cup fresh blueberries

1 cup fresh raspberries

3 medium peaches, peeled, sliced (about 3 cups)

2 teaspoons grated lemon peel

1 tablespoon lemon juice

1) Heat oven to 400°F. Grease 2-quart glass casserole with butter or cooking spray.

2) In medium bowl, stir together 1¼ cups flour, ⅓ cup sugar, the baking powder, salt and nutmeg. Cut in butter, using pastry blender or fork, until mixture looks like coarse crumbs. Stir in milk just until combined; set aside.

3) In 2½-quart saucepan, stir together ¾ cup sugar and 2 tablespoons flour. Stir in blueberries, raspberries, peaches, lemon peel and lemon juice. Heat to boiling over medium-high heat, stirring constantly. Spoon fruit mixture into baking dish.

4) Immediately drop biscuit dough by 8 spoonfuls onto hot mixture. Sprinkle sugar crystals over dough.

5) Bake 25 to 35 minutes or until biscuits are golden brown. Cool at least 15 minutes before serving.

HIGH ALTITUDE (3500-6500 FT.): No change.

Nutrition Information Per Serving:

Calories:	290	From Fat:	60
Total Fat			7g
Saturated Fat			4g
Trans Fat			0g
Cholesterol			15mg
Sodium			290mg
Total Carbohydrate			55g
Dietary Fiber			3g
Sugars			35g
Protein			3g

Cranberry-Orange Upside-Down Cake

PREP TIME: 20 MINUTES (READY IN 1 HOUR 25 MINUTES)
SERVINGS: 9

e EASY

CRANBERRY TOPPING

2 tablespoons butter or margarine

³⁄₄ cup sugar

1 tablespoon grated orange peel

1¹⁄₂ cups fresh or frozen cranberries

¹⁄₂ cup sweetened dried cranberries

CAKE

1 cup sugar

¹⁄₄ cup butter or margarine, softened

1 tablespoon grated orange peel

2 eggs

1¹⁄₄ cups all-purpose flour

1¹⁄₂ teaspoons baking powder

¹⁄₂ teaspoon salt

¹⁄₃ cup milk

¹⁄₄ cup orange juice

1) Heat oven to 350°F. Grease the bottom and sides of 8-inch square pan with shortening or cooking spray.

2) In 10-inch skillet, melt 2 tablespoons butter over medium-low heat. Stir in ³⁄₄ cup sugar, 1 tablespoon orange peel and the fresh or frozen cranberries. Cook 5 to 7 minutes, stirring frequently, until cranberries start to soften and juice is thickened. Stir in the dried cranberries. Remove from heat; set aside.

3) In large bowl, beat 1 cup sugar, ¹⁄₄ cup butter, 1 tablespoon orange peel and the eggs with electric mixer on medium speed until fluffy. On low speed, beat in flour, baking powder and salt until mixed. Beat in milk and orange juice until mixed. Beat on medium speed 1 minute longer.

4) Spread cranberry mixture in pan. Carefully spoon batter over cranberry mixture, starting around outside edge and filling in the middle.

5) Bake 40 to 50 minutes or until toothpick inserted in center comes out clean. Run metal spatula around edge of pan to loosen cake. Place large heatproof serving plate upside down over pan; carefully turn plate and pan over. Let stand 2 minutes so the topping drizzles over cake; remove pan. Spread any topping from bottom of pan over cake. Cool 5 to 10 minutes before serving. Serve warm or cool.

HIGH ALTITUDE (3500-6500 FT.): In Step 2, use medium-low to medium heat. Decrease sugar in cake to 3/4 cup and increase eggs to 3.

Nutrition Information Per Serving:	
Calories: 360	From Fat: 230
Total Fat	26g
Saturated Fat	13g
Trans Fat	1.5g
Cholesterol	330mg
Sodium	420mg
Total Carbohydrate	14g
Dietary Fiber	0g
Sugars	5g
Protein	18g

Sweet Potato Pudding Cups

PREP TIME: 15 MINUTES (READY IN 1 HOUR 40 MINUTES)
SERVINGS: 6 (1/2 CUP EACH)

e EASY

1 can (23 oz) sweet potatoes in syrup, drained

¼ cup packed brown sugar

1 teaspoon ground cinnamon

1 teaspoon ground nutmeg

¼ teaspoon salt

¼ teaspoon ground cloves

2 eggs

1 can (14 oz) sweetened condensed milk (not evaporated)

3 tablespoons chopped pecans

Sweetened whipped cream, if desired

1) Heat oven to 325°F. Grease 6 (6-oz) ovenproof custard cups or ramekins with butter or cooking spray.

2) In blender or food processor, blend all ingredients except the pecans and whipped cream until smooth. Pour into custard cups.

3) In 13x9-inch pan, place the filled custard cups. Carefully place the pan with cups in oven. Pour enough very hot water into pan, being careful not to splash water into cups, until the water is within ½ inch of the tops of cups.

4) Bake 30 minutes. Sprinkle the tops of the puddings with chopped pecans. Bake 20 to 25 minutes longer or until tops are set. Using tongs or grasping tops of custard cups with pot holder, carefully transfer cups to cooling rack. Cool 30 minutes. Just before serving, top with sweetened whipped cream.

HIGH ALTITUDE (3500-6500 FT.): No change.

Nutrition Information Per Serving:		
Calories: 370	From Fat: 90	
Total Fat		10g
Saturated Fat		4.5g
Trans Fat		0g
Cholesterol		95mg
Sodium		420mg
Total Carbohydrate		50g
Dietary Fiber		3g
Sugars		44g
Protein		9g

5 cups soft white bread crumbs (about 10 slices bread)

¼ cup granulated sugar

6 tablespoons butter or margarine, melted

¾ cup packed brown sugar

2 teaspoons apple pie spice

4 large baking apples (about 2 lb), peeled, sliced (8 cups)

16 medium dried figs, quartered (1 cup)

½ cup apple cider

Apple-Fig Brown Betty

PREP TIME: 25 MINUTES (READY IN 1 HOUR 20 MINUTES)
SERVINGS: 6

1) Heat oven to 350°F. Grease bottom and sides of 12x8-inch (2-quart) glass baking dish with butter or cooking spray.

2) In medium bowl, stir together bread crumbs, granulated sugar and butter. Spread ⅓ of crumb mixture in bottom of baking dish.

3) In medium bowl, stir together brown sugar and apple pie spice. Add apples and figs; stir to coat with sugar mixture. Spoon over crumb mixture in dish. Pour apple cider evenly over apple mixture. Top with remaining ⅔ of crumb mixture.

4) Bake 50 to 60 minutes or until apples are tender and topping is golden brown. Serve warm.

HIGH ALTITUDE (3500-6500 FT.): Increase apple cider to 1 cup.

Nutrition Information Per Serving:		
Calories: 220	From Fat: 45	
Total Fat		5g
Saturated Fat		2g
Trans Fat		0g
Cholesterol		0mg
Sodium		5mg
Total Carbohydrate		41g
Dietary Fiber		4g
Sugars		24g
Protein		2g

Pear-Rum Crisp

PREP TIME: 20 MINUTES (READY IN 1 HOUR 5 MINUTES)
SERVINGS: 6

e EASY

FRUIT MIXTURE

- $1/2$ cup packed brown sugar
- 3 tablespoons all-purpose flour
- $1/2$ teaspoon ground cinnamon
- $1/2$ teaspoon ground nutmeg
- 3 firm ripe medium pears, peeled, sliced (6 cups)
- $1/4$ cup sweetened dried cranberries
- $1/4$ cup dark rum, apple juice or apple cider

TOPPING

- $1/2$ cup all-purpose flour
- $1/2$ cup packed brown sugar
- $1/2$ teaspoon ground cinnamon
- $1/2$ cup cold butter or margarine, cut into pieces
- $1/2$ cup quick-cooking oats

Nutrition Information Per Serving:

Calories:	470	From Fat:	150
Total Fat			16g
Saturated Fat			10g
Trans Fat			0.5g
Cholesterol			40mg
Sodium			125mg
Total Carbohydrate			77g
Dietary Fiber			6g
Sugars			53g
Protein			3g

1) Heat oven to 350°F. Grease bottom and sides of 8-inch square (2-quart) glass baking dish with butter or cooking spray.

2) In large bowl, stir together $1/2$ cup brown sugar, 3 tablespoons flour, $1/2$ teaspoon cinnamon and the nutmeg. Add pears, cranberries and rum; stir to coat fruit with sugar mixture. Spread in baking dish.

3) In medium bowl, mix $1/2$ cup flour, $1/2$ cup brown sugar and $1/2$ teaspoon cinnamon. Cut in butter, using pastry blender or fork, until mixture looks like fine crumbs. Add oats; stir until crumbly. Sprinkle evenly over fruit mixture.

4) Bake 40 to 45 minutes or until pears are tender when pierced with a fork and topping is golden brown. Serve warm or at room temperature.

HIGH ALTITUDE (3500-6500 FT.): No change.

Butternut Squash Cake with Butter-Rum Frosting

PREP TIME: 20 MINUTES (READY IN 2 HOURS 15 MINUTES)
SERVINGS: 15

e EASY

CAKE

- 1¼ cups packed brown sugar
- 1 cup vegetable oil
- 2 teaspoons vanilla
- 3 eggs
- 2½ cups all-purpose flour
- 1½ teaspoons baking soda
- 1½ teaspoons pumpkin pie spice
- ½ teaspoon salt
- ⅔ cup buttermilk
- 2 cups shredded peeled butternut squash (about 1 lb)
- ½ cup sweetened dried cranberries, if desired
- ½ cup chopped toasted hazelnuts (filberts), if desired

FROSTING

- ½ cup butter or margarine, softened
- 4 oz (half of 8-oz package) cream cheese, softened
- 2 tablespoons rum or 2 teaspoons rum extract plus 4 teaspoons milk
- 4 cups powdered sugar
- ¼ cup chopped toasted hazelnuts (filberts)

1) Heat oven to 350°F. Spray bottom and sides of 13x9-inch pan with baking spray with flour.

2) In large bowl, beat brown sugar, oil, vanilla and eggs with electric mixer on medium speed until creamy. On low speed, beat in flour, baking soda, pumpkin pie spice and salt until mixed. Add buttermilk; beat on low speed until mixed. Beat on medium speed 1 minute longer. Stir in squash, cranberries and hazelnuts. Pour into pan.

3) Bake 45 to 55 minutes or until toothpick inserted in center comes out clean. Cool completely, about 1 hour.

4) In medium bowl, beat butter and cream cheese on medium speed until creamy. Add rum and powdered sugar; beat on low speed until mixed. Beat on medium speed until smooth and creamy. Frost cake. Sprinkle with ¼ cup hazelnuts. Store covered in refrigerator.

HIGH ALTITUDE (3500-6500 FT.): No change.

Nutrition Information Per Serving:		
Calories: 530	From Fat: 230	
Total Fat		26g
Saturated Fat		8g
Trans Fat		0g
Cholesterol		65mg
Sodium		300mg
Total Carbohydrate		70g
Dietary Fiber		1g
Sugars		50g
Protein		5g

tip To toast hazelnuts, place them in a shallow baking pan. Bake at 350°F for 6 to 10 minutes, stirring occasionally, until fragrant and golden brown. Cool slightly and rub them between your hands to loosen some of the skins.

Ginger-Peach Cheesecake

PREP TIME: 20 MINUTES (READY IN 8 HOURS 50 MINUTES)
SERVINGS: 16

e EASY

CRUST

1½ cups crushed gingersnap cookies (about 30 cookies; 8 oz)

¼ cup butter or margarine, melted

FILLING

4 packages (8 oz each) cream cheese, softened

⅔ cup sugar

½ cup sour cream

1 tablespoon vanilla

4 eggs

1 can (15.25 oz) peach slices in heavy syrup, drained, coarsely chopped

TOPPING

¾ cup peach preserves

1 tablespoon finely chopped gingerroot

2 teaspoons lemon juice

1) Heat oven to 300°F. Wrap foil around outside of bottom and side of 9-inch springform pan to catch drips. In medium bowl, stir together crust ingredients. Press on bottom and 1 inch up side of pan.

2) In large bowl, beat all filling ingredients except eggs and peaches with electric mixer on medium speed until smooth. On low speed, beat in eggs until blended. Gently stir in peaches. Pour into crust.

3) Bake 1 hour 25 minutes to 1 hour 30 minutes or until edge of cheesecake is set but center still jiggles slightly when moved. Turn oven off; open oven door at least 4 inches. Leave cheesecake in oven 30 minutes longer.

4) Remove cheesecake from oven; place on cooling rack. Without releasing side of pan, run knife around edge of pan to loosen cheesecake. Cool in pan on cooling rack 30 minutes. Cover loosely; refrigerate at least 6 hours but no longer than 24 hours.

5) In small bowl, mix topping ingredients. Carefully spread over top of cheesecake. Run metal spatula along side of cheesecake to loosen. Remove side of pan; leave cheesecake on pan bottom to serve. Store covered in refrigerator.

HIGH ALTITUDE (3500-6500 FT.): No change.

Nutrition Information Per Serving:	
Calories: 410	From Fat: 240
Total Fat	27g
Saturated Fat	16g
Trans Fat	1g
Cholesterol	130mg
Sodium	300mg
Total Carbohydrate	36g
Dietary Fiber	1g
Sugars	24g
Protein	7g

tip

Won't need the entire cake at once? Spoon the topping over wedges of cake rather than over the whole, uncut cake. The unused topping can be reheated and served over the remaining cake at a later time.

Caramel-Glazed Spice Cake

PREP TIME: 20 MINUTES (READY IN 1 HOUR 35 MINUTES)
SERVINGS: 12

EASY

CAKE

- 1/3 cup butter or margarine, softened
- 1/2 cup granulated sugar
- 2 eggs
- 1 cup all-purpose flour
- 2 teaspoons ground ginger
- 1 teaspoon ground cinnamon
- 1/4 teaspoon baking soda
- 1/4 teaspoon baking powder
- 1/4 teaspoon salt
- 1/4 teaspoon ground cloves
- 1/3 cup sour cream
- 1/4 cup finely chopped walnuts

CARAMEL TOPPING

- 1/4 cup butter (do not use margarine)
- 3/4 cup packed brown sugar
- 1 tablespoon light corn syrup
- 3 tablespoons whipping cream
- 1/2 teaspoon vanilla

1) Heat oven to 350°F. Spray bottom only of 9-inch round cake pan with baking spray with flour.

2) In large bowl, beat 1/3 cup butter, the granulated sugar and eggs with electric mixer on low speed until blended; beat on medium speed until creamy. On low speed, beat in flour, ginger, cinnamon, baking soda, baking powder, salt and cloves until mixed; beat on medium speed 1 minute. Stir in sour cream and walnuts just until blended. Pour into pan.

3) Bake 30 to 35 minutes or until toothpick inserted in center comes out clean. Cool 10 minutes. Run table knife around edge of pan to loosen cake. Place heatproof serving plate upside down over pan; carefully turn plate and pan over and remove pan. Cool at room temperature 30 minutes.

4) In 2-quart saucepan, melt 1/4 cup butter over medium heat. Stir in brown sugar and corn syrup. Heat to boiling over medium-high heat, stirring constantly. Stir in whipping cream; boil and stir 3 minutes. Remove from heat; stir in vanilla. Cool about 25 minutes at room temperature, stirring occasionally.

5) Spread caramel topping over top of cake, allowing some to run down side of cake.

HIGH ALTITUDE (3500-6500 FT.): No change.

Nutrition Information Per Serving:		
Calories: 270	From Fat:	130
Total Fat		14g
Saturated Fat		8g
Trans Fat		0g
Cholesterol		65mg
Sodium		170mg
Total Carbohydrate		32g
Dietary Fiber		0g
Sugars		23g
Protein		3g

Pear-Walnut Crumble Pie

PREP TIME: 20 MINUTES (READY IN 1 HOUR 35 MINUTES)
SERVINGS: 8

e EASY

PIE

- 1 Pillsbury® refrigerated pie crust (from 15-oz box), softened as directed on box
- 5 cups sliced peeled pears (about 5 large)
- 2 tablespoons granulated sugar
- 1 tablespoon all-purpose flour
- 1 teaspoon grated lemon peel
- ¼ teaspoon ground ginger
- Dash salt

TOPPING

- ½ cup all-purpose flour
- ⅓ cup packed brown sugar
- ½ teaspoon ground cinnamon
- ¼ teaspoon ground ginger
- ¼ teaspoon ground nutmeg
- ⅓ cup cold butter or margarine, cut into pieces
- ½ cup chopped walnuts

1) Heat oven to 400°F. Place pie crust in 9-inch glass pie plate as directed on box for One-Crust Filled Pie.

2) In large bowl, lightly toss pears and remaining pie ingredients. If pears are very juicy, add additional 1 tablespoon flour. Spoon into crust-lined plate.

3) In medium bowl, mix ½ cup flour, the brown sugar, cinnamon, ginger and nutmeg. Cut in butter, using pastry blender or fork, until mixture is crumbly. Stir in walnuts. Spoon over pear mixture.

4) Cover crust edge with strips of foil to prevent excessive browning. Bake 35 to 45 minutes or until topping is golden brown. Cool at least 30 minutes before serving. Serve warm or cool.

HIGH ALTITUDE (3500-6500 FT.): Bake 40 to 50 minutes.

Nutrition Information Per Serving:	
Calories: 370	From Fat: 180
Total Fat	20g
Saturated Fat	8g
Trans Fat	0g
Cholesterol	25mg
Sodium	190mg
Total Carbohydrate	47g
Dietary Fiber	3g
Sugars	21g
Protein	2g

Berry–Pear Crisp Pie

PREP TIME: 25 MINUTES (READY IN 3 HOURS 45 MINUTES)
SERVINGS: 8

CRUST

1 Pillsbury® refrigerated pie crust (from 15-oz box), softened as directed on box

FILLING

3 ripe pears, peeled, cored, thinly sliced (about 3 cups)

1 cup fresh blueberries

1 cup fresh raspberries

1 tablespoon lemon juice

$\frac{1}{3}$ cup granulated sugar

3 tablespoons cornstarch

TOPPING

1 cup old-fashioned or quick-cooking oats

$\frac{1}{2}$ cup all-purpose flour

$\frac{1}{2}$ cup packed brown sugar

1 teaspoon ground cinnamon

$\frac{1}{2}$ cup butter or margarine, softened

$\frac{1}{2}$ cup chopped walnuts, if desired

Vanilla ice cream, if desired

1) Heat oven to 425°F. Unroll crust. Place in 9-inch glass pie plate; flute edges. Line crust with 10-inch round of cooking parchment paper or foil. Fill with dried beans or pie weights. Bake 8 to 9 minutes or until crust is set. Remove parchment and beans. Cover edge of crust with strips of foil to prevent excessive browning. Bake 6 to 7 minutes longer or until crust is golden. Cool completely on cooling rack, about 15 minutes.

2) In large bowl, gently toss filling ingredients. Spoon filling into pastry-lined pie plate.

3) In large bowl, beat topping ingredients with electric mixer on medium-low speed until crumbly. Sprinkle topping evenly over filling.

4) Line cookie sheet with foil. Place pie plate on foil-lined cookie sheet. Cover pie with foil; bake 15 minutes. Reduce heat to 375°F; bake 45 to 50 minutes longer or until bubbly. Remove foil from pie; bake 20 to 25 minutes longer or until topping is golden brown. Cool completely on cooling rack, 2 to 3 hours.

HIGH ALTITUDE (3500-6500 FT.): No change.

Nutrition Information Per Serving:		
Calories: 450	From Fat: 180	
Total Fat		19g
Saturated Fat		10g
Trans Fat		0g
Cholesterol		35mg
Sodium		200mg
Total Carbohydrate		66g
Dietary Fiber		5g
Sugars		31g
Protein		3g

Grilled Banana Boats

PREP TIME: 25 MINUTES (READY IN 45 MINUTES)
SERVINGS: 6 BANANA BOATS

6 ripe firm large bananas, unpeeled

6 tablespoons chocolate chips

6 tablespoons miniature marshmallows

2 tablespoons chopped pecans

1) Cut 6 (12-inch) sheets of heavy-duty foil. Heat gas or charcoal grill, or heat oven to 350°F.

2) With sharp knife, make deep lengthwise cut along the inside curve of each banana, being careful not to cut all the way through. Open the slit to form a pocket. Crimp and shape 1 sheet of foil around each banana, forming boats.

3) Holding each banana in hand, fill pocket with 2 tablespoons chocolate chips, 2 tablespoons miniature marshmallows and about 1/2 heaping teaspoon chopped pecans.

4) Return each banana to its foil boat. Seal top of foil, leaving 2 to 3 inches headspace. Place on grill over medium heat. Cover grill; cook 8 to 10 minutes or until the marshmallows soften. Or bake 15 to 20 minutes in oven until marshmallows soften. (Can also place in campfire coals to cook.)

HIGH ALTITUDE (3500-6500 FT.): No change.

Nutrition Information Per Serving:	
Calories: 220	From Fat: 45
Total Fat	5g
Saturated Fat	2g
Trans Fat	0g
Cholesterol	0mg
Sodium	5mg
Total Carbohydrate	41g
Dietary Fiber	4g
Sugars	24g
Protein	2g

Caramel-Pecan-Apple Pie

PREP TIME: 35 MINUTES (READY IN 3 HOURS 20 MINUTES)
SERVINGS: 8

CRUST

1 box (15 oz) Pillsbury® refrigerated pie crusts, softened as directed on box

FILLING

6 cups thinly sliced, peeled apples (6 medium)

3/4 cup sugar

2 tablespoons all-purpose flour

3/4 teaspoon ground cinnamon

1/4 teaspoon salt

1/8 teaspoon ground nutmeg

1 tablespoon lemon juice

TOPPING

1/3 cup caramel topping

2 to 4 tablespoons chopped pecans

1) Heat oven to 425°F. Make pie crusts as directed on box for Two-Crust Pie using 9-inch glass pie plate.

2) In large bowl, gently mix filling ingredients; spoon into crust-lined pie plate. Top with second crust; seal edges and flute. Cut slits or shapes in several places in top crust. Cover edge with 2- to 3-inch-wide strips of foil to prevent excessive browning; remove foil during last 15 minutes of baking.

3) Bake 40 to 45 minutes or until apples are tender and crust is golden brown. Immediately after removing pie from oven, drizzle with caramel topping; sprinkle with pecans. Cool on cooling rack at least 2 hours before serving.

HIGH ALTITUDE (3500-6500 FT.): No change.

Nutrition Information Per Serving:	
Calories: 410	From Fat: 140
Total Fat	15g
Saturated Fat	5g
Trans Fat	0g
Cholesterol	10mg
Sodium	340mg
Total Carbohydrate	66g
Dietary Fiber	1g
Sugars	34g
Protein	0g

Cherry-Pear Tart

PREP TIME:	25 MINUTES (READY IN 1 HOUR 5 MINUTES)
SERVINGS:	8

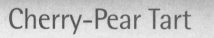 EASY

CRUST

1 Pillsbury® refrigerated pie crust (from 15-oz box), softened as directed on box

FILLING

1 tablespoon cornstarch

1 tablespoon water

1 ripe large pear, peeled, cored, thinly sliced (about 1 cup)

1 can (21 oz) cherry pie filling with more fruit

2 teaspoons grated orange peel

CRUST TOPPING

1 egg

1 tablespoon water

1 teaspoon sugar

1 tablespoon sliced almonds, toasted

1) Heat oven to 425°F. Line large cookie sheet with cooking parchment paper. Unroll pie crust onto cookie sheet.

2) In small bowl, stir together cornstarch and 1 tablespoon water. In medium bowl, stir cornstarch mixture and remaining filling ingredients. Spoon filling mixture onto center of crust within 2 inches of edge. Carefully fold 2-inch edge of crust over filling, pleating crust slightly as necessary.

3) In small bowl, beat the egg and 1 tablespoon water; brush over the edge of crust. Sprinkle sugar over crust edge.

4) Bake 20 to 25 minutes or until pears are tender and crust is golden brown. Sprinkle with almonds. Cool 15 minutes. Cut tart into wedges; serve warm. Cover and refrigerate any remaining tart.

HIGH ALTITUDE (3500-6500 FT.): No change.

Nutrition Information Per Serving:		
Calories: 190	From Fat:	70
Total Fat		7g
Saturated Fat		2.5g
Trans Fat		1g
Cholesterol		20mg
Sodium		430mg
Total Carbohydrate		21g
Dietary Fiber		0g
Sugars		0g
Protein		9g

Ruby Raspberry Crescent Cobbler

PREP TIME: 20 MINUTES (READY IN 45 MINUTES)
SERVINGS: 12

● EASY

1 box (10 oz) frozen raspberries in syrup, thawed, drained and liquid reserved

1 bag (16 oz) frozen cut rhubarb, thawed, drained and liquid reserved

1/2 cup sugar

1/2 teaspoon ground cinnamon

3 tablespoons cornstarch

1 can (8 oz) Pillsbury® refrigerated crescent dinner rolls or 1 can (8 oz) Pillsbury® Crescent Recipe Creations™ refrigerated flaky dough sheet

1 tablespoon butter or margarine, melted

2 teaspoons sugar

1/2 teaspoon ground cinnamon

1/4 cup chopped pecans

Vanilla ice cream, if desired

1) Heat oven to 375°F. Spray 11x7-inch (2-quart) glass baking dish with cooking spray.

2) In 1-cup measuring cup, mix raspberry and rhubarb liquids. If necessary, add enough water to make 1 cup. In 2-quart saucepan, mix 1/2 cup sugar, 1/2 teaspoon cinnamon and the cornstarch; stir in the 1 cup reserved liquid. Cook over medium heat 4 to 5 minutes, stirring constantly, until thickened; remove from heat. Stir in raspberries and rhubarb. Spoon into baking dish.

3) Unroll dough (if using crescent rolls, pinch seams to seal). Place over raspberry-rhubarb mixture; tuck in edges. Brush with melted butter. In small bowl, mix 2 teaspoons sugar, 1/2 teaspoon cinnamon and the pecans; sprinkle evenly over dough.

4) Bake 18 to 24 minutes or until bubbly and golden brown. Cool 5 minutes. Cut into 4 rows by 3 rows. Serve with ice cream.

HIGH ALTITUDE (3500-6500 FT.): Bake 24 to 30 minutes.

Nutrition Information Per Serving:		
Calories: 160	From Fat:	50
Total Fat		6g
Saturated Fat		2g
Trans Fat		0g
Cholesterol		0mg
Sodium		160mg
Total Carbohydrate		26g
Dietary Fiber		2g
Sugars		16g
Protein		1g

Bananas Foster Biscuit Shortcakes

PREP TIME: 40 MINUTES (READY IN 40 MINUTES)
SERVINGS: 8

BISCUIT

½ cup flaked or shredded coconut

¼ cup granulated sugar

1 can (16.3 oz) Pillsbury® Grands!® refrigerated buttermilk biscuits

3 tablespoons butter or margarine, melted

FILLING

¼ cup butter or margarine

½ cup packed brown sugar

4 medium bananas, sliced

1 tablespoon light rum (or ½ teaspoon rum extract and 2½ teaspoons water)

WHIPPED TOPPING

1 cup whipping cream

2 tablespoons packed brown sugar

1) Heat oven to 375°F. In small bowl, mix coconut and granulated sugar.

2) Dip tops and sides of biscuits into melted butter, then into coconut mixture. On ungreased large cookie sheet, place biscuits, coconut sides up, 2 inches apart. Sprinkle any remaining coconut mixture over tops of biscuits.

3) Bake 14 to 18 minutes or until biscuits and coconut are light golden brown. Cool 5 minutes.

4) Meanwhile, in 10-inch skillet, melt ¼ cup butter over medium-high heat; stir in ½ cup brown sugar. Cook until brown sugar is dissolved, stirring occasionally. Remove from heat; fold in bananas and rum.

5) In medium bowl, beat whipped topping ingredients with electric mixer on high speed until stiff peaks form.

6) To serve, split warm biscuits. Fill and top biscuits with banana filling and whipped topping.

HIGH ALTITUDE (3500-6500 FT.): No change.

Nutrition Information Per Serving:		
Calories: 540	From Fat: 260	
Total Fat		29g
Saturated Fat		17g
Trans Fat		3.5g
Cholesterol		60mg
Sodium		700mg
Total Carbohydrate		64g
Dietary Fiber		2g
Sugars		37g
Protein		5g

tip

Add some crunch to this yummy banana shortcake by sprinkling the whipped topping with toasted pecans.

Chocolate-Peanut Butter Truffle Pie

PREP TIME:	50 MINUTES (READY IN 2 HOURS 50 MINUTES)
SERVINGS:	12

CRUST

1 Pillsbury® refrigerated pie crust
(from 15-oz box), softened as
directed on box

TRUFFLE FILLING

1/2 cup whipping cream

1 cup dark chocolate chips

1/2 teaspoon vanilla

PEANUT BUTTER FILLING

1 cup whipping cream

1 package (8 oz) cream cheese,
softened

1 cup creamy peanut butter

1 cup powdered sugar

TOPPING

1/4 cup dark chocolate chips

1 tablespoon shortening

2 tablespoons coarsely chopped
salted peanuts

1) Heat oven to 450°F. Bake pie crust as directed on box for One-Crust Baked Shell, using 9-inch glass pie plate. Cool completely on cooling rack, about 15 minutes.

2) Meanwhile, in 2-quart saucepan, heat 1/2 cup cream over medium-high heat until hot. Remove from heat; stir in 1 cup chocolate chips and the vanilla until smooth. Spread truffle filling in bottom of baked crust. Freeze 15 minutes.

3) Meanwhile, in medium bowl, beat 1 cup cream with electric mixer on high speed until stiff peaks form. Set aside. In another medium bowl, beat cream cheese, peanut butter and powdered sugar with electric mixer on medium speed until smooth; fold in whipped cream. Carefully spread over truffle filling. Refrigerate until set, about 2 hours.

4) In small microwavable bowl, microwave 1/4 cup chocolate chips and the shortening uncovered on High 30 to 60 seconds, stirring every 15 seconds, until melted. Drizzle chocolate over pie; sprinkle with peanuts. Cut into wedges to serve. Cover and refrigerate any remaining pie.

HIGH ALTITUDE (3500-6500 FT.): No change.

Nutrition Information Per Serving:		
Calories: 520	From Fat:	350
Total Fat		38g
Saturated Fat		17g
Trans Fat		0.5g
Cholesterol		55mg
Sodium		240mg
Total Carbohydrate		36g
Dietary Fiber		2g
Sugars		22g
Protein		8g

Key Lime Cheesecake Pie

PREP TIME: 30 MINUTES (READY IN 3 HOURS 15 MINUTES)
SERVINGS: 8

1 Pillsbury® refrigerated pie crust (from 15-oz box), softened as directed on box

FILLING

1 envelope unflavored gelatin

1/2 cup fresh lime juice

1 cup sugar

2 eggs, beaten

2 packages (3 oz each) cream cheese, softened

1/4 cup butter or margarine, softened

1 cup whipping cream

1 1/2 teaspoons grated lime peel

1/2 cup whipping cream, whipped, sweetened

Lime slices

1) Heat oven to 450°F. Make pie crust as directed on box for One-Crust Baked Shell. Cool completely on cooling rack, about 15 minutes.

2) In 1-quart saucepan, sprinkle gelatin on lime juice. Let stand 5 minutes to soften. Using wire whisk, beat in sugar and eggs. Heat mixture to boiling over medium heat. Reduce heat; boil gently 3 minutes, stirring constantly.

3) In medium bowl, beat cream cheese and butter. Pour in hot lime juice mixture; beat until smooth and well blended. Refrigerate about 45 minutes or until cool, stirring occasionally.

4) In medium bowl, beat 1 cup whipping cream until stiff peaks form. Fold in cooled lime juice mixture and grated lime peel. Spoon into cooled pie shell. Refrigerate until firm, about 2 hours. Garnish with whipped cream and lime slices as desired. Cover and refrigerate any remaining pie.

HIGH ALTITUDE (3500-6500 FT.): No change.

Nutrition Information Per Serving:

Calories:	500	From Fat:	320
Total Fat			35g
Saturated Fat			20g
Trans Fat			1g
Cholesterol			145mg
Sodium			250mg
Total Carbohydrate			41g
Dietary Fiber			0g
Sugars			27g
Protein			5g

Chocolate Mousse Macadamia Tart

PREP TIME: 30 MINUTES (READY IN 2 HOURS 30 MINUTES)
SERVINGS: 12

CRUST

1 Pillsbury® refrigerated pie crust (from 15-oz box), softened as directed on box

1 oz bittersweet chocolate (from 6-oz bar), chopped

1/2 teaspoon vegetable oil

MACADAMIA NUT FILLING

1/4 cup granulated sugar

2 tablespoons light corn syrup

1/3 cup butter or margarine, softened

1/3 cup whipping cream

1 cup chopped macadamia nuts

CHOCOLATE FILLING

1 cup powdered sugar

1 package (3 oz) cream cheese, softened

1 teaspoon vanilla

5 oz bittersweet chocolate (from 6-oz bar), melted

1 1/2 cups whipping cream

TOPPING

1/2 cup whipping cream

1 tablespoon powdered sugar

1/4 teaspoon vanilla

GARNISH, IF DESIRED

1/3 cup toasted macadamia nuts, coarsely chopped

1) Heat oven to 450°F. Bake pie crust as directed on box for One-Crust Baked Shell, using 10-inch tart pan with removable bottom or 9-inch glass pie plate. Cool completely on cooling rack, about 15 minutes.

2) In small bowl, microwave 1 oz chocolate and the oil uncovered on High 20 to 30 seconds, stirring every 10 seconds, until melted. Spread in bottom of crust.

3) In 1-quart saucepan, mix granulated sugar and corn syrup; cook over medium heat 4 to 6 minutes (do not stir). Stir in butter, 1/3 cup whipping cream and 1 cup macadamia nuts. Cook 4 to 5 minutes, stirring frequently, until hot. Carefully spread in crust. Freeze until set, about 20 minutes.

4) Meanwhile in large bowl, beat 1 cup powdered sugar, the cream cheese and vanilla with electric mixer on high speed until smooth. Add melted chocolate; beat until smooth. Gradually add 1 1/2 cups whipping cream, beating until soft peaks form. Spread chocolate filling over nut filling. Refrigerate until filling is set, 2 to 3 hours.

5) In medium bowl, beat topping ingredients with electric mixer on high speed until stiff peaks form. Spoon over chocolate filling. Top with toasted macadamia nuts.

HIGH ALTITUDE (3500-6500 FT.): No change.

Nutrition Information Per Serving:

Calories:	520	From Fat:	370
Total Fat			41g
Saturated Fat			21g
Trans Fat			1g
Cholesterol			75mg
Sodium			150mg
Total Carbohydrate			33g
Dietary Fiber			3g
Sugars			18g
Protein			4g

Alphabetical Index

General Recipe Index

This handy index lists every recipe by food category, major ingredient and/or cooking method, so you can easily locate recipes to suit your needs.

Cherry-Pear Tart, 338
Chocolate Mousse Macadamia Tart, 343
Chocolate-Peanut Butter Truffle Pie, 341
Cream Cheese-Apple Danish Tart, 317
Key Lime Cheesecake Pie, 342
Pear-Walnut Crumble Pie, 335
Pistachio and White Chocolate Mousse
    Tartlets, 316
Pumpkin Pie, 280
Raspberry-Lemon Cream Pie with Almond
    Crust, 314
Rhubarb Crunch Pie, 318
Sour Cream-Apple Pie, 319
Spiced Chocolate Chip-Pecan Pie, 320

Pizzas
Baked Potato Pizza, 116
BBQ Chicken Pizza, 59
Chicken Alfredo Pizza, 59
Chicken 'n Bacon Ranch Pizza, 133
Chili and Olive Pizza Snacks, 52
Chipotle Chicken Pizza, 217
Double Crust Pizza, 139
Ham and Chile Brunch Pizza, 16
Mega-Meat Pizza, 162
Pizza Bread Salad, 96
Rustic Chicken Pizza, 145
Spicy Thai Pizza, 58

Pork
Carolina Pulled-Pork Sandwiches, 186
French Country Pâté, 45
Green Chile Pulled-Pork Burritos, 178
Harvest Pork Stew, 175
Italian Pork Tenderloin with Roasted Sweet
    Potatoes, 167
Pork Chops with Apple Chutney, 189
Pork Chops with Cranberry-Cornbread
    Stuffing, 201
Pot Stickers with Sweet Soy Dipping Sauce, 61
Pulled-Pork Fajitas, 252
Southwest Pulled-Pork Sandwiches, 75
Texas Two-Meat Chili, 195

Potatoes & Sweet Potatoes
Asparagus-Potato Brunch Bake, 9
Bacon-Ranch Potato Salad, 86
Baked Potato Pizza, 116
Brown Butter Snap Peas with New
    Potatoes, 107
Chili Potato Dippers with Cheddar Jalapeño
    Dip, 221
Crusty Mummy Fingers, 269
Easy Grilled Baked Potatoes, 111
Ground Beef- and Corn-Topped Potato
    Skins, 168
Italian Pork Tenderloin with Roasted Sweet
    Potatoes, 167
Mashed Potato Monsters, 263
Parmesan-Ranch-Chicken Packets, 148
Perfect Mashed Potatoes, 114
Pot Roast and Vegetables, 185
Pot Roast with Creamy Dill Sauce, 173
Potato and Ground Beef Gratin, 149
Roasted Red Pepper Potato Salad, 83

Rhubarb
Rhubarb Crunch Pie, 318
Ruby Raspberry Crescent Cobbler, 339

Rice & Barley
Arroz con Pollo, 210
Beefy Wild Mushroom and Barley Soup, 200
Easy Chicken-Rice Burritos, 230
Garden-Style Red Rice, 124
Green Poblano Rice, 113
Grilled Salmon Paella Packets, 136
Maple-Glazed Turkey with Wild Rice
    Stuffing, 278
Mediterranean Vegetable Bulgur Salad, 256
Rice with Pasta, 121
Sweet Potato and Barley Risotto, 188
Turkey and Rice Salad, 88

Salads & Coleslaw
Antipasto Rotini Salad, 239
Apple and Celery Salad with Creamy Lemon
    Dressing, 79
Bacon-Ranch Potato Salad, 86
Black-Eyed Pea Salad Bowl, 259
Brie, Lettuce and Tomato Salad, 92
Bruschetta-Style Tortellini Salad, 250
Buffalo Shrimp Salad, 95
Cannellini Bean and Tuna Salad, 82
Chicken Waldorf Salad, 76
Chipotle Chicken Salad, 151
Confetti Quinoa Salad, 254
Crunchy Asian Chicken Salad, 253
Escarole-Pear Salad, 93
Fruited Jicama Salad, 86
Garden Bounty Fontina Salad, 81
Greek-Style Pasta Salad, 255
Grilled Bell Pepper Panzanella Salad, 257
Grilled Chicken Garden Salad, 96
Grilled Flank Steak Salad with Parmesan
    Crisps, 130
Grilled Margarita Chicken Salad, 91
Grilled Salmon Caesar Salad, 157
Honey-Mustard Coleslaw with Apples, 249
Italian Bean and Tuna Salad, 94
Jicama, Zucchini and Red Pepper Salad, 74
Layered Pizza Salad, 251
Layered Summer Fruits with Creamy Lime
    Dressing, 245
Layered Tortellini Pesto Chicken Salad, 84
Mediterranean Vegetable Bulgur Salad, 256
Napa Cabbage Slaw, 87
Peach-Berry Bellini Salad, 73
Peppered Roast Beef Salad, 249
Pico de Gallo Salad, 77
Pizza Bread Salad, 96
Pomegranate and Almond Salad, 99
Refreshing Ginger Fruit Salad, 89
Roasted Beets and Nectarine Salad, 85
Roasted Red Pepper Potato Salad, 83
Rotisserie Chicken Salad with Cherries and
    Gorgonzola, 138
Sesame-Wheat Berry Salad, 254
Smoked Salmon-Avocado Sushi Salad, 78
Southwestern BLT Taco Salad, 216
Spicy Mexican Cabbage Slaw, 227

Super-Simple Picnic Potato Salad, 246
Taco Lettuce Cups, 90
Thai Beef-Noodle Salad, 154
Tilapia Salad with Strawberry-Pineapple
    Salsa, 71
Tostada Chicken Salad, 228
Turkey and Rice Salad, 88
Wheat Berry, Grilled Corn and Spinach
    Salad, 72

Sandwiches
Buffalo Pepper-Chicken Sandwiches, 76
Carolina Pulled-Pork Sandwiches, 186
Chicken Fajita Crescent Braid, 144
Chicken Louis Sandwiches, 93
Chicken Niçoise Salad Sandwiches, 98
Easy Reuben Sandwich Slices, 157
French Dip Sandwiches, 183
Grilled Ham and Cheese Boo Bites, 273
Ham and Cheese Pull-Apart Sandwich
    Loaf, 258
Italian Meatball Heroes, 181
Make-Ahead Dagwood Sandwiches, 238
Mediterranean Stuffed Burgers, 165
Mexican Sloppy Joes, 83
Open-Face Chicken Pitas, 70
Pulled-Beef Sandwiches, 247
Shanghai Sliders, 80
Sloppy BBQ Joes, 97
Southwest Pulled-Pork Sandwiches, 75
Turkey Teriyaki Sandwiches, 194

Sausage & Pepperoni
Black Bean-Chorizo Dip, 233
Bruschetta-Style Tortellini Salad, 250
Burrito Grande, 223
Cornbread and Sausage Dressing, 105
Double Crust Pizza, 139
Egg and Sausage Breakfast Ring, 20
Greek-Style Pasta Salad, 255
Grilled Salmon Paella Packets, 136
Halloweenies with Mustard Dip, 270
Italian Sausages and Peppers with Rotini, 177
Layered Pizza Salad, 251
Magic Potion Meat Sauce for Spaghetti, 160
Mega-Meat Pizza, 162
Mini Bacon-Wrapped Sausages, 293
Pizza Pinwheels, 284
Scary Slow-Cooked Chili, 264
Sinister Pepperoni-Ravioli Supper, 262

Side Dishes
Baked Butternut Squash with Apples, 118
Bread Stuffing, 277
Broccoli and Tomatoes, 123
Brown Butter Snap Peas with New
    Potatoes, 107
Caramelized-Onion Bread Pudding, 244
Cauliflower and Broccoli with Fresh Herb
    Butter, 104
Chili Potato Dippers with Cheddar Jalapeño
    Dip, 221
Cilantro Corn, 119
Corn with Fresh Herbs, 114
Cornbread and Sausage Dressing, 105